Community Policing

A Contemporary Perspective

anderson publishing co.
2035 reading road
cincinnati, ohio 45202
(513) 421-4142

Robert Trojanowicz
Bonnie Bucqueroux

Michigan State University

COMMUNITY POLICING
A Contemporary Perspective

Second Printing—September 1990

Copyright © 1990 by Anderson Publishing Co., Cincinnati, OH

ISBN 0-87084-875-5
Library of Congress Catalog Number 89-80504

Kelly Humble *Managing Editor*

Cover Design by Cyndi Symanek

To the men and women who serve as Community Policing Officers, because they are the ones who translate this new philosophy into action every day.

— *Robert Trojanowicz*

To my father, Henry McLanus, for arguing these issues with me – and to my mother, Helen, for mediating the debates. And sincerest and most profound thanks to soulmate Drew Howard and baby sister Tina McLanus for their unstinting affection, support, and assistance – you both gave me a helping arm when my damaged one threatened to prevent me from finishing my share of this work on time.

— *Bonnie Bucqueroux*

FOREWORD

No field of public service has changed as dramatically or as rapidly as has policing. For those not involved with policing during the 1960s and early 1970s, it is hard to imagine its isolation, insularity, and sense, almost to the point of paranoia, of being under threat. The metaphor of the *thin blue line* conveyed policing's belief that it – misunderstood, unappreciated, alone and lonely – stood between the forces of good and evil on city streets. Moreover, as Egon Bittner has pointed out, no field of public endeavor was as utterly devoid of rigorous self-assessment or self-scrutiny as policing.[1] Research by police on police was virtually nonexistent. And, as Herman Goldstein has suggested, no agency of city government was as unaccountable as public police.[2] Having successfully mystified their functioning during the 1940s and 1950s, the idea that police should be held accountable to mayors or city managers was rejected and attacked by those in policing, under the rationale that such accountability was tantamount to political *meddling* in police affairs.

Barely more than 15 years later, policing is almost the diametric opposite. No field has placed its core functioning, in the case of police its tactics to deal with crime (patrol, rapid response to calls for service, and criminal investigation), to as systematic and withering scrutiny as have police. And no profession has asked questions about its *raison d'etre* as thoroughly and as painfully as have police.

Understand, this was not done to police; it was done by police. True, some of the early research, primarily that conducted on criminal investigation, was neither instigated nor conducted by police, but virtually all of the first wave of research on preventive patrol, rapid response to calls for service, and foot patrol was conducted at minimum in collaboration with police; much was conducted at the instigation of police themselves, aided by researchers. The Kansas City Preventive Patrol Experiment, for example, was conceived of, executed, and ultimately published in a joint enterprise between researchers and police. And, a fact largely forgotten or ignored, those police involved in the project were primarily practicing patrol officers, not administrators or staff from research and/or planning.

Those involved in the early days of research on the effectiveness of police can remember the painfulness of self-scrutiny for police. Nothing seemed to work: preventive patrol, rapid response to calls for service, criminal investigation. Even those approaches that initially offered promise, team policing, for example, followed a recurrent pattern: enthusiastic endorsement of the concept, successful implementation, initial promising findings, and, then, with maddening regularity, an inability to hold the innovation in place in the police department. Cincinnati's experience in team policing was the most well documented example of this phenomenon.

Moreover, whether tactics had proved effective or not, the significance of the findings was unclear. Some, for example, misunderstood the findings of the Kansas City Preventive Patrol Experiment and suggested that the numbers of police officers could be reduced in cities, believing that the study tested the impact of numbers of patrol officers rather than a police tactic. Even when some tactics had dramatic pay-offs – foot patrol, for example, with its impact on fear, citizen attitudes, and officer satisfaction – it was unclear just what those findings meant. Could anybody seriously argue that all departments should return to foot patrol? How important were the findings about reduction of fear? Was concentration on fear reduction a legitimate goal of police?

Other issues confounded police during this era as well. The urban fiscal crisis of the late 1970s and early 1980s limited the size of police departments: few grew; many shrank. Citizen demands for policing seemed to be changing; increasingly they were demanding foot patrol. Community crime control and private security were burgeoning fields. In almost every field, consumers were demanding new levels of quality and, in the case of governmental services, new forms of accountability.

It was during this era of flux that Professor Robert Trojanowicz, director of Michigan State University's School of Criminal Justice, worked with the Flint Police Department and the Mott Foundation to conduct the Flint Neighborhood Foot Patrol Experiment. Later, Michigan State's National Neighborhood Foot Patrol Center (now the National Center for Community Policing) was created in an effort to provide education about, and consultation in, the development of foot patrol programs in cities throughout the United States. In his capacity as director of the Center, Trojanowicz listened, taught, and consulted in more than 168 police departments in the United States and Canada. In 1987, Trojanowicz also joined the Program in Criminal Justice Policy and Management, as a Research Fellow in the Kennedy School of Government at Harvard University, where, in addition to his other responsibilities, he continued his research and writing.

Like others of us working in or writing about policing, Trojanowicz has been attempting to make coherent the myriad of innovations, research findings, and organizational modifications now extant in policing. Looking back, it is now clear that, somewhere during the first few years of the 1980s, a pattern began to emerge in police practice, research, and thinking that gave structure to what had been both so frustrating and apparently divergent during the 1970s. Police work in Flint (MI), Santa Ana (CA), Madison (WI), Houston (TX), Newport News (VA), New York (NY), and elsewhere gave organizational shape and form to the changes in policing. Foot patrol research in Newark (NJ) and Flint was suggestive of other themes. Herman Goldstein's work in problem-oriented policing and the *Broken Windows* metaphor provided further structure to the emerging themes in professional police practice.

What was being discovered was that police were not just developing new tactics; instead, they were developing a whole new – and here the language is not agreed upon – philosophy, organizational strategy, model, or paradigm. Using my own preference, organizational strategy, policing was developing new or alternate sources of authority, definitions of function, organizational structures, administrative practices, sources of demand, relationship to their environment, tactics, and measures of performance. Indeed, just as the first generation of police leaders such as August Vollmer and O.W. Wilson developed a police strategy during the 1930s that would supplant what they termed "the old model of policing," so today, police executives are embarking in new directions – respectful of the past, but attuned to the responsibility of taking policing into the 21st century.

This book describes what is perhaps the most significant police effort to identify, label, and implement a new organizational strategy: Community Policing. Moreover, this book is prescriptive. As a consequence, this is not a dispassionate or *academic* (in the pejorative sense of the term) book. The authors believe in the viability of Community Policing because they believe in its benefits to the community and its contributions to the profession of policing and because of its effects on individual officers. They understand that police protect and represent many values in American society, not just the values of crime control. Even should Community Policing prove not to be as effective as they suggest and hope, the movement of police to embrace community and neighborhood values – aware of the potential tyranny of neighborhoods and prepared to restrain such tyranny – represents a significant advance to the development and maintenance of a truly civil authority.

The authors, along with others, are attempting to define a model of policing and to assist city and police officials implement and maintain Community Policing. Unabashedly, this volume advocates and describes. Its goal is to help policing into the 21st century.

George L. Kelling
Research Fellow
Program in Criminal Justice
Policy and Management
Kennedy School of Government
Harvard University
and
Professor of Criminal Justice
Northeastern University

[1]Bittner, Egon, *Police Research and Police Work, Police Yearbook* (Lexington, MA: Lexington Books, 1973).

[2]Goldstein, Herman, *The Urban Police Function* (Cambridge, MA: Ballinger Publishing, 1977).

PREFACE

Community Policing, the first major reform in a half-century, changes the way the police think and act. This revolutionary movement broadens the police mandate beyond a narrow focus on fighting crime, to include efforts that also address fear of crime, social and physical disorder, and neighborhood decay. The Community Policing philosophy provides an organizational strategy that challenges police officers to solve community problems in new ways. It says that the police must form a partnership with people in the community, allowing average citizens the opportunity to have input into the police process, in exchange for their support and participation. Community Policing rests on the belief that contemporary community problems require a new decentralized and personalized police approach, one that involves people in the process of policing themselves.

This book also details the evolution of the Community Policing Officer (CPO), who acts as the police department's community outreach specialist. Freed from the isolation of the patrol car and the incessant demands of the police radio, CPOs operate as full-fledged law enforcement officers, but their expanded mission allows them the flexibility and autonomy to develop short- and long-term, community-based efforts to improve the safety and quality of life in the communities they serve.

Much of the challenge in writing this book has been to keep up with the ways in which this new way of policing continues to evolve – it is like trying to mount a butterfly to a board while its wings are still beating. The goal has been to describe as fully as possible what Community Policing can and is doing, without pinning it down in ways that might inhibit its continued growth. As Professor David Carter has said, Community Policing is at the "cutting edge" of what is happening in policing today, which means that no single book can hope to capture all the creative ways in which it is and will be applied.

Most promising of all, perhaps, are the ways in which Community Policing addresses the pernicious problems posed by illicit drugs in this society. We have all recoiled in horror at the sight of what armed troops have done to average citizens on the streets of Beijing, a grim reminder of why we must explore all police alternatives before succumbing to the temptation to send our military troops into areas of our major cities where open drug dealing has careened out of control. As a result, we have devoted two chapters to how Community Policing offers new ways in dealing with the drug problem, which may well be the most serious criminal justice issue of our times.

As the police stand poised on the brink of the 21st century, the need to provide a comprehensive look at the Community Policing movement seemed a particularly urgent task. This book was written with today's criminal justice student in mind, because of the need to make tomorrow's police officers – and ultimately the police administrators of the future – aware of the Community Policing contribution. Yet the book is also intended to provide today's police professionals an important resource that may spark new ideas that they can implement now.

This book is also intended for government policymakers and administrators, community leaders, and concerned citizens. For Community Policing to succeed in fulfilling its promise, everyone in the community must understand what it can and cannot be expected to do. Community Policing is not a cure-all for society's ills as much as it serves as a catalyst to involve people in the process of making their neighborhoods better and safer places in which to live. Maybe the biggest obstacle to Community Policing's widespread acceptance is that it requires a profound, but subtle, shift in thinking. It is not a simple tactic that can be conveyed in a catchy slogan, but a new way of looking at old problems. Embracing the Community Policing approach means more than tinkering with the system; it implies re-thinking the way in which the police deliver service to those they serve.

The authors also hope this book will inspire debate and discussion. While the necessity of putting ideas into words on paper is akin to pinning down those fluttering butterfly wings, readers should not infer that the authors assume that they know what the future will bring. Much of the impetus in writing this book was to inspire a dialogue about Community Policing with others who are equally concerned about helping the police contend with the exciting and daunting challenge of finding new ways to achieve excellence. We hope that this book serves as an important first step in developing a new roadmap that will allow us all to find the best route to a better future.

Robert Trojanowicz
Bonnie Bucqueroux

AUTHOR'S NOTE: Anyone who writes for publication today faces difficult decisions concerning proper terminology. Grammar rules have long dictated that the third-person singular form requires using the masculine pronouns *he, his,* and *him,* yet women have valid concerns that this ignores them. Various alternatives – *he or she, s/he,* or recasting sentences into convoluted forms – often appear awkward. The authors are sensitive to this issue, in particular because of the valuable contribution that women have made as Community Policing Officers; however, to make this book as readable as possible, we have conformed with traditional grammar usage.

We have also had to decide what terms to use for various other groups. For example, we have elected to use the term *black* rather than *African American*. Though *African American* has been suggested as a better alternative, it is not yet clear whether it will emerge as the preferred term. We have also elected to use the term *undocumented alien* as opposed to *illegal alien,* because of the negative connotations implicit in the latter.

The goal was to make this book as grammatically correct and as easily readable as possible. To anyone who may disagree with the choices made, the authors can only reply that no offense was intended. We remain sensitive to such issues and sincerely hope that no offense is taken.

THE TEN PRINCIPLES OF COMMUNITY POLICING

1. Community Policing is both a philosophy and an organizational strategy that allows the police and community residents to work closely together in new ways to solve the problems of crime, fear of crime, physical and social disorder, and neighborhood decay. The philosophy rests on the belief that law-abiding people in the community deserve input into the police process, in exchange for their participation and support. It also rests on the belief that solutions to contemporary community problems demand freeing both people and the police to explore creative, new ways to address neighborhood concerns beyond a narrow focus on individual crime incidents.

2. Community Policing's organizational strategy first demands that everyone in the department, including both civilian and sworn personnel, must investigate ways to translate the philosophy into practice. This demands making the subtle but sophisticated shift so that everyone in the department understands the need to focus on solving community problems in creative, new ways that can include challenging and enlisting people in the process of policing themselves. Community Policing also implies a shift within the department that grants greater autonomy to line officers, which implies enhanced respect for their judgment as police professionals.

3. To implement true Community Policing, police departments must also create and develop a new breed of line officer, the Community Policing Officer (CPO), who acts as the direct link between the police and people in the community. As the department's community outreach specialists, CPOs must be freed from the isolation of the patrol car and the demands of the police radio, so that they can maintain daily, direct, face-to face contact with the people they serve in a clearly defined beat area.

4. The CPO's broad role demands continuous, sustained contact with the law-abiding people in the community, so that together they can explore creative new solutions to local concerns involving crime, fear of crime, disorder, and decay, with private citizens serving as unpaid volunteers. As full-fledged law enforcement officers, CPOs respond to calls for service and make arrests, but they also go beyond this narrow focus to develop and monitor broad-based,

long-term initiatives that can involve community residents in efforts to improve the overall quality of life in the area over time. As the community's ombudsman, CPOs also link individuals and groups in the community to the public and private agencies that offer help.

5. Community Policing implies a new contract between the police and the citizens it serves, one that offers the hope of overcoming widespread apathy, at the same time it restrains any impulse to vigilantism. This new relationship, based on mutual trust, also suggests that the police serve as a catalyst, challenging people to accept their share of the responsibility for solving their own individual problems, as well as their share of the responsibility for the overall quality of life in the community. The shift to Community Policing also means a slower response time for non-emergency calls and that citizens themselves will be asked to handle more of their minor concerns, but in exchange this will free the department to work with people on developing long-term solutions for pressing community concerns.

6. Community Policing adds a vital proactive element to the traditional reactive role of the police, resulting in full-spectrum police service. As the only agency of social control open 24 hours a day, seven days a week, the police must maintain the ability to respond to immediate crises and crime incidents, but Community Policing broadens the police role so that they can make a greater impact on making changes today that hold the promise of making communities safer and more attractive places to live tomorrow.

7. Community Policing stresses exploring new ways to protect and enhance the lives of those who are most vulnerable — juveniles, the elderly, minorities, the poor, the disabled, the homeless. It both assimilates and broadens the scope of previous outreach efforts, such as Crime Prevention and Police/Community Relations units, by involving the entire department in efforts to prevent and control crime in ways that encourage the police and law-abiding people to work together with mutual respect and accountability.

8. Community Policing promotes the judicious use of technology, but it also rests on the belief that nothing surpasses what dedicated human beings, talking and working together, can achieve. It invests trust in those who are on the front lines together on the street, relying on their combined judgment, wisdom, and expertise to fashion creative new approaches to contemporary community concerns.

9. Community Policing must be a fully integrated approach that involves everyone in the department, with the CPOs as specialists in bridging the gap between the police and the people they serve. The Community Policing approach plays a crucial role internally, within the police department, by providing information and assistance about the community and its problems, and by enlisting broad-based community support for the department's overall objectives.

10. Community Policing provides decentralized, personalized police service to the community. It recognizes that the police cannot impose order on the community from outside, but that people must be encouraged to think of the police as a resource they can use in helping to solve contemporary community concerns. It is not a tactic to be applied, then abandoned, but an entirely new way of thinking about the police role in society, a philosophy that also offers a coherent and cohesive organizational plan that police departments can modify to suit their specific needs.

CONTENTS

SECTION ONE

WHAT COMMUNITY POLICING MEANS

CHAPTER 1
What Community Policing Is
– and Is Not

The legitimate object of government is to do for a community of people whatever they need to have done, but cannot do at all, or cannot so well do for themselves, in their separate and individual capacities.
　　　　　　　　　　　　—Abraham Lincoln

The Community Policing Revolution

Community Policing is the first major reform in policing since police departments embraced scientific management principles more than a half-century ago. It is a dramatic change in the way police departments interact with the public, a new philosophy that broadens the police mission from a narrow focus on crime to a mandate that encourages the police to explore creative solutions for a host of community concerns, including crime, fear of crime, disorder, and neighborhood decay. Community Policing rests on the belief that only by working together will people and the police be able to improve the quality of life in the community, with the police not only as enforcers, but also as advisors, facilitators, and supporters of new community-based, police-supervised initiatives.

The Community Policing philosophy also embodies a new organizational strategy that allows police departments to decentralize police service, with a new breed of police officer as the department's direct link to average citizens. This new Community Policing Officer (CPO) is a mini-chief in a specific beat area, a generalist who considers making arrests as only one of many options that can be used to solve problems. As the community's catalyst for positive change, the CPO enlists average citizens in the process of policing themselves. The CPO also serves as the community's ombudsman to other public and private agencies that offer help. By stationing these officers permanently in the community, police departments can look beyond addressing immediate problems today, toward making substantive, long-term changes that will enhance the overall quality of community life over time. By empowering average citizens and allowing them a new voice in setting local police priorities, Community Policing challenges both police officers and private citizens to find creative, new ways to solve both old and new problems.

What started as an experiment has now exploded into a widely accepted, growing movement. More than 300 departments now report that they already have some form of Community Policing.[1] While that number is only a fraction of the thousands of police departments nationwide, it includes only those who have formally notified the National Center for Community Policing, and among those who have embraced Community Policing are the trendsetting police departments in New York City and Los Angeles. As professor David Carter of Michigan State University says, "This is the cutting edge of policing in America today."[2]

Yet despite impressive progress, many people both inside and outside police departments still do not know precisely what Community Policing is and what it can do. Though many have heard that Community Policing offers important new answers to pressing problems, far fewer actually know how it works and what kind of future it portends. Does Community Policing work in practice or is it just a pipe-dream? Is Community Policing simply a new name for Police/Community Relations? Is it foot patrol? Is it Crime Prevention? Is it Problem-Oriented Policing? Is it a gimmick, a fad, a promising trend – or is it an unstoppable new way of policing?

Much of the confusion surrounding Community Policing stems from three basic factors:

- Community Policing had a long and difficult birth, which has raised some questions about its goals and uses.

- The movement continues to suffer because some police departments claim to have Community Policing, but they violate the spirit or the letter of what true Community Policing demands.

- Community Policing threatens the status quo, which always generates resistance and spawns controversy, even more so because Community Policing also challenges basic beliefs. It also requires substantive changes in the organizational structure of police departments and the definition of the patrol officer's mission.

What It Is

Before discussing these factors in detail, the following is a basic definition of Community Policing:

> Community Policing is a new philosophy of policing, based on the concept that police officers and private citizens working together in creative ways can help solve contemporary community problems related to crime, fear of crime, social and physical disorder, and neighborhood decay. The philosophy is predicated on the belief that achieving these goals requires that police departments develop a new relationship with the law-abiding people in the community, allowing them a greater voice in setting local police priorities and involving them in efforts to improve the overall quality of life in their neighborhoods. It shifts the focus of police work from handling random calls to solving community problems.
>
> The Community Policing philosophy is expressed in a new organizational strategy that allows police departments to put theory into practice. This requires freeing some patrol officers from the isolation of the patrol car and the incessant demands of the police radio, so that these officers can maintain direct, face-to-face contact with people in the same defined geographic (beat) area every day. This new Community Policing Officer (CPO) serves as a generalist, an officer whose mission includes developing imaginative, new ways to address the broad spectrum of community concerns embraced by the Community Policing philosophy. The goal is to allow CPOs to *own* their beat areas, so that they can develop the rapport and trust that is vital in encouraging people to become involved in efforts to address the problems in their neighborhoods. The CPO acts as the police department's outreach to the community, serving as the people's link to other public and private agencies that can help. The CPO not only enforces the law, but supports and supervises community-based efforts aimed at local concerns. The CPO allows people direct input in setting day-to-day, local police priorities, in exchange for their cooperation and participation in efforts to police themselves.
>
> Community Policing requires both a philosophical shift in the way that police departments think about their mission, as well as a commitment to the structural changes this new form of policing demands. Community Policing provides a new way for the police to

provide decentralized and personalized police service that offers every law-abiding citizen an opportunity to become active in the police process.

While that statement and the **Ten Principles** at the beginning of the book make Community Policing sound so appealing that it would seem that all police departments would be eager to jump on board the bandwagon, a closer look shows that it demands profound changes in the way traditional police departments view their role. Though an oversimplification, traditional policing implies that the police department imposes law and order on the community, while Community Policing makes the all-important shift to understanding that the police role must be to encourage and support people's efforts to police themselves.

In that sense, Community Policing adds the *carrot* to the *stick,* providing *full-spectrum* policing that embraces a broad range of community needs and concerns, as diverse as the need to provide a quick response to a crisis that motor patrol provides best, to the police-supervised neighborhood initiatives that are the hallmark of Community Policing. Crucial as well is that Community Policing is not an add-on – deploying a handful of CPOs does not constitute a commitment to Community Policing. It is, instead, a new way of looking at the business of policing, an approach that reinvigorates the way that police departments think and act.

Though these ideas and themes will be examined many times throughout the book, the following are key words that can help define what Community Policing is:

- **Philosophy/Strategy/Tactic** – Though a semantic debate about whether a new concept is a philosophy, a strategy, or merely a tactic may sound like quibbling, experience shows that a failure to understand how broadly a new concept must be applied can doom a promising new idea before it has a chance to demonstrate what it can do. In this context, a *philosophy* is defined as what you think and believe, a *strategy* is how you put the philosophy into practice, and a *tactic* is one method that can be used to achieve a narrowly defined goal.

  To understand the distinctions, for the sake of argument, suppose that you have decided to adopt a personal philosophy based on *brotherly love.* The next step is for you to develop a coherent strategy to express that philosophy in your behavior. This might require making a personal commitment that all future personal interactions must be based on honesty, respect, compassion, courtesy, and sensitivity to the other person's needs. One tactic you might choose to employ would be to make a habit of saying *please* and *thank you.* Another might be to mark a calendar with all your friends' birthdays, so that you never forget to send a card or make a call.

As this illustrates, a philosophical change must find its expression in a coherent strategy – just believing in brotherly love is not enough if it does not alter your behavior. A tactic plays a far more limited role – after all, people can say *please* and *thank you* without having any commitment to brotherly love.

This helps explain why it is crucial to understand that Community Policing is a new philosophy that offers a coherent strategy that departments can use to guide them in making the structural changes that allow the concept to become real. Community Policing is not just a tactic that can be applied to solve a particular problem, one that can be abandoned once the goal is achieved. It implies a profound difference in the way the police view their role. Just adopting one or more tactics associated with Community Policing is not enough. Conversely, departments that embrace Community Policing must not only change the way they think, but the way they act.

- **Foot Patrol** – Adding to the confusion, many people have good reason to wonder whether Community Policing and foot patrol are the same thing, since the two terms have often been used interchangeably. The distinction is that Community Policing is a philosophy, whereas foot patrol is just one tactic that can be used to put line officers in closer contact with people. A police department can have true Community Policing without using foot patrol, and a department can have foot patrol without a true commitment to Community Policing.

The reason the misnomer of foot patrol stuck for so long stems from the fact that Community Policing has its roots in two experimental foot patrol programs, one in Newark (New Jersey) and one in Flint (Michigan), which were launched and evaluated during the late 1970s and early 1980s. In Newark, the initial foot patrol experiment used foot patrol as a limited tactic – the goal was to see whether putting officers back into the community on foot would deter crime. The Flint experiment went substantially further, using foot patrol officers as part of a strategy to involve officers directly in community problem-solving, with the officers trained to do far more than act as a visible deterrent to crime. Both experiments reflected the growing realization that something important may have been lost in the process of putting officers into patrol cars, and that there might be a way to update the role of the old-fashioned beat cop to address contemporary community problems.

The promising research results from the Flint experiment persuaded the C.S. Mott Foundation of Flint to fund the National Neighborhood Foot Patrol Center at Michigan State University's School of Criminal Justice in 1984. At that time, no one quite knew what to call this new approach, so it made sense to refer to the tactic used in Flint. Many new names continued to crop up – Community-Oriented Policing, Neighborhood Policing, Neighborhood-Oriented Policing. Finally, in 1988, the center changed its name to the National Center for Community Policing as the best expression of what this new philosophy represents.

Part of the confusion concerning what Community Policing is and what it can do results from the years during which people used the term foot patrol as a synonym. Foot patrol conjures up the image of a beat cop rattling doorknobs and smiling at people on the street, and it also harkens back to the days when this close contact with the community was tainted by corruption. A modern-day CPO plays a vastly more demanding role, as a true professional who serves as an autonomous mini-chief, involving people in a wide variety of new initiatives. Deploying officers on foot for crowd control along parade routes, or using foot patrol solely as a visible deterrent to maintain order in business districts, is not Community Policing. It is also important to note that CPOs who walk a beat on foot have not suffered problems of corruption like the foot patrol officers of the past, since the community acts as an additional check on their behavior, as will be discussed in depth later.

- **Problem-Oriented Policing/Problem-Solving Policing** – Confusion also surrounds the relationship between Community Policing and Problem-Oriented Policing (also called Problem-Solving Policing), which are different but compatible concepts. Essentially, Problem-Oriented Policing asks line officers to use their heads, to look for the underlying dynamics behind a series of incidents, rather than to focus on the individual occurrences as isolated events. The confusion arises because Community Policing urges CPOs to use Problem-Solving techniques, but it also demands that police departments make substantive structural changes, so that CPOs can act as the department's specialists in identifying, carrying out, and monitoring long-term solutions.

Noted proponents of Problem-Oriented Policing, such as Herman Goldstein of the University of Wisconsin School of Law and the leadership of the Police Executive Research Forum (PERF),[3] recognize the benefits of involving officers directly in the community. But the definition of Problem-Oriented Policing does not expressly demand this commitment to restructuring departments to promote continuous community involvement.

The quintessential example used to explain how Problem-Oriented Policing works is the problem of a series of pursesnatchings at a bus stop, where young predators snatch a pocketbook from one of the bus patrons standing inside an L-shaped pipe barrier, then they dash down the alley immediately nearby. The traditional police response is to send an available motor patrol officer to the scene each time the department receives a call. Like so many crime problems, a call for service triggers the police response, but the call rarely comes until after the crime has been committed, defeating much of the usefulness of rapid response. By the time the officer arrives, he usually does little more than take a report, since the culprits are long gone.

Problem-Oriented Policing instead suggests that a technique like crime-mapping or crime analysis would flag the department to the persistent problems at that corner. An officer skilled in Problem-Oriented Policing would investigate why that particular bus stop had so many pursesnatchings. In this case, the solution lies in making two obvious changes. First, move the bus stop away from the alley, so that the predators cannot simply disappear. At the same time, it also makes sense to eliminate the pipe barrier completely, since it simply herds potential victims into one restricted spot. If it is important to identify where patrons should stand, it makes much better sense to paint lines on the sidewalk so potential predators know that someone might pursue them as they run away.

Traditional police, trained to think solutions lie in responding to calls and catching the bad guys, must be educated to make the shift from an agenda driven by responding to isolated incidents to one focused on solving the underlying problem in new ways. Critics of Problem-Oriented Policing worry that this kind of solution does nothing to take the bad guys off the street and that the crimes will simply be displaced when those pursesnatchers find a different site where they can ply their trade. Yet crime is opportunistic, and anything that the police can do to make it tougher for the bad guys to commit crimes and get away with them holds the promise of reducing crime overall.

Community Policing approaches problems somewhat differently and it may focus more on quality of life concerns. To show both the overlap and the distinctions, we can use this example to illustrate the Community Policing approach – same bus stop, same pursesnatchings. In this case, the CPO assigned to the beat area would be likely to uncover the problem on his own, rather than to have it flagged to his attention by central headquarters. In fact, a CPO might well discover the problem even if the department never did. Many victims never report crimes to the police, especially in cases where it is unlikely the police will be able to recover their stolen property or they have no need for a police report to give the insurance company. In a traditional department, unless enough victims report pursesnatchings to the police, there may never be enough pins clustered at that spot on the map at headquarters to alert the department that there is a problem at that site. With Community Policing, the CPO stands a much better chance of hearing about the situation from the victims, other bus patrons, or from the people who live nearby.

A CPO would also employ the same problem-solving tactics – moving the bus stop and eliminating the pipe barrier – but his continued presence in the community would also allow him to find out whether those solutions worked. Again, not everyone who is victimized reports the crime to the police, so a department without Community Policing might never know whether the changes actually solved the problem or not.

The CPO also has more of an opportunity to pursue the problem further, over time. As part of routine home visits with neighbors in the area, the CPO may generate information about the kids who may have been causing the problem, especially since people learn to trust their CPOs, which makes it more likely they will tell what they know. Another consideration is that those who fear retaliation may be less willing to share their suspicions with a motor patrol officer. People tend to become silent when they realize that the relatively rare sight of a patrol car parked outside their home may be a red flag to the kids who committed the crimes. In contrast, CPOs routinely stop and chat with people and make home visits, which allows people to share information without calling undue attention to themselves. The CPO's continued presence also means people can pass on new or remembered information long afterward, without the need for them to make any special effort to contact the police.

A CPO can follow up potential leads without focusing on arrest as the only solution to the problem. Once given the names of likely perpetrators, the CPO can talk to the parents and to the kids. The CPO is not there to make an arrest, but to share his concerns; he can warn the kids that he is watching them – and he can offer them help as well. Enterprising CPOs have initiated many creative efforts targeted at high-risk kids, including enlisting them in efforts to help make the community safer, thereby transforming them from predators to protectors. CPOs also routinely work on developing enriching community-based activities for kids that offer the promise of helping to keep them out of trouble, especially since the CPO's supervision allows the officer informal opportunities to reinforce positive values.

Depending on the particular circumstances, the CPO might also choose to enlist Neighborhood Watch in special efforts to monitor the bus stop. Or the CPO might also make periodic stops at the new site at times when the crimes usually occur, to involve the regular patrons in efforts to look out for one another and to share with him any information about kids they see hanging around. By demonstrating that the police take the problem seriously, the CPO encourages people to provide information, without which the police cannot hope to solve problems.

As this comparison shows, Community Policing and Problem-Oriented Policing are not the same, but they mesh together so well that many people mistakenly think they are identical. In essence, solving problems is an important aspect of Community Policing, and a department that encourages its officers to use Problem-Oriented techniques can make greater use of their potential as part of a Community Policing approach. As Edmonton (Canada) Superintendent Chris Braiden says, Problem-Oriented Policing "walks the talk" of Community Policing.[4]

In this book, readers should be made aware that the term Community Policing embraces the idea that all officers in the police department will be trained in and encouraged to use Problem-Oriented tactics, and that CPOs can make particular use of such tactics because they can anticipate and identify problems, tailor solutions to local needs, and provide sustained, street-level evaluation and follow-up.

- **Working Together** – Community Policing dramatically alters the relationship between police officers and the people they serve. In the traditional approach, administrators tell supervisors what to do, then supervisors tell officers what to do, and then the officers tell people in the community what to do. "Just the facts, m'am," was *Dragnet* Sgt. Joe Friday's famous line.

  Back in the 1950s, when that series was on TV, everyone seemed to agree that that was how the police should handle the job. A police officer commanded respect and demanded answers – he was the person holding all the power in any interaction with the public. His narrow mandate – solve the crime – meant that he could not allow anything to interfere with that goal. He had no time to listen to anyone's *petty* concerns, such as rowdy kids in the neighborhood, barking dogs, or potholes in the street. Sgt. Friday showed little sympathy or concern even for frightened victims, since their emotions simply got in the way of his opportunity to get the facts.

  Imagine if Joe Friday had said, "Please go ahead and tell me about the problems and concerns you see in this neighborhood. Maybe we can work together not only to solve this particular crime, but to tackle some of the other things that you and your neighbors are worried about." Equally as shocking to the traditional mindset is the thought that Sgt. Friday would then inform his superiors that he and some people in the community planned to work together on ridding the area of problems such as panhandling and vandalism.

  As this demonstrates, the Community Policing philosophy rests on two important departures from the past:

- **Developing Trust** – Community Policing suggests that to get "the facts," the police must do more than attempt to impose their authority, that they must find new ways to promote cooperation between citizens and the police. Information is the lifeblood of policing. Without the facts, police officers cannot solve problems. The challenge the police face in getting information is that there are two kinds of people who have information about crime – the perpetrators and their associates and the law-abiding people who consciously or unconsciously possess information that the police need. Traditional efforts focus on the former, while Community Policing broadens the focus to solicit information from the law-abiding people, through both formal and informal contacts.

  The traditional police approach offers only limited opportunities for officers to tap the information that law-abiding people possess. Many times, the only contact that motor patrol officers have with law-abiding people is as part of a formal effort to gather information from victims or possible witnesses shortly after a crime has been committed. Obviously as well, such occasions often mean the people are under unusual stress, which makes it even more difficult for them to share what they know with someone they may never have seen before. Another difficulty lies in the fact that an armed, uniformed officer who is a stranger can seem intimidating – and this is an image that many traditional officers strive to cultivate. In addition, the unbalanced power relationship, where the officer appears to have all the power and the person has none, can make people feel their own power lies in just saying *no.*

In contrast, a CPO has numerous opportunities for formal and informal talks with the law-abiding people in the community. During routine home and business visits, neighborhood meetings, and chats on the street, people can pass vital information without arousing suspicion that they are *squealing to the cops.* When CPOs follow up after a crime has been committed, they can often elicit more and better information from victims and witnesses because they have already established a bond of trust.

- **Sharing Power** – The second dramatic departure from the past is that the CPO's agenda is influenced by the community's needs and desires, not just the dictates of the department. It provides a *quid pro quo,* with the CPO saying to people in the beat area: If you provide information and assistance, in exchange, you receive an opportunity to have input into the police priorities in your community. That sounds like common sense, and it is. Yet it also implies a distinct threat to the power enjoyed by the department under the existing system, where the top officials reserve the exclusive right to decide local police priorities.

Empowering average citizens also requires an important adjustment in the line officer's thinking. Traditional officers who believe their authority should be sufficient to demand compliance may find it difficult to make the shift to sharing power demanded by Community Policing. A traditional officer like a Joe Friday would find it tough to chat about seemimgly petty concerns, but going that important step further to allow people greater control of his daily agenda would no doubt trouble him even more. The best CPO's understand that people aren't obstacles the officer must overcome to do the job, but a tremendous resource that can be tapped to make the community a better and safer place overall. It also takes the sustained presence of a CPO to persuade people that the department now sees them in this new light, and that the commitment to sharing power is real.

The CPO's challenge also includes involving people directly in efforts to solve problems in the community. Not only does Community Policing encourage people to act as the eyes and ears of the department 24 hours a day, but it solicits their direct participation in solving problems far beyond basics such as Neighborhood Watch. It might mean encouraging volunteers to help staff the local office. It could mean urging groups of parents to volunteer their time to coach summer athletic activities for kids. It often means asking businesses to donate goods, services, or expertise. The goal is for the CPO to recruit as many volunteers as possible, so that the community has dozens of new workers trying hard to make a positive difference, yet taxpayers only have to pay for the CPOs.

Chief Gary Leonard of the Alexandria (Virginia) Police Department has made tremendous use of volunteers, including two retired colonels who help analyze intelligence and a statistician who spends four hours each week providing sophisticated crime analysis. Leonard also uses volunteers to make callbacks to property crime victims whose cases are not assigned for further investigation. Those calls often uncover that the "crime" has been "solved" – that stolen bicycle or lawnmover was actually borrowed by a friend, but the apparent victim never thought to call the department to let them know. Leonard said this effort alone has dramatically improved the department's clearance rates, and people single him out when he gives speeches to tell him how much they appreciated being called, even though they could offer no new information and the department could offer no new help.

- **Creative** – The Community Close-Ups in this book demonstrate that Community Policing will work in any kind of police department, from those in big cities to small towns. Community Policing's flexibility is a reflection of its focus on creativity and innovation. In one Florida community, CPOs are making a difference in kids' lives by rewarding any youngster who brings in a bag of litter with a football or softball donated by local merchants. A midwestern Community Policing effort held Neighborhood Watch meetings across the street from open dope dealing, which ultimately drove the dealers away, without engaging the rest of the expensive criminal justice system that all too often seems to operate like a revolving door. With Community Policing, the shape of the solution is dictated by the nature of the problem.

  In the Flint experiment, an enterprising CPO convinced the teenagers who had been terrorizing park visitors that they should instead accept the responsibility for maintaining the park and protecting both the young and the old who wanted to use the facility. The CPO's ability to convert these kids from being the problem to being the solution shows how Community Policing can enhance the quality of community life without relying on the threat of arrest as the primary means to effect positive change.

  The explosion of new ideas generated by Community Policing efforts nationwide certifies that the approach is bounded only by the imagination of the people involved and the particular needs of the community. Departments can also trade ideas and then tailor them to local resources and local needs. Community Policing provides *accountable* creativity, because new ideas must meet the needs of both the department and the community, since both set the boundaries concerning what the police role should be.

- **Crime, Fear of Crime, Disorder, and Quality of Life** – As this list implies, the Community Policing philosophy defines the police mission broadly. Other chapters will discuss in greater detail why *crime* should not always be viewed as a series of single, isolated events, but as part of a process that often includes social and physical disorder and neighborhood decay. For now, it is important to understand that Community Policing says that police officers must do more than concentrate only on specific crime incidents, by looking for pressure points in the underlying dynamics that might lend themselves to providing new solutions.

    Community Policing also means that the police must accept new responsibilities in dealing with fear of crime, disorder, and quality-of-life issues in addition to a narrow focus on crime. Experience shows that many people worry as much or more about seemingly petty problems, such as vandalism or barking dogs, as they do about crimes like murder, because they realize the threat of being murdered is relatively small, but the dog that keeps them up all night so they go to work exhausted is a real and immediate problem that directly affects their quality of life.

    Like any other full-fledged law enforcement officer, a CPO's first priority is crime, but as we have already learned, arrest is only one of the tools in the arsenal that they can use to battle crime. Community Policing demands a subtle, sophisticated shift in thinking, so that the entire department learns to focus on how certain problems can be solved, not on how many cases can be cleared. When Bruce Benson was with the Flint Police Department, he spent a year working on B&E's (breaking and enterings). As a result of that year-long effort, only one case actually went to trial – the others never resulted in an arrest or the accused plea bargained to lesser charges. In the case that went to court, the suspect was found guilty – he received five years' probation. That made Benson reflect on how much he had really accomplished for all his hard work. Like many officers in the traditional system, Benson began to question whether there might be a better way than relying on arrest and conviction to cure the social disease of serious crime.

    Not only does a CPO attack crime in ways that may not involve arrest, but Community Policing also recognizes that fear of crime can be as much of a problem as crime itself – it is fear of crime that can trap the elderly in their homes, that makes women afraid to venture out alone. Traditional efforts have little if any ability to reduce fear, unless some aggressive effort targeted at crime succeeds in making people feel safer. Community Policing addresses the problem in new ways. In Brampton, Ontario (Canada), outside Toronto, a creative CPO realized that the elderly's biggest fear is the young – older people often see kids as potential predators who can overpower them, steal from them, and hurt them. To ease both real and unwarranted fears, the CPO recruited high-school students and trained them in Crime Prevention, then he had the youngsters work with the elderly, telling them what they could do to help themselves. The two groups got along famously, especially since both often suffer from needing special attention and someone to listen, and the effort also helped ease the elderly's fears.

As the research shows, most of the calls the police receive have nothing to do with a crime in progress. The bulk of calls involve other problems, often physical or social disorder – a loud party, an abandoned car, uncollected garbage stacking up, a group of rowdy teens on the corner, or drunks who have taken over a neighborhood park. The traditional police mindset that sees officers as law enforcement officers and not peace officers considers such calls as nuisances – they interfere with the real business of policing, which is catching the bad guys. Yet the department's failure to help people cope with these kinds of problems fosters alienation between the police and the people they are supposed to serve. The CPO bridges that gap by acting as the community's catalyst for change, and as their ombudsman to other public and private agencies that can help.

The CPO understands that decaying neighborhoods act as magnets for crime. Even cities such as Washington, D.C., and Detroit, known nationwide as having high rates of violent crime, are actually places where most people are safe, and most people live within the law. What these cities have are hot spots – crime-riddled neighborhoods where the violent few dominate the law-abiding many. And these hot spots are typically places plagued by the so-called *signs of crime* – graffitti, litter, abandoned homes, potholes in the street, weed-choked vacant lots. These are the neighborhoods where drunks and addicts sleep in doorways, teen gangs roam the streets, dope dealers and prostitutes ply their trade openly, and mainstreamed mental patients beg for money or rave at passersby. People need not know anything about crime statistics to sense instinctively that it is far less safe to walk those streets alone at night than a street in an upscale suburban neighborhood, with its manicured lawns and freshly painted homes.

Almost without exception, when a police department announces a new Community Policing effort and solicits input from average citizens, the people do not list Part I or serious crimes – murder, rape, robbery, and aggravated assault – as their primary concerns. People instead usually name relatively petty problems, such as vandalism, noise, street people, and low-level dope dealing. Again, the shift required in embracing the Community Policing philosophy requires that the police department must learn to listen to what people want, not what the police think they should care about.

In a Community Policing effort in Windsor, Ontario (Canada), the six constables who operate out of a Cooperation Station, a facility in a public housing project where the police share space with social services, have a unique way of addressing two important problems at the same time in an effort that directly enhances the quality of life in the area. All first-time juvenile offenders in the county are routinely assigned to diversion. This means that CPOs now supervise these youngsters twice a week as they plant flowers, pick up litter, and do many other chores that help the area look better. This effort allows the youngsters and the constables to get to know each other on a first-name basis – at the same time it allows the constables to identify these high-risk youngsters on sight, which reminds the kids that they cannot operate anonymously anymore.

Besides providing the youngsters with a structured and meaningful way to pay the community back for their transgressions, it offers these youngsters the chance to experience the satisfaction of a job well done, one that makes a visible improvement in how the neighborhood looks. That sense of pride can help boost self-esteem, and the kids have the chance to feel what it is like to contribute by doing something that people appreciate. Such efforts can also help the entire area reverse the downward cycle, where decay begets further decay which promotes crime.

To many traditionalists, this sounds suspiciously like a *touchy-feely,* New Age, social-work orientation – worrying about having youngsters plant flowers does not sound much like *real* police work. Real officers save lives and catch crooks, yet as we will see in later chapters, the police play only a limited role in the overall dynamics of crime, but a community in obvious chaos makes everyone feel afraid, and people look to the police for answers.

- **Community Policing Officers (CPOs)** – A CPO is a new breed, an officer who sees himself as a community problem-solver and not just as a crime-fighter. A CPO answers calls and make arrests, just like any other police officer, but that is only the minimum requirement. The CPO acts as a innovator, looking beyond individual incidents for new ways to solve problems. The CPO is the police department's direct link to the community, providing policing with a human touch, an officer that people know on a first-name basis and as a friend who can help.

  The CPO acts as a catalyst, involving people in efforts to police themselves. The CPO operates as a mini-chief in the assigned beat area, with the autonomy to do what it takes to solve the problems people care about most. The CPO also acts as a referral specialist, the community's ombudsman who can link people to the public and private services that can help and who can jog reluctant bureaucracies to do the jobs they are supposed to do. The CPO acts as the Crime Prevention and Police/Community Relations specialist, but those aspects of the CPO's job are the result of providing full-fledged police service on a daily basis.

The hallmark of Community Policing is that the effort is tailored to local needs, which also means that elements of how the CPO operates in the community reflects local resources and local concerns. In some programs, the CPOs operate out of offices in schools, public housing complexes, or even in shopping malls. As mentioned before, the CPOs in Windsor operate out of a multi-purpose Cooperation Station – the name itself was the winning entry in a contest held for school kids in which the winner received a skateboard donated by a soft-drink manufacturuer.

Some CPOs walk the beat, while others may ride a horse or a bike. The mode of transportation is not as important as the commitment to ensuring the CPO has the time and opportunity to talk with people formally and informally. It is also important that CPOs take calls like any other officer, though some departments have decided to phase this in over time, as a way to reduce internal dissent by allowing the CPOs to prove their worth first.

Aurora (Colorado) may prove to be the wave of the future, because its Community Policing effort requires each area within the department to identify ways it can express the Community Policing philosophy, to make sure that CPOs are not forced to carry the whole load alone. The department has changed its slogan from *Serve and Protect* to *Community Commitment,* and a special committee has been formed to evaluate proposals concerning how every area in the department can help make the shift real. Among the dozens of proposals submitted, one idea already approved is to develop an internal and external reference directory, so that anyone who calls the department will ideally be referred to the right person in the right agency or department on the first try. That might sound trivial, but it focuses on helping people avoid the maddening traditional bureaucratic response, where people are shuffled around in a telephone version of Russian roulette. Another proposal involves restructuring the investigations unit, to allow more time with victims, focusing on their needs.

Obviously, the shift to Community Policing also requires a shift in how the department assesses performance, both the performance of the department as a whole and also how it rates various jobs. In the case of CPOs in particular, the department faces a new challenge in finding ways to measure quality, not quantity. As David Carter (author of the upcoming chapter on research) learned in his days as a police officer, the traditional system typically evaluates line officers on factors such as miles driven and tickets issued, as well as on subjective determinations about appearance and *bravery.*

Not only do these measures have little to do with a CPO's effectiveness, Carter also suggests they probably have little to do with a traditional line officer's effectiveness either. When Carter worked as a motor patrol officer himself, he found these measures pressured even the most dedicated officers to learn how to manipulate the system to generate the numbers explicitly or implicitly required to win a supervisor's approval. Carter discovered that he had difficulty racking up enough miles patrolling his tiny beat area, but then an old hand showed him how taking a big loop on the interstate on the way to and from his beat would keep the supervisor happy. That same officer also told Carter which traffic signal to visit at rush hour – an easy way to ticket enough drivers running red lights to ensure meeting the unofficial daily quota. By mastering these gimmicks, looking neat, and acting macho, an officer could please his superiors and enhance his chances for promotion without anyone worrying much about whether all this effort had much to do with an officer's effectiveness and whether there was any direct benefit to the community.

Contrast that system with the one that Chief Alex Longoria has instituted in MacAllen (Texas), where CPOs are handed a blank sheet of paper and told they must write about what they want to accomplish and what they have done and will do to achieve those goals. Or the system in Aurora where all personnel, both sworn and civilian, are evaluated (at least in part) on how they are working to implement this new commitment to the community. The traditional policing system focuses on generating numbers, while the Community Policing approach focuses on producing results.

- **Particular Geographic (Beat) Area** – The importance of stationing a CPO permanently in a specific beat area rests on allowing the officer to *own* that particular piece of the overall turf. The optimal size of each beat can differ dramatically from place to place. The goal is to keep the geographic area small enough so that the officer can get around the entire beat area often enough to maintain direct contact. In high-density, high-crime areas, a CPO might only be able to handle a few blocks at most, while in a relatively tranquil residential area of single-family homes, the CPO's ability to cover the physical distance might be the primary limiting factor.

Another important consideration in setting up beats is for the department to identify areas of community cohesion. Whenever possible, it pays not to divide a distinct neighborhood so that it falls into two or more beat areas. The goal is to decentralize police service by dividing the area into logical and manageable units, so that people can receive *small-town* police service regardless of whether they live in MacAllen, Texas, or mid-town Manhattan.

A major misunderstanding about Community Policing stems from the misconception that the goal in freeing the officer from the patrol car is so that the officer serves as a visible deterrent to crime on the street. While that may be a useful by-product of freeing CPOs from the patrol car, the more important purpose is to involve the officer in the life of the community, so that the CPO knows what is going on and can find new ways to solve problems with the aid of the law-abiding people in the area who care.

In the Flint foot patrol project, there was roughly one foot officer for each 2,500 people, so some residents at first complained that they were not seeing the officer in front of their homes often enough. The department must educate people about how Community Policing works, because false expectations will lead them to feel disappointed. Again, this also certifies why it is important to stop using the term foot patrol as if it meant Community Policing, since that only adds to confusion about how this new approach works.

- **Direct, Daily, Face-to-Face Contact** – Community Policing also rests on maintaining the same CPO in the same beat every day. The goal is to involve CPOs so deeply in the life of the community that the officers feel responsible for what happens in their beat areas, and the people who live there learn to trust them and work with them – and hold them accountable for their successes and failures. CPOs should not be used as *pinch hitters* to fill vacancies elsewhere in the department, nor should they be rotated in and out of different beats. The only way that Community Policing can work is when both the officers and the residents can count on the CPO's continued, daily presence.

    Considerable debate swirls around the question of whether CPOs should be allowed to use cars for at least part of the day, simply so that they can get around their beat areas more quickly. The optimal situation allows CPOs to walk or ride a horse, motorscooter, or bicycle around the beat area, to make it easy to stop and chat and to reassure people that the officer is willing to take the same risks on the street that they are. In high-density, high-crime areas, freeing officers from patrol cars altogether may be an essential step in reversing the downward spiral, so that people begin to find the courage to reclaim their streets from predators. That may make less sense in residential areas that serve as bedroom communities, especially since many are virtually empty during the day.

    The danger in the traditional system's reliance on the patrol car is that it becomes a barrier to communication with the law-abiding people in the community. Officers trapped inside cars become slaves to the police radio, which serves less as a link to people in the community than as a means for the department to control the officer's agenda. Especially in big cities, if CPOs use patrol cars with police radios, they can find they no longer have the time or opportunity to talk directly to people, since they dare not risk missing an important call. The temptation is for officers to spend uncommitted time on random patrol, which produces random results. The goal of Community Policing is to focus on working with people directly to solve problems.

One solution might be to provide CPOs who have large areas to cover a patrol car outfitted with a cellular telephone, so that they can use that to talk to people in the community and set up and verify appointments as they go from place to place. Depending on local conditions, some departments are experimenting with using CPOs as part of a team, where the motor officers assigned to the area provide the rapid response, while the CPO acts as the outreach specialist, handling calls for service that do not require an immediate response and focusing on efforts to involve people in proactive efforts.

There is an obvious danger in suggesting that police administrators can consider the elements that make up Community Policing as a shopping list from which they can pick and choose the things that sound easy to adopt and ignore those that are difficult to implement. Yet Community Policing can take different forms in different areas, depending on the internal dynamics of the department and the external situations in the community. Ultimately, the sincerity of the commitment to the concept probably matters more than the particulars, and some departments may have good reason to phase in aspects of the approach over time, in the hope of reducing internal resistance.

It usually does not take much time for the community to trust its new CPOs, but if often takes far longer for everyone in the department to see that Community Policing delivers. To succeed, Community Policing must be nurtured within the department, even as it thrives in the community. Community Policing must not only be tailored to the external environment of the community, but to the internal environment of the department as well.

What It Is Not

To reinforce understanding of what Community Policing *is,* it also pays to look at what Community Policing *is not:*

- **Community Policing is not a technique.** The two philosophies that dominate modern policing are traditional (professionalized) policing, personified by the aloof motor patrol officer zooming to the scene in a patrol car to catch the bad guys, and Community Policing, embodied in the accessible CPO working with neighborhood people to find creative new solutions to local problems. Community Policing is not a technique that departments can apply to a specific problem until it is solved, but an entirely new way of thinking about the role of the police in the community. It says that the police must focus on addressing community concerns, rather than separate crime incidents.

The entire department must be infused with the Community Policing philosophy, with CPOs as the department's community specialists who provide direct, personalized police service, as the department's direct link to average citizens. Community Policing is not something to be used periodically, but it is a permanent commitment to a new kind of policing that provides decentralized and personalized community problem-solving.

- **Community Policing is not public relations.** Improved public relations is a welcome by-product of Community Policing, not its sole or even primary goal. Research shows that people like Community Policing, and its popularity transcends race. Yet unlike Police/Community Relations programs, Community Policing is not a program, an add-on, a unit whose mission is to improve the department's image. Though well intentioned, such limited outreach efforts of the past were criticized for offering sizzle without providing much steak.

  Community Policing instead enhances the department's image because it is a sincere change in the way the department interacts with people in the community. It treats law-abiding people as partners, a new relationship based on mutual trust and shared power. The traditional system often makes people feel that the police do not care about their wants and needs. In traditional departments, officers often see people in the community as *them,* those nameless and faceless strangers whose reluctance to cooperate and share what they know makes them indistinguishable from the criminals. Community Policing instead treats law-abiding people in the community as an extension of *us.*

- **Community Policing is not anti-technology.** The news media loves to cover stories about new crime-fighting technologies – voice prints, gene mapping, sophisticated computer profiling. These advances make it seem that policing has now become a science, not an art, and that crime will soon disappear in the face of the onslaught of these new technological and scientific marvels.

  Canada's Chris Braiden insists that view is a delusion. What the police need to get a handle on solving a crime is a lead – some scrap of information that points them in the right direction. Braiden says forensic science clears less than 1 % of all cases, and that in traditional policing, officers spend only about 2 % of their time with the victims and witnesses who are most likely to have the information that can provide police a likely lead.[5] An additional irony is that the most basic technology – the patrol car, the telephone, the police radio, the computer – have often done much to distance the police further from the people who have the information they need.

  Many people erroneously assume that Community Policing rejects technology, because it refuses to lock the officer into a patrol car and handcuff him to the police radio. In reality, CPOs can make tremendous use of new technologies, such as hand-held computers, remote telephone answering machines, and cellular telephones. Yet Community Policing also recognizes that no technology can compete with a fully functioning, creative human being, whether the person is a police officer or a law-abiding citizen willing to help.

What people often fail to realize is that sophisticated techniques such as gene mapping or voice prints can only confirm whether a suspect is or is not the culprit. There is no centralized computer bank of every citizen's voice print or gene map to identify perpetrators. Before such technologies can make a contribution, good, solid police work must generate the information that leads to arresting a suspect who can be tested.

The amazingly sophisticated techniques that crime labs can use to determine whether someone did or did not commit a crime like rape serves as a useful example. To use those techniques first requires that the victims report the crime to the police, and many women have heard horror stories about how insensitive police officers have made their experience more traumatic than it should have been. The victims must also know about the importance of preserving evidence. CPOs have an obvious role to play, because a rape victim may find it easier to talk to an officer she already knows, and CPOs also conduct workshops and provide information on topics such as rape, including discussions about the importance of preserving evidence.

If the woman did not know her attacker, solving the rape may depend on piecing together shreds of information from the victim and any possible witnesses. People who see the police as strangers are less likely to come forward than those who view the police as friends. The Community Policing approach also means that the CPO is there in the community every day for months afterward, so that witnesses have the opportunity to pass along what may prove to be a crucial shred of information that they just remembered, information that they might not deem important enough to place a call to the department to talk to a stranger. This demonstrates that Community Policing can enhance the department's ability to apply new technologies, by improving the odds that people will provide the information that will allow them to be used.

- **Community Policing is not soft on crime.** Critics suggest that Community Policing's broad mandate and its focus on using tactics other than arrest to solve problems detract from a proper focus on serious crime. CPOs often face derision within the department, from fellow officers who call them *lollicops* or the *grin-and-wave squad*. The reality is that CPOs make arrests just like any other officer does, but CPOs deal with a broader variety of community concerns *in addition to* crime, not as *a substitute* for addressing serious crime. As the chapter on research will show, motor patrol officers typically spend vast amounts of uncommitted time on random patrol, which has little, if any, real impact on serious crime. In contrast, CPOs spend their time between calls on a variety of proactive efforts designed to prevent crime and solve problems.

Crime analysis routinely shows that the majority of calls for service come from a relatively small number of locations. The CPO who makes routine home and business visits to places that are plagued by serious problems may be able to identify new solutions to persistent problems that offer the hope of averting even more serious problems in the future. Who can say whether a CPO's visit to a troubled family where neighbors often call to report they hear a woman or child screaming might prevent a murder. A home visit could help link the family to affordable counseling that the people would not have found on their own. Such proactive efforts may actually deserve credit as a *negative response time* – the police arrive and handle the problem before a crime occurs or someone places a call for service.

- **Community Policing is not flamboyant.** When a SWAT team swoops in and disarms a sniper, everyone cheers and the story makes headlines. When a CPO helps organize a summer softball league for idle youngsters, the long-term impact may be equally as dramatic, but the effort will not rate a lead-off feature on the nightly TV news. The media reinforces the image of the macho police officer whose job is glamorous, tough, and often dangerous. That hero myth also appeals to police officers themselves, which is part of why many officers refuse to volunteer for duty as a CPO. For Community Policing to succeed, however, the entire department must embrace the wisdom of this approach. All officers must focus on working together among themselves and with people in the community on solving community concerns.

In recognition of this new agenda, the police must also learn to reward creativity. In Alexandria (Virginia), the officer who received the Officer of the Year honors in 1988 was not part of a daring sting or a dangerous undercover assignment or an officer who thwarted a bank robbery. The award was instead given to an officer who solved a nagging and potentially dangerous problem by remembering the importance of the human touch. The story begins when this officer left the courthouse one morning, frustrated to find the case at which she was to testify had been continued yet again. Just outside the courthouse, the officer spotted a local drunk who we will call "Jimmy," during one of his rare sober moments.

Jimmy had long been a problem for the department, because when he drank, he became belligerent. Inevitably, someone would call the police, and every officer had good reason to worry that Jimmy would one day seriously injure someone. Over the years, Jimmy had racked up 27 arrests for being drunk and disorderly, and resisting arrest.

Amazed to see Jimmy sober, the officer confronted him about why he became so abusive when he drank – for which Jimmy had no good answer. By talking further, the officer was, however, able to discover that Jimmy survived on two small pensions, one linked to the military. After spending some time on the phone later, the officer was able to confirm this made Jimmy eligible for residential care at a facility that offered treatment for substance abuse. So the officer tracked Jimmy down and cajoled him into visiting the facility with her. He agreed to move in, and now Jimmy lives – alcohol-free – in a place that he enjoys, and the people in the community and the police no longer have to worry he will harm them.

Creativity and persistence solved a potentially serious problem that had plagued the department for years, and the officer received the credit she deserved for finding an innovative solution to an old problem. The fact that the department also cited her as Officer of the Year for this achievement certifies that it has embraced the values of Community Policing – and it also sends a message to everyone in the department that this approach is valuable and that those who adopt this philosophy will be rewarded.

- **Community Policing is not paternalistic.** Police departments are organized as a paramilitary hierarchy where those at the top expect to set the agenda, based on their superior experience and expertise – *father knows best.* This organizational structure also extends beyond the police department itself the way officers typically interact with the community. The message to the average citizen is that the police think people do not know enough about police work to do much more than pay taxes and answer questions, if asked. The traditional, paternalistic police attitude suggests that solving and combatting crime is so complex and difficult that it must be left in the hands of skilled professionals specifically trained for the job. Community Policing threatens those who enjoy the traditional system, because it says that police superiors must stop treating line officers like children who must be watched constantly. It also says that police officers must stop acting like parents to people in the community and must begin treating them like respected partners.

  It also implies a new set of trade-offs. Traditional departments often seek to make friends with the community by providing services such as helping people when they lock their keys in the car. Finding the resources to fund CPOs may require eliminating some services – for example, it might mean that a driver who suffers a fenderbender and needs a police report for the insurance company would be asked to drive to the station instead of expecting the police to dispatch an officer to the scene.

  A shift to Community Policing also means the department will respond more slowly to non-emergency calls. A family that returns home after vacation to find the TV set gone must be educated to understand why it may make better sense to send a

CPO the next day rather than to dispatch a motor officer immediately. Community Policing is predicated on the belief that an informed public will support intelligent choices about what the police role should be, especially once they see that Community Policing treats them as respected partners in the policing process.

- **Community Policing is not an independent entity within the department.** The Community Policing philosophy must infuse the entire department, but the change-over can generate tremendous pressure on the CPOs, who are the most visible expression of the new commitment. The challenge that many new efforts face is finding ways to demonstrate to others in the department how the Community Policing philosophy and those newly deployed CPOs benefit them directly. Detectives and narcotics officers need to understand how cooperating with their CPOs can make their jobs easier, by providing them a new link to the information that law-abiding people have that they are afraid to share with police officers who are strangers. Motor patrol officers in particular must be shown that CPOs not only help them by providing information, but also because they help ease tensions between the police and the community, which can be a particular problem in minority neighborhoods.

  In the Flint experiment, a foot patrol officer arrived on the scene shortly after motor patrol officers had responded to a call about a man brandishing a gun. The foot officer was able to tell his motor patrol peers that the man inside was known as a heavy drinker, and that his wife routinely visited her sister when he got drunk. A phone call there confirmed that the wife was safe and had her children with her, and that the man was probably asleep in the back bedroom. When the officers entered, they found the man passed out in bed as predicted. By working together, the motor officers and the CPO solved the problem with the least risk to themselves and others.

  Departments launching a new Community Policing effort can use *war stories* from elsewhere to educate everyone in the department about how Community Policing benefits the entire department. Police officials should also make a special effort to make sure that any initial successes are touted within the department in ways that do not seem to set CPOs apart from their fellow officers. Integrating the Community Policing philosophy into the day-to-day operation of the entire department is a challenge, one that requires care and feeding over time.

- **Community Policing is not cosmetic.** Unlike Crime Prevention and Police/Community Relations programs, Community Policing goes beyond providing information and expressing goodwill, to making substantive changes in how the department interacts with the public, by broadening the police mandate to focus on proactive efforts that hold the promise of paying off over time. Community Policing is not limited to a special unit or program. CPOs are simply the patrol officers who serve as community outreach specialists, offering direct, decentralized, and personalized police service as part of a full-spectrum Community Policing approach that involves the entire department in new community-based efforts to solve problems.

Unlike limited proactive or community-oriented efforts of the past, Community Policing not only broadens the agenda to include the entire spectrum of community concerns related to crime and disorder, but it offers greater continuity, follow-up, and accountability. Important as well is that Community Policing goes far beyond handing out brochures, making speeches, talking with community leaders, telling people how to guard against crime, and urging fellow officers to treat people with respect. As line officers directly involved in the community, CPOs have the opportunity to make far-reaching changes.

In Florida, a CPO concerned about the poverty and high unemployment in his beat area actively solicited leads on jobs that he posted in the neighborhood office. An innovative officer in the Flint experiment initiated activities for juveniles designed to boost their self-esteem. Community Policing's proactive focus goes beyond target hardening and other relatively superficial solutions, to initiating creative efforts that hold the promise of long-term changes whose full impact may not become fully evident for years. What has been lost in many communities is the continuing presence of a respected agent of social control who not only keeps watch but offers help to make sure good intentions translate into concrete action. A resourceful and attentive CPO can help generate and maintain positive enthusiasm, guarding against back-sliding, so that the police are involved in making visible changes in the quality of life in the community.

- **Community Policing is not a top-down approach.** In traditional policing, the power to make decisions concerning how the police will operate resides in the centralized authority of the police command. They tell the community what the police agenda will be, and they issue orders to underlings in the department concerning how policy will be implemented. Community Policing decentralizes decision-making, opening up departments so that new ideas can surface. Community Policing provides the department grass-roots input from both community residents and line officers, which can help overcome a bureaucracy's inherent tendency to become more stodgy and stagnant over time.

Community Policing goes beyond previous outreach efforts that talked almost exclusively to community leaders, who may or may not have an accurate feel for the concerns of average people on the street. The shift from imposing solutions from the top to soliciting input and support from below not only creates a climate where innovation can flourish, but it can help overcome citizen apathy. Equally as important is that Community Policing can also directly restrain any impulse to vigilantism, by directing that energy into lawful, police-supervised efforts.

- **Community Policing is not just another name for social work.** The broad constellation of problems associated with crime and disorder that plague this society, especially in the inner city, defy simple solutions. Yet critics of Community Policing think that involving officers in efforts that have not traditionally been viewed as part of the police mandate is not only wasteful, but silly. Traditionalists insist that the police have their hands full trying to battle serious crime, so efforts that detract from that effort not only waste valuable time and money, but they can erode the credibility and authority of the police. Their attitude is that the police should leave social work to the social workers, so that the police can focus all their energies on their real and important job of fighting crime.

  Yet this ignores the fact that many police officers are already involved in many efforts that have little, if anything, to do with serious crime – crowd control at public events, protecting politicians, issuing traffic tickets, providing people directions. The question is not whether the police should become involved in efforts that do not directly focus on serious crime but on what kinds of other services they should provide.

  As the only government social agency open 24 hours a day, seven days a week, people call the police for help with a host of problems that have little or nothing to do with serious crime. Yet if the police refuse to help, if only by offering advice on alternative solutions, this further alienates people from the police, which can make people less eager to cooperate when the police later ask for their help.

  The fact is, social work has always been an important element of police work. When line officers talk about the use of police discretion, they mean that the job requires doing more than just sticking to rules and procedures. It also means allowing police officers the freedom to make immediate decisions on their own, including the freedom to solve problems in ways that have nothing to do with arresting bad guys. Though it conflicts with the *superhero* myth, good police officers have always tried to encourage youngsters to live within the law and help the elderly feel less vulnerable.

  Community Policing not only sanctions but also broadens this role, urging all officers to focus on solving community problems and specifically allowing CPOs to use their uncommitted time to initiate efforts to address a wide variety of community concerns. As we will see in succeeding chapters, traditional policing at best has only a limited impact on most serious crime – the officer is almost never there when a drunken husband unexpectedly reaches for a knife in a family fight, when a clandestine dope deal goes sour, or when a mugger in an alley panics and shoots. Yet many people both inside and outside policing think society's crime problems would disappear if the police just crack enough heads and the courts do their part by locking up all the bad guys. This mindset ignores three important realities:

- **Rebellion** – Many people, especially the juveniles who commit the majority of crimes, respond to aggression with rebellion. If the police limit their approach to *getting tough,* they risk alienating the law-abiding people who cross their path, and they also risk abetting the transformation of petty miscreants into hard-core offenders. As we learn more about human dynamics, we see that real or implied violence simply begets more violence – today's abused child stands an increased chance of being tomorrow's abuser. The police must find ways to contribute to an overall reduction in the level of violence in this culture, not only because it is morally right, but because it is also in their enlightened self-interest – unnecessary aggression today may play a role in creating tomorrow's *cop haters.*

  At a practical level, limiting an officer's response to a get-tough approach can also limit effectiveness. A helping hand can often be far more effective in solving a problem than a kick in the pants. The virtue of a Community Policing approach is that CPOs stand a better chance of knowing which response to apply, information that they can share with their peers. CPOs have the opportunity to become so immersed in the lives of the people in their beat areas that they can spot the manipulators and the charming sociopaths who know how to con strangers, including fellow officers whose job does not allow them much opportunity to know people well.

- **Limitations** – Another obvious obstacle in the get-tough approach is that there is not enough jail and prison space to lock up all the bad guys. The reality in many areas today is that there is barely enough room to keep the most serious offenders behind bars – and many of them will commit new crimes again once released. In many high-crime areas, the criminal justice system operates like a revolving door, where offenders are quickly back on the street, and arrest simply provides an inducement to commit more crimes to pay legal fees.

  Not only does this mean that arresting more and more people may ultimately prove futile, experience also shows that prisons often fail to rehabilitate. The system can do little to turn around a serial rapist, which is why scarce prison space is devoted to keeping the most violent offenders off the street. Yet the message to many criminals is that the system does not take property crime seriously, which makes it even harder to use sanctions as a way of turning this pool of career criminals around.

Longer-term solutions may lie in urging the police to explore new ways to intervene with youngsters who are at the greatest risk of pursuing criminal careers as adults. And this means taking the so-called petty crimes of juveniles far more seriously than the current system allows. The sad fact is that the traditional police approach often gives short shrift to crimes like vandalism, despite the fact spending a little more time on that young offender's problem today can save lots of time in the future. The additional irony is that it is far easier for the police to have a positive impact on a youngster whose criminal career begins when he throws a rock through a window than expecting the police to solve the problem posed by a 50-year-old burglar who is far less likely to mend his ways as the result of anything a police officer can do.

A Community Policing approach assists the police in finding new ways to handle juveniles at risk, especially since it encourages officers to consider arrest as only one option they can employ. The juvenile justice system dramatically restricts the use of formal sanctions, so CPOs who are skilled in employing a range of innovative approaches to encourage positive change are the logical candidates to develop new strategies aimed at kids. The benefit to the community is that this approach holds the promise of making streets safer in the future, without the need to keep building more and more jails and prisons.

- **Scope of Service** – The third reality ignored in a narrow, get-tough approach is that roughly four of every five calls for service to any police department do not involve a crime in progress. The romantic vision of the officer as crime fighter, tracking down vicious killers and clever jewel thieves, bears little relationship to how most police officers spend their days and nights. It is far more likely that someone calls needing help with a barking dog, a loud party, a disheveled panhandler who is scaring customers away, or a drunk sleeping in the hallway.

  By labelling these as *nuisance* calls, the police send the message to people that they do not appreciate being asked to waste their time on these annoyances, when they should be out on the streets putting *real* bad guys away. Yet if people who call the police for relatively minor problems are made to feel they are merely bothering the police, the department should not be shocked to find that people are increasingly reluctant to risk their own personal safety to help the police by providing information or direct assistance – or when they are asked to pay more in taxes for police service. People resent a system where the police always seem to have the time to issue them a traffic ticket for speeding on the way to work, yet they cannot find the time to have an officer help stop the neighbor's dog from barking all night.

This is not to say that the police must try to be all things to all people, but they must allow average citizens to have a say in police priorities. Traffic tickets, even those for relatively petty infractions, generate revenue whereas dealing with the barking dog does not. The police must take care to ensure that they do not let economics dictate their total agenda, but they must allow people some voice in what kinds of services they should provide.

This is also not to say that the CPO's job is to pamper people and handle problems that people should be handling for themselves, but it does imply a new way of dealing with so-called nuisance calls. Take, for example, the situation where a CPO received a call from a man who was upset about a group of teens making a racket outside his window playing street hockey. The exasperated man demanded that the officer do something to help. Though it was a tough sell, the CPO challenged the man to go outside and talk to the kids himself – he even gave the man his home number in case the man ran into trouble after the CPO left the office. More than an hour and a half later, the caller phoned again to report he'd had "the time of his life" playing hockey with the kids, and he was simply calling to thank the CPO for persuading him to handle the problem face-to-face by himself.

The police officer must be many things – law enforcement officer and peace officer, armed symbol of authority and part-time social worker. It is this blend of force and compassion that makes the job so potent and unique. No other job in civilian society permits a person to choose from an array of responses that range from flashing a friendly smile to shooting to kill. For many years, the British *bobbies* were famous for not needing to carry guns because they were not only respected but loved by the people they served. Though that has changed in the face of modern realities, it serves as a reminder that verbal aggression and physical force can never provide the total answer to contemporary community problems. Pressuring the police to restrict their options to this narrow range of responses makes as little sense as urging them to load their gun with only one bullet.

- **Community Policing is not elitist.** One of the biggest difficulties that CPOs often face is that they are heroes in the community, but objects of derision among their peers. Some of the resentment stems from the fact it makes little sense to have CPOs walking the beat at night when very few people are awake, so CPOs tend to work what their envious peers consider *banker's hours.* This seemingly preferential treatment can breed internal resentment, especially when people in the community treat CPOs as special friends – in the Flint experiment, community residents organized a picnic that more than 300 people from the beat area attended to honor their foot officer when he was promoted to sergeant. Motor patrol officers often grumble that people do not understand that they are the *real* cops who put their lives on the line for an ungrateful public.

  Left unchecked, this friction can erupt into outright hostility. As we will see in later chapters, departments that launch new Community Policing efforts must pay particular attention to educating everyone in the department about the Community Policing philosophy, the role of the CPO, and how this new way of policing can benefit everyone in the department directly. It takes constant reinforcement from the top to explain that CPOs are not being treated like an elite corps, but as the department's direct link to the community.

  An added irony is that the traditional system is also often called professionalized policing, yet it fails to treat officers like true professionals. A professional is someone whose education and training focus on helping the candidate inculcate the mission and values of the job, in addition to teaching the skills involved. The goal is for the individual to internalize a commitment to the goals and standards of the profession, so that the person can be trusted to use proper judgment without the need for constant supervision.

  If the department makes a sincere commitment to Community Policing, all officers will be accorded greater trust and respect by being treated as true professionals. Community Policing also implies allowing all line officers greater autonomy and according them greater respect – not just CPOs. Experience shows that CPOs often work beyond quitting time, without any overtime pay, because they act like professionals who focus on the task and not on the clock. In essence, the Community Policing commitment offers true professionalization of the police role. It is the traditional system that treats officers like robots, as interchangeable cogs in a wheel, and it is Community Policing that elevates the status of all officers in the department to that of professionals.

- **Community Policing is not designed to favor the rich and powerful in the community.** The dramatic surge in drug-related murders in Washington, D.C., at the end of the 1980s prompted more than one commentator to suggest that if these murders were occurring in an affluent enclave nearby such as Georgetown, the police would be forced to take more action. That damning indictment that the police pay more attention to the problems of the rich and powerful deserves a closer look, because while part of the argument unfairly stacks the deck against the police, it also offers a kernel of truth.

The fact is, of course, that the odds are that an upscale community like Georgetown will never suffer a similar spate of drug-related murders. The mistake is to think that this is because most of the residents of Georgetown obey the law, while the majority of those who live in decaying, crack-riddled neighborhoods in the District of Columbia do not. But what it does mean is that the high price tag required to afford to live in Georgetown means the community does not suffer from poverty, unemployment, illiteracy, overcrowded classrooms, declining health care, despair – the myriad of social ills that plague many inner-city neighborhoods. Crime clusters in neighborhoods that already suffer problems of social and physical disorder, and these problems can overwhelm the law-abiding majority forced by circumstances to live there in fear.

Yet there may well be more than a little truth to the persistent allegations that the police often accede to pressures to pay more attention to the wants and needs of the rich and powerful. Though this can include paying attention to even the most serious crime of murder, any gap in the level of service between rich and poor is likely to grow even wider in the level of response for less important calls for service.

It is easy to see why the police might hustle faster to investigate an abandoned car, up on blocks with no wheels, if the call comes from a senator in Georgetown rather than someone from a bad section in the District. The first reason is that the police in Georgetown may well be far less busy, because there are fewer emergency calls demanding an immediate response. Second, that abandoned car would be a relative rarity in Georgetown, which makes it seem more suspicious – perhaps a bomb? And the unfortunate and unavoidable third reason is that a senator who is unhappy with the police response can do far more to make life miserable for the department. He may well know the chief personally and will have few qualms about calling him at home to complain. That senator also has access to the media, a bully pulpit from which he can denounce the department's inefficiency. And in this case particularly, the senator may also have some say in setting the police budget – or his friends do.

That third reason why the rich and powerful tend to receive better police service makes us feel squeamish, because Americans believe deeply in equality. Yet it is naive to think that the rich and powerful do not have special clout, and that the overall level of police service can decline a bit each rung further down the socio-economic ladder. The mistake lies in thinking the solution is to find some way to curb or eliminate clout at the top. A better and more practical solution is to find ways to even the scales for those who live closer to the bottom, which is precisely what Community Policing can do.

Most departments that phase in CPOs put them first in the decaying, high-crime neighborhoods where the greatest problems of crime and disorder cluster. Upscale communities with expensive homes will benefit from having a department committed to the Community Policing philosophy, but it may – or may not – make sense to station a CPO directly in those neighborhoods, at least at first. CPOs often are so popular that everyone, including those who need their services least, demands equal treatment, yet the most urgent need is usually in the *hot spots,* the neighborhoods where poverty and crime travel together – the places where people suffer from being on the bottom of the power pyramid.

Community Policing is egalitarian in the sense that it says that regardless of whether you have money and power – and despite whether you do or do not vote or pay taxes – law-abiding citizens deserve direct assistance and support from the police. Community Policing empowers people whose lack of economic or political clout makes it hard for them to compete for police attention against the rich and powerful in the community who find it easier to be heard.

- **Community Policing is not a quick fix or panacea.** Perhaps the greatest lesson this country has learned in the past few decades is that social problems such as crime and disorder do not lend themselves to simple solutions. Part of the difficulty in educating people about Community Policing is that it cannot be captured in a slogan – it cannot be conveyed in 10 words or less. It is not a nifty, new tactic that can be instituted overnight to solve a particular problem. Community Policing is instead a sophisticated, subtle, logical, and flexible approach that focuses on street-level problems and concerns.

Community Policing cannot solve all of the community's problems of crime and disorder, and most new initiatives will take time before the results are apparent. Also, as Edmonton's Chris Braiden says, "Lying in the belly of any new solution are many new problems."[6] The first thing that Community Policing will probably *not* do is help much with high-level crime. Because it focuses on the kinds of problems that people face at home and on the street, Community Policing can do little to uncover sophisticated stock fraud, exotic computer crime, or a complex embezzling scheme hatched in the bowels of a corporation – the kinds of crimes that are so complex that it can require special training just to tell if they have occurred at all.

What Community Policing excels at is finding new solutions to street-level problems, by challenging the department and the community to find new answers. By accepting that the police should not dash about randomly trying to catch all the bad guys, especially since there is not enough room to lock them all away anyhow, Community Policing frees the police to look at a greater range of options. Sometimes this means the police bounce the problem back at people with some advice about how they can solve the problem themselves. Other times, the police enlist their aid in working together to find solutions. It can mean linking people to other agencies that can help. Sometimes the best solution is to make an arrest, sometimes not.

The CPO plays a unique role because the job allows the officer the continuity in one place to initiate efforts that require nurturing. The traditional police response focuses on the here and now – take the call, handle the problem, move on to the next call. The CPO has the luxury of continuity, which means that he can develop interventions that offer payoffs over time.

A few situations lend themselves to immediate solutions – if the problem is a loud stereo at night, the CPO who forces neighbors to talk may be the catalyst who helps prod the offender into wearing headphones at night. It would no doubt take longer for a CPO to organize a successful campaign to wipe out graffitti and have all the abandoned and decaying buildings torn down. It can take a decade for a troubled youngster to become a hardened criminal, and some grow out of their problems on their own. Yet the traditional system holds little promise of making a positive difference when the police response is limited to brief bursts of negative attention, usually from a different officer each time. A CPO can do more than issue warnings about dire consequences, by offering praise and support for any encouraging signs of better behavior.

Quantifying the results of such efforts is virtually impossible – who knows if another fight about the stereo could have ended in assault or murder? How much graffitti and how many decaying buildings must a dope dealer see before deciding this is a good place to open up shop? Can that CPO possibly do enough to turn that youngster around?

And as Braiden suggested, Community Policing brings with it a new set of problems as well, primarily internal resistance within the department. Though there are ways that the department can head off and reduce hostility from within, the fact remains that it will take time and energy to do so.

Community Policing makes an important contribution, but it cannot and should not be expected to do more than it can. Enthusiasts tend to oversell the concept, as if it could work miracles overnight. As society changes, the day will no doubt come when Community Policing may also seem dated and out of touch. For now, it provides the necessary tonic for a system that tended to view the officer as a chess piece whose moves are controlled by the police radio.

- **Community Policing is not "safe."** – Allowing officers the freedom to attempt creative solutions to problems carries with it the risk of mistakes that can range from the embarrassing to the disastrous. The traditional system instead focuses on routinizing tasks and codifying procedures as a way to eliminate the potential for bungles that can threaten the department's reputation.

At issue, of course, is whether police officers are educated professionals who can be trusted to do more good than harm. Community Policing says that police departments must learn to suffer the occasional foul-up, so that officers can bring the full impact of their education, training, experience, professional instincts, and imagination to bear on solving community problems. History shows that the traditional approach is far from error-free, and that you do not eliminate problems by treating personnel as if they cannot be trusted.

Community Policing says that the system benefits from treating people as individuals, allowing them to capitalize on their strengths and work on minimizing their weaknesses. The foot patrol officer in Flint who loved to fish transmitted this enthusiasm to the kids who participated in the fishing derby that he organized. The point is not therefore to order all the other officers to organize fishing events – or to cancel that one if a child is accidentally snagged by an errant hook.

Allowing people the opportunity to fail also offers people the chance to succeed brilliantly. One of the hardest things departments often face in a new Community Policing effort is restraining the impulse to second-guess or censor. If a CPO writes a newsletter for distribution in the community, the department must not look over the officer's shoulder. It means backing an officer if a well-meaning effort does not pan out – even if it causes some embarrassment.

The Medical Model

Disease often serves as a useful metaphor for crime. We suffer from illness, as individuals and as a society, just as we separately and collectively suffer the ravages of crime. The problem can range fron a nagging hangnail to a life-threatening heart attack, from a broken picture window to murder, but both disease and crime carry with them the fear of permanent damage and death. Carrying the comparison further, psychosomatic illness substitutes for fear of crime. Victims of psychosomatic disorders suffer *real* pain, even though there is no underlying disease, just as people can become virtually paralyzed by fear of crime, though they may never actually fall victim to crime themselves.

Viewed in this context, there are obvious parallels between the doctor and the police officer. Both must try to solve individual problems that range from the real to the imaginary, and by doing so effectively, they hope to make a contribution to the overall health of society. For the sake of argument, let us compare how the motor patrol officer acts like an emergency room physician, while the CPO's role more closely parallels that of the family doctor.

Both the motor patrol officer and the emergency room physician are *reactive* -- the job demands that they stand ready to act when the next crisis hits, bringing to bear their years of training and experience to handle the emergency as best they can. It is vitally important not to bog them down with other demanding or distracting duties, since their primary responsibility is so important – and stressful – that the goal is to keep them as fresh and ready as possible so that they can act quickly when an emergency occurs.

The emergency room physician never knows whether the next case will be a heart attack or heartburn, just as the motor patrol officer never knows whether he risks facing a vicious killer or a frightened child. Yet both must be trained and ready to make split-second decisions that can mean the difference between life and death.

The CPO and the family doctor play a broader proactive role. Both may be called upon to deal with a crisis, a situation where their action makes the difference between life and death, yet the role also involves dealing with a wider range of concerns. They must also be specialists in focusing on long-term care and prevention.

Both kinds of doctors and both kinds of police officers must also rely on a host of other important specialists who can fill in the gaps. Yet the average citizen relies most on these two kinds of doctors and two kinds of police as the primary providers in their respective full-spectrum approaches.

Analyzing the model further, the first lesson to be drawn is that it makes as little sense to argue that CPOs do not perform *real* police work as it does to suggest family doctors do not do *real* medicine. Both deal with serious problems, but their additional proactive focus means their goals extend beyond treating immediate catastrophes to promoting overall well-being in the future. Their mandate is to offer advice and support on ways to make changes today that can prevent serious problems tomorrow.

Another useful lesson is that the professional standards used to assess the performance of one job make little sense when applied to the other. Quick response is the hallmark of the emergency room physician, but the family doctor must be allowed to spend the extra time it takes to find out all about the total person – stresses on the job, family problems, personal habits, amount of daily exercise, diet. A good family physician takes the time to develop rapport and trust, to enlist the patient's support in making positive changes. An emergency room physician must be encouraged to develop a good bedside manner, but the job does not provide as many opportunities for its full expression.

Of interest as well are the parallels between the history of the delivery of police service and health care in this country. Early in this century, old-fashioned foot officers walked a beat, while old-fashioned country doctors made house calls. Without overly romanticizing the past, both the foot patrol officer and the country doctor did a pretty good job. Not that some people did not die because the system could not respond fast enough or well enough, but most people were happy with the kind and quality of the service they received.

The advent of new technology and the pace of modern life increased the pressure to centralize these services to make them more efficient. It did not take a time-study expert to see that sending the country doctor on house calls was wildly inefficient – someone might die of a heart attack while the doctor was on his way to treat someone with the flu. Analyzed in terms of new principles such as cost effectiveness, it made no sense to allow a highly trained professional to waste time travelling out into the community.

Yet the shift to demanding that the patient must always come to the doctor injected alienation into the equation. In place of the kindly country doctor who treated patients like friends came the crisply efficient, impassionate new breed of physician. The doctor had all the answers and the patient's job was to answer questions and follow orders – it was even considered bad form for the patient to ask the name of the medicine the doctor prescribed. As long as the string of medical miracles kept coming, as killer diseases like smallpox and polio were eradicated by new breakthroughs, it seemed like quibbling to complain about the warm, human touch that had been lost somewhere in the process.

Yet after most of the infectious killer diseases were conquered, people discovered that the new killers – cancer and heart disease – did not lend themselves to easy answers, no magic pill or shot. Instead, preventing and treating these new *lifestyle* diseases required changes in the patient's behavior: quit smoking, cut down on saturated fats and cholesterol, lose weight, start exercising. Doctors no longer had the exclusive power to effect a cure alone, because issuing orders does not always mean they will be followed.

To convince patients that they had to take steps to make changes to prevent disease and heal themselves, doctors found they had to develop rapport with their patients, so that they would trust and adopt their advice. Doctors began to see that they had to treat their patients as partners in the health-care process, providing them encouragement and support.

Physicians also faced increased pressure to change their relationship with their patients because more and more patients were filing malpractice suits, a problem the country doctor almost never faced, even though there is good reason to suppose they made at least as many errors. Doctors as well as patients began to understand the benefits of personalizing health-care service. Together all these changes have resulted in a subtle but important shift in thinking, from a system that focused on curing illness to one that pays as much attention to promoting wellness, just as the advent of Community Policing signifies a shift from a system that focused on fighting crime to one that also promotes enhancing the quality of life in the community.

In policing, the old-fashioned beat cop gave way to the educated, highly trained police professional. People missed that friendly beat cop on the corner, and the new breed of officer whizzing by in a patrol car seemed far more aloof, but again that seemed a small price to pay, especially since new technology seemed to offer the hope of eradicating crime. Yet not only did crime not go away, in the late 1960s, crime rates exploded, college campuses erupted, and race riots flared across the country. Minorities in particular began to file lawsuits alleging police brutality, and people clamored for civilian review boards to allow them a voice in how the police should act.

Especially in periods of transition, the past, present, and future all inhabit today. The medical establishment has not yet completely adopted a wellness-oriented phi-losophy – there are still many doctors who resist treating patients as equals and who think it is folly to ask doctors to do more than cure disease. Yet doctors at the cutting edge of this new thinking about what constitutes quality medical care enjoy the challenge of working with people on finding ways for them to be as fit and healthy as they can. It is also true that many police traditionalists are clinging to the past, though innovative CPOs continue to prove that Community Policing is policing's pre-scription for a new emphasis on community wellness. Only time will tell whether these new approaches can fully succeed in fulfilling their promise. But what is cer-tain is that people will not allow either system to retreat and abandon the progress that has already been made.

NOTES

[1]Information provided by the National Center for Community Policing, Michigan State University, School of Criminal Justice, East Lansing, MI, on April 17, 1989.

[2]Dr. David Carter of Michigan State University, quoted in an article by Andrew H. Malcolm, *Cities Try Out New Approach in Police Work,* New York Times, March 29, 1989.

[3]For further information on Problem-Oriented Policing, see:

Goldstein, Herman, *Policing in a Free Society* (Cambridge, MA: Ballinger, 1977).

Goldstein, Herman, *The Urban Police Function* (Cambridge, MA: Ballinger, 1977).

Goldstein, Herman, *Improving Policing: A Problem-Oriented Approach, Crime and Delinquency,* 25:236-258, 1979.

Eck, John, and Spelman, William, *Problem Solving: Problem-Oriented Policing in Newport News, VA* (Washington, DC: Police Executive Research Forum – PERF, 1987)

Eck, John, *Managing Case Assignments: Burglary Investigation Decision Model Replication* (Washington, DC: Police Executive Research Forum – PERF, 1979).

Eck, John, *Solving Crimes: The Investigation of Burglary and Robbery* (Washington, DC: Police Executive Research Forum – PERF, 1984).

Pierce, Glenn, et al., *Evalution of an Experiment in Proactive Police Intervention in the Field of Domestic Violence Using Repeat Call Analysis* (Boston, MA: The Boston Fenway Program, Inc., March 13, 1987).

Greenwood, Peter W.; Chaiken, Jan M.; and Petersilia, Joan, *The Criminal Investigation Process* (Lexington, MA: DC Health, 1977).

[4]Braiden, Chris, *Nothing New Under the Sun,* Footprints (Newsletter) (East Lansing, MI: National Neighborhood Foot Patrol Center – now called National Center for Community Policing, Spring/Summer 1988).

[5]Braiden, Chris, speech at the Foot Patrol Training Seminars held at Michigan State University in East Lansing on April 6 & 7, 1989.

[6]*Ibid.*

CHAPTER 2
The History of
Community Policing

History is philosophy learned from examples.
—Dionysius of Halicarnassus

Perhaps it is not true that history repeats
itself; it is only that man remains the same.
—Walter Sorrell

The Lessons of History

The homily that people receive the kind of policing they deserve ignores the role power plays in both the kind and quality of police service. The police are social control agents, the branch of government that imposes the authority of law on the public at large. Primary power, therefore, resides among those who make the laws; then, by extension, it is vested in those who determine police structure, set the police agenda, and choose the tactics that the police will employ.

In totalitarian countries, all power is vested in government leaders, an obvious invitation to abuse, since the system permits the few to impose their will on the many, with the police controlled by the power elite. In democratic societies, the people make the laws, through their elected representatives, but the organization and operation of the police can vary greatly from agency to agency, and from place to place.

The main challenge in the United States has been to fashion a structure for the police that insulates departments from the corrupting influence of partisan politics, without risking a department so autonomous that it is isolated from the wants and needs of those it is sworn to serve. Finding the proper balance between the need for police independence and the need for public accountability has been difficult. Examining the history of American policing can help us see what we have learned – and forgotten – as modern policing evolved.

As policing shifted from an informal to a formal system, this progress also meant a shift away from direct community input and control. As we will see, most changes were the inevitable result of four important, interrelated pressures:

- Continued population growth.

- The shift from an agrarian to an industrial economy.

- The crowding of people into cities.

- Advances in technology.

However, viewed from another perspective, the history of modern policing begins and ends with the community. In the beginning, hundreds of years ago in England, people simply policed themselves. The bulk of modern policing's history shows how each succeeding advance inadvertently distanced the police further and further from the people they must serve:

- The use of citizen volunteers to help apprehend wrongdoers.

- The organization of regular night watches manned by volunteers.

- The move to a paid police force.

    Expanding police protection to 24-hour-a-day service.

- Consolidation of police service into organized city, county, state, and federal police agencies.

- The substitution of motor patrol for foot patrol.

- The reform movement to *professionalize* (bureaucratize) and *depoliticize* the police and narrow their mandate to crime-fighting.

- The influx of modern technology such as the computer.

Each effort to improve police efficiency and effectiveness was a response to an obvious problem, but few recognized that the downside to each change was increasing isolation from the general public. The riots and civil unrest of the late 1960s were a vivid reminder that a democratic society will not accept a police force that is alienated from any segment of society.

The purpose in looking backward is to identify the best of the past we must keep, as it warns us of mistakes we dare not repeat. The history of modern policing therefore serves to show why the emergence of Community Policing was the inevitable response to a system that had lost touch with its initial function, which was to find ways to involve all citizens in the police process.

When people feel the police do not understand or respond to their wants and needs, the result is either vigilantism or apathy or both. History proves that safety and order are not commodities the police impose on communities from the outside; instead they are the hallmarks of communities where people accept responsibility for improving the overall quality of life. Critics contend Community Policing is no more than old wine in new bottles, but, as this brief history will show, the movement is more like a fine, old wine that has been filtered to take out impurities and pollutants.

American Policing's British Roots

The United States is undeniably a polyglot culture, a hearty stew made up of the various ethnic groups who continue to arrive in search of the American dream. While this unlikely mix has blended together to produce a uniquely American psyche, with its distinct way of doing things, most of this country's institutions still show the profound early influence of the British, seasoned with a hint of Puritan values.

Therefore, to understand this country's law enforcement tradition requires a brief excursion into British police history. According to William H. Hewitt, the history of law enforcement in England can be divided into three distinct, successive periods:

- The era when citizens were responsible for law and order among themselves.

- A system where the justice of the peace both meted out justice and maintained the peace.

- A paid police force.[1]

Viewed from the context of today, it is hard to imagine a time when there were no paid police officers and the community residents policed themselves. Under Alfred the Great (870-901), citizens had to help apprehend wrongdoers or risk being fined. During that era, communities were organized into *tithings, hundreds,* and *shires.* Every ten citizens constituted a tithing and every ten tithings made up a hundred. A *constable,* appointed by a local nobleman, was in charge of each hundred; his job was to make sure citizens reported problems and tracked down offenders.

A group of hundreds was organized into a shire, the rough equivalent of a county. Shires were supervised by a *shire-reeve* – or *sheriff* – whose role narrowed over time to apprehending lawbreakers. During the reign of Edward I (1272-1307), the constable was formally given an official police force to help protect property in large towns; the force was funded by pledges and manned by unpaid citizen volunteers.

In 1326, Edward II established a new office, *justice of the peace,* filled by noblemen appointed by the king. The justice of the peace, with the constable serving as his assistant, eventually refined his role to that of judge – the first official split of the judicial and law enforcement functions.

It is important to understand that the king and his noblemen had a vested interest in maintaining social order, because both crime and rebellion ultimately threatened the taxes upon which the feudal system depended. The citizens supported the upper classes, in exchange for which they received some protections. As economic pressures began to erode the feudal system, the pledge system that supported these local law enforcement efforts broke down and citizen participation decreased.

The dramatic rise of the Industrial Revolution at the end of the 18th century dramatically accelerated the pace of social change, as people flocked to the cities and the older forms of community control broke down. By mid-century, vast, crime-riddled slums had sprung up in the industrial cities, and frightened officials and citizens created a host of erratic and overlapping groups that launched a draconian war on crime. At one point, stealing a loaf of bread was a hanging offense, one of 160 capital crimes. In that era, citizens vied for rewards paid for turning in offenders, and the guilty were given long sentences or deported to America or Australia, yet crime continued to plague urban areas.

The need for new solutions became even more urgent when the citizens began to rebel against military intervention. In 1818, troops were called in to quell a disturbance at a lecture in Manchester and eleven people were killed, with many more injured. For the first time, the people balked at using soldiers to deal with civil unrest, and the resulting public outcry set the stage for dramatic reform.

Against this backdrop of chaos, Sir Robert Peel became Home Secretary in 1822, inheriting a fragmented system where there was one police force for business, one for shipping, one for parishes, as well as a host of vigilante groups. The visionary Peel, acknowledged as the father of modern policing, introduced the Metropolitan Police Act of 1829. How the bill passed without dissent remains a mystery, since it radically restructured the status quo. The act abolished existing efforts and, in their place, established a Police Office, administered by *justices* (commissioners) in charge of planning. It also created the Metropolitan Police District, staffed by paid constables.

The virtually unknown Charles Rowan and Richard Mayne were the commissioners Peel appointed to organize and run the new department. The duo set up operation in the back of London's Whitehall Place, which opened onto a courtyard used by the kings of Scotland – Scotland Yard. There they fashioned a plan to deploy six divisions of 1,000 men each, with each division divided into eight patrol sections, with those sections divided into eight beats.

To be an officer, candidates had to provide three character references and prove they could read and write. Despite the dismal pay – and the fact that becoming an officer cost the men their right to vote in parliamentary and municipal elections – more than 12,000 applied for the 6,000 jobs as a *Bobby* (a nickname honoring Sir Robert that has stuck ever since).Yet turnover was high, with more than 11,000 officers leaving the force during the first three years, in part because of low pay, but also because the general public initially resisted the new police force.

After the first year, the citizens actually called for the force to be disbanded. Yet the police persisted, battling night-long riots during their first four years, with only their batons for protection, winning respect because the Bobbies never inflicted serious injury and did not resort to calling in the military. As the crime rate began to drop and the streets became safer, the *Peelers* gained acceptance.

Yet the twin problems of low status and low pay persisted even after the force won acceptance. For years, British police officers were considered unskilled laborers, and it was not until 1890 that they were granted pensions. A police strike in 1918 led to legislation the following year that established a police federation which set pay scales and adopted a professional code. Of the nine principles typically attributed to Peel (which were, in fact, drafted by Rowan and Mayne), the seventh addresses how the police should treat the public:

> To maintain at all times a relationship with the public that gives reality to the historic tradition that the police are the public and that the public are the police; the police being only members of the public who are paid to give full-time attention to duties which are incumbent on every citizen in the interests of community welfare and existence.[2]

Colonial Law Enforcement in Cities and Towns

Against this backdrop of British history, we can now trace the American law enforcement tradition to its beginnings in Colonial times. Perhaps the earliest organized law enforcement effort was the *night watch,* first established in a Boston town meeting in 1636. Unless they could provide a good excuse, all males older than 18 were expected to serve. No doubt the most famous *night watchman* of all time was Paul Revere, the Revolutionary War hero who roused the citizenry with the cry, "The British are coming, the British are coming."

In New York, a *schout* and *rattle watch* was established in 1651. The rattle was an actual rattle, used to sound the alarm by a *rattle watcher,* who made 48 cents for his 24-hour duty. The system was not without problems, particulary because offenders were often sentenced to this duty as punishment. However, once pay rates rose, so did the number of applicants eager for the job.

Over time, watch systems in various towns became more sophisticated and more organized. By 1705, in Philadelphia, the Common Council divided the city into ten patrol areas, each with a constable who recruited citizen volunteers to keep the watch with him. Incredible as it seems today, all these early law enforcement efforts only provided formal protection at night. In fact, captains assigned to various areas of New York City chose to interpret sunrise as occurring anywhere from 3 a.m. to 5 a.m., so they could shorten their duty.

Though the system had serious flaws, night watches functioned fairly well as long as America remained primarily an agrarian society – keep in mind that it was not until 1790 that six cities finally reached a population of 8,000. However, at the turn of the 19th century, the drawbacks were becoming difficult to ignore. One major problem was that local watchmen were notoriously lax, to the degree that they had become the butt of jokes about their ineptitude.

As commerce and population in the eastern states grew, crime problems there began to mirror those in England that were fueled by the Industrial Revolution. Meanwhile, continued western expansion into the seemingly unlimited frontier created a different set of law enforcement problems. How these different traditions were ultimately wedded into one distinctly American approach requires looking at each historical trend separately.

The Rise of Municipal Police

As noted above, early law enforcement efforts in the few American cities large enough to require organized efforts consisted primarily of night watches, manned by citizens who were supervised by constables assigned to various districts. Major problems with this system were that they operated only at night, enforcement was erratic and inefficient, and the competence and character of the individuals selected or forced to serve were often suspect.

Between the Revolutionary War and the Civil War, rapid population growth and increasing industrialization pressured police departments to become more effective and more efficient. However, the downside to organizing the police into one structured department was that concentrating power into the hands of paid police without providing the proper safeguards ushered in an era marked by widespread corruption.

Much of the impetus to consolidate the police into a single, unified force stemmed from the inability of the existing system to respond to the growing number of civil disorders of the mid-1800s. In 1837, the Boston fire company and the Irish clashed, with as many as 15,000 people involved in the riot, which did not end until the militia was called in. The next year, in Philadelphia, the first of a series of so-called Negro riots occurred, causing widespread death and destruction, including the burning of Pennsylvania Hall. The rioting broke out again in 1842 and 1844.

As early as 1833, Philadelphia made a dramatic effort to organize an independent, competent, 24-hour-a-day police force, supported by patron Steven Girard, who left a large inheritance to fund police reform. Philadelphia passed a model ordinance that provided two dozen police, who would serve both day and night, with officers appointed by the mayor's office and control of the force vested in one officer. In addition, the new law required that promotions would be based on skill and integrity.

While this sounds like a giant leap forward – and it was – within two decades, partisan politics undid Girard's good intentions, with the police force consolidated under a marshal (later a police chief), elected for a two-year term. While that change may sound benign, it meant that the police department was no longer insulated from partisan politics. Without safeguards, such as Civil Service, the *spoils system* prevailed.

That term comes from the motto, "To the victors go the spoils," used in this sense to mean that the political party that wins can use *patronage* (political favors) as a means of consolidating and perpetuating its power. The *Spoils Era* in American history referred to the period prior to passage of the Civil Service Act of 1883 as a time when many federal officials considered a government post as a virtual private fiefdom. Once elected, politicians solidified their power by taking care of the cronies who had helped them win election. Every decision, from who would receive lucrative government contracts to who would be hired or promoted, was dictated by politics rather than merit.

State and local governments were far from immune to political corruption. Within local police departments, the spoils system meant that political favoritism dictated who was hired and who was promoted. In their dealings with the public, corrupt departments did the politicians' bidding, which meant looking the other way when politicians and their friends broke the law, while using the law to punish political enemies. This kind of corruption also promoted the harassment of blacks and other immigrant ethnic minorities, many of whom could not vote, and the police were also used to wage outright war against strikers who threatened powerful business interests.

Adding to opportunity for corruption as well was the fact that the police in those days also handled a number of other administrative tasks totally unrelated to what we think of today as part of the police role. In many cities, the police issued licenses for everything from taverns to ice-cream parlors, boarding houses to dog breeders. Even honest cops who were not tempted by monetary bribes could do little to defy a system where such licenses were dispensed as political favors.

In the Spoils Era, police departments were routinely headed by a police chief whose sole qualification was that he would do the bidding of the politician or politicians who gave him his job. Lack of qualified and independent leadership at the top was a major problem in American policing for many years.

In cities such as Baltimore and Cincinnati, the police force was used primarily to rig elections. Until 1844, New York City had actually had two police forces, one for daytime duty, one at night, with each dispensing patronage. The New York police reform act passed that same year became a model for the American police system, though it lagged years behind Peelian reform in England. The major problem with the law was that it allowed aldermen and assistant aldermen to appoint the police captain, assistant captains, and patrolmen for their wards to one-year terms. The police chief, appointed by the mayor, was little more than a figurehead. While the new system attempted, in theory, to consolidate and upgrade the police into one unit controlled by a police chief, in practice, it institutionalized political corruption.

In some municipalities, police officials were elected; in others, they were appointed by the mayor, the city council, or some other administrative body. Even uniforms were not standardized. As late as 1853, New York policemen wore civilian clothes and could only be identified by the 33-inch clubs they carried. Initial efforts at standardization often did little to lessen confusion, since each ward adopted its own style. For instance, the summer uniforms in some wards consisted of suits made of white duck cloth, while others opted to wear colors, and some even chose to wear straw hats.

By 1860, Philadelphia decided to adopt a standard police uniform, which consisted of single-breasted blue frock coats with brass buttons, gray pants with black stripes down the sides, and an old-style broad-top cap with a leather visor. It was not until the next year that a new badge was adopted, and a few years later the trousers were changed to matching blue, inaugurating the *men in blue* look associated with police uniforms today.

As these anecdotes demonstrate, the history of policing in this era was marked by occasional enlightened efforts to upgrade the force, but few efforts addressed the underlying corruption in any systematic way. For example, in 1871, leading police officials of the time met in Philadelphia, where they devised and implemented the first uniform crime reporting system, a valuable attempt to find new ways to identify crime trends. By that time, pay scales for police officers had also improved, and, by the mid-1880s, police officers in many metropolitan areas could retire at half pay after 20 years of service.

The bad news was that graft was also endemic. The Lexow investigation of the New York City Police Department in 1894 confirmed that officers had to pay a $300 to be hired, with higher payoffs for promotions. From their first contact with the department, rookies learned that bribery and political *pull* were part of the system.

Civil Service reform helped clean up some abuses, particularly in hiring and promotion, and periodic, highly touted investigations of corruption in big-city departments also spurred change, though in many cases, those gains faded when the headlines stopped. However, as long as police leadership remained deeply politicized, the taint of corruption hovered around many municipal police departments well into the 20th century.

While 19th century law enforcement in the eastern United States was primarily a study in learning how to develop structures suited to increasingly populous cities, the law enforcement challenge in the *Wild West* during this period focused on how to make the frontier a safer place, which involved different kinds of problems, since people were scattered far apart and communication between settlements was almost non-existent. As we will see later, no sector of the United States was free of vigilantism, but, on the frontier, even authorized efforts dispensed rough justice.

Frontier Justice

The westward expansion that characterized the 19th century meant that people ventured into the wilderness first and then formal institutions followed. Movies about this era tend to glorify the violence associated with the lawlessness of the frontier, but there were many bloody clashes between various interest groups – sheepherders versus cattlemen, farmers versus ranchers, settlers versus Indians, various ethnic groups against others. Settlers were also not only easy prey for con men and swindlers offering phony land deals, but isolated families alone on the prairie had little protection from thieves and rustlers.

The laws in place were also a curious blend of criminal codes and so-called *blue laws,* a peculiarly American phenomenon where religious groups successfully lobbied to make custom part of the criminal law. Many of these laws related to the selling and consumption of alcohol, either restricting sale to certain times or places or banning it outright in specific areas. In other cases, blue laws regulated everything from store hours to public dancing. There was a certain irony in the fact that many frontier communities had rigid laws governing such social behavior, when, at the same time, it was doubtful they had the mechanisms in place even to enforce the laws against major crimes.

In many cases as well, it was difficult to tell much difference between formal law enforcement and vigilantism. The typical system in most frontier towns was that the sheriff was the chief law enforcement official. When the town or territory could afford to do so, the sheriff was a paid official, but the candidates for the job often had few skills beyond a willingness to take what was often a thankless job. The sheriff could deputize citizen volunteers to track down offenders, and visiting circuit judges made periodic rounds of outlying territories to conduct trials.

Vigilantism

Because of the lack of swift and sure justice and the violent nature of frontier life, many people had few qualms about taking the law into their own hands. Drawing the line between responsible efforts of organized civilian volunteers and *vigilantism* can be difficult. After all, looking back on the British experience, groups of unpaid citizens constituted the bulk of early law enforcement efforts. However, as the concept of justice evolved, it recognized that victims and their families and friends must be removed from the formal process, since they should not be expected to be objective – if you damage my property, that should be a capital crime, whereas if I damage *yours,* that is merely a forgivable accident.

What makes vigilantism different from responsible citizen action is that it operates *in addition to* and often *in opposition to* existing formal efforts. As more than one sheriff learned, standing in the way of vigilantes intent on enforcing their own brand of justice could often be more dangerous than dealing with the criminal. When citizens pursue suspected felons, they are assisting the police, but when they seek to inflict punishment, they have crossed the line into vigilantism. Vigilantes inject emotion into a process where reason should prevail; their subjectivity undermines their claim to justice.

Among the first recorded examples of vigilantism were the South Carolina *regulators* who operated between 1767 and 1769. This extralegal citizens' group served as a model for later vigilante efforts. Astute film-goers will note that Marlon Brando played a *regulator* hired to kill rustlers in *The Missouri Breaks,* certifying this was the preferred term for a vigilante until the mid-19th century.

According to Richard M. Brown in *Violence in America,* vigilantism is based on three rationalizations:

- **Self-preservation** – Just as self-defense is a valid defense for what would otherwise be murder, this idea justifies vigilantism by arguing that citizens must be willing to *kill or be killed,* when the official system fails to provide adequate protection. Newspapers of the era often endorsed this sentiment. An editorial in the *San Francisco Herald* in 1851 said: "Whenever the law becomes an empty name, has not the citizen the right to supply its deficiencies?"[3]

- **Right of revolution** – Unlike the Canadians, for instance, citizens of the United States come from a tradition of violent revolution, and early framers of the Constitution argued that periodic revolt might be necessary to prevent government tyranny. Part of the American psyche embraces the idea that when something fails to work properly, revolution is as valid a response as reform.

- **Economic rationale** – The development and maintenance of an effective criminal justice system is an expensive proposition, and this position argued that frontier towns should not bear the expense, when vigilantism did the job efficiently for free.[4]

Echoes of all three justifications can be heard in this particular warning, posted outside Las Vegas, New Mexico, in 1880, a citizen manifesto similar to many of that era:

The citizens of Las Vegas are tired of robbery, murder, and other crimes that have made this town a byword in every civilized community. They are resolved to put a stop to crime, even if, in obtaining that end, they have to forget the law and resort to a speedier justice than it will afford. All such characters are notified that they must either leave this town or conform themselves to the requirement of the law or they will be severely dealt with. The flow of blood must and shall be stopped in this community and good citizens of both the old and new towns have been determined to stop it if they have to hang by the strong arm of force every violator of law in this country.
—*Vigilantes*[5]

The impulse to vigilantism may be understandable, but a system with no controls is an invitation to abuse. All too often, the innocent were hung along with or instead of the guilty. In addition, whenever groups operate with no oversight, there is nothing to prevent people's worst instincts from taking over. On the frontier, in the South, and also in the major cities of the East, prejudice ran high against various groups – Indians, Negroes, and immigrants. Many formal law enforcement efforts were often tainted by a two-track system of justice, where offenses committed by members of unpopular groups rated punishment far beyond what native white Americans suffered, especially if the victims were white.

Because vigilantes, by definition, have no external restraints, lynch mobs had a justified reputation for hanging minorities first and asking questions later. Because of its tradition of slavery, which rested on the rationalization that blacks were sub-human, the South had a long and shameful history of mistreating blacks, long after the end of the Civil War. Perhaps the most infamous American vigilante group, the Ku Klux Klan, was notorious for assaulting and killing black men for transgressions that would not be considered crimes at all, if they had they been committed by a white man.

More than one Southern black was hanged by a lynch mob for such *crimes* as whistling at a white woman or failing to show proper respect to a white person. Adding to the climate of terror such outrages perpetuated was the fact that some law enforcement officers participated in or gave tacit approval to Klan activities, adding to the popular perception that some vigilante groups enjoyed a quasi-legal status or were at least tolerated by the establishment. A later section will deal in more detail with the history of the relationship between the police and minorities and other sub-groups, such as strikers and students.

20th Century Policing

While the foregoing might seem like a uniformly grim and pessimistic view of the history of law enforcement, there were undeniable problems in law enforcement at the turn of the century, including the taint of corruption, shortcomings and confusion in leadership, the threat of vigilantism, and inequities in application of laws. Though Civil Service reform helped introduce increased fairness into hiring and promotion, without effective leadership at the top, many police departments continued to wallow in corruption.

Part of the problem was structural, since many big-city departments were controlled by police boards that rarely provided a single, strong leader who could speak with authority *for* the department and *to* the department. Awareness of this flaw led to efforts to invest leadership in one person, so that by 1921, only 14 out of the 52 cities in the United States with a population of 100,000 or more were still run by police boards. However, this reform served to highlight another major defect – too many departments were headed by men who had no practical or educational background in law enforcement.

Once New York City adopted the single-administrator form, during roughly the next two decades, a parade of army officers, newspapermen, lawyers, and professional politicians were tapped to fill the post. In Philadelphia during the first 20 years of the 20th century, the position of director of public safety was filled by a candy manufacturer, an insurance broker, a banker, an electric company official, and five lawyers.

This also indicates the tremendous problem many departments had with turnover, since Civil Service reforms often did nothing to insulate the top spot from politics. Not only were most top police administrators ill-equipped for the job, they served at the whim of politicians. Police Commissioner Woods of New York City testified in 1912: "The police department is peculiarly the victim of this principle of transient management. Most of the commissioners are birds of passage. The force gets a glimpse of them flying over, but hardly has time to determine the species."[6]

At that time, New York had had 12 commissioners in 19 years, with an average life span in the job of less than two years and the shortest term only 33 days. In comparison, by 1912, London had had only seven police commissioners during the preceding 91 years.

The problem was not limited to New York; in the early 20th century, the director, chief, or commissioner's office in major cities seemed to have a revolving door:

- Philadelphia had 13 directors in 33 years.

- Cincinnati had 4 in 7 years.

- Cleveland had 5 in 12 years.

- Chicago had 25 in 49 years.

- Detroit had 9 in 19 years.

Adding to the host of problems that plagued police departments in that era was the legislative control that tied the chief's hands, making him an instrument of the law, so that he could not innovate or experiment. In addition, low pay for police added to problems with morale and increased the likelihood of bribery. In 1900, a blue-ribbon commission known as *The Fifteen* found New York City officers had been blackmailing prostitutes, requiring a sliding scale of payoffs to look the other way.

In September 1919, the Boston police went on strike for higher wages. That night, when word spread that there were no police on duty, people looted stores and smashed windows, forcing the mayor to call out the troops. A hastily organized group of citizen volunteers was deployed to maintain order, but when they killed two citizens, that touched off intermittent rioting and violence that lasted for days. Massachusetts Governor Gompers then made his famous announcement: "There is no right to strike against the public safety by anybody, anywhere, anytime."[7] In response, Boston recruited a entirely new police force, but the incident left a black mark against the police that extended far beyond the city, since the story made headlines nationwide.

Corruption also increased with passage of the Volstead Act of 1919, which made Prohibition the law of the land. This ushered in the *Roaring Twenties,* also called the *Jazz Age* or the *Flapper Era.* It was a time when bootleggers and owners of *speakeasies* openly paid off police, and many people winked at the no-alcohol law. Mirroring in some ways today's problems with illegal drugs, the huge profits from rum-running often meant huge payoffs to police. While many decried this open rebellion, a large segment of society viewed Prohibition as a laughable nuisance, and even murderous gangsters like Al Capone and Lucky Luciano were portrayed as folk heroes.

The blatant disregard of Prohibition also fostered widespread disrespect for the law in general and, by extension, disrespect for police. The 1920s were a heady time, a live-for-today response to the grimness of World War I. It was also the era of the easy buck, when people could buy stock on margin for as little as 10 % down, which meant even busboys and cab drivers were playing the Stock Market. More than a few became millionaires overnight, as a result of a stock tip from a well-connected patron with insider information.

It should also be noted that one of the quickest ways for an ambitious politician to further his career was to launch an investigation of corruption in police departments. In New York, both Theodore Roosevelt and, much later, Thomas Dewey, catapulted onto the national political scene by using the springboard of police reform. The press was also eager to jump on this issue, since expressions of moral outrage about police corruption, coupled with sordid examples of abuses, helped sell newspapers.

This is not to suggest that there were not serious problems within police departments, but honest and dedicated individuals who were trying to make a difference faced tremendous odds, in no small part because the general public held the police in such low regard. A widely read article of the period said:

> Every large American police department is under suspicion. The suspicion amounts to this: that for-money crimes are not only tolerated but encouraged. The higher the rank of the police officer, the stronger the suspicion. Now it is only one step from the encourage-

ment of vice, for the purposes of loot, to an alliance with criminals. Indeed, in some of our large cities, the robbery of drunken men is permitted already by police on the profit-sharing plan.[8]

The Stock Market Crash of 1929 and the resulting Great Depression ended the giddy atmosphere of the 1920s with a bang, touching off a politically volatile period of re-examination. The crisis of confidence in the police set the stage for the dramatic police reform movement launched in the 1930s that determined the face of American policing for almost the next half-century.

Police Reform in the 1930s

Just as the principles attributed to Sir Robert Peel provided the foundation for British policing, Oakland (California) Police Chief August Vollmer is credited with launching the American police reform movement. As head of the National Commission on Law Observance and Enforcement established by President Herbert Hoover in 1929, Vollmer supervised the preparation of 10 principles he considered vital in reforming the police:

1. The corrupting influence of politics should be removed from the police organization.

2. The head of the department should be selected at large for competence, a leader, preferably a man of considerable police experience, and removable from office only after preferment of charges and a public hearing.

3. Patrolmen should be able to rate a "B" on the Alpha test, be able-bodied and of good character, weigh 150 pounds, measure 5 feet 9 inches tall, and be between 21 and 31 years of age. These requirements may be disregarded by the chief for good and sufficient reason.

4. Salaries should permit decent living standards, housing should be adequate, eight hours of work, one day off weekly, annual vacation, fair sick leave with pay, just accident and death benefits, when in performance of duty, reasonable pension provisions on an actuarial basis.

5. Adequate training for recruits, officers, and those already on the roll

is imperative.

6. The communication system should provide for call boxes, telephones, recall system, and (in appropriate circumstances) teletype and radio.

7. Records should be complete, adequate, but as simple as possible. They should be used to secure administrative control of investigations and of department units in the interest of efficiency.

8. A crime-prevention unit should be established if circumstances warrant this action and qualified women police should be engaged to handle juvenile delinquents' and women's cases.

9. State police forces should be established in states where rural protection of this character is required.

10. State bureaus of criminal investigation and information should be established in every State.[9]

Though some of Vollmer's specifics may seem dated, this progressive doctrine established important concepts that served as the underpinning for modern policing:

- The necessity of eliminating political corruption.

- The need for an independent chief.

- The importance of an educated and trained police force that would be compensated as professionals.

- The judicious use of the latest technology.

- An awareness of the benefits of preventing crime.

- The beginning of an expanded role for women.

- An understanding of the need for different police approaches for urban and rural areas.

- The importance of the service role in policing.

In their analysis of this reform movement, Harvard University's George L. Kelling and Mark H. Moore propose that Vollmer's moral vision, coupled with O.W. Wilson's work in police administration, revolutionized policing in seven areas:

- **Authorization** – In the past, police authority rested on *politics and the law;* the Reform Era replaced that underpinning with *professionalism and the law.*

- **Function** – The reform movement also narrowed the police function from a broad array of *social services* to *crime control.*

- **Organizational design** – Reformers also shifted departments from their previous *decentralized* model into a *classical, centralized* form.

- **Demand for services** – In the past, police *responded* to a *community's needs,* but the reform movement instead *sold* the public on the police role as *crime-fighters.*

- **Relationship to environment** – To insure against corruption and improve professionalism, the police were encouraged to abandon their *intimate* community ties and instead adopt a sort of *professional aloofness.*

- **Tactics/technology** – The *foot patrols* of the past gave way to *preventive motor patrol,* with an additional emphasis on *rapid response* to calls for service.

- **Outcomes** – The police of the past sought to *satisfy* both *politicians and mainstream citizens,* whereas the reform movement *measured success* by how well the police *controlled crime.*[10]

As Kelling and Moore point out, big-city police departments took a lesson from J. Edgar Hoover, who made the Federal Bureau of Investigation (FBI) a widely popular and respected unit by narrowing its mandate to specific crimes that were both highly visible and relatively easy to solve, then selling the public on the force's successes. Though local police did not have the luxury of picking and choosing which crimes they would pursue, the reformers could see great wisdom in narrowing the police function to crime control, not only because relative success would be easier to measure, but because involving the police in a whole host of other duties, such as issuing liquor licenses, seemed to invite inevitable corruption.

It is also important to understand the panorama of societal change that provided the backdrop against which these reforms took place. Not only had Hoover *professionalized* the FBI, but this was a time when it seemed every problem, including social ills, could be solved by properly applying scientific principles and the new science of management theory. As proof, believers could point to the giant strides made by industry, where moguls such as Henry Ford introduced revolutionary concepts such as the assembly line that dramatically increased productivity by stressing efficiency. It was an era when change was synonymous with progress, and there appeared to be no limits on what could be achieved.

That seems naive today, now that we have learned there is always a price, though sometimes initially hidden, that must be paid when any new technology is introduced and that people do not always behave rationally. However, back then, as the country struggled to overcome the effects of the Great Depression, the idea that American ingenuity could create a perfect world was an article of faith, certified over time by examples such as this country's victory in World War II.

Vollmer's precepts signalled an organized approach to resolving the problems of the past, while offering a new course for the future. Change does not come overnight, but these principles gained momentum as the wave of the future for policing, which meant many metropolitan police departments adopted new ways to extract politics from the process. As Kelling and Moore point out, such efforts helped make many police chiefs more autonomous than any other local government official. For example, Los Angeles and Cincinnati adopted Civil Service examinations for chief, while Milwaukee provided police chiefs lifetime tenure, with removal only for cause.

Meanwhile, as the reform movement took hold in urban police departments, the frontier and Southern sheriff tradition continued to evolve into the model for rural areas nationwide, and state police departments were initiated to fill important gaps between local and federal efforts. Pressures to professionalize the police increased throughout the system, but history proves that concentrating groups of people into confined spaces in cities appears to increase the number and seriousness of crime and disorder problems, which means urban police face challenges in scope and scale beyond what other departments do. Because crime and disorder cluster together in poorer neighborhoods, this also helps explain why minorities can serve as convenient scapegoats for the frustrations of both society and its police.

The Police and Minorities

The history of policing is, in reality, a record of how one group of people attempts to control the behavior of others, as individuals and in groups. A closer examination of early law enforcement efforts in England shows that even within a seemingly cohesive culture, where everyone shared the same ethnic roots, the same language, and the same customs, differences in class determined how the law was applied. Under the feudal system, the nobility claimed rights that the serfs did not enjoy. A group of noblemen on a fox hunt could destroy crops. The infamous *droit du seigneur* gave landlords the right to deflower the virginal daughters of their tenants, a legalized rape.

While the United States was founded on the ideal of establishing itself as a classless society, in practice, various groups have been discriminated against because of their skin color, ethnic heritage, immigrant status, religious beliefs, gender, or income level. Since law enforcement is part of the overall social fabric, many of these groups also suffered at the hands of police.

Prejudice depends on stereotyping – Jews are money-gougers, blacks are shiftless and sex-crazed, Italians are oily racketeers, the Irish are drunks, and Poles are stupid. Among the most common slurs attributed to all minorities and immigrant groups are that they are dirty and lazy. Because the police are, in reality, simply people and therefore not immune to prejudice, without bias-free leadership and firm guidelines to prevent abuse, it is easy to see why the police often found it easier to certify success by arresting members of unpopular groups than by risking the arrest of a well-connected person who could make waves for the officer and the department.

In addition, especially during the Spoils Era, it was not uncommon to find entire departments harassing unpopular minorities, as a way of solidifying mainstream support. In a capitalist society, supply and demand operate unfettered, at least in theory. This means the job goes to the lowest bidder, which therefore means that impoverished immigrants and disenfranchised blacks willing to work for low wages were perceived by businessmen as a boon – and as a serious threat by workers who feared being displaced. Until or unless these groups could establish political and economic clout, it was understandably popular to use the police to "keep them in line."

In a capitalist, democratic society, money and votes mean power. Immigrants often arrived with little more than the clothes they were wearing, and the process of becoming a naturalized citizen takes time. In the South, poll taxes and literacy tests were effective ways of excluding blacks from the electoral process, and statistics verify that blacks have never enjoyed income levels comparable to whites in this country. Even today, the poor, the Underclass, and many minority groups are the least likely to vote. The powerless make inviting targets for exploitation – and for society's frustrations.

Sadly, the history of modern policing includes numerous incidents where police unfairly harassed minorities, and a white skin was no protection against abuse. Jews faced widespread anti-Semitism, including harsh treatment by police, especially in cities like New York where immigrant Jewish families often settled. The Irish, Poles, Italians, Germans, and other central and eastern European immigrants also suffered injustice, a sadly predictable rite of passage in the transition to assimilation.

As this litany confirms, the have-nots, those without substantial clout, often had good reason to fear the police. Waves of immigrants hit this country's shores because of problems at home – the Irish faced famine, eastern Europeans fled revolution, the Jews tried to escape persecution. Lured by the myth that this country's streets were paved with gold, hordes of displaced persons flooded into the land of opportunity only to face the stark reality of low-paying and often dangerous jobs as unskilled workers.

One bloody episode occurred in 1897 when 21 Polish and Hungarian strikers who had organized a march outside Hazleton, Pennsylvania, were killed when the local police fired upon them after the owners of the local coal company convinced the police the protest was illegal. As this example demonstrates, police violence against minorities often exhibited the interwoven themes of rich against poor, as well as *us* against *them*.

As Jack L. Kuykendall explains, such incidents are evidence of power clashes that reinforce the negative stereotyping of one group by another.[11] Ethnic minorities cling together because of culture, heritage, language, and rejection and oppression by the mainstream, yet this in turn is perceived by the mainstream as evidence of secretive and clannish behavior that justifies further abuse. Completing the vicious cycle, minorities that suffer indignities and brutality at the hands of police learn, in turn, to see the police as paid thugs and oppressors. Once people are divided by the *us against them* mindset, it becomes much easier for each side to justify aggression against the other.

Though a white skin did not prevent discrimination, being white undoubtedly made it easier for ethnic minorities to assimilate into the mainstream. The additional burden of racism has made that transition much more difficult for those whose skin is black, brown, red, or yellow.

In no small part because of the tradition of slavery, blacks have long been a target of abuse. The use of citizen patrols to capture runaway slaves was one of the precursors of formal police forces, especially in the South. This unfortunate legacy persisted as an element of the police role. In some cases, police harassment simply meant blacks were more likely to be stopped and questioned, while at the other extreme, blacks have suffered beatings, and even murder, at the hands of white police. Questions still arise periodically today about the disproportionately high numbers of blacks killed by police in some major cities.

Most worrisome is that some law enforcment officials made it clear that they not only tolerated but encouraged their officers to keep blacks "in their place." Though we still wince at news footage of notorious southern Sheriff "Bull" Connor loosing police dogs on Civil Rights marchers in Selma, Alabama, the police in the North have not always treated blacks much better. Even in the recent past, more than one big-city northern police chief has used racism to secure his power, by currying favor with whites by thinly veiled assurances that he will use police power against blacks.

Hispanics have fared little better, and border states in particular have a check-ered record in their dealings with Mexican immigrants, dating back even before the notorious incident in the 1940s, when *zoot suiters* and police clashed in riots in Los Angeles in 1943. Cubans in Miami and Puerto Ricans in New York have also reported notable problems with police brutality. The same holds true for Native Americans in various areas.

Orientals have also been the target of hostiity. *Coolies* who worked laying rail-road track were seen by some as taking jobs away from *real* Americans, which led to riots in 1871. American citizens of Japanese extraction were interned in concentra-tion camps during World War II. Even today, the *boat people* from Viet Nam and Cambodia face problems in many communities, where they are perceived as straining the local economy, as evidenced in the bloody clashes between white and Oriental fishermen in Texas.

This uniformly depressing aspect of police history confirms that even when individual officers feel prejudice, the system must do all it can to prevent discrimina-tory behavior. Institutionalized racism and discrimination undermine a respected and respectable police force. Such abuses are fostered when police officers are isolated from continuous, informal contact with the community, and when police adminis-trators are insulated from the wants and needs of all citizens.

Initial Attempts to Reach the Community

The police reform movement launched by Vollmer in the 1920s, which took hold in the 1930s, seemed to offer the promise that society was on the brink of solving the riddle of crime. Police departments were now increasingly insulated from the political pressures that had spawned a variety of abuses, and they were organized according to the principles of scientific management theory, which promised increased efficiency and effectiveness. Over time, more and more departments were manned by educated and highly trained officers, roaming the streets in new squad cars that gave them the mobility to swoop down quickly wherever problems occurred. As home telephones became increasingly affordable, it seemed there would soon be no way crooks could escape the ever-tightening net.

By the 1950s, however, blemishes had begun to appear in that model of perfection. Many police departments found themselves the target of mounting citizen complaints. Many accusations seemed relatively trivial – perhaps the officer appeared indifferent to the caller's seemingly petty concerns such as broken streetlights or a barking dog. Sometimes the charges were serious, such as when minorities accused the police of harassment or outright brutality.

While concern about the isolation of the police from their constituency had not reached crisis proportions, the increasing pressure to find a way to build bridges to the community-fostered interest in *Police/Community Relations (PCR)* efforts. The best PCR programs were a sincere effort to reach out and address a host of community concerns. The worst were half-hearted, understaffed, and underfunded attempts to blunt public criticism without making any substantive change.

The three main components of PCR programs were *efficiency, responsiveness,* and *representation.* PCR efforts targeted six program areas:

- Communication and education programs.

- Programs to involve citizens in crime prevention.

- Programs to improve law enforcement service to the public.

- Youth programs.

- Other programs, such as critical-incident programs involving police relations with minorities.

- Training programs.

In 1955, the National Institute of Police/Community Relations, co-sponsored by the School of Police Administration and Public Safety of Michigan State University and the National Conference of Christians and Jews, convened to help police become aware of their problems. Later, the National Association of Police/Community Relations Officers outlined seven objectives of a good PCR program, paraphrased below:

- Improve communication, reduce hostility, and identify tensions between the police and the community.

- Assist both the police and the community in acquiring skills to promote improved crime detection and prevention.

- Define the police role, emphasizing equal protection.

- Adopt a teamwork approach, including the police department, the public, and other public service agencies.

- Instill in each officer a "proper attitude and appreciation of good police/community relations."

- Enhance mutual understanding between the police and the community.

- Stress that the administration of justice is a total community responsibility that necessitates total community involvement.[12]

As these laudable goals suggest, PCR efforts aimed high, but they fell short on structure and tactics. In practice, PCR units operated as separate entities within the department, never fully integrated into the police milieu. In the organizational scheme, the PCR unit was usually in the service track, not part of the operations bureau, which meant the jobs were filled with *staff* and not *line* officers. While this made sense, given the unit's mandate, it meant PCR officers were not viewed as *real cops.* The officer's mission was not to handle crime and disorder on a daily basis, but to "make nice." In some cases, the PCR director was a civilian, further distancing the effort from *true policing.*

With the benefit of 20/20 hindsight, another structural flaw was to have PCR officers communicate with the community through community leaders. Tactics included organizing an advisory council made up of civic and church leaders. Though this seemed wise at the time, experience shows that community leaders are not always fully in touch with the real concerns in the community, so PCR units rarely received the broadest possible input about the community's real concerns.

In part because of these structural weaknesses, PCR tactics often translated into well-meaning activities of limited scope. PCR officers staffed a speaker's bureau that gave talks on crime prevention or recruiting to various civic groups. Officers also made presentations in schools. Another typical PCR function was press relations. PCR officers also served as liaison to other public and private agencies. Many PCR officers spent much of their day hosting tours of police facilities. Though PCR officers were encouraged to solicit *suggestions,* many were under orders not to handle actual *complaints,* but to refer those to the administration.

While most PCR officers winced at being labelled public relations flak-catchers, the structure of the unit and nature of their daily activities made it difficult for them to do more. The friendly PCR officer who discussed concerns with minority leaders often bore little resemblance to the tough motor patrol officer who arrived later to handle a call. Their role in press relations was often perceived as putting a good face on a department's mistakes.

PCR programs overall suffered two major interrelated problems because of the inherent lack of follow-up and accountability. Though citizens might feel flattered by the attention when a PCR officer asked for suggestions, the officer lacked clout within the department to address specific complaints. In addition, the PCR officer who gave the talk on crime prevention to the Senior Citizens Club was never the officer who had to handle the call later, if those preventive efforts failed.

The stated objective of using PCR officers to reverse minority abuse within the department was obviously doomed, since the most aggressive officers were usually the first to call PCR officers wimps. Also, especially in departments where PCR units were established as a reluctant gesture to defuse community criticism, police administrators used the unit as a dumping ground for problem officers, further undermining internal and external credibility. However, in spite of these structural and tactical drawbacks, many PCR efforts achieved notable success.

The 1950s also saw the introduction of new *Crime Prevention* units, a proactive approach aimed at the community. Depending on the size of the department and the funding available, some departments provided a separate Crime Prevention officer or unit, while others rolled both Crime Prevention and PCR into one.

Like PCR, Crime Prevention was manned by *staff* rather than *line* officers. The unit's goal was to educate the businesses and community residents about specific measures they could take, such as target-hardening, to reduce their likelihood of victimization and thereby help decrease the crime rate overall. Obviously, the unit's strengths and weaknesses mirror those of PCR units, though many such efforts helped inform the public about things they could do to help the police in their battle against crime.

Despite their drawbacks, many communities applauded and appreciated both PCR and Crime Prevention efforts as the first sincere evidence of a willingness by the police to reach out to the community and address their concerns in an organized way.

The Challenge of the Late 1960s

Though PCR efforts were decidedly a step in the right direction, the program's inherent weaknesses became dramatically apparent during the domestic upheaval that began in the late 1960s. As Baby Boomers will attest, the early 1960s were a time of great optimism, fueled by the idealism of the millions of young people who dominated the culture by their sheer numbers. President John Kennedy tapped into this youthful enthusiasm when he challenged the entire generation to "ask not what your country can do for you, but what you can do for your country." His new Peace Corps attracted thousands of energetic young people who believed in their collective ability to change the world overnight.

Despite Kennedy's assassination in 1963, his successor, Lyndon Johnson, announced his commitment to carry on Kennedy's civil rights agenda, embodied in the Great Society programs that were designed to promote equality between black and white and narrow the gap between rich and poor. This was the era when Martin Luther King's dream of a colorblind society seemed within reach. Within policing, it seemed that the continued adoption and expansion of Police/Community Relations and Crime Prevention units would provide the last link in fulfilling the promise of a full-service, professionalized police force, capable of handling any challenge.

Shockingly, within just a few short years, the country was instead plunged into domestic chaos. Talk of revolution filled the air, as cities burned, and crime rates soared. The civil rights movement spawned the militant Black Power movement, which included groups such as the Black Panthers, whose bloody clashes with police heightened tensions on both sides. Race riots erupted summer after summer – in Watts, Newark, Detroit, then in cities nationwide the spring of 1968 when Martin Luther King was assassinated (see Chapter 5 for further discussion).

Meanwhile, protests on college campuses became increasingly violent, as the focus narrowed to the pressing issues of the Vietnam War and the draft. The nightly news was filled with images of students armed with lists of nonnegotiable demands taking over university administration buildings as riot police lobbed teargas into the crowds.

The upheaval pitted hawks against doves, blacks against whites, students against the establishment, young against old, in an atmosphere of increasing fury on all sides. As representatives of the establishment whose job included maintaining domestic peace, the police often found themselves on one side of the barricades facing any one of a number of widely diverse groups collectively known as the *New Left*.

The New Left was a loose coalition of radical groups clamoring for a variety of social changes, under the overall umbrella term of social justice. Their unifying slogan was *Power to the People*. The agenda ranged from legalizing marijuana and other drugs to ending the draft, from sexual freedom to equality for blacks and women. Protests covered the spectrum from non-violent actions, such as the bizarre attempt by the Yippies to levitate the Pentagon by chanting, to outright urban terrorism, including bombings conducted by small, ultra-radical groups like the Weathermen, who had split from Students for a Democratic Society (SDS) over the issue of violence. The underground Weathermen served as a model for other violent groups, such as the Symbionese Liberation Army (SLA) that made headlines when they kidnapped heiress Patty Hearst.

To the New Left, the police were *pigs,* brutal agents of establishment oppression. To the police, the New Left was made up of *hippies* and *longhairs,* an unlikely mix of spoiled college kids and draft-dodgers, who had turned their backs on the culture that subsidized them, and murderous black criminals, who cloaked their reverse racism in rhetoric about equality.

Perhaps the most dramatic confrontation occurred in Chicago during the 1968 Democratic convention, when TV cameras rolled as the late Mayor Daly's police waded into crowds of young protestors. Wielding nightsticks, their badge numbers hidden, the police *cracked heads* in what the Kerner Commission would later call a *police riot.*

As if to add insult to injury, the 1960s were also a time when the rates of serious crime exploded. Even after adjusting for the increase in population, between 1965 and 1970, murder rates jumped rose 55 %, aggravated assault 48 %, and robbery 124 % .[13] While part of that increase might be attributable to improved reporting techniques, there was an undeniable surge in both the number and severity of crimes committed.

Some experts attribute the dramatic rise in crime during that era to the bulge of Baby Boomers hitting their most crime-prone years of 18 to 25 years old. Others cite the boom in drug use, while some claim society's refusal to legalize marijuana fostered a scofflaw attitude similar to what happened during Prohibition. Another view held that the dramatic increase in the number of single-parent homes was the key, while another targeted poverty and racism. Whatever the cause or causes, the police bore the brunt of much of the resulting frustration. Though they obviously had little or no control over any of the possible root causes of the dramatic increase in serious crime, by emphasizing crime-fighting as their primary mission, the police invited accusations they had failed whenever crime rates rose.

The increasing polarization of society into opposing factions made it hard for the calm voice of reason to be heard above the shouting. Those on the political right issued a call for *law and order* – which those on the left interpreted as a euphemism for a heavy-handed police crackdown on minorities and students. Those on the political left protested against police brutality, suggesting the police had become the Gestapo. Despite the infusion of new technology funded by the Law Enforcement Assistance Act (LEAA), escalating criminal and political violence continued into the early 1970s, underscoring the need for the police to find new ways to heal old wounds.

In this climate, the growing rift within society could not be healed by well-meaning but often ineffectual PCR and Crime Prevention efforts. Quite obviously, the bitterness brewing between the police and various splintered and polarized elements within communities required a bolder approach. Though many police departments that had not previously adopted a PCR or Crime Prevention program now did so as a way of addressing the need to find ways to break down barriers between the police and the community, these efforts lacked the structural and tactical clout to deliver the knockout punch required to stem the onslaught of crime and disorder problems.

As the limitations of both PCR and Crime Prevention efforts became increasingly obvious, numerous experiments were conducted to see if some new way could be found to build bridges to the community and fight crime and disorder at the same time. One promising new approach that became popular beginning in the early 1970s was *team policing,* which involved maintaining a permanent team of officers that responded to crime problems within a particular geographic area.

Team policing recognized that one of PCR's main defects was its reliance on staff and not line officers. However, though team policing involved line officers, it was often applied as if it were no more than a limited tactic, rather than as a strategic approach, so it typically lacked the commitment required to make any substantive and lasting impact on improving overall, long-term police relations within the community. And while team policing was effective in solving specific crime problems, it did not demonstrate that it could stem the rising tide of crime. Many times, a team policing effort in one area simply displaced crime somewhere else. In essence, team policing also suffered because it was still basically a reactive approach, with officers rushing from one crisis to the next.

Again, hindsight makes it easy to identify the shortcomings in all the ambitious attempts to find a new way for the police and the community to make peace and work together in the face of the dramatic increase in crime. These were the evolutionary phases that set the stage for the Community Policing revolution.

The Birth of Community Policing

As history demonstrates, many factors set the stage for the birth of Community Policing:

- The isolation of officers in police cars.

- The narrowing of the police mission to crime fighting.

- A scientific approach to management that stressed efficiency more than effectiveness.

- Increased reliance on high-tech gadgetry instead of human interaction.

- Insulation of police administration from community input.

- A long-standing concern about police violation of minority civil rights.

- Initial attempts by the police to reach the community, such as PCR, Crime Prevention, and team policing units.

Most of these elements share one theme in common – the isolation of the police from the public at large. The resulting alienation fostered an *us against them* mindset on the part of both the police and the community. Community Policing therefore rose like a phoenix from the ashes of burned cities, embattled campuses, and crime-riddled neighborhoods, a positive new response to the chaos of that turbulent era. Beginning in the early 1970s, the basic issues and ideas that would ultimately coalesce into the Community Policing concept were discussed in various books and articles, though the cohesive philosophy and the specific organizational changes that would have to be made to achieve these new goals had not yet solidified.[14] Later, in some cases, it was called foot patrol, then Neighborhood Policing, Neighborhood-Oriented Policing, Community-Oriented Policing, Community-Based Policing, or Community Policing. But regardless of the name used, this growing new movement learned from the past, saving the best from each successive advance.

From the reform movement of the 1930s, Community Policing retains:

- The commitment to upgrading the education and training of police officers.

- The judicious use of new technology.

- Efforts to use the talents of women officers.

- Most importantly, the insulation of the police from politics, so that today's CPO cannot fall into the trap of the foot patrol officer of the past whose agenda was dictated by politicians and special-interest groups.

From Police/Community Relations and Crime Prevention efforts, Community Policing retains:

- A sincere commitment to improving police relations with minorities.

- Outreach into schools, in the hope of preventing problems in the future.

- A liaison with other organizations and agencies.

- Efforts to end police brutality.

From team policing, Community Policing retains:

- The primary mandate of providing effective law enforcement, which includes carrying a gun and making arrests.

- An effort to deal with crime trends rather than attacking isolated crimes one by one.

To these virtues, Community Policing brings:

- A new mandate that expands the police beyond crime-fighting, to include efforts targeted at physical and social decay, disorder, and fear of crime.

- A proactive focus.

- Daily, face-to-face contact with the community, with the same officer in the same neighborhood, as a means of developing long-term rapport and mutual trust.

- An opportunity for meaningful community input into the police agenda, in exchange for which citizens must share the responsibility for helping to police their communities.

- An emphasis on encouraging the officer to experiment with creative and innovative solutions aimed at problems and not just isolated incidents.

Policing Today

August Vollmer's dream of a professionalized police force has been realized, though he might be stunned by its size and shape, and by the problems it faces. From 1977 to 1982, the percentage of police officers in urban areas rose from 68% to 82%. While there are 3,000 county sheriff's offices nationwide, an increasing number are retaining the detention function, but shifting law enforcement duties to a county police department (79 such multi-purpose county offices were in operation as of 1986). Today, more than 90% of all municipalities of 2,500 or more people have their own police forces.[15]

While more police units are adopting the metropolitan policing model, vast differences in the levels of police protection persist. According to the National Insitute of Justice *Report to the Nation on Crime and Justice – Second Edition,* published in 1988, the number of officers per 100 square miles ranged from zero in some places in Alaska, to 8,667 in some boroughs of New York City. While three-quarters of all counties have somewhere between one and three officers for each 1,000 residents, the range overall is from zero to 55. Despite the pressure to add more officers as population density increases, great variations remain. As the report shows, both San Diego County in California and Knox County in Tennessee employ roughly two officers for each 1,000 population, yet the former houses 1.8 million people, compared to only 300,000 for the latter.[16]

Vollmer's commitment to upgrading police officers is evident in the dramatic increase in the educational levels of police officers. In 1982, an FBI survey found that 79% of all officers had at least some college, with 23% holding a bachelor's degree. Almost all departments also provide their own basic and in-service training, and there are now more than 670 training centers nationwide.[17]

Though still underrepresented compared to the population at large, women constituted 7% of all police officers in 1985. And blacks have made even greater strides, increasing their percentage of officers and detectives to 12% as of the same year.[18]

The explosion of technology now pervades all law enforcement agencies. According to the report, there were fewer than 1,000 police cars in 1922, and only one police department was using a computer in 1964. Today, motor patrol dominates most law enforcement efforts, and a study in 1981 confirmed that all jurisdictions with a population of 50,000 or more use computers.[19]

Overall, the twin traditions of big-city policing and frontier law enforcement have been welded into a multi-level system, spanning all units of government, so that by 1986, there were 50 federal law enforcement agencies and 11,743 municipal, 79 county, and 1,819 township general-purpose agencies. Municipal, county, and township agencies together employ 533,247 full-time equivalent employees.[20]

Those figures document the progress the police have made since the reform movement of the 1930s, but it is still too early to tell the full impact of the Community Policing reform movement. No doubt changing times and changing needs will spawn yet another reform movement in the future, but today's Community Policing revolution is the most dynamic and innovative response to finding ways to involve the community in policing itself that has come along in 50 years. From its birth as pilot programs in places like Newark and Flint to its widespread practical application nationwide today, Community Policing has made the crucial transition from being a promising experiment to an accepted norm.

As we learn more about how to follow criminal activity up the ladder to those at the top, we must also recognize that much of the crime and disorder that plagues people's lives is not the result of sophisticated and elegantly planned schemes by a criminal elite. New concepts such as *strategic policing* allow departments to fashion efforts aimed at the superstructure of crime. Departments must always strive to become more effective against the criminal elite – high-level drug dealing, organized crime, political corruption, car-theft rings, white-collar crime, and computer, credit card, and stock fraud.

While it is important for the police to perfect techniques that allow them to match wits with those at the top, the lesson of history teaches that the biggest challenge the police face is finding a way to enlist the cooperation and support of average citizens in efforts to make their lives safer and more enjoyable, a way that accords them the dignity and respect they deserve. Community Policing reminds us of the importance of balancing efforts aimed at the top with those that focus on the street where most people live. It also reminds us that people are the police department's most valuable resource and should be treated as valued partners in the police process.

What history also shows is that change takes time and that, at any given moment, the past and the future co-exist together. Even today, some departments have not fully embraced all the reforms Vollmer outlined in the 1930s, meanwhile other departments are leading the way into the future that others will follow. What we do know today is that Community Policing has now reached *critical mass,* so that it is now recognized as being at the cutting edge of what is new in policing.

NOTES

[1]William H. Hewitt, *British Police Administration* (Springfield, IL: Charles C Thomas 1965), p. 4.

[2]Charles Reith, *The Blind Eye of History* (London: Faber & Faber Ltd., 1952), p. 154.

[3]Wayne Gard, *Frontier Justice* (Norman, OK: University of Oklahoma Press, 1949), p. 158.

[4]Richard M. Brown, *The American Vigilante Tradition, Violence in America,* A Staff Report to the National Commission on the Causes and Prevention of Violence (Washington, DC: U.S. Government

Printing Office, 1969), p. 140.

[5]Miguel Antonio Otem, *My Life on the Frontier,* 1864-1882 (New York: The Press of the Pioneers, 1935), pp. 205-6.

[6]Raymond B. Fosdick, *American Police Systems* (New York: The Century Co., 1921), p. 68.

[7]Frederick Lewis Allen, *Only Yesterday* (New York: Harper & Row, Publishers, 1959), p. 44.

[8]Franklin Matthews, *The Character of the American Police, The World's Work 2* (New York: Doubleday, Page & Co., May 1909, October 1901), p. 1314.

[9]*Report on Police* (Wickersham Commission) *National Commission on Law Observance and Enforcement* (Washington, DC: U.S. Government Printing Office, 1931), p. 140.

[10]George L. Kelling and Mark H. Moore, *From Political to Reform to Community: The Evolving Strategy of Police,* a paper produced at Harvard University's Kennedy School of Government (Cambridge, MA: 1987), p. 38.

[11]Jack L. Kuykendall, *Police and Minority Groups: Toward a Theory of Negative Contacts, Police,* 15, No. 1 (September-October 1970), pp. 47 & 52.

[12]*Get the Ball Rolling: A Guide to Police Community Relations Programs* (New Orleans: National Association of Police Community Relations Officers, 1971).

[13]Charles Murray, *Images of Fear,* Harper's Magazine (May 1985), p. 41.

[14]Among the books and articles published during the 1970s that raised issues and concerns that set the stage for what has since become Community Policing are:

Trojanowicz, Robert C., *Juvenile Delinquency: Concepts and Control* (Englewood Cliffs, NJ: Prentice-Hall, 1973).

Trojanowicz, Robert C., and Dixon, Samuel L., *Criminal Justice and the Community* (Englewood Cliffs, NJ: Prentice-Hall, 1974).

Trojanowicz, Robert C.: Trojanowicz, John M.: and Moss, Forrest M., *Community Based Crime Prevention* (Pacific Palisades, CA: Goodyear Publishing Co., 1975).

Goldstein, Herman, *Policing in a Free Society* (Cambridge, MA:Ballinger, 1977).

Goldstein, Herman, *Improving Policing: A Problem-Oriented Approach, Crime and Delinquency,* 25:236-258, 1979.

[15]*Report to the Nation on Crime and Justice,* Second Edition, U.S. Department of Justice (Washington, DC: Bureau of Justice Statistics, March 1986) p. 63.

[16]*Ibid,* p. 64.

[17]*Ibid,* p. 63.

[18]*Ibid.*

[19]*Ibid.*

[20]*Ibid.*

CHAPTER 3
The Changing Meaning
of Community

The difference between the right word and the almost right word is the difference between lightning and the lightning bug.
—*Mark Twain*

The Importance of Definitions

Like any professional field, modern policing abounds in jargon – terms understood by insiders, which function as a kind of shorthand so that they can communicate ideas to each other easily and quickly. The danger, however, is that jargon can cause confusion, both inside and outside a field, when people do not understand a term's true meaning.

As noted in Chapter 1, some early experiments that paved the way for Community Policing relied on the tactic of using foot patrol officers to put police officers in daily, face-to-face contact with the community. This helped fuel misunderstanding about how modern, directed foot patrol differed from foot patrol in the past, and whether foot patrol and Community Policing were synonymous. Not only did this spawn confusion, but it also meant that the taint of corruption surrounding foot patrol efforts of the past raised unwarranted concern about contemporary efforts.

Confusion and misunderstanding can also arise when two people think they are talking about the same thing, when they both use the same term, without realizing each has a different idea concerning what the word means. The likelihood of this kind of misunderstanding is magnified with a term like Community Policing, since those two simple words are used to convey a subtle but sophisticated new philosophy, as well as a new organizational strategy that departments can use to put the philosophy into practice.

Because accurate and complete definitions are so important, the first chapter defined what Community Policing is – and is not. The purpose of this chapter is to clear up any confusion concerning what the word *community* means in the context of Community Policing.

Community as a Force in Social Control

At first glance, debating what is meant by the word *community,* when it is used in the term *Community Policing,* sounds like a boring academic exercise – reminiscent of the arguments among theologians about how many angels could dance on the head of a pin. However, even a cursory review of the literature shows that community can mean very different things to different people, at different times, so unless we define what we mean by community, it can be difficult to understand clearly the goals of Community Policing.

In terms of preventing and controlling crime and disorder, it is important to understand the dynamics of people, both as individuals and as members of groups. The primary responsibility for social control resides in the individual. Each person is ultimately accountable for his behavior, because it is the individual who decides what he will or will not do, according to the dictates of his conscience.

The next most important unit that affects social control is the family. The family communicates values and expectations that help shape individual conscience. Though some individuals sink below or rise above the standards set by the family, the family remains a potent force in determining how people behave. Beyond the family, the next most important force in shaping people's values and behavior is the community, which includes other powerful social institutions such as the church and schools. From strongest to weakest, the full progression includes:

- the individual (conscience)

- the family

- the community (including institutions such as churches and schools)

- the region

- the country

Though we will deal in detail later with the precise definition of community, at issue as well is the obvious weakening of the many of the social institutions, including community, that have traditionally played crucial roles in the development and shaping of individual conscience. Perhaps the most important changes have occurred within families. Dating from prehistoric times, the extended family or some variant of this model has been the primary social unit responsible for rearing the young in ways that encourage them to adopt the values and mores of the group.

However, in less than 50 years, since the end of World War II, we have seen the rapid decline of the *extended family* in favor of the *nuclear family*. While experts continue to debate the full consequences of this shift, the obvious fact is that this means we now have two people doing a job previously shared by many. No longer do grandparents or aunts and uncles live in the home – or even nearby. Undeniably, this reduces the number of powerful adults in daily, face-to-face contact with the family's children as they grow up.

Even more recently, we have seen the decline of the traditional nuclear family. The Bureau of Census now projects that only 39 % – a distinct minority – of the children born in 1987 will live with both natural parents until age 18.[1] Death, divorce, and separation have always taken a toll, but the increased incidence of divorce in the United States now means more children are raised by stepparents or in single-parent homes. While this in no way denigrates the modern parent's skills in raising children, the dramatic increase in the number single-parent families, so that now one in four (26 %) of all families are headed by a single parent,[2] means that the entire burden of instilling in children a strong sense of right and wrong now often rests on only one person.

This has obvious economic implications as well, since the single parent is typically the mother, and a woman's standard of living drops, on average, 73 % in the year following a divorce (a man's rises 43 %).[3] Because women still earn far less than men, for half the children raised in single-parent homes, this means a below-average family income.[4]

Adding to the burden of the single parent is the continued erosion of the community as a strong source of support. Though much of this chapter will be devoted to defining what we now mean by community and the changes it has undergone, at this point, suffice it to say that the impact of the community in helping to provide and promote a coherent and consistent set of expectations concerning what is – and is not – acceptable behavior has weakened. In addition, as we shall see later, the power of other community institutions, such as the church and the schools, has eroded.

As if to fill the vacuum, we have also seen the explosion of mass media. Nielsen Media Research reports that children two through five years old watch an average of 25 hours and 26 minutes of TV each week. At six to 11 years old, this declines slightly to 22 hours and 46 minutes. It rises again to 23 hours and 13 minutes per week of TV viewing for teenage girls, and 24 hours and 16 minutes a week for teenage boys.[5]

Adults watch even more television than children; the lower the family income, the more TV people watch; and, as a frame of reference, the total number of hours of television watched in American households in 1985 topped more than 224 billion.[6]

Also of concern is that the average child has seen 18,000 murders on TV by age 16.[7] According to George Gerbner of The Annenberg School of Communications at the University of Pennsylvania, research shows that six to eight incidents of violence (defined as overt acts that could kill or maim) occur during each hour of prime time programming (which excludes the news), 20 to 25 per hour on weekend, children's, daytime TV – figures that have remained stable for decades.[8]

In addition, since the advent of TV, people spend so many hours viewing – instead of reading about the world or interacting with others – that television becomes many people's "window on the world." Gerbner also says that violence on television should be of particular concern to law enforcement for two reasons – research indicates that viewing violent images on television can incite aggression in some children, but even more pervasive is a lingering sense of insecurity, fear, and mistrust that desensitizes all viewers to violence – children and adults. Though images of violence occur far more frequently on TV than in real life, people tend to mistake this illusion for reality. This produces the so-called *mean world syndrome* that makes people fearful of venturing out among others, which has an obvious impact on our ability to build a sense of community.[9]

The profound consequences of these economic and social changes cannot yet be fully understood. Yet it takes little imagination to see that these trends portend a different world. For thousands of years, an inquisitive child relied on asking a family member for answers about right and wrong. Today, instead, a new generation of *latchkey kids* returns home from school and pops on the television for company. According to a Lou Harris poll, 41% of the 2,000 parents surveyed said they leave their children on their own between the end of school and 5:30 p.m. at least once a week – roughly one out of four left their children alone every school day.[10] Important as well is that fear of being home alone ranks first among children's most common fears, according to *Sprint* magazine.[11]

Without engaging in the *nature versus nurture* debate concerning how individual conscience is formed or the conservative versus liberal controversy concerning how best to promote family values, the fact remains that the majority of children growing up today are being raised very differently than they were in the days of the extended family, an era when the community also played a more forceful role in shoring up traditional values about right and wrong. In today's world, many single parents do not have the option of not working so that they can stay home with their children. In 1988, 65% of all mothers reported either that they held jobs or were looking for work,[12] and a growing number of two-parent families now depend on two full-time incomes to maintain their desired standard of living. These changes are occurring during a time when the increasing fragmentation of traditional communities also means these new kinds of families cannot depend on them as much for extra help in the all-important job of raising children to become law-abiding adults.

In terms of crime and disorder, the implications of these changes are enormous. We have built a society that depends on individual conscience as the primary source of social control – that almost everyone will stop at a red light even if there is no police officer in evidence. Traffic laws and police officers are in place, to make sure that occasional offenders learn their lesson by being penalized and because we hope that making sure people know such a system is in place will act as a deterrent, as will the occasional punishment of transgressors. Yet considering the tremendous social changes of the past half-century, we must question whether we are shifting to a society where ever greater numbers of people will not stop at society's red lights unless there is an officer visible. Can we, as a society, afford that many *watchers* – and do we want to live in that kind of world?

To maintain a safe and orderly society, we must rely on external controls when internal controls fail. If our social institutions, such as the family and the community, fail to instill the virtue of self-control in the young, we will be increasingly forced to depend on external controls, such as the criminal justice system. However, recent history shows that we may lack the will or the ability to provide enough money to fund formal efforts at the level needed to ensure public safety. Many police departments today still have not bounced back from the recession of the 1970s, which means they have fewer sworn officers than they did 10 years ago. Yet crime rates now stand at levels that would have been considered totally unacceptable prior to the late 1960s.

This underscores the threefold importance of Community Policing as a new way for the police to address contemporary concerns:

- In the short term, Community Policing involves the community in efforts designed to reduce crime, fear of crime, and disorder today. This encourages law-abiding people to reclaim their streets and enhance the immediate quality of life in their neighborhoods.

- Many Community Policing efforts specifically target the young. Since juveniles commit a disproportionate share of crime in this country, such efforts offer the short- and long-term promise of reducing crime today and deterring criminal activity in the future. Because of its proactive approach, Community Policing promotes community-based activities that can help keep kids out of trouble. The traditional police approach depends primarily on sanctions – break the law and you will be punished. Community Policing not only includes sanctions against bad behavior but it helps provide support for kids who learn to live within the law – break the law and you will be punished, but if you act responsibly, you will be rewarded.

- Long-term, Community Policing can offer the potential for the police to play an important role in helping to rebuild a sense of community where it is declining or has disappeared. The goal is to shore up communities as places where everyone participates in assisting today's beleaguered families transmit important values, such as respect for the law, to the next generation. By making neighborhoods safer and more attractive places to live, Community Policing adds to the sense that community life is an important and integral aspect of life, one worth struggling to achieve and maintain.

The History of the Meaning of Community

To understand the full implications of these goals therefore requires a clear understanding of what is meant by community and how communities have changed in recent times. The definition of community has evolved over time to take into account the changing reality, as the kind and character of communities themselves have changed. In the past, defining community was simpler, because a sense of community based on a *community of interests* typically overlapped the *geographic community,* but, as we shall see, that need not always be the case today. Technological and economic changes have had a dramatic impact on community life.

Part of the challenge for Community Policing therefore is to help revive the idea that those who live in the same area can improve the quality of community life by understanding how they share a community of interest. Perhaps ironically, the threat of crime and disorder can be the catalyst to make people see that they do share a community of interest based on mutual geography. Of great consequence as well is that unless this corrosive fear is channelled into positive change, it can degenerate into apathy – or into outbursts of vigilantism. Community Policing holds the promise of using that fear and anger as the impetus and foundation for efforts to improve the overall quality of community life.

At the turn of the century, when this country was primarily an agrarian society with less than 10 % of the population living in cities, the term community hardly seemed to require definition. Community expressed the idea of a distinct area where people shared both a common geography and a common culture, as well as elements of mutual interdependence. Increasing industrialization drove people from the farms into the cities, but the term community still seemed to serve fairly well in describing how even the largest cities broke down into smaller communities that still met these criteria.

According to Donald R. Fessler, (rural) sociologists defined community as "any area in which people with a common culture share common interests."[13] The problem with that broad a definition is that it could span "a rural village of half a hundred families" to "one of our major cities."[14] As Fessler noted, large cities were not what people meant when they talked about communities, because the inherent depersonalization that dominates large cities militates against the cohesive sense of community.[15]

In the 1920s, the so-called *Chicago School*, comprised of sociologists such as Robert E. Park, continued attempts to refine the rural model so that it could be applied to communities within major metropolitan areas.[16] According to sociologist Thomas M. Meenaghan, the Chicago School technique relied on identifying central locators, such as businesses, churches, and schools, and then drawing the community's boundary lines by finding those living the furthest away who still used those services.[17] As Meenaghan wrote in his treatise, *What Means Community*, "...Park saw the community as a group of people living in a specific geographic area and conditioned by the subcultural or life processes of competition, cooperation, assimilation, and conflict. The unplanned life processes created so-called natural areas that not only had a defined territorial frame, but also shared special or unique cultural and social characteristics."[18]

In less formal terms, this means people take on identifiable marks of membership in the community just by living there; that even when individuals or groups within a community do not much like each other, their constant interaction helps shape their identity and their values; and that living in the community is a potent force in influencing what people think, how they feel, and what they believe. People do not make a conscious decision to take on the colorations and nuances of their communities, but instead this occurs as a natural outgrowth of living in the community and bumping up against the behavior and attitudes of other community members in the routine course of daily life.

By the 1950s, there were so many definitions of community that George A. Hillery, Jr., of the University of Atlanta, attempted to classify 94 different definitions, by content, to see whether he could identify areas of common agreement.[19] His conclusion was that, "Most... are in basic agreement that community consists of persons in social interaction within a geographic area and having one or more additional ties."[20]

This makes it easy to see how the term *community* began to become synonymous with *neighborhood*. Yet sociologists and ecologists continued to draw distinctions between these two terms that often tended to confuse rather than explain any difference. In Hillery's time, a decade after World War II, when most cities were still dominated by clear-cut, virtually self-contained, ethnic neighborhoods, drawing such distinctions seemed like needless hairsplitting.

In her paper, "The Neighborhood," published in 1982, Suzanne Keller defined neighborhood in terms that echo past definitions of community, demonstrating that confusion about these terms persists today. "The neighborhood, viewed as an area or a place within a larger entity, has boundaries – either physical or symbolic and usually both – where streets, railway lines, or parks separate off an area and its inhabitants or where historical and social traditions make people view an area as a distinctive unit. Usually these two boundaries reinforce each other: the physical unit encourages symbolic unity, and symbolic boundaries come to be attached to physical ones."[21]

Though community study had, to a great degree, fallen out of fashion in the 1960s, efforts to update and refine the definition of community in the 1970s focused on identifying new unifying principles. The University of Chicago's Albert Hunter, in his book, *Symbolic Communities,* noted the close association among the words *common, communication,* and *community.* He argued that both language and shared symbols help identify what he called the *natural community.*[22] Meenaghan focused on social area analysis, which used census tract information to break out urban groups of 3,000 to 6,000 people, so that data on the homogeneity of economic, family, and ethnic characteristics could then be used to identify the boundaries of communities.[23]

As these definitions demonstrate, the terms *neighborhood* and *community* could be used interchangeably with little argument when most cities consisted of distinct ethnic enclaves. After the turn of the century, wave after wave of immigrants arrived, primarily from Europe, settling most often into expanding ethnic neighborhoods in major cities, where they could also continue to maintain their various cultural traditions. In addition, native blacks from the rural South continued to migrate to northern cities in search of higher-paying jobs in industry. They settled in specific city neighborhoods, dictated not only by choice and income but by discriminatory housing practices.

As we shall see, the economic changes and the explosion of technology that have occurred since the end of World War II disrupted the status quo, so that established definitions of community and neighborhood began to take on new meaning. What many researchers failed to take into account was that a community of interest did not have to be tied to a particular geographic area. In particular, the impact of mass transit, mass communications, and mass media, as well as economic pressures, disrupted previously stable communities, leaving in their wake areas in many major cities where people still live together in a definable geographic area, but they do not interact in the same ways as before.

Assaults on the Community

A serious danger in any discussion about changes in what is meant by the word *community*, and changes that have occurred within communities, is that such discussion is unconsciously colored by a wistful longing for what may only *seem* like a better past. As Victor Azarya of the Hebrew University in Jerusalem wrote about many of the definitions of community analyzed by Hillery: "These approaches are clearly mixed with some nostalgia for a glorious past in which people were thought to be more secure, less alienated, and less atomized."[24]

What Azarya ignores, however, is that we look to the family and the community not only to teach us values, but to provide emotional support, a sense of identity, and the warmth that comes from belonging to a group that cares about us. Without romanticizing the past, there are disturbing differences between yesterday's communities and today's reality in terms of the level of emotional support they provide.

One major difference is that more of us live in cities than ever before. In 1988, three of every four people live in a *major metropolitan area*, defined as cities of 50,000 people or more and their surrounding areas. This is up from roughly 63 % during the 1970s.[25]

U.S. cities have also become blacker and poorer. The *white flight* of the 1950s from the cities to the suburbs was succeeded by the *black flight* of middle- and upper-class blacks that began roughly a decade later, as the explosion of serious crime discussed in the previous chapter persuaded those who could to move to the suburbs. This shift was also fueled by the continuing rise in the overall standard of living created by an expanding economy, which allowed more and more people the opportunity to be upwardly mobile.

White flight from cities was also the result of a notoriously unethical real estate practice, called *blockbusting*. Blockbusting stampeded white home owners into selling their houses because of the fear that black families moving in would inevitably cause property values to plunge. Some unscrupulous real estate agents would intentionally line up a black home buyer for a house in an all-white neighborhood, and the agents would either keep the buyer's race secret or offer the seller an inflated price to ensure the sale would go through. Then they would prey on the racial fears of the other white home owners, warning them that unless they sold quickly, they would be trapped in homes worth a fraction of their current value. This practice exploited a self-fulfilling prophecy, since panic selling did depress price, which meant those previously stable neighborhoods quickly degenerated into chaos.

Not only did the influx of newcomers have no shared history together, the fact that late arrivals were able to purchase homes for a fraction of what the early arrivals had paid often meant the new community suffered inevitable internal tensions in trying to blend people of vastly different socio-economic classes in one confined area. Only the real estate agents profited, since they were able to turn tidy profits on the huge volume of sales that blockbusting promoted.

The full implications of these dislocations were somewhat masked, as long as the rising standard of living held the promise of offering ever-increasing opportunities for advancement to anyone willing to work hard – the American dream. Then the dramatic rise of oil prices in the early 1970s, followed by stagflation, then the recession of 1982, culminated in the loss of high-paid unskilled jobs in industry and manufacturing, with more of the new jobs created in the lower-paying service fields, and with many of those jobs in the suburbs. Adjusted for inflation, median family income in 1988 stood at $30,850, almost precisely the same as 15 years earlier.[26] As a society, we have not yet grasped the full implications of what it will mean if most people cannot expect to improve their condition, and the young have good reason to worry they may not be able to achieve the same standard of living enjoyed by their parents.

Using Detroit as an example, since the 1950s, the city has lost 850,000 people – enough to qualify as this nation's 11th largest city.[27] According to the *Detroit Free Press,* during that same time, other important community assets have been also been lost: "Detroit has lost about 100 movie theaters, J.L. Hudson's flagship department store, the headquarters of the AAA-Michigan, Stroh's brewery, the *Pistons* professional basketball team, the *Lions* pro football team, countless factories."[28] In addition, Cardinal Szoka announced in the fall of 1988 that he planned to close one-third (43) of Detroit's remaining Catholic churches, leaving the city with only half the number it boasted in 1968.[29]

In 1956, Michigan employed 412,000 in the auto industry, down to 288,000 in the second quarter of 1988.[30] While this suggests future workers will need more education to secure good jobs, two studies of ninth grade classes in Detroit (in 1982 and 1983) showed that roughly four of every 10 of those students left school by graduation.[31] As if to fill that gap, illegal drug trafficking in Detroit is expected to reach $1 billion in 1988.[32] The *Drug Abuse Trends* report prepared by the Michigan Department of Public Health's Office of Substance Abuse Services reports that the rate of cocaine use statewide in 1986 was 64.2 per 100,000, but that rate jumps to an alarming 491.7 per 100,000 for non-white males.[33]

While this stands as a glaring example of the problems plaguing northern *Rust Belt* cities, the influx of newcomers into the Sun Belt cities of the South and West face problems as well. Since 1973, the overall number of people living in poverty in the U.S. rose from 23 million to 35.3 million.[34] Since 1977, the inflation-adjusted income of the poorest 10 % of American families has fallen more than 10 %.[35]

New as well is what is now called the *Underclass,* the one-fourth of those poor families that *Time* magazine called:

> ...the poor who are more than just temporarily down and out, the ones caught in a vicious cycle of poverty and despair. For the most part they are black and live in the decayed heart of American cities. But the Underclass is defined less by income than by behavior. Members are prisoners of a ghetto pathology, the denizens of a self-perpetuating culture marked by teenage pregnancy, fatherless households, chronic unemployment, crime, drug use, and long-term dependency on welfare.[36]

Among children from all kinds of families, one in four is born poor, and at least one in three will be on welfare at some point, with one in two living in a single-parent household headed by a female.[37] According to Senator Daniel P. Moynihan, "About 10 years ago, we became the first nation in history in which the poorest group in the population was the children. This is intensifying. Today, the poorest children are the youngest children."[38]

The *Time* article on the Underclass also notes that more than half of all black infants are born out of wedlock and that figure reaches 90 % in the inner cities. In addition, nearly half of all black females are pregnant by age 20. Two out of five black children depend on welfare, with at least 100,000 homeless.[39]

While ethnic neighborhoods in the past also suffered the cruelties associated with poverty, for many, the combination of white skin, opportunities for a decent education, access to high-paid unskilled jobs, and community reinforcement of the value of education and the hard-work ethic allowed many struggling immigrant groups to work their way out of their ghettos. Minorities have demonstrably had a more difficult time, with the result that many cities consist of a poor and black inner city, dotted here and there with affluent neighborhoods whose gentrification dislocates the poor who lived there before. Beyond the city core are neighborhoods of varying fortune, encircled by middle- and upper-class suburbs that are most often predominantly white.

What does the term *community* mean in this new context? In American cities, neighborhood and community could be used interchangeably as long as the phenomenon described could be symbolized by this scenario: An Italian (Polish, Jewish, etc.,) grandmother and mother send their youngest son to the store for butter to make dinner before the rest of the family came home from work. Passing the police officer on the corner, the boy arrives at the shop, where the owner shares the same nationality. The store owner's relationship with the family is such that he may well extend interest-free credit if the father is sick or unemployed, and he is also sure to march the young boy home to his folks if he catches him shoplifting. If that happens, no doubt the young man's offense would be discussed at the dinner table, as well as afterward when the family passes time together before bed. Within that confined geographic area was a support system made up of family and community that worked together to inculcate the young with a strong sense of right and wrong.

The economic changes, as well as the dislocations wrought by mass transportation, mass communication, and mass media, have ruptured the tie between geography and community. In the rural model of 100 years ago, individuals were forced to depend on each other, in great part because they had no connection to people who lived outside their immediate area. A farmer whose barn burned could usually count on his neighbors to help him rebuild. The altruistic impulse was bolstered because people stuck together since they also knew they might be the ones to need a helping hand tomorrow.

Affordable technology, such as the automobile and the telephone, now allow those with sufficient resources to make bonds based on community of interest without regard for geography. If trouble strikes, a person today picks up the telephone to call a friend across town or across the country. If the problem is serious enough, that friend can climb into a car or board a plane to come help. In addition, because of inter-marriage among various nationalities, fewer people identify themselves first as an ethnic, weakening ethnic ties as a basis for a community of interests in favor of other factors that may not offer as much tradition.

In the rural past and in city neighborhoods before the advent of the telephone and the automobile, people were forced to trust their neighbors, whether they shared much in common or not. Today, it takes less effort to call a friend hundreds of miles away for advice, comfort, or assistance, than to walk 10 feet to the person who lives next door. This makes it far easier to associate with people of the same class, same educational level, same religion, same politics, same interests, regardless of whether they live nearby. A couple whose identity centers on being liberal, non-smoking joggers who both work outside the home and who enjoy spending their weekends camping with the kids, may not want much contact with the conservative family next door, a family where the wife does not work and they spend their leisure time in front of the TV.

Though the effects of mass transportation and mass communication on the community have been well documented, the role of mass media also deserves explanation. Journalists and advertisers alike understand *demographics,* which means that their audience breaks down in part by geography, but more strongly by *lifestyle,* made up of age, income, race, religion, marital status, education, career, politics, social status, and leisure-time interests.

Many in our society now define themselves by labels, reinforced by the mass media – Baby Boomer, born-again Christian, feminist, yuppie, New Ager. Many people identify most strongly with career, while others find identity in their leisure-time activities – antique buff, triathlete, hospital volunteer. Freed from the link to place, many people can shift gears into and out of various communities of interest during the day.

Using politics as an example, it becomes clear how this context of community has changed. Before television, politicians and their supporters relied on campaigning door-to-door within neighborhoods for support. Today, the politician stages a photo-opportunity in a particular neighborhood where background symbols that appeal to particular demographic groups nationwide are manipulated to transmit a message to those who share that community of interests, regardless of where they live – community as media backdrop.

Cynics like Azarya can argue that communities of the past were far from being glorious, but that does not mean today's communities do not fall ever farther short of that imperfect model. Statistics alone do not tell the full story about the impact these changes in our sense of community make in the lives of people who find less fulfillment in community life than ever before. No research can be done to see whether people today would feel happier, safer, and more secure if they were living in the kind of communities that existed in the past, yet we instinctively feel this is true.

The answer in such cases lies not in looking at what science tells us, but at literature. As author Kurt Vonnegut notes, this need to be part of a community tied to a place where people interact together in their daily lives is universal:

> This is a lonesome society that's been fragmented by the factory system. People have to move from here to there as jobs move, as prosperity leaves one area and appears somewhere else. People don't live in communities permanently anymore. But they should: Communities are very comforting to human beings. I was talking to a United Mine Workers lawyer in a bar down in the Village the other day, and he was telling me how some miners in Pennsylvania damn well will not leave, even though the jobs are vanishing, because of the church-centered communities there, and particularly because of the music. They have choirs that are 100 years old, some of them extraordinary choirs, and they are not going to go to San Diego, and build ships or airplanes. They're going to stay in Pennsylvania because that's home.... Until recent times, you know, human beings usually had a permanent community of relatives. They had dozens of homes to go to. So when a married couple had a fight, one or the other could go

to a house three doors down and stay with a close relative until he was feeling tender again. Or if a kid got so fed up with his parents that he couldn't stand it, he could march over to his uncle's for a while. And this is no longer possible. Each family is locked into its little box. The neighbors aren't relatives. There aren't other houses where people can go and be cared for.... We're lonesome. We don't have enough friends or relatives anymore. And we would if we lived in real communities.[40]

Vonnegut says the craving for community runs so deep that people who have no drinking problem join Alcoholics Anonymous, because of the extended family and sense of community it provides them. He cites the longing for community as a factor in drug use. "The fact that they use drugs gives them a community. If you become a user of any drug, you can pick up a set of friends you see day after day, because of the urgency of getting drugs all the time. And you'll get a community where you might not ordinarily have one."[41]

The emotional need to belong in a society where few opportunities exist has produced what Vonnegut calls *granfalloonery,* "a proud but meaningless association of human beings."[42] For example, if two people sitting side-by-side in an airplane discover they share something in common, perhaps both are graduates of the same university, they will be quick to pretend this makes them part of some important community. In fact, they may share nothing else in common but that fact. The theme in many of Vonnegut's writings is that a true sense of community has been lost, replaced by the illusion of community that fails to satisfy the basic human need of belonging.

What is clear as well is that many who live in poverty, including the Underclass, lack the resources to enjoy even this weakened sense of community based solely on interests. While some may be able to tune in to the mass culture offered on TV, fewer have the money for a telephone or a car, so they have no easy access to people outside their neighborhoods (including the social workers they depend on). The obvious dangers of the street, reinforced by what they see on TV, perpetuate the mean world syndrome that, in their case, is rooted in reality.

When we stop to compare a young boy's trip to the corner store in an inner-city neighborhood today, perhaps the first and most obvious difference is that the young man is probably black. How he approaches that walk takes on new meaning in light of the fact that the leading cause of death for young black men is murder at the hands of another young black man.[43] In Detroit, which has the highest rate of juvenile homicides among the nation's 10 largest cities, 35 children 16 years old or younger were shot dead in 1987, with that figure rising to 37 for just the first nine months of 1988.[44]

THE CHANGING MEANING OF COMMUNITY 89

In a city such as Detroit, that trip to the store also means the youngster will likely pass by at least one of the estimated 10,000 crack houses there.[45] Different as well is the increased likelihood that the person behind the counter in the neighborhood store is probably not also black. Chances are as well that the person behind the counter is not the owner, but a hired clerk, one who has no authority to extend credit or make allowances for family problems. The underlying racial tensions, cultural differences, and pervasive mistrust make it far more likely that if the young boy shoplifts, the clerk will not confront the family privately but call the police instead – or even take the law into his own hands. And somehow, though the law makes no distinction, shoplifting from an impersonal corporation rather than the Mom-and-Pop stores of old seems a different kind of crime.

Again using Detroit as an example, frustrated citizens who have lost faith in law enforcement to maintain order in the community are resorting to vigilantism. In 1988, neighborhood residents who said the police were no help in dealing with a crack house in their neighborhood burned it down. When the case went to trial, the jury found the two admitted arsonists not guilty, tacitly condoning vigilantism by saying the community was "absolutely fed up with crack dealers."[46]

These changes mean that today we see a three-tiered hierarchy of community based on class:

- **Underclass and lower-class** inner-city neighborhoods, awash in crime and drugs, house those too poor to escape, either permanently, through upward mobility, or symbolically and temporarily, by automobile or telephone. These blighted areas have lost many important anchors, including industry, businesses, shops, schools, and churches – institutions that helped hold the community together. Despite a shared geography and the common threat posed by high rates of crime, many people in such communities are too fearful to interact in ways that can rebuild a sense of community.

- For the **middle class,** community spans a wide range of options. On one end are lower-middle class neighborhoods which may or may not show active signs of community life, filled with people who hope to rise higher, but fear slipping lower. On the other end of that spectrum are upper-middle-class communities – gentrified areas in major cities and upscale suburban and ex-urban enclaves. In those areas, people usually have the resources that allow them to interact with others who share their interests, regardless of geography. As disposable income goes up, people can also afford to partake of social and cultural activities both within the geographic community and else-where – movies, plays, clubs, sporting events, health clubs. The more dollars an individual or family has, the more they can afford to develop and enjoy a community of interests that need not be tied to the geographic area in which they live. Participation in any commun-ity life available within the geographic area where they live becomes voluntary, a matter of choice for those who have the resources to choose from a broad range of options.

In varying degrees, fear of crime impels members of many mid-dle-class communities to band together for mutual support, but many can also substitute money for time and effort. Individually and collec-tively, they can choose to buy additional security – such as a sophisti-cated burglar alarm system, or doormen and security guards to check on in-coming visitors.

- By virtue of their income, the **upper classes** can afford all the secu-rity they want and need, yet, even with bodyguards, the affluent cannot guarantee perfect safety, especially since their wealth makes them inviting targets for crimes like kidnapping, crimes that the less fortunate rarely face. There is also, no doubt, a sense of community tied to place in wealthy areas such as Palm Springs and Grosse Pointe, but community involvement usually means heading charitable organ-izations or becoming a patron of the arts, which implies service to others rather than mutual dependence. The affluent also have the wherewithal to travel wherever a community of interests draws them.

Not only has American society become stratified in this three-tiered hierarchy, communities have also changed because of the fairly recent emergence of planned communities. Hunter noted that a *natural* community springs up when people live together in places that also support an underlying community of interests and mutual interdependence. Planned communities upset the natural balance, whether it is a low-income public housing project or an upscale suburban enclave (though the resulting problems are obviously very different). What all planned communities share in common is that their rapid appearance thrusts large numbers of people together who have no past history.

In both cases, sparking an immediate sense of community is difficult because there is no established base upon which to build. In the case of many suburban developments, a sense of community may develop over time, because the people who move there share enough in common, though it may never run deep. This is far different than when an organic community assimilates an infusion of newcomers into an already functioning system. The emotional loss may be masked in affluent suburbs, because people in such circumstances often have the money to travel and indulge their hobbies and amusements. Among those who are financially strapped, however, the move from a stable city neighborhood to a new suburb offers undeniable improvements, yet it may also exact a penalty in the loss of an important source of support.

In the case of public housing projects, the same kinds of barriers to generating a natural community exist, but experience also shows they are prone to even more serious problems. The kinds of low-income housing projects popular during the 1950s and 1960s put huge numbers of people into a confined space virtually overnight. Unlike the suburbs, such projects normally housed renters, not owners. This meant the new residents had less of a stake in maintaining the property, and they typically also had fewer resources to do so.

The lack of an existing cohesive community allowed the predators among them to exploit this lack of community, which, in turn, could prevent or at least slow the growth of a natural community. Unlike the suburbs, where home owners typically enjoyed a rising standard of living, many of the people trapped in housing projects found their standard of living declining instead, especially as welfare payment failed to keep pace with inflation. Home ownership also allowed those who bought a home in a new suburb to enjoy the benefits of increasing equity, inflating home prices, and a write-off on mortgage interest on their income tax. Their counterparts in low-income public housing were not building any equity, and, for them, inflation simply meant an increased risk of rising rents and expenses beyond what their income could cover. The additional irony, of course, is that their rent was not tax-deductible.

For those whose basic standard of living is comfortable, the loss of community may simply mean learning greater self-reliance, perhaps explaining the boom in self-help books offering advice to people on how they can become their own best friends and handle personal problems on their own. As Suzanne Keller wrote, "It is now possible for individuals to travel throughout the globe without ever leaving home, while others are at home wherever they set foot. Expanding spiritual and physical horizons have severed the original link between place and community."[47] For those left behind without access to new technologies and a raise each year, the gap between the life of the *haves* and the *have-nots* can seem an unbridgeable gulf.

This has added a new meaning to communities defined by community of interest. As Rita Mae Kelly writes, "Prior to the riots in Watts, Hough, and other ghetto areas of large cities, the word 'community' was almost never applied to neighborhoods or blocks in cities."[48] Today, when someone talks about the *black community*, a black person's membership within that definition of community depends on the context. For example, if the term black community is used in a discussion of rates of unemployment among black youth, middle- and upper-class blacks may not be implicitly included. Yet if discussion concerns certain subtle forms of racism, all blacks would automatically feel included.

Once the definition of community was divorced from place and focused instead on shared interests, an individual's inclusion or exclusion can be problematic. Membership in this kind of weak and shifting community cannot offer the same kind of emotional sustenance as a community based on constant, face-to-face interaction. While there may be some feeling of closeness implicit in being a member of the black community – or any other community based on interests – there may not be direct, concrete benefits in daily life.

Without overly romanticizing the past, the alienation fostered by the loss of a sense of community takes an increasing toll on people. Membership in a strong community of the past implied belonging to a group of *us* who held fast together against the world. If community no longer provides that emotionally satisfying feeling of security and shared struggle, people are forced to rely more on themselves or on family. For those without the resources to enjoy the culture beyond what a TV screen provides, the loss of geographically viable communities threatens to erode an important link to the values the mainstream culture holds dear, including a respect for law.

Perhaps the most telling evidence of the depth of despair implicit in this loss of a sense of community tied to place was expressed in the riots of the late 1960s and early 1970s. Angry, frustrated blacks destroyed their own neighborhoods, and people would not do that to communities that they loved.

How Community Policing Builds a Sense of Community

The purpose in this analysis is not to belabor or assign blame for the growing gap between rich and poor, the problems posed by racism, the blight of the inner-city, and the pernicious problems of the Underclass. Instead the goal is to examine today's reality and the dynamics that have eroded the strong communities of the past, to better understand the unique role Community Policing can play in meeting the obvious challenges.

Social activist Saul Alinsky proposed viewing community through the prism of issues, since they constitute the most urgent community of interest.[49] The issues of crime, fear of crime, and disorder within any geographic community offer police their best and most logical opportunity for unifying people in ways that help rebuild that traditional sense of community.

As discussed before, much of the reason previous well-meaning police efforts designed to address community concerns, such as Police/Community Relations programs, ultimately failed was because their primary goal was not to address real issues, such as crime. Community Policing improves community and race relations as a by-product of confronting the issues people care about most. The physical and social decay so evident in inner-city neighborhoods acts as a magnet for crime. What Community Policing recognizes is that law-abiding citizens in these areas need the kind of help only the police can provide to reclaim their communities. It is not racist to target black, inner-city neighborhoods for help first; it would be racist to ignore their urgent needs, as if to suggest that the people who live there do not care about building decent communities.

Yet as the discussion of the three-tiered class hierarchy of community also shows, money can mask some of the downside of a loss of a sense of community, and Community Policing can play an important role wherever people cluster together. The department in Clearwater, Florida, for instance, first introduced community policing in the Greenwood Avenue area, a low-income, high-crime community. The approach's success there persuaded the administration to implement community policing on the beach, where many problems involved helping local businesses and residents cope with the influx of tourists. In the new effort, CPOs in shorts patrol the beach, easing tensions when young visitors who are far away from home often feel the urge to behave in ways they would not in their home communities – which also shows how a sense of community can shape people's behavior.

Regardless of the neighborhood, any new Community Policing effort starts first with face-to-face meetings with average citizens, not just so-called community leaders. This part of the start-up process involves average citizens in setting the priorities the police should pursue first and that alone can help people regain a sense of personal control over their collective destiny. In addition, the CPO's role is also to challenge the community into accepting its share of responsibility for reducing crime and disorder. This can include individual initiatives, such as target hardening of stores and residences, and also working together as a group in efforts that go far beyond Neighborhood Watch.

In some communities, CPOs and volunteers shepherd seniors on shopping trips. In others, they target activities for young people. Many persuade area businesses to provide resources to extend efforts far beyond what the police budget could justify. While critics argue that anything not directly aimed at specific crimes is a misuse of police resources, Community Policing recognizes that building stronger communities means reducing the number of places where crime can find a foothold and flourish.

Robert Cooley Angell argues that solving the problem of juvenile deviance, so important because juveniles commit most of this country's crimes, requires that the system help those who stray find their way back into the mainstream culture. The theory Angell propounds to determine where this support exists is called the *concept of the threshold:*

> Below a certain threshold of neighborhood life, the reorientation of deviant groups is so difficult as to represent an unsound approach to the reduction of delinquency; above it, such reorientation becomes feasible. It is probable that all areas in most small cities, and the better residential areas in larger cities, are above this threshold. Only the most deteriorated areas in the metropolis seem beyond redemption by this method.[50]

As Angell also points out, upper-class juveniles may well exhibit deviance, but their communities not only offer support but opportunity. While Community Policing cannot create jobs where none exist, many efforts offer programs designed to help those who can be reclaimed find ways to be productive. Where Community Policing takes exception to Angell's otherwise valid analysis is that the inner city need not be the write-off he suggests it is, nor are communities above the threshold as solid as they could be. Community Policing holds the promise of being a catalyst for positive change in communities at all levels.

In his book *Criminology*, Donald R. Taft lists a number of changes that might help bring about a crimeless society, including some that might prove unpalatable, and with the understanding that not all might be necessary to achieve at least substantial improvement. One suggestion that goes to the heart of Community Policing is, "A crimeless society might have to reverse the trend toward impersonal relationships and restore the personalized culture of the past."[51] Community Policing's virtue in that regard is that not only does this approach help to revive community life, it personalizes police service through its CPOs, and the philosophy changes the nature and character of all the department's interactions with law-abiding citizens.

As Bruce Benson, who was a lieutenant in the Flint foot patrol experiment, noted, a survey comparing why people chose one bank over another, despite the fact all the banks in the area offered virtually the same services and benefits, related strongly to whether the patrons felt they received personalized service. If tellers smiled and made comments about anything other than the business at hand, people responded positively to this personalized attention. A police department infused with the Community Policing philosophy understands that the benefits of making law-abiding people feel they are being treated as human beings not only makes the police more popular within the community, but it enhances the feeling of community cohesion.

In summary, we see that the sense of community that existed in many neighborhoods has disappeared, as a result of dramatic economic and technological changes in a relatively short period of time. Those above the poverty line at least have some opportunity to use their resources to find the emotional sustenance once provided by neighborhood life, but many problems, including crime, fear of crime, and disorder, are magnified where people cannot escape decaying communities, either physically or symbolically.

In many ways, these changes occurred so suddenly that people stunned by the changes have not yet fully identified how to set things right. The advent of a society rich enough so that the majority can afford their own automobiles, telephones, and televisions seemed to offer unlimited progress. Given enough time, it seemed those left behind would catch up. What we see today instead, however, is a culture still reeling from the surge of crime that exploded in the 1960s. Though the bulge of Baby Boomers has aged beyond their crime-prone teenage years, rates of crime persist at levels that consistently make crime one of the top presidential campaign issues.

As our understanding grows, we see that a community based solely on a community of interest, with no geographic tie, can provide some level of emotional sustenance, as long as it is reinforced with meaningful, face-to-face involvement. The problem of crime, however, requires that people who live in the same area find ways to revitalize that sense of community in their neighborhoods, especially in those places where people cannot afford to buy as much protection as they want and need.

Community Policing, as noted in the first chapter, is not a panacea – it alone cannot be expected to revive that sense of community overnight to the degree that the neighborhood reaches the threshold where those who break the law can always find the reinforcement they need to become law-abiding citizens. What Community Policing does provide, however, is an important first step in many ways:

- CPOs can bring neighborhood people together in efforts to enhance the community, so that they can begin to establish a pattern of interacting face-to-face, which fosters the mutual trust and support that is necessary to build a sense of community.

- As creative new initiatives begin to control or reduce crime, fear of crime, and physical and social decay, law-abiding people can reclaim their streets from predators, reversing the cycle that erodes a sense of community life. By making communities safer and more attractive places to live, people can begin to enjoy the emotional support that participating in community life can provide.

- By allowing people direct input into setting the police agenda for their area, in return for which they must agree to provide continued support and participation, Community Policing can help people develop confidence in their ability to control their collective destiny.

- In contrast to the adversarial relationship implicit in the traditional system, the Community Policing philosophy encourages the department to humanize all interactions with law-abiding citizens, focusing on new ways to help them solve community concerns. By decentralizing police service through CPOs, and by personalizing all the department's interactions with average citizens, Community Policing helps foster an atmosphere of mutual trust and respect, which are essential in promoting a positive community atmosphere.

- Many Community Policing efforts specifically target the most vulnerable – the elderly, women, children. Singling them out for protection offers the promise of encouraging everyone to participate more fully in a community life enriched by their involvement.

- Fear of crime traps many people in their homes, where television reinforces the perception the streets are even more dangerous than, in fact, they are. By encouraging people to band together for support and by providing personal protection, Community Policing reduces the fear of crime that stifles community involvement.

- Vigilantism appears to be a growing problem, one that threatens to make communities even more dangerous. Community Policing attempts to channel that impulse in lawful – and ultimately more effective – ways. It demonstrates that responsible collective action can reverse the downward cycle that plagues so many neighborhoods.

- At least initially, many cities using Community Policing focus new initiatives in inner-city neighborhoods, where the most serious crime and drug problems persist. Besides the logic of addressing the most serious problems first, a renewed sense of community may provide part of the answer in addressing the decay that often makes such areas magnets for serious problems. This offers the promise of involving the police in new efforts to reach the Underclass, encouraging and supporting their efforts to make positive changes.

- A welcome by-product of Community Policing is improved race relations, and racial tensions remain a major barrier in developing a true sense of community.

As this demonstrates, Community Policing attempts to renew the link to a place that was historically an important part of the definition of community. It says that people who live in the same place must again become sensitive to the need to care for their neighbors, and that the police must become good neighbors to the people they serve.

NOTES

Note: This chapter is an expanded version of the material contained in *The Meaning of Community in Community Policing,* by *Robert C. Trojanowicz* (Director and Professor, School of Criminal Justice, Michigan State University, and Research Fellow, Program in Criminal Justice Policy and Management, John F. Kennedy School of Government, Harvard University) and *Mark H, Moore* (Daniel and Florence Guggenheim Professor of Criminal Justice Policy and Management and Faculty Chair, Program in Criminal Justice Policy and Management, John F. Kennedy School of Government, Harvard University), published as Community Policing Series No. 15 (East Lansing: National Neighborhood Foot Patrol Center, School of Criminal Justice, Michigan State University, 1988)

[1] Moynihan, Daniel P., *America's Children: Half are born without a fair chance,* from a copyrighted article in the New York Times, reprinted in full in the *Detroit Free Press,* October 3, 1988, p. 7A.

[2] Lapham, Lewis H.; Pollan, Michael; and Etheridge, Eric, *The Harper's Index Book,* (New York: An Owl Book/Henry Holt and Company, 1984-1987), citing U.S. Bureau of Census.

[3] Lapham, *et al.,* citing Weitzman, Lenore J, *The Divorce Revolution: The Unexpected Social Consequences for Women and Children in America* (New York: Free Press/MacMillan, 1985).

[4] Moynihan.

[5] *1988 Nielsen Report on Television,* privately printed by Nielsen Media Research (Northbrook Illinois: Nielsen Media Research, 1988), p. 9.

[6] Lapham, *et al.,* citing A. C. Nielsen.

[7] Lapham, *et al.,* citing National Institute of Mental Health (Bethesda, MD).

[8] Gerbner, George, The Annenberg School of Communications, University of Pennsylvania, interviewed by telephone on October 7, 1988.

[9] Gerbner, George; Gross, Larry; and Signorelli, Nancy of The Annenberg School of Communications, University of Pennsylvania; and Morgan, Michael, University of Massachusetts, *Television's Mean World: Violence Profile No. 14-15,* published by The Annenberg School, Philadelphia, PA, September 1986, and the interview with George Gerbner cited above.

[10]Harris, Lou, & Associates, from a survey conducted for the Metropolitan Life Insurance Company, verified by telephone interview to New York City office on October 5, 1988.

[11]Lapham, *et al.,* citing *Sprint* magazine (Scholastic, Inc., New York).

[12]Church, George J., *Are You Better Off?, (Time* magazine, October 10, 1988), p. 28.

[13]Fessler, Donald R., *Facilitating Community Change: A Basic Guide* (San Diego: University Associate, 1976), p. 7.

[14]*Ibid.,* p. 7.

[15]*Ibid.,* p. 7.

[16]Watman, William S., *A Guide to the Language of Neighborhoods* (Washington, DC: National Center for Urban Ethnic Affairs, 1980), p. 35.

[17]Meenaghan, Thomas M., *What Means Community?, Social Work,* 19(6), 1972, p. 94.

[18]*Ibid.,* p. 94.

[19]Hillery, George A., Jr., *Definitions of Community: Areas of Agreement, Rural Sociology,* 20(4), 1955, p. 111.

[20]*Ibid.,* p.111.

[21]Keller, Suzanne, *The Neighborhood,* in *Neighborhoods in Urban America,* edited by Ronald H. Baylor (Port Washington, NY: Kennikat Press, 1982), p. 9.

[22]Hunter, Albert, quoted in William S. Watman's *A Guide to the Language of Neighborhoods.*

[23]Meenaghan, p. 95.

[24]Azarya, Victor, *Community* in *The Social Science Encyclopedia,* edited by Adam Kuper and Jessica Kuper (London: Routledge & Kegan Paul, 1985), p. 135.

[25]*USA Today,* October 5, 1988, p. 1.

[26]Church, p. 28.

[27]McGraw, Bill, and Blossom, Teresa, *Closings deal another blow to a city losing people, businesses, institutions, Detroit Free Press,* September 30, 1988, p. 2B.

[28]*Ibid,* p. 2B.

[29]Ager, Susan, *Catholics took road to closings, Detroit Free Press,* October 2, 1988, p. 15A.

[30]Jackson, Luther, *State's auto jobs continue decline, Detroit Free Press,* August 15, 1988, p. 1C.

[51]Finkelstein, Jim, *Campaign aims to keep students in school, Detroit Free Press,* August 26, 1988, p. 1A.

[52]*The State of Michigan Strategy – 1988 Update of the 1986 Anti-Drug Abuse Act,* prepared by the Michigan Office of Criminal Justice, a quote from Joel Gilliam of the Detroit Police Department, July 1988, p. 1.5-2.

[53]*The State of Michigan Strategy – 1987 Update of the 1986 Anti-Drug Abuse Act,* prepared by the Michigan Office of Criminal Justice, taken from *Drug Abuse Trends,* prepared by the Michigan Department of Public Health's Office of Substance Abuse Services, Statistical Division, by Richard Calkins.

[54]Church, p. 28.

[55]*Ibid.*

[56]Stengel, Richard, *The Underclass: Breaking the Cycle, Time* magazine, October 10, 1988. p. 41.

[57]Moynihan.

[58]Moynihan.

[59]Stengel.

[40]Vonnegut, Kurt, Jr., *Wampeters, Foma & Granfalloons (Opinions),* (New York: Delacorte/Seymour Lawrence, 1965-1974), pp. 241-242.

[41]Vonnegut, p. 250.

[42]Vonnegut, p. *xv.*

[43]Stengel.

[44]Swickard, Joe, *Detroit tops big cities in rate of youths slain, Detroit Free Press,* September 11, 1988, p. 15A.

[45]*The State of Michigan Strategy – 1988,* a quote from Detroit Mayor Coleman Young, p. 1.5-1.

[46]Swickard, Joe, and Trimer, Margaret, *Jury acquits 2 vigilantes of burning down house, Detroit Free Press,* October 7, 1988, p. 1A.

[47]Keller, Suzanne, *Community and Community Feeling,* in *The Encyclopedia of Urban Planning,* edited by Arnold Whittick (New York: McGraw-Hill, 1984), p. 288.

[48]Kelly, Rita Mae, *Community Control of Economic Development* (New York: Praeger. 1977), pp. 35-36.

[49]Meenaghan, p. 97.

[50]Angell, Robert Cooley, *Free Society and Moral Crisis,* (Ann Arbor, MI: Ann Arbor Paperbacks/The University of Michigan Press, 1965), p. 116.

[51]Taft, Donald R., *Criminology* (New York: MacMillian, 1942), p. 681.

SECTION TWO

WHAT COMMUNITY POLICING DOES

CHAPTER 4
Community Policing's Impact
on Crime and Disorder

*We are in bondage to the law in order that
we may be free.*

—*Cicero*

Assessing Community Policing's Impact

In any discussion of Community Policing's obvious virtues, the underlying question that must ultimately be confronted is: "How effective is Community Policing in the battle against crime?" Since the reform movement of the 1930s, the primary job of the public police has narrowed to that of crime-fighter. While the merits of paring the police role down to this narrow yardstick can be debated, it has become the minimum standard against which any new police program or activity must be measured – especially when resources are tight.

Indeed, part of the impetus for finding new ways of policing stemmed from the apparent failure of traditional policing to meet the challenge posed by the explosion of serious crime that began in the 1960s. By 1975, the first year of the National Crime Survey, the study showed that one in every three households was touched by crime that year.[1] Rates of serious crime in this country are far higher than for other Western, industrialized nations. Crime has become such an emotional topic in the United States that it has consistently emerged as one of the top issues in every presidential campaign of the past two decades. People look to the police for answers, and pressure to find new ways to combat crime helped persuade the police to experiment with new ideas, including Community Policing.

Does Community Policing do a better job of reducing and controlling crime? Does expanding the police role to address problems of physical and social disorder improve or detract from a police department's impact on crime? Such questions are much easier to pose than to answer. As we will see in a succeeding chapter, research on early efforts in Flint, Michigan, and Baltimore County, Maryland, showed reductions in certain crime rates, though studies of other initiatives did not.[2] By 1985, the National Crime Survey reported that the number of households touched by crime had declined from the one in three level to one in four,[3] roughly the same period that Community Policing went from being a promising abstract idea to concrete reality. Does this prove that Community Policing works?

Though supporters of Community Policing can point to data that suggest that the movement has at least contributed to the recent decline in crime, it also pays to remember Mark Twain's warning that there are three kinds of lies – "lies, damn lies, and statistics."[4] At the same time that crime rates were falling, unemployment was declining, as the country bounced back from the recession. At the same time as well, the percentage of the population in its most crime-prone teenage years was falling, as the last of the Baby Boomers matured. Another obvious factor was that the number of offenders behind bars also soared during this time. In 1970, roughly 100 of every 100,000 people in this country were incarcerated, and this figure doubled to 200 per 100,000 by 1985.[5]

In a complex society undergoing rapid and constant change, there are simply too many variables to be able to determine, with any certainty, how much of a role any single factor may play in the rise and fall of overall crime rates. Unlike a controlled lab experiment, studying changes in the world at large depends on how wisely the researchers choose which factors they will look at. After all, during that same period, there were also dramatic increases in the number of coronary bypasses performed, as well as in the number of compact disc players purchased, yet no one would argue these changes made any difference in overall crime rates. At a certain point, we must rely on logic and reason to determine which changes hold the greatest promise of making a significant impact on crime.

Therefore, to understand how well and in what ways Community Policing addresses crime requires contending with a number of underlying issues, including some questions for which there are no easy answers:

- How much crime is there?

- Which crimes are a priority – to society as a whole and to different people? What can and should the police do to combat serious crime, petty crime, and disorder?

- How do traditional efforts attempt to combat crime? Where and when do such efforts succeed – and fail?

- How does Community Policing contribute? What are its strengths and weaknesses? What role does disorder play in the entire matrix of crime, and does Community Policing's focus on neighborhood control offer the promise of better long-term crime control?

Crime – What Do We Know?

The answer to how much crime exists in the United States is simple – no one knows. At best, indicators such as the Uniform Crime Reporting (UCR) statistics compiled by the FBI show trends, but they do not provide a true picture of the number of crimes actually committed at any specific time. As the National Crime Survey verifies, most crimes are never reported to the police. According to the *Report to the Nation on Crime and Justice – Second Edition,* only about one-third of all crimes are reported.[6] Even when the police are notified, changes in reporting procedures and complications within the system make it likely that many crimes are omitted from national totals.

The more serious the crime, the more reliable the figures, though all suffer underreporting. We assume (correctly) that murder rates are the most accurate of all, since people are very likely to report the discovery of a dead body to the police. Yet even in this case, no one knows for sure how many missing persons are actually murder victims whose bodies will never be found. Accounts given by a number of self-confessed killers routinely allude to victims whose disappearance was never reported. When figures for even this most serious of crimes cannot be considered complete, the less serious the crime, the more likely that the statistics should be considered highly suspect as an indicator of what is happening in the real world.

An important issue beyond mere numbers concerns which crimes we consider the most serious, as a society and as individuals. The UCR data focuses on eight so-called Part I (Index) or "serious" crimes – four violent crimes (murder, rape, robbery, aggravated assault) and four property crimes (burglary, larceny/theft, motor vehicle theft, arson). While it might seem that everyone would agree these are the crimes that deserve the greatest attention – and nearly all countries in the world define these crimes as top priorities – they do not always reflect the full range of major concerns.

Using murder as an example, the UCR figures show there were 18,980 murders committed in the United States in 1985.[7] In comparison, of the 43,800 traffic-related deaths that same year, half involved alcohol (40 % involved drinking above the legal limit, with 10 % below).[8] Though a direct comparison of both problems ignores obvious difficulties, the realization that drunk driving kills even more people each year than this country's horrendous murder rate has made us rethink our collective priorities. People understand that they can make changes in their lifestyle to help protect themselves from the threat of murder more easily than they can protect themselves from a random drunk driver on the roads, so they now look to the lawmakers, the police, and the courts to provide them greater protection.

This reflects the reality that what we define as serious crime changes over time. While monitoring trends for Part I crimes over time provides a snapshot of what is happening in society, the picture remains incomplete. Prior to the Sullivan Act, for example, narcotics were legal, whereas by 1985, drug abuse violations ranked fifth among all arrests, at 811,400.[9] Manufacturing, selling, and consuming alcohol were illegal acts under Prohibition, but since Repeal, the police role has been narrowed primarily to controlling open drinking, public drunkenness, drunk driving, and problems with underage drinking. Twenty years ago, the crime of child abuse received relatively little attention, but now the American Humane Society found that 1,713,000 cases were reported to authorities in 1984.[10] Many states have decriminalized so-called *status offenses* (acts by juveniles, such as violating curfew or running away, that would not be considered as crimes if committed by an adult), but part of the price for protecting young people's civil rights may be that these changes contributed to problems such as the 5,000 runaways buried in unmarked graves each year, which means the pendulum may begin to swing back.[11]

Certain ideas about crime seem to go in and out of fashion, as our knowledge and sensibilities change over time. For example, not only is increasing attention now paid to all rapes, but within the past few years, the *new crime* of date rape has been more clearly defined as an offense that victims should report to the police for prosecution. Advances in technology and changes in business practices have also spawned new categories of crime. Prior to the widespread use of computers, unleashing a computer *virus* could not have been a crime. This country's increasingly complicated financial system has unleashed new variants of white-collar crime, including electronic embezzlement of funds and new wrinkles in stock manipulations. And where should we now rank the threat posed by organized crime, since their illegal gains have been shifted into legitimate businesses? Consider the additional costs incurred to monitor doctors, not only for prescription violations, but for Medicare and Medicaid fraud.

To address the complexity of determining the relative severity of different crimes, the National Survey of Crime Severity (NSCS), conducted in 1977, asked respondents to rank 204 illegal activities. As expected, people viewed violent crime as more serious than property crime. It also appeared the people surveyed consistently made distinctions based on five other factors:

- The relative vulnerability of the victim.

- The extent of injury or loss.

- In property crimes, the type of business (a theft from a museum was considered more serious than one from a railroad yard, even when the dollar loss was identical).

- The relationship of the offender to the victim (if a man beat his wife so severely that she ended up in the hospital, respondents tended to view that as substantially more serious than when the same injury resulted from a fight among male classmates).

- In drug offenses, the type of drug makes a difference (sale and use of heroin rated significantly higher than for marijuana).

Of interest as well is that victims generally rated crimes higher than non-victims, and whites were harsher than minorities. While most people rated the severity of different kinds of thefts based on the dollar amount stolen, regardless of background, older people rated thefts with large losses as slightly more severe than people in other age groups.[12]

While this shows how individuals make distinctions about crime priorities, as a society, we show our collective priorities by how we deploy our resources. In an elegant analysis comparing the impact of bank robberies versus stolen bikes, Edmonton (Canada) police inspector Chris Braiden questioned whether police are out of touch with the wants and needs of average citizens. His study showed that in 1984, 1,069 banks in Canada were robbed, with total losses of $2.8 million. Because of the importance of the crime and because such losses are typically recoverable by insurance or tax write-offs, bank robberies are always reported to the police.

In contrast, that same year, 182,000 bikes were reported stolen. Since the reporting rate for bicycle thefts is only 29 %, Braiden conservatively calculated that these crimes cost Canadians $45 million that year. Comparing the two crimes shows that bicycle thefts involve roughly 100 times as many victims as bank thefts, with 15 times the dollar loss.[13] Yet he notes that when a bank robbery occurs, every available officer responds. When a bike is stolen, many departments will not even send an officer to investigate – instead they ask for a report over the phone.

Braiden's point is not that the police pay too much attention to bank robberies, but that they pay far too little to so-called petty crimes. This does not mean that a fleet of squad cars should come screaming to the scene of a bike theft, sirens blaring, but that the police must have a strategy that allows them to monitor and play a role in dealing with such offenses. One crucial reason that petty crime must not be ignored is that it can serve as the training ground for more serious crime. The youngster who steals a bike and gets away with it learns the wrong message, which is that there are no consequences for breaking the law. A system too busy to care about that bike theft today contributes to producing the potential bank robber of tomorrow. The traditional system ignores the wisdom implicit in the adage that it pays to nip problems in the bud – and far too many police officers think *wasting* time on finding the youngster who steals a bike detracts from the *important* job of catching bank robbers.

It is easy to understand the justification for relegating widespread but relatively trivial crimes to lesser status. Compared to an armed bank robbery, a bicycle theft does seem petty – except to the victim. Human nature dictates that comedy is when you slip and fall on a banana peel – tragedy is when I prick my finger. In our quest for justice, we have tried to fashion a criminal justice system where the greatest resources are concentrated on what appear to be the more serious threats. But the danger is that police departments can lose touch with average citizens and become indifferent to their valid concerns, and petty crime affects far more people than so-called serious crime.

We expect crime victims to take their victimization seriously, but when the police fail to do so, that reinforces their already heightened sense of vulnerability and fear. Police departments that appear to ignore petty crime contribute to the pervasive sense of dread that crime is spiralling out of control – and that the system will not help because it does not care.

While the next chapter will deal in greater depth with the problem of fear of crime, any discussion of crime must include recognition of how the threat of victimization affects people. We expect the police to do all they can to protect us. We understand, intellectually, that if a serial killer is on the loose, the police department must shift resources from other services to help protect us from that threat, even though relatively few people are actually at greater risk. But what reinforces our collective fear that we are unable to cope with serious crime is the casual acceptance of petty crime as routine, or that it is somehow part of the price we must pay for our democratic freedoms.

An average person on the street probably has no idea what the ups and downs in the statistics show about the crime rate in the neighborhood. But when the woman across the street returns home for the second time in six months to find the TV stolen, teens begin brazenly smoking marijuana on the corner and verbally abusing passersby, and a stream of late-night visitors frequent an increasingly dilapidated house two doors down, that person may have good reason to fear that their personal risk of victimization is increasing. Those incidents may not individually or collectively make a noticeable difference in the crime statistics, and even the most sophisticated crime analysis may not identify a trend, but someone attuned to life in that neighborhood knows problems are brewing.

To understand more clearly the special niche that Community Policing fills, it is important first to understand how traditional policing confronts the entire matrix of crime. Only then can we assess the impact Community Policing makes on the full range of crime and disorder problems that plague our society.

The Traditional Police Effort

There are three times that any police action can influence crime:

- Police action can prevent a crime from occurring.

- Police intervention during the commission of a crime can influence the outcome.

- Police efforts after the crime has occurred can resolve the situation, ideally by solving the crime, arresting the perpetrator, and, in appropriate cases, restoring stolen property.

Traditional police efforts rely primarily on motor patrol as the first line of offense and defense. Special units, high-tech gadgets, sophisticated lab analyses, and investigative follow-up are all designed to complement the use of motor patrol as the primary weapon in the traditional police arsenal aimed at fighting crime. Yet even a cursory examination of this approach demonstrates serious structural shortcomings in how traditional policing approaches the three times intervention can make a difference:

- **Prevention** – The rationale for having motor patrol officers cruise streets on free patrol is that their visible presence in the community should act as a deterrent to crime. Yet one of the few research studies ever funded to test this hypothesis raised serious questions about motor patrol's overall effectiveness in this regard.

  The controversial Kansas City (Missouri) Preventive Patrol study divided the South Patrol Division's 15 districts into three kinds of beats. In five reactive-only beats, routine preventive patrol was eliminated entirely; patrol cars were dispatched only when calls for service were received. In the five control beats, routine preventive patrol remained at the standard one-car-per-beat ratio. In the five proactive beats, the intensity of routine preventive patrol was increased by doubling or tripling the normal ratio.

Among the findings:

- Rates of crimes reported showed no difference among the beats.

- Victimization studies showed the proactive approach made no discernible impact on the number of burglaries, auto thefts, larcenies involving auto accessories, robberies, or vandalism – the kinds of crimes considered to be most susceptible to deterrence through preventive motor patrol.

- Citizen attitudes toward police showed few consistent differences and no apparent pattern across the three different types of beats.

- Fear of crime did not decline.

- Citizen satisfaction with police did not improve in the experimental areas.

- Experimental conditions showed no effect on police response times or citizen satisfaction with response times.[14]

This study obviously raises concerns about motor patrol's immediate ability to prevent crime by its mere presence. It also shows citizen satisfaction does not appear to depend on how often they see a patrol car – not only did satisfaction not rise in the beats where patrols were doubled, but it did not decline in areas where officers only responded to calls. The assumption was that motor patrol would provide short-term prevention, while the addition of Crime Prevention Units would address the need for longer-term, educational efforts. Yet because no one can count crimes that have not been committed, there is no easy way to determine how well Crime Prevention Units perform. (See Chapter 6 for a fuller discussion of the research.) As discussed earlier, however, many well-meaning efforts suffered from lack of accountability within the community, as well as lack of clout within the department.

- **Crimes in Progress** – In theory, this is the area where motor patrol's ability to provide a rapid response should make its greatest contribution to reducing and controlling crime, but another study done on Kansas City raised troubling concerns. It showed that response time was unrelated to the probability of making an arrest or locating a witness for the Part I crimes described earlier. Success or failure depended less on how fast the officer arrived and more on how quickly the citizen reported the crime.[15]

A follow-up study conducted in four cities by the Police Executive Research Forum supported this conclusion. About delay in reporting crimes to the police, the report said, "Most of the time, the delays are so substantial that even our fastest response to the crime will be ineffective in producing arrests. In short, we have focused on using high-technology dispatching equipment and sophisticated deployment schemes to reduce police response time, when we should also have focused on reducing citizen delays."[16] Research confirms that rapid response led to response-related arrests for Part I crimes in only 3 % of all calls.[17]

- **Resolving Crimes Already Committed** – Traditional police efforts after the crime has occurred include both motor patrol and investigation. In 1983, about 20 % of all reported crimes – one in five – resulted in arrests.[18] Again, the rationale for relying primarily on motor patrol's quick response is based on the assumption that the officers can therefore do a better job of preserving evidence and locating witnesses. After this initial assessment, many departments then assign investigators to follow up further. Yet even when the police make a felony arrest, less than three in 10 result in imprisonment of the offender.[19] And while the police can do little to influence the rate of incarceration, these figures contribute to the widespread perception that traditional police efforts and the criminal justice system as a whole are not doing enough to make people safe. (Again, for a fuller discussion of the research, see Chapter 6.)

As this discussion shows, traditional motor patrol efforts have no discernible impact on preventing crime, very rarely do they thwart crimes in progress, and they accomplish less than people hope for in resolving crimes after the fact. This analysis is not meant as an indictment of traditional efforts. As pollster Lou Harris found, "And, most of all, perhaps far better than the establishment, they (people) know about the kind of job being done by law enforcement officials, whom they are prepared to pay higher tribute to, especially at the state and local levels."[20] Instead, these findings are offered as an effort to understand the structural limitations of a basically reactive response. Not only are the police powerless to influence economic and social trends in society that contribute to crime, but the likelihood that their crisis-oriented actions will make a significant dent in reducing overall crime limits what such efforts should be expected to achieve.

Perhaps as early as 1964, there were ominous warnings that the traditional police approach, with its focus on reacting to calls for service, would prove unable to control serious crime. That was the year that Kitty Genovese was mugged and murdered in New York. Though she screamed for help for half an hour as her attackers stabbed and beat her, none of those 38 middle-class neighbors who heard her cries called the police. In a series of articles in the New York Times, some of those neighbors said they were too afraid to get involved, while others said they simply did not consider the problem any of their business – that it was a problem for the police to handle, not them.[21]

Some commentators tried to write off the incident as peculiar to New York City, but the case raised serious concerns that something had gone severely wrong with the relationship between people and the police and also that something was seriously wrong with the system. The traditional approach relies on that all-important call for service before the police can spring into action. The millions of dollars spent each year recruiting and training top-notch officers and equipping them with the latest technology ultimately relies on persuading just one person to lift up the phone.

What the *Kitty Genovese* case did was demonstrate that the police had oversold themselves as society's crime-fighters, to the degree that people wanted to believe they could delegate all responsibiity to police professionals – that crime was not their responsibility and getting involved was too risky. That famous case also vividly brought home the depth of the estrangement between people and their police. None of those people in Queens apparently saw the police as trusted friends who could protect them, but as nameless and faceless strangers that they dared not count on. This incident brought into stark relief the terrifying prospect that the alienation between people and their police was so profound that no one was safe. It also verified to predators that people no longer cared enough to make that crucial phone call, without which the traditional system is virtually impotent. It drove home the point that a society in which people are not part of the police process cannot expect to control serious crime, and that the police had to find better ways to involve people in efforts to police themselves.

The Dynamics of Serious Crime

As a society, we have labelled Part I (Index) crimes as our top priority. We shift resources away from petty crimes, such as the aforementioned bicycle thefts, because the severity of these crimes demands extra attention. While we may argue whether other crimes should also merit special attention, we should accept that these deserve priority status and then look more closely at what we are asking our police officers to do, when we say we want them to be more effective in battling serious crime.

To understand the special contribution that Community Policing can make in extending the overall impact of the police, we will examine the most heinous crime, murder, in great depth, to show how Community Policing augments motor patrol's attempts to prevent, thwart, or solve this crime. With that understanding, we will then briefly examine the special dynamics involved in the other three violent Index crimes of rape, robbery, and assault. In conclusion, we will highlight the contribution Community Policing makes in the overall police effort to cope with the four Index property crimes.

- **Homicide** (including murder, nonnegligent man-slaughter, and negligent man-slaughter) – Murder is often a crime of passion or profit. In 58% of known murders, the victim knew or was related to the killer.[22] One out of every five murders occurs during the commission of another felony,[23] and, in many major cities, half or more of all homicides are drug related.[24] While TV dramas perpetuate the image of psychopathic killers roaming the country, picking off victims at random, the vast majority of murders committed in the United States stem from the escalation of domestic quarrels, arguments between friends or acquaintances, or battles that result from the intoxicating effects of drug use or those that erupt from conflicts about drugs and drug profits.

  Murder can be premeditated or impulsive, but, in either case, the police face obvious limits on their ability to make a difference. As the murder of President Kennedy – and then his killer – affirmed, even being encircled by police is not always enough to prevent premeditated murder. In impulsive murders that occur when a robbery or burglary goes awry, the police cannot hope to provide much protection except by striving to eradicate and control these other crimes.

  One of the most intractable problems is finding ways to prevent domestic violence from escalating to murder. When we look at the dynamics of murders involving family or friends, the reactive nature of traditional police efforts makes dealing with such problems extraordinarily challenging. Until or unless a call is made to the police, either by the victim or by neighbors or other witnesses, there is little chance that a patrol car driving by can have any impact on people arguing behind closed doors, so preventive patrol can do little. Once a call is made, motor patrol officers can reduce the likelihood of repeat violence that always holds the threat of ending in murder by arresting the attacker.

  The Minneapolis Domestic Violence Experiment in 1981-1982 showed arrest was the most effective of the three standard methods police use to reduce domestic violence (the other two are *advising* or *sending the suspect away* for at least eight hours). The research showed that when the police arrested the suspect, the incidence of repeat violence over the next six months was only 10%, compared to 19% for advising, and 24% when the suspect was sent away.[25]

  This study also shows that factors traditionally considered outside the province of the police seem to play a role in this potentially murderous violence. One striking finding was that roughly six out of 10 suspects and victims alike were unemployed, while the overall unemployment rate in the area was only 5%. Also, 45% of suspects were the unmarried male lover of the victim; 35% were the victim's current husband. Eight of 10 victims said they had been assaulted by the same person within the past six months, and six of 10 had called the police to intervene within that same period. Slightly more than one in four couples were in counseling at the time. In addition, six in 10 suspects had a prior arrest, and four in 10 had been arrested for an alcohol offense.[26]

This paints a vivid picture of couples struggling with problems beyond what a 10-minute visit from a motor patrol officer can hope to solve. Over and over, the police arrive to find a troubled couple, stressed by economic problems, where alcohol helped trigger potentially murderous rage. No wonder the police have been vocal about their reluctance to handle such calls, not only because they face unpredictable violence themselves, but because of their frustration in making a long-term improvement.

Yet this research demonstrates that even a one-time, reactive police intervention can make an impact – if someone calls the police – and this is where Community Policing can begin to expand the police department's impact. One of Community Policing's stated goals is to boost people's confidence in the police as a valid source of help, so that they will be quicker to report crimes to the police. By focusing on domestic violence as an example, here are other ways a creative Community Policing effort could be devised to target murders stemming from this problem:

- CPOs could be charged with the responsibility to make follow-up home visits periodically, as part of their regular beat activity. If the additional sanction of arrest can make such a substantial impact in reducing short-term future violence, repeated visits by a uniformed, armed officer at least offers the promise of convincing the aggressor that the police are watching him and that they take the matter seriously.

- In his role as liaison to other public and private agencies, a CPO might also be able to urge more of the three out of four troubled couples into appropriate and affordable counseling. CPOs can also offer information about alcohol abuse programs. He can also offer to escort the victim to a shelter for battered women.

- Long-range, proactive Community Policing efforts, ranging from career counseling to providing lists of available jobs, help address some of the underlying dynamics, such as unemployment. In addition, Community Policing efforts that provide relief for families under pressure, such as activities for juveniles, can help ease tensions that can trigger violence. Because we now know that children who see physical violence in their homes while they are growing up often learn to mimic that behavior when they become adults, Community Policing's added impact in reducing violence today also holds the promise of reducing such violence years from now.

The dynamics of so-called *crimes of passion* defy easy answers. While traditional, reactive efforts can help, the underlying factors that can impel some people to murderous violence require longer-term interventions, which is where Community Policing offers the promise of playing a broader role. The difficulty in outlining precisely how Community Policing can dramatically extend the police role relates to the fact that its strategies and tactics are bounded only by the imagination of the officers involved. Perhaps in ethnic neighborhoods where male macho behavior tacitly condones wife beating, the CPO might work with local religious leaders to develop workshops on how to change cultural attitudes. Prevention efforts might also include having CPOs talk on domestic violence in various high-school classes aimed at both sexes, separately and together. The CPO's opportunity to work with young people, one-on-one and in small groups, in informal give-and-take conversations over a long period of time, can also help to counter-balance the negative impact of growing up in a violence-prone environment. Another virtue of Community Policing is that it does not rest on a rigid, textbook approach, but instead each effort can be tailored to the needs of the particular community.

In areas where murders are related to drug problems, the CPO must contend with finding ways to address the dynamics associated with drug abuse and drug trafficking. The succeeding chapters devoted to drug problems will discuss Community Policing's unique contribution to attacking both the supply and demand side of drugs in greater detail. But in terms of targeting the drug-related murders that appear to be an ever-larger percentage of total murders, it is important to understand that Community Policing augments traditional efforts by targeting street-level drug sales and drug use.

Basically, traditional efforts are designed to follow the chain upwards, in the hope of arresting top-level dealers. By focusing downard instead, Community Policing complements traditional efforts, thereby completing a full-spectrum approach. As this chapter will explain, targeting street-level sales has the virtue of solving problems without raising the overall price of drugs, which helps wring the profits out of drug dealing, the profits for which dealers seem all too willing to kill. This also means that Community Policing efforts do not result in higher prices that force addicts to steal more to support their habits, so this approach holds the promise of indirectly reducing murders committed during robberies and burglaries. As this chapter will also show, a CPO's rapport with the community also means they often gather intelligence on drug dealing beyond what more expensive and dangerous undercover operations generate, and, as community liaison, CPOs can help addicts who want help in finding appropriate and affordable treatment.

As this example shows, Community Policing's unique ability to generate more and better information than traditional efforts contributes to resolving all the various kinds of homicides. By employing problem-solving techniques, Community Policing can be used to tackle the prevention and resolution of homicides that follow a pattern, such as the one in five murders that occur during another felony, such as assault, robbery, rape, or burglary.

The purpose of this lengthy discussion has been to identify how departments that adopt Community Policing can address a far broader range of the dynamics involved in the many different kinds of murder, as a way of illustrating the principles that apply to a wide array of other serious and petty crimes. To complete the picture, here is a brief look at some of the dynamics involved in the other violent Index crimes:

- **Rape** (by force or without consent) – Victimization studies show that 8% of all women will be raped at least once during their lifetime – one in 100 will be raped twice.[27] More a crime of aggression than sex, rape is a crime where victims often decide not to involve the police, especially when the victim knows her attacker. This society's complicated and conflicting attitudes about sex often contribute to the victim's reluctance to expose her personal life to the police and then in court.

  Traditional efforts to prevent, thwart, or resolve this problem mirror the limitations the police face with murder. The circumstances surrounding the incident dramatically influence the likelihood that the police can make a difference. If the rapist stalks victims and accosts them on the street or breaks into their homes, the problem for the police is obviously different than in so-called *date rape,* where the attacker proceeds despite the victim's protests, with or without the use of force.

  Many departments rely on their Crime Prevention Units to provide rape prevention instruction to women's groups. Motor officers on free patrol can target areas where rapes are most likely to occur. But as statistics show, the likelihood of interrupting a crime in progress is small, and reactive efforts depend on how quickly the police receive a call.

  Resolving rapes after the fact is obviously easier in cases such as date rape, where the victim typically knows the identity of her attacker. As noted earlier, however, many women hesitate to report this kind of crime to the police, which often means the rapist remains free to strike again.

- **Robbery** (taking property by force or threat of force) – Of the 14,681,000 robberies between 1973 and 1984, the 63 % that were completed caused losses totalling $4.4 billion. Also, according to the NCS, one in every three victims was injured, one in 10 seriously enough to seek emergency room treatment, and a chilling one in four not only lost property but was also injured as well.[28] Adding to police frustration, slightly less than two-thirds of all completed robberies are reported to the police, and only about one-third of attempted robberies are reported to the authorities.[29]

  Perhaps more than any other crime, robbery fits the nightmare image most people extend to all crimes – a stranger picks you, seemingly at random, and threatens your life to take what he wants. In eight of 10 robberies committed by more than one person, the victim either did not know his assailants, or he knew them only by sight (seven in 10 when the robbery is committed by a lone attacker), and robbery is a crime most often committed on the street. Whether it is called a mugging, a stickup, a holdup, or a robbery, a gun is actually discharged in one-fifth of all cases.[30]

  Without belaboring what we already know about how traditional efforts impact on crime, this is a crime where a patrol car driving by may prevent someone from being robbed, though obviously there is no way to know how often that happens – or how often it means the robber picks the next likely target he sees after the car goes by. Logic also suggests that many crimes are prevented or thwarted when an average citizen happens by, though in some major cities, some robbers are even bold enough to accost victims on subways and streets despite the presence of onlookers. Roughly one in 10 of all murders occurs as a result of robbery.[31]

  Though robbery is a daunting challenge, this is a crime where the police presence can make an obvious impact, but traditional efforts alone cannot hope to do as much as when they are combined with Community Policing. While a man who stabs his wife to death may never again find himself in circumstances where he would murder again, a robber who gets away with his crime may feel encouraged to repeat. The National Institute of Justice's Drug Use Forecasting (DUF) data also shows that the overwhelming majority of those arrested for any crime in many major cities had taken some kind of illegal drug within the previous 48 hours,[32] adding to the suspicion that many crimes, such as robbery, are committed by addicts seeking money for drugs.

- **Assault** (ranging from simple assault to attempted murder) – In essence, this crime is *symbolic* murder – violence or the threat of violence aimed at another, therefore many erupt as a result of domestic disputes and drug-related incidents. As such, the opportunities for the police to control this crime are limited by the same frustrations they face in dealing with homicides.

  As the dynamics involved in these most serious violent crimes indicate, the traditional police response offers little opportunity for officers to make meaningful interventions that hold the promise of making people safer. All too often, the best the police can hope to do is deal effectively with the problems after the fact, and even in that regard, Community Policing's ability to generate more and better information holds the promise of doing a better job than traditional efforts. Moreoever, because of Community Policing's emphasis on treating citizens as partners in the police process and on encouraging CPOs to develop their interpersonal skills to the maximum, it allows the department to do a better job of working with victims and witnesses.

Community Policing's focus on solving problems rather than just answering calls and handling crimes as individual incidents also makes better sense than traditional efforts because of the relative difficulty in making a difference in the dynamics that result in serious crime. CPOs gather information beyond what traditional efforts can achieve, which allows the department to concentrate its efforts where they will do the most good. CPOs provide a sustained presence in the community, so that they can initiate efforts targeted at troubled families and potentially exposive situations in ways that traditional approaches never could. As people learn to trust their CPOs, they turn to them for help, and CPOs skilled in knowing other communities resources that can be tapped for assistance have made dramatic strides in helping to defuse the overall climate of violence by concentrating their efforts on those relatively few families and addresses where the greatest potential problems cluster.

By focusing on neighborhood decay, CPOs can help make sure that abandoned buildings do not make inviting locations for new dope houses, whose customers often rob the law-abiding people who are closest. Even making sure that burned out streetlights are repaired promptly holds the promise of reducing the opportunities for muggings and rape. CPOs can work with area businesses to make sure their employees know how to take precautions against victimization. They can target high-risk kids in the hope of turning them around before they narrow their options to the degree they accept being bounced in and out of custody as an accepted fact of life. As we will see, CPOs also have an opportunity to intervene in street-level drug dealing in ways that hold the promise of reducing the overall climate of violence over time. Community Policing seeks to work with law-abiding people in humanizing and enhancing the local environment so that people can live in communities that offer a sense of hope for the future.

A glimpse at some examples of how Community Policing contributes to preventing, thwarting, or resolving the four Part I property offenses shows its value in controlling all kinds of crime:

- **Burglaries** – One-third of all burglaries involve businesses, therefore two of three target residences where, in 1985, 42 % did not require forced entry.[33] While Crime Prevention Unit efforts try to persuade people of the importance of hardening their homes against crime, their inherent lack of follow-up and direct, community accountability make Community Policing a better proactive option.

- **Larceny/theft** – Though less than 5 % of personal larcenies involve contact between the offender and the victim, pocket-picking and purse-snatching are two crimes that affect the elderly as often as other age groups.[34] Community Policing often targets special groups, such as the elderly, for special attention, which can include activities such as shopping trips for the elderly so that they are less vulnerable to such crimes.

- **Motor vehicle theft** – Because insurance companies demand a police report, almost nine of every 10 car thefts are reported to the police, and recovery of the stolen property is also more likely than for any other property crime.[35] Community Policing's focus on examining the underlying dynamics rather than responding to individual incidents makes obvious sense, since the dynamics are far different if the problem stems from teenagers joyriding or an organized car-theft ring operating in the area.

- **Arson** – This crime breaks down into obvious categories – people set fires because of a compulsion, for profit (typically insurance), or for revenge. While prevention is important and the fire department is most responsible for reducing damage once the crime is in progress, resolving arson greatly depends on good information. Determining the reason for the crime spotlights the likely perpetrators, therefore Community Policing's unique ability to generate greater quantities of high-quality information is an obvious plus.

Community Policing's Strengths

One reason for the lengthy analysis of the dynamics involved in major crimes is to show the tremendous difficulty the police face in making a positive difference. The police can do little about obvious root causes of crime, such as poverty and unemployment, nor can they do much to influence policy concerning people's access to guns, social support for single parents, or any of the other factors that may play a role in the overall matrix of crime. While individual conscience may be the single biggest determinant concerning whether any specific person will – or will not – commit a particular crime, the police can play only a limited role in controlling crimes of passion, and society's emphasis on the acquisition of material possessions as a yardstick of success is an attitude that the police can do little to alter.

Crime encompasses such a broad range of human activity and unpredictability that no single agency in a democratic society, no matter how powerful, can be expected to provide all the answers. Of importance as well is the recognition that the police are only one element in the overall criminal justice system. To protect our cherished civil rights, the *system* often appears to err on the side of letting the guilty go free rather than to risk punishing the innocent. The system is based on the ideal that imposing swift and sure penalties on those who cross the line into illegal activity will help deter others from doing so, yet today's overcrowded court dockets, bureaucratic bottlenecks, and overflowing jails and prisons show how far we are from achieving that goal.

Yet what this analysis is also designed to demonstrate is that the traditional police approach holds little promise of doing a better job than it already does. There is good reason to suppose that tinkering with the traditional approach in the hope of dramatically improving police departments' ability to solve the riddle of serious crime is like rearranging the deck chairs on the *Titanic* – too little, too late. What has become glaringly apparent is that the traditional system focuses the vast bulk of its resources on only one of three times that police action can influence the ultimate outcome of a potentially criminal act.

Current efforts target most sworn personnel, the department's first line of defense, toward maintaining the overall ability to respond immediately to those relatively few times where a quick response is vital. One obvious problem with the traditional system therefore is that proactive and follow-up efforts often suffer from lack of resources as a result. Yet an even more serious problem is that the rationale for relying primarily on motor patrol rested on the assumption that encouraging these officers to use their free patrol time on preventive patrol would make a substantial contribution in the fight against serious crime. Unfortunately, this appears to have little, if any, practical value in reducing or controlling crime. Though it rattles the foundations of traditional thinking, research tends to confirm that preventive motor patrol efforts are often no more than an expensive waste of time.

While that may overstate the case, the fact remains that history fails to show that the traditional approach can cope effectively with the explosion of serious crime that began in the late 1960s. Admittedly, the rates of serious crime in recent years have continued to decline, but these may have as much to do with the maturing of the Baby Boomers out of their most crime-prone years and the unprecedented strength of the sustained economic boom, as to the contribution the police have made in doubling the number of people behind bars in recent years. The fact remains that this society continues to suffer rates of serious crime that would be considered intolerable in other industrialized Western nations. This reality has sparked and continues to fuel a radical re-assessment concerning whether police departments might find better ways to approach the challenge posed by serious crime.

What Community Policing proposes is that the riddle of serious crime requires understanding that serious crime incidents cannot be solved in isolation – separate from each other and separate from their relationship to the social and physical environment in the community. Though it may sound illogical on the surface, the Community Policing philosophy suggests that only by broadening the police mandate beyond a narrow focus on serious crime incidents as they occur can the police provide short- and long-term answers to the dilemma posed by serious crime.

As noted before, the subtle and sophisticated Community Policing approach rests on recognizing that coping with serious crime demands approaching it in context. It is possible that anyone in the United States may at some point in his life be swept away by the passion of the moment to commit an irrational act totally out of character, an act that ends up as a crime statistic. In such cases, the police can often do little more than to make sure that they will arrive on the scene as soon as reasonably possible after receiving the call, and both the traditional police approach and Community Policing guarantee that. But an important flaw in the traditional approach is that it is not much of an exaggeration to suggest the prevailing system supposes a world in which it is equally likely that President Bush may one day bludgeon Barbara in a fight as that this will happen at an address where domestic disputes routinely escalate into violence.

The traditional approach only superficially recognizes that many criminal acts follow their own internal logic, that they have a context within the community. As in the case of those purse snatchings at the bus stop discussed in Chapter 1, that one site acted as a magnet for such crimes, just as households with a history of domestic disputes often end up as places where aggravated assaults and even murders are more likely to occur. It comes as no surprise that muggings can flourish in places where relatively affluent people congregate next door to open drug dealing; that daytime burglaries can erupt in bedroom communities where both parents work and kids are in school; that dilapidated areas dominated by drug-abusing school dropouts suffer theft rates higher than well-tended neighborhoods where kids shuttle from one after-school activity to another.

The traditional response to these obvious realities is simply to add more patrol cars in problem areas, at problem times. Since the sight of a patrol car whizzing by is rarely much of a deterrent, this simply makes it more likely a car will be available to respond rapidly to the flow of calls for service. This reactive mode means the police do not accomplish much until the call is placed, and most people either cannot or will not call fast enough so that speed of arrival ends up making much difference in the final outcome. As David Carter notes, random patrol produces random results.

What Community Policing does is open up the thinking of the department, so that the police learn to see crime in a broader context. The first challenge is to infuse all officers with the Community Policing approach, so that they learn to look beyond isolated crime incidents, at the underlying dynamics where creative interventions might help solve the problem in ways that need not require arrest. In many cases, this requires looking at the physical environment in a new way, such as recognizing that replacing streetlights may help cut the rate of muggings and rapes in dimly lit areas that people frequent alone at night. That fencing off an abandoned lot where dope dealers congregate may discourage open drug dealing that plays a role in burglaries in the area.

Yet Community Policing goes beyond adopting problem-solving police techniques (1) by broadening the police mandate beyond a narrow focus on crime, and (2) by restructuring the department to carry out this expanded mission more effectively. Though it would seem sensible that the best way to reduce and control serious crime is to for the police to focus even more attention on just these crimes alone, Community Policing approaches the problem from a different direction. It says that serious crime is the *heart attack* that the police must treat, but that they must also find a way to address the broad underlying causes – they must involve the patient in efforts that promote good health. The challenge is to make the all-important shift from focusing on illness to promoting wellness. This means doctors must at least attempt to educate their patients about high-risk behavior. The best doctors go further, by providing support for patients who try to quit smoking, embark on a sensible exercise program, diet off any extra pounds, and reduce their intake of cholesterol and saturated fats.

In the case of curing sick communities, this means the police must educate people about what they can do to combat crime. Then the department's community outreach specialists, its CPOs, must go further by involving people in efforts to deal with the social and physical disorder that promote neighborhood decay – fixing potholes in the street, helping the homeless find shelter, providing meaningful activities for idle teens, and helping people with the persistent, nagging problems such as unrelenting noise that escalate the underlying tensions.

Critics contend that Community Policing detracts from a proper focus on crime, by dissipating the energies of the department in efforts that have nothing to do with serious crime. They argue that this broadening of the police mandate squanders resources better spent addressing the serious crime problems that this society faces. One problem lies in thinking that serious crime occurs in a vacuum, whereas it is instead part of the fabric of the community, which cannot be separated from its cultural context. Another problem is that this argument supposes that the traditional approach focuses more time and energy on serious crime than the Community Policing approach does, whereas the reverse may well be true.

Because it is basically reactive, the traditional approach usually requires a call for service to trigger action – the dispatcher receives a call that a serious crime is in progress and sends a motor patrol officer in response. A department that adopts Community Policing does the same. The next level of priority is a call about a serious crime that has already ocurred – someone discovers a body, the bank robbers have fled, a rape victim arrives at the emergency ward. Again, regardless of whether the call comes into a traditional department or one that has adopted Community Policing, a motor patrol officer is dispatched to the scene. The major difference here concerns what happens after the officer arrives, since a department infused with the Community Policing philosophy asks the officers to look beyond the individual incidents to see whether there are underlying pressure points that could influence the likelihood of similar problems in the future.

The question then becomes how the department uses its resources beyond fulfilling these most basic functions. In traditional departments, motor patrol officers spend their time between calls involving serious crime on answering relatively minor calls and on preventive patrol. Those calls can include a so-called petty theft, helping people who are locked out of their cars or homes, tagging an abandoned vehicle, issuing a traffic ticket, or responding to a call about a loud party in progress. Most motor patrol officers see those kinds of calls as *nuisance calls,* trivial matters that occupy their time until the *real* business of policing – a call about serious crime – comes over the radio. If they have the luxury of time between even these kinds of nuisance calls, a motor patrol officer may cruise areas known for their open dope dealing and prostitution, knowing full well that the activity heats up again once their taillights disappear around the corner. As this shows, the traditional approach may well squander precious resources in efforts that hold little promise of addressing the challenge posed by serious crime.

The first important shift that Community Policing demands is accepting that property crime in general deserves serious attention. While it is obviously true that violent crime deserves top priority, the existing system often fails to recognize the importance of taking property crime equally seriously. People sense something is askew with police priorities when the department insists it cannot afford to send an officer when a person calls to report that his car has been stolen, yet that same driver knows the police always seem to find the time to write him a ticket when he tries to make an illegal left-hand turn. And even departments that send officers to take a report on a stolen car may send the wrong message when they refuse to do the same for that 12-year-old whose bike was stolen.

They especially risk sending the wrong message to the 12-year-old who steals a bike. In essence, it says that police do not care much about property crime, especially those typically committed by juveniles. This seems particularly misguided, since the point is not to let juveniles who commit such crimes fall through the cracks until they commit a violent act or escalate to bigger and bigger property crimes. As a former lieutenant in the Flint foot patrol experiment contends, our collective inability to find ways to turn around a 40-year-old burglar should help us recognize the importance of finding a way to make sure that a 12-year-old who commits his first property crime does not find that the police do not care enough to send an officer to investigate.

The point is not that the police department must be at the immediate beck and call of each person who asks for service, but Community Policing allows the department to use the CPO's free patrol time to follow up on reports about property crime. A dispatcher who grasps how Community Policing works explains to the caller that the CPO will stop by in the next day or so to discuss the problem, since dispatching a motor patrol officer immediately holds no promise of altering the outcome. During that follow-up visit, the CPO has a chance to find out whether there has been a rash of similar incidents in the neighborhood, and whether the person has any ideas concerning who might be involved. Perhaps that stolen bike was one of five that have disappeared, but only this family placed a call to the police.

If nothing else, making that home visit provides the CPO a hook to attempt to involve that family in the police process. This could mean challenging them to recruit five other neighbors for an organizing meeting where the CPO can explain Neighborhood Watch and offer some Crime Prevention tips. It could mean the CPO succeeds in enlisting various family members for new community-based initiatives, whether that means recruiting a coach for the new softball league or someone in the family to handle calls at the CPO's local office.

Maybe that visit allows the family to share concerns about other problems in the community, as well as their insights and suggestions about possible solutions. Perhaps that casual visit elicits information about the teenager down the street that is rumored to be selling drugs, the unexplained bruises on the child next door that they can hear screaming in the night, the group of teenagers they heard shouting racial epithets at passersby. Unlike motor patrol officers whose focus is on handling this call as quickly as possible so that they can move on to the next, the purpose in freeing CPOs from those constraints is so that CPOs have the time and opportunity to use informal interchanges to find out valuable information about the community context of crime, including serious crime.

Freeing CPOs to act as the department's community outreach specialists also allows the department to involve itself in efforts to combat social and physical disorder. Again, critics of Community Policing see this as distracting from a proper focus on serious crime, because they fail to see the community context. Unless the department educates everyone about the contribution that CPOs make in carrying out the Community Policing mandate, motor patrol officers in particular may see what CPOs do as unimportant – or even stupid. On the surface, it seems ridiculous to suggest that a CPO is helping the department and its motor patrol officers by haranguing the city sanitation department to pick up the garbage on time. Traditionalists suggest it is tantamount to insanity to allow officers to waste their time on such trivial problems, especially in a decaying neighborhod notorious for violent clashes between drug dealers vying for new customers.

Yet that CPO probably stands a better chance of getting timely garbage service for the area than a barrage of calls from people whose address verifies they carry little clout with City Hall. And that achievement can help the CPO gain credibility and inspire confidence among the people whose support is vital in organizing efforts targeted at reducing open drug dealing. An enterprising CPO may also be able to capitalize on that initial first step by recruiting kids in the neighborhood to begin picking up litter in exchange for which they receive a donated toy. Perhaps the local shop teacher could involve students in fixing broken benches in the park where drug dealers congregate. The next step might be to involve area businesses in donating paint and shrubs to help spruce up the facility. The park might be a good place to host Neighborhood Watch meetings, so that drug dealers begin to realize that this is no longer a safe place to deal.

By itself, that CPOs effort to have the garbage picked up on time is trivial. But as part of a long-range effort to reverse the downward cycle of decay, it can be an important first step. Areas that look bad attract problems because predators understand the visual cues – the people here don't care. As the area begins to improve, this also emboldens and empowers more people to participate, and the more people participate in community life, the less inviting the area becomes for those who seek to exploit signs of a community's indifference. As momentum builds, each improvement holds the promise of making the area a place that people can enjoy rather than fear.

The process of revitalizing the community produces other positive spinoffs. When CPOs involve young people in such efforts, they learn about responsibility, hard work, and doing things for others. Properly structured, they also have the opportunity to learn skills that can enhance their ability to land a part-time job. It also provides CPOs informal opportunities to reinforce positive values. These opportunities demonstrate that the police are not uniformed thugs who thrive on giving kids a hard time, but caring human beings who are willing to help make the community a better and safer place to live.

Involving the police in efforts aimed at juveniles also holds the promise of breaking down the barriers between the police and the adults in the community. Jowanne Barnes-Coney, a foot patrol officer in the Flint experiment, said that by working first on programs aimed at the young people in her beat area, she was able to make in-roads with the parents. Kids are basically more open and trusting, so once she had them on her side, they provided her access to their parents.

Admittedly, the link between Community Policing's proactive focus and any potential impact on serious crime in the future seems tenuous. Fix a few potholes and someday the murder rate will decline? Teach a kid to plant flowers today and he won't rob someone five years from now? The first thing to remember is that the traditional system does far less. An officer whizzing by in a patrol car on preventive patrol accomplishes little. Investing scarce resources in a new radar gun and patrol car to catch a few more speeders will do virtually nothing to cut tomorrow's rates of serious crime. The second important realization is that the link between crime and disorder is real. As the next chapter will show, research confirms that efforts to improve the social and physical environment in the community pay off in reducing the overall rates of crime. Many communities are dotted with *hot spots,* areas that look unsafe and are unsafe. The police, if only by default, must begin to address the need to reverse this downward cycle.

Given the choice, does it make better sense to imprison two educated and highly trained police officers into one patrol car, where they spend most of their time talking to each other, or should departments consder freeing some of those officers so that they can talk to people in the community instead? As the chapter on the Flint research shows, the foot officers there felt safer than their motor patrol counterparts. The research also showed that this outreach effort significantly reduced racial tensions between the police and the minority community.

History reveals that serious crime is a stubborn problem, not given to easy or quick solutions. Community Policing suggests that creativity and innovation are required to approach serious crime from new angles, making incremental improvements that hold the promise of making long-term substantive improvement. It recognizes the importance of treating all crime, including property crime, as serious police business. It says arrests alone are not the cure. It focuses special attention on those at risk of becoming offenders and victims. It involves people in efforts to make their communities more crime-resistant, including participating in projects to reduce neighborhood decay. It involves CPOs as community outreach specialists, allowing them to function as the community's ombudsman to other agencies that can help. Community Policing pays particular attention to juveniles, not only because young people commit more than their share of crime, but because of the hope that positive police intervention at an early age holds a greater promise of encouraging youngsters to live within the law as adults.

For some, such efforts still sound more like social work than police work. Traditionalists sincerely believe that the proper police response to serious crime is embodied in the tough cop rolling up to the scene, sirens blaring, even though that may only account for a fraction of the time spent on the job. Faced with this ambitious list of other duties that Community Policing demands, traditionalists ask, why the police? Proponents of Community Policing argue instead, who better?

NOTES

[1]*Report to the Nation on Crime and Justice, Second Edition,* U.S. Department of Justice (Washington, DC: Bureau of Justice Statistics, March 1988), p. 14.

[2]Trojanowicz, Robert C., *An Evaluation of the Neighborhood Foot Patrol Program in Flint, Michigan* (East Lansing, MI: National Neighborhood Foot Patrol Center, Michigan State University), and *Fighting Fear: The Baltimore County Cope Project* (Washington, DC: Police Executive Research Forum, February 1986), p. 20.

See also, *Crime and Policing* by Mark H. Moore, Robert C. Trojanowicz, and George L. Kelling, *Perspectives on Policing* series No. 2, a publication of the National Institute of Justice, U.S. Department of Justice, and the Program in Criminal Justice Policy and Management, John F. Kennedy School of Government, Harvard University, June 1988.

[3]*Report to the Nation on Crime and Justice,* p. 14.

[4]Twain, Mark, *The International Thesaurus of Quotations,* compiled by Rhoda Thomas Tripp (New York: Perennial Library, Harper & Row), p. 925.2.

[5]*Report to the National on Crime and Justice,* p. 104.

[6]*Ibid,* p. 34.

[7]*Ibid,* p. 7.

[8]*Ibid.*

[9]*Ibid,* p. 67.

[10]*Ibid,* p. 33.

[11]Axthelm, Pete, "Somebody Else's Kids," *Newsweek,* April 25, 1988, p. 64.

[12]*Report to the National on Crime and Justice,* p. 16.

[13]Braiden, Chris, inspector for the Edmonton (Canada) Police Department, in remarks delivered during the National Neighborhood Foot Patrol Training Seminars, Michigan State University, East Lansing, MI, April 1987.

[14]Kelling, George, *et al.*, *The Kansas City Preventive Patrol Experiment: A Summary Report* (Washington, DC: The Police Foundation, 1974).

[15]Kansas City (Missouri) Police Department, *Response Time Analysis Report* (Kansas City: Board of Police Commissions, 1977).

[16]Larson, Richard C., and Cahn, Michale F., *Synthesizing and Extending the Results of Police Patrol Studies* (Washington, DC: National Institute of Justice, 1985).

[17]Kelling, George, *The Newark Foot Patrol Experiment* (Washington, DC: The Police Foundation, 1981).

[18]Lapham, Lewis, "Images of Fear," *Harper's* (May 1985), p. 43.

[19]*Ibid.*

[20]Harris, Lou, *Inside America* (New York: Vintage Books, Random House, 1987), p. 185.

[21]Goulden, Joseph C., *Fit to Print: A.M. Rosenthal and his Times* (New York: Lyle Stuart, 1989).

[22]*Report to the Nation on Crime and Justice,* p. 2.

[23]*Ibid.*

[24]Gropper, Berhard A., Ph.D., "Probing the Links Between Drugs and Crime" (Washington, DC: National Institute of Justice, February 1985), p. 2.

[25]Sherman, Lawrence W., and Berk, Richard A., "The Minneapolis Domestic Violence Experiment" (Washington, DC: Police Foundation Reports, Police Foundation, April 1984).

[26]*Ibid.*

[27]*Report to the Nation on Crime and Justice,* p. 29.

[28]*Ibid.*, p. 5.

[29]*Ibid.*

[30]*Ibid.*

[31]*Ibid.*, p. 4.

[32]"Drug Use Forecasting" (Washington, DC: National Institute of Justice, May 1988), p. 5.

[33]*Report to the Nation on Crime and Justice,* p. 3.

[34]*Ibid.*

[35]*Ibid.*

CHAPTER 5
Community Policing's Impact
on Fear of Crime

*Neither a man nor a crowd nor a nation can
be trusted to act humanely or to think sanely
under the influence of a great fear.*
—*Bertrand Russell*

Fear of Crime as a Separate Issue

Man is programmed to respond to threats. Our very survival as a species depends on our ability to cope with danger. When we sense impending peril, chemicals flood our bodies so that we are fully mobilized to fight or flee. But today in the United States, one of our greatest fears is fear of crime, and the ways in which people try to cope with that fear produces new stresses that take an additional toll:

- A woman turns down a promotion because it would mean making sales calls at night and memories of her sister's brutal rape make her too fearful to drive alone after dark.

- An elderly couple no longer feels safe walking to local stores, even during daylight, so they now wait for their daughter to take them with her when she shops. Not only do they worry about what they will do if she cannot come, they miss the outings they used to take together, stopping at local shops where everyone knew their names.

- A sixth-grader begins feigning illness, as an excuse to stay home from school, because a classmate was attacked by older boys, and he is afraid he will be next.

- A man and wife have watched their middle-class neighborhood decline, but they vowed to stay – until a rash of burglaries and muggings nearby. To their shock, they find their home is worth less than it was a few years ago, but they sell and move to the suburbs, though it means additional time and expense to commute to their jobs.

Crime alone costs this society somewhere between $26.9 and $136.9 billion each year, just in the actual gross receipts of criminal activity.[1] Even this does not include the medical costs incurred by victims, their lost productivity and earnings, the cost of private security and protective devices, property damage, declining property values, and the staggering $45.6 billion tax dollars it took in 1985 to fund this country's criminal justice system.[2] How do we calculate the additional cost of fear of crime?

In each of the all-too-common scenarios cited above, no one was the victim of a particular crime, though all were victimized by crime's evil and insidious shadow – fear of crime. The damage that each person suffered was very real and as serious as what many crime victims endure. What we must never forget is that whenever one person is victimized by crime, that individual's family, friends, co-workers, and acquaintances are also victimized by the reminder that we are all vulnerable. And even reading about lurid crimes in the newspaper or seeing an innocent victim on TV reinforces the message that no one can be completely safe. In that sense, criminals must be held responsible not only for the havoc they wreak on their victims, but for the damage they do to us all.

The economic and social damage done to us, as individuals and as a society, by fear of crime has become as important an issue today as crime itself. We must also remember that the damage done by the corrosive fear of crime extends beyond individuals and families, to businesses and to communities as well. Downtown in many cities today is a place that people flee as soon as they leave work. The large department stores and other retail businesses that could afford to do so have followed people to the demonstrably safer suburbs, to shopping malls guarded by hired security. Many businesses that could not afford to make the transition or that waited too long to try have simply disappeared – the family-owned drug store, the ethnic bakery, the corner grocery, the shoe repair shop – taking local jobs with them.

In major cities, the damage can seem dramatic – so many stores and homes have been abandoned and destroyed that entire areas look as if they had been bombed. In faltering northern industrial cities like Detroit, even many comfortable homes now stand empty, a cruel irony in an era when the ranks of the homeless have been swelled by platoons of new recruits, including families with children.

This discussion is not intended as nostalgia for the past. Change has always brought social and economic dislocation, and, as the buggy-whip makers and itinerant scissors-grinders will attest, the challenge lies in learning to adapt. But the difference is that the changes wrought by industrial or technological advances, though wrenching, could be more easily accepted as the price of progress. Changes that result from fear of crime are instead the painful and hidden tax we all bear on top of the burden of crime itself.

The traditional police response to fear of crime has been to attack crime, in the hope that reducing crime overall will ultimately lessen fear. Since traditional policing relies primarily on motor patrol, which is basically reactive, there are obvious structural limitations that make it difficult to provide an effective means of confronting fear of crime separately and directly. Though Crime Prevention and Police/Community Relations programs have helped broaden the traditional police role in ways that impinge on fear of crime, these peripheral attempts tended to chip away at problems that demand a bulldozer.

As we learned in the last chapter, the number of households touched by crime dropped from one in three in 1975, to one in four in 1986, though it is virtually impossible to verify the extent to which various factors have contributed to this decline. Reflecting this good news is the equally good news that fear of crime appears to have declined as well. According to pollster Lou Harris, in 1975, 55 % of the total U.S. population reported feeling uneasy when they walked their own streets. By 1983, this figure had dropped to 32 % . Those groups who continued to be the most fearful remained the same – women (42 %), older people (35 %), blacks (36 %), those who live in big cities (37 %), and low-income residents (40 %).[3]

While the trend is encouraging (and part of the overall improvement may be attributable to Community Policing), these figures still show that millions of people are afraid. And while more people feel safer than they did in the mid-1970s, the rates are still far higher than in the substantially safer period of the early 1960s. When we look at the profound demographic changes that have occurred at the same time, we see that many crime-riddled, northern industrial cities have lost population to the suburbs and to the Sun Belt – where crime rates are now on the rise. This not only raises questions concerning the quality of life for those left behind, but about the ability of new communities to keep crime and the fear it spawns in check.

This chapter will explore the complex issues involved in fear of crime:

- What kinds of crime are people afraid of and are such fears justified? Are various groups afraid of different threats? What role does physical and social disorder play in fear of crime?

- How does Community Policing address fear of crime? How should we assess Community Policing's impact on disorder as a way to reduce these fears? When does fear of crime provide an impetus for positive action and when does it become a problem in itself?

Before addressing these important questions, we first must tackle one of the most distressing and most debated issues related to fear of crime – the problem of crime and race.

Race as an Issue in Fear of Crime

No one can approach the controversial and volatile topic of the link between crime and race without great trepidation, because of the tremendous opportunity for being misunderstood – just raising the issue is interpreted by some as offensive. Commenting on minority crime and victimization must be done with great care and sensitivity. Yet these crucial factors must be dealt with in any responsible analysis of fear of crime, because the racial tensions in our society make it difficult to separate fear of crime from racial fear and bigotry, and minorities often feel their fears and concerns are too often ignored or neglected.

To understand today first requires looking back to yesterday. As Chapter 2 detailed in depth, many immigrant groups have been the target of indigenous bigotry. And, as the agents of social control wielded by the establishment, all too often the police were badly misused as an instrument of discrimination. With the exception of Native Americans and blacks, most minorities came to this country for one of two reasons – either to escape problems at home or because of what they perceived as increased opportunities here. In most cases, their assimilation followed predictable rites of passage, from initial discrimination, to tacit acceptance, then full-fledged participation. In most cases as well, skin color played at least some role in the length of that timetable, as did an individual's ability to speak English without an accent.

While people from numerous countries continue to arrive here in search of a new home, since the Vietnam era, the new immigrants have included large numbers of Hispanics from Mexico, Puerto Rico, and Central America; Orientals from Cambodia, Laos, and Vietnam; and blacks from Haiti. Blacks and Hispanics today constitute the two largest minorities, with blacks totalling roughly 12 % of the U.S. population and Hispanics 6 % .4 Though we often lump minorities together, as if they were a monolithic whole, a comparison of both the victimization and arrest rates of blacks and Hispanics highlights important differences that verify the seriousness of *black-on-black* crime.

The Bureau of Justice Statistics analyzed 1984 and 1985 data on victimization rates by race and origin per 1,000 persons age 12 and older:[5]

	Personal Crimes of	
	Violence	*Theft*
White	29	70
Black	38	63
Other	25	73
Hispanic	30	60
Non-Hispanic	30	70

The most striking deviation shows that blacks are far more likely than whites or other minorities to be the victims of violent crimes – the crimes people fear most. Looking just at murder, a black man's lifetime risk of being murdered is a shocking 1 in 30 (1 in 132 for black females), compared to 1 in 179 for white males (1 in 495 for white females).[6] As noted before, murder is the leading cause of death for young black males in this country. A black person in the United States is five times more likely to be murdered than someone who is white.[7] A study of the National Crime Survey by Wesley G. Skogan showed black women report being raped twice as often as their white counterparts.[8] Skogan also found that blacks are not only more likely to be assaulted, but those assaults tend to be more serious and more likely to require hospitalization overnight – and the victims are less likely to be insured.[9]

Also noteworthy is that these statistics also show most minorities suffer less property crime, though this does not make them feel any safer. Since some studies seem to confirm there is no significant difference in the reporting rates of property crime between blacks and whites, this disparity appears to confirm that because minorities are generally poorer, they simply have less worth taking.

Looking at the other end of the spectrum, at arrests, UCR data show that 47 % of those arrested for violent crimes were black and 15 % Hispanic.[10] While UCR statistics are far from perfect, arrest data tend to be fairly reliable, especially for serious crimes. Separate victimization studies where victims are asked the race of their attacker also support these basic findings.[11]

Another question is whether these figures may reflect a possible racial bias because the police might be more likely to arrest a black person compared to someone who is white. While that may have been a problem in the past, even if the practice persists – and increasing numbers of minority officers make it less likely – the chances are this would not hold true for these most serious crimes of murder, rape, robbery, and aggravated assault, though it might still be a factor in arrest rates for all crimes combined.

A closer look at those arrest statistics shows that Hispanics were 2.5 times more likely to be arrested for a serious violent crime than their representation in the overall population would suggest. While the rate confirms that violence committed by Hispanics is a serious problem, even more staggering is that blacks are arrested for these crimes four times more often than their relative share of the population would indicate.

Another analysis, comparing black and Hispanic arrests for violent crimes committed in New York City, cited by Charles E. Silberman in *Criminal Violence, Criminal Justice,* verified a marked discrepancy in the rates for these two minorities. While poverty undeniably plays a role in the higher rates of violent crime among minorities overall, Silberman also noted that the median family income for New York's substantial Puerto Rican population was 20 % below that of blacks (their educational levels were lower as well).[12] If poverty alone were the predictor, we would expect Hispanics to commit proportionally more violent crimes than blacks, yet the reverse is true.

As Silberman writes:

> It is essential that we understand why black offenders are responsible for so much violent crime. The explanation does not lie in the genes.... Black crime is rooted in the nature of the black experience in this country – an experience that differs from that of other ethnic groups. To be poor and black is different from being poor and Puerto Rican, or poor and Chicano, or poor and a member of any other ethnic group.[13]

Discrimination is obviously an important key, and Joseph Darden, Dean of Michigan State University's Urban Affairs Programs, explains why race is one of the most potent sources of discrimination. Darden says that people tend to discriminate against those who they perceive as having distinguishable differences, but that they reserve the most virulent discrimination for people who differ in *kind* rather than in *degree.* Differences in kind relate to factors such as race and gender – we perceive men and women as very different from each other, and we do the same with skin color. Differences in degree related to factors such as class – the middle class may perceive itself as distinguishable from the lower class, but the differences are a matter of degree, not of kind. Since discrimination is based on objectifying the other group, people typically exhibit the greatest discrimination for those they perceive as the most different, which is why race proves so important in understanding such problems.

Darden also notes that segregating people with perceived differences into specific areas serves to intensify discrimination. Segregation contributes to making it easier to focus on differences rather than similarities. This also explains why discrimination on the basis of gender, though it is a difference in kind, is mitigated because it is less likely they will be segregated from each other than that people of different skin color will be isolated from each other. "People find it easier to treat a segregated group as less human, and they are more hostile to people who are not among them all the time," says Darden.[14]

In essence, this is the process that made it easier for the Nazis to escalate their institutionalized violence against the Jews. The more that Jews were restricted from opportunities to interact with the mainstream, the easier it became to exaggerate supposed differences, which then becomes the rationale for increasing harshness, culminating in the *Final Solution,* the *Holocaust* that cost six millions Jews their lives.

These aspects of the dynamics of discrimination are evident in the black experience, beginning when they were kidnapped and brought to the South as slaves, where they were treated as sub-human animals to be bought and sold. While many today bridle at the suggestion that events so long ago could still have any significant influence today, we must remember that slavery meant legalized white violence against black slaves, and the institution of slavery destroyed generations of black families. For a profit, for punishment, or just on a whim, a slave owner had the power to split up couples and sell off grandparents, parents, and children, with no regard for family ties. And while black males were valued for their physical strength, they were most feared for it as well.

After emancipation, blacks faced an unprecedented challenge far more daunting than what any other minority had to tackle. In a climate of white bigotry and hostility, blacks had to find ways to re-establish families, forge a new black culture in an adopted land, test the limits of their personal and collective freedom, and find ways to make a living with relatively few skills (even teaching slaves to read was a crime). The Ku Klux Klan burned crosses in the yards of those they thought pushed too far or too fast, and black males also had good reason to fear being lynched. At the turn of the century, a total of 115 black men were lynched during 1900, more the next year.[15]

As the economy shifted away from farming to factories, many blacks abandoned the rural life of the segregated South to seek jobs in northern industrial cities, only to find *de facto segregation* meant they were still isolated from the white mainstream. According to an analysis of the War on Poverty by Nicholas Lemann published in *The Atlantic,* during the period from the start of World War II to the end of Lyndon Johnson's presidency, more than four-million blacks moved from the rural South to the urban North, a migration whose consequences were little noted at the time. The prevailing wisdom was that lucrative factory jobs would mean blacks would follow the patterns of other ethnic groups and ultimately work their way out of the ghetto. Yet instead, mirroring what again happened in the 1980s, in the early 1960s, the number of jobs in manufacturing actually dropped in many major Northern industrial cities, despite the overall economic boom.[16]

The War on Poverty

Lemann's analysis deserves close attention, not only because it is one of the few detailed examinations of the history of the War on Poverty, but because it shows how the themes of poverty, race, and crime became so closely intertwined in the debate about how this country should deal with issues such as black-on-black crime. As Lemann notes, the decline in the poverty rate for black families went down even more dramatically than for whites in the decade from 1947 to 1957, yet few policy-makers paid much attention when the rate of exit from poverty began to slow in the late 1950s, except to suggest that isolated *poverty pockets* were residual problems that demanded attention.[17] Meanwhile, in black urban ghettos, welfare rates were rising, as were the rates of serious crime and the influx of hard drugs.

Lemann argues that the impetus to use government to address such problems gained momentum because both President John F. Kennedy and his brother Robert, the Attorney General, became persuaded that opportunity was a decisive factor in juvenile delinquency. While social workers tended to view delinquency as strongly linked to failed parenting, many sociologists of that era took the larger view and held that juvenile crime erupted when teenage males confronted an obvious gap between what they wanted and what they could hope to achieve. An evolving consensus of the sociologists of the so-called Chicago School, influenced by Robert Park (see Chapter 3), focused on *anomie* as part of the key – that young people in poverty-stricken neighborhoods were alienated from the broader culture.

Both Kennedy brothers became proponents of the theory propounded by Richard Cloward and Lloyd Ohlin in *Delinquency and Opportunity* that opportunity and delinquency are directly linked as cause and effect.[18] As Lemann notes, once you accept the contention that increasing opportunity is at least part of the key to addressing persistent problems such as poverty, racism, and crime (and not everyone does), the challenge then is to decide the proper role of government in enhancing opportunity.

Conservatives basically argue that government's proper role should be limited to stimulating and maintaining a healthy economy, so that wealth will eventually *trickle down* to those in need. Liberals generally favor a more activist role for government, using the Robin Hood ideal of taking money from the rich to give to the poor through strategies such as the progressive income tax – *redistribution of wealth*. How to use such funds to benefit the poor sparks other controversies. Most efforts fall into one of four basic approaches:

- direct payments to poor people (welfare, negative income tax, guaranteed annual income)

- public works projects that provide assistance in the form of jobs

- community action (efforts aimed at the deficits people face as the result of being poor, such as programs to provide job training and early education)

- community development (efforts aimed at improving the living conditions and work environment in poor areas)

Though any analysis risks gross oversimplification and each philosophy expands or contracts to accept or reject different notions at different times, conservatives have traditionally resisted passing new laws as a way to end discrimination, insisting that laws already protect minorities and that laws do little to change attitudes in society. In general, conservatives favor a *strict construction* approach to the Constitution, which means the court should interpret the law narrowly and decide issues based on what is expressly addressed in the Constitution. To go further risks *legislating from the bench,* and conservatives therefore typically prefer to allow the states to decide issues for themselves through the legislative process.

In the case of discrimination, *states' rights* was the rallying cry conservatives used to argue that the federal government should not usurp the right of the states to make their own decisions. The landmark school desegregation case, *Brown v. the Board of Education* in 1954, was viewed as a threat to states' rights. Today, conservatives particularly resist the use of *quotas* to guarantee minorities a portion of the jobs available as a way to redress past discrimination.

An unfettered capitalism was viewed as the best way to allow those willing and able to work to achieve the American dream. Over time, conservatives accepted that government should provide some form of welfare for widows and orphans, as well as for the physically and mentally handicapped, since they were viewed as being prevented from enjoying the fruits of the system through no fault of their own. Beyond that, conservatives view welfare as a necessary evil, a temporary helping hand to tide families over until the potential wage-earners can find employment.

Conservatives see individual initiative as the most important key to overcoming poverty, and they fear that ambitious efforts by government risk fostering dependence and raising expectations that cannot be met through government actions. For the most part, conservatives favor decentralized, low-cost welfare programs, because they believe that local control allows such efforts to be tailored to local needs. Conservatives also favor tying welfare to work – what has come to be called *workfare*.

Liberals see the Constitution as a document whose intent must be interpreted in the light of the new challenges that the framers could not have foreseen. They view the Supreme Court as an important force in guaranteeing the states do not pass laws that abridge the freedoms guaranteed by the Constitution, and this has generally come to mean that liberals favor using the law as a guarantor of efforts, such as *affirmative action*, to address the residual problems of past discrimination.

While liberals see personal initiative as an essential ingredient that explains why some individuals can overcome the obstacles that stand in their way to achieving full participation, they contend that government has a valid role to play in levelling the playing field so that disadvantaged groups can reach their full potential. Liberals see welfare as the minimum that keeps people fed, clothed, and housed, but that government must do more to help those at the bottom rungs of the socioeconomic ladder.

Liberals see the national government as the best instrument to promote social change, by using tax laws to transfer a share of the wealth generated by the capitalist system into initiatives designed to enhance equal opportunity. As Lemann points out, liberals succeeded in passing legislation for Social Security and the G.I. Bill over protests from conservatives, and those indirectly addressed the problems of poverty and discrimination. What was new in the 1960s was that liberals began to target initiatives aimed at enhancing opportunity as a way to address poverty and discrimination directly.[19]

Until relatively recently, liberals did not appear to worry much about the potential for welfare to promote dependence, therefore they have been less enthusiastic about tying welfare to work requirements, though that appears to be changing. Liberals instead tended to see offering government jobs as something that could be used in addition to welfare, both as a way to stimulate the economy and as a way to enhance opportunity for the poor. President Franklin Roosevelt's $9 billion *New Deal* verifies that such efforts are expensive.[20] While First Lady Eleanor Roosevelt was famous for struggling to improve conditions for blacks, it was not until the Kennedy-Johnson era that efforts to help the poor became so strongly linked in the public consciousness to the issue of race.

President John F. Kennedy's policy included elements of both conservative and liberal thinking. The tax cut Kennedy succeeded in passing in 1963 to stimulate the economy was an idea later championed by President Ronald Reagan's conservative *supply-side* economists. Kennedy planned to counterbalance the tax cut, which most benefited the middle and upper classes, with *community action* initiatives that would be launched prior to the 1964 presidential campaign. According to Lemann, the purpose was not to attract votes among the poor, who traditionally voted Democrat, as much as to win support away from Nelson Rockefeller, head of the liberal wing of the Republican Party.

The consequences concerning whether the liberal or conservative view holds sway are enormous, in terms of what happens in society as a whole and in the black community. History shows that, given an unfettered choice, employers in both the private and public sector will typically hire and promote white males first. If continued economic expansion means the existing labor pool begins to run thin, other groups get their chance. But they also suffer problems if there is an economic downturn, since they are often last-hired, therefore first-fired, because of the role of seniority in such decisions.

What particularly skewed the opportunity for black males to participate fully in the *go-go* economy of the 1960s was the emergence of women as a viable second choice for employers. The emerging Women's Liberation movement certified that there was a ready and willing pool of women eager to fill both skilled and unskilled jobs. Though women remember that era as one of struggle to make gains in the workplace, in retrospect, it appears that, if forced to make a choice between hiring females of any race or black males, women usually won the nod. Racial and sexual stereotyping no doubt played a role, since it appears that women were viewed as more docile and reliable, especially compared to "volatile" black males.

Yet, of course, employers did not enjoy unfettered choice in hiring, especially following the landmark Civil Rights Act of 1964. Though the law was intended primarily to promote equality for blacks, it also empowered women, much to the surprise of many who had did not realize the full impact of their inclusion in the new law. By that time, of course, President Kennedy had been assassinated and his successor, Lyndon Johnson, then launched his profoundly different, broader, and more expensive War on Poverty.

Lemann says that Kennedy only planned to spend $1 million on 10 modest community action efforts. Johnson instead targeted $1.75 billion for his *Great Society* programs, which included community action, the Job Corps, and other programs. Johnson named the Kennedys' brother-in-law, R. Sargent Shriver, as the head of the Office of Economic Opportunity that would oversee the new initiatives. The most popular of all the war-on-poverty programs, Head Start, was added in 1965, and community development, embodied in the Model Cities program, was added in 1966.

A firm believer in politics, Johnson also believed in using the federal government as the protector of black voter registration efforts in the South as a way to help end discrimination. Welfare continued to provide direct cash payments to the poor, but to win enough conservative votes for passage, liberals had to accept regulations that barred payments to women and children if there was a husband or boyfriend in the home. Not until the late 1980s were most such regulations omitted, though they arguably promoted the break-up of families and contributed to removing male role models in the home.

As this also shows, the War on Poverty was not exclusively targeted at blacks –

there have always been more whites than blacks living below the poverty line and on welfare, though blacks constitute a proportionally larger share of the poor than their numbers in the overall society should justify. Yet Johnson's vocal commitment to civil rights and equal opportunity was linked to the War on Poverty, which indelibly marked it as a program designed to redress the twin problems of poverty and racism.

Johnson launched his War on Poverty with great enthusiasm, yet within a decade, it was dismantled as an expensive and misguided flop. Even by 1988, associating the Democratic presidential nominee with the dreaded "L" word meant tarnishing him with reminders about those "free spending" liberals and their "failed efforts of the past." As the last expensive and ambitious effort of national scope designed to "cure" poverty and racism, and thereby indirectly, it was hoped, reduce crime, the War on Poverty and the events of that era intensified and focused the debate about these issues in ways that continue to resound today.

To understand what happened requires knowing a bit about the profound changes that were occurring in the civil rights movement. Martin Luther King remained committed to non-violence, based on the successful campaign waged by Mahatma Ghandi to end British colonial rule in India. Frustrated by the slow pace of change, many young blacks in particular began to question whether such methods would work here. During the 1960s, the optimistic *Black Pride* movement began to lose ground to the militant *Black Power* movement, which spawned the *Black Panther Party* and other separatist groups. Many of these groups rejected King as an *Uncle Tom* and began discussing violence as an alternative.

King had faced substantial resistance among whites, and the more militant groups faced even greater resistance by heightening fears of violence. In addition, increasingly militant groups also began to alienate or exclude white sympathizers on the Left, by rejecting their participation except as sources of funding. Over time, the perception of the Black Panthers began to change, as their focus appeared to shift from positive community efforts, such as their breakfast program in Watts, to fundraising tactics that appeared to border on extortion and controversial shootouts with the police.

In his incendiary book *Soul on Ice,* Black Panther leader Eldridge Cleaver also complicated the dialogue by arguing that his earlier rapes committed against white women should be viewed as political acts, an expression of black rage against white oppression and the stereotyping of black males as consumed by lust for white women.[21] By this attempt to blur the line between criminal acts and political acts, Cleaver added to the perception that those who supported civil rights activism were *soft* on crime.

Yet the biggest trauma in race relations had to be the riots that first broke out in the black Los Angeles ghetto called Watts in 1965. Many hoped Watts would prove to be an isolated incident, but instead each long, hot summer brought new incidents. Newark and Detroit erupted in 1967, prompting Johnson to establish the Kerner Commission to investigate the causes. The report laid the blame in great part to the growing split between black and white society, and it urged spending billions in new programs.

The Kerner report was controversial, with conservatives arguing that government may have helped spark the riots by launching programs that promised more than they could deliver, and that spending more was not the answer to problems that only individual initiative could solve. While liberals countered that the riots were the harvest reaped by allowing smoldering problems to fester unaddressed for so long, Lemann notes that by coming after most Great Society programs had been launched, those programs could be construed as part of the cause. Another problem was that announcing expanded funding for such efforts might appear tantamount to paying ransom, an inducement for those who wanted more help to use riots as a threat.

The riots, combined with rising crime rates, not only frightened white voters, but they found themselves increasingly pinched trying to pay for both a frustrating and protracted foreign war in Vietnam and an expensive War on Poverty that had yet to provide them much protection. Funding both *guns and butter* also overheated the economy, fueling rising inflation that ate further into the pocketbooks of the middle class. In addition, headlines about the mismanagement and corruption in various Great Society programs and widely publicized incidents of violence among the recruits in the Job Corps eroded the confidence that these programs were the answer.

Lemann also notes that many local politicians had reason to want to see programs fail, since they were calculatedly excluded from the process. While there were valid reasons for the national government to want to circumvent the local power structure and fund community action efforts directly, this had the effect of transforming potential friends into outright enemies. Community action initiatives also covered a broad spectrum, since they could target whatever priorities the local groups deemed most important, which meant that some aimed to confront the local power structure.

Though various authors purport to have probed LBJ's mind to explain all the reasons why he chose to escalate the war in Vietnam and retreat from his War on Poverty, the fact is that Republican Richard Nixon was elected in 1968, with support from what Vice-President Spiro Agnew called the *Silent Majority.* Nixon ran on his *secret plan* to end the Vietnam War and a promise to restore law and order, which some perceived as code words for cracking down on student protestors and militant blacks.

Nixon named as urban affairs advisor former Democrat Patrick Moynihan, who had been forced to leave the Johnson administration when a furor broke out over his report on *The Negro Family.* In it, Moynihan appeared to criticize black families, citing statistics that showed that though black unemployment was declining, the number of new welfare cases and illegitimate births continued to rise. He came under attack from the political Left, especially from blacks who not only resented a white intellectual setting himself up as an expert on the black experience, but because raising the possibility of some underlying *pathology* in the black family was viewed as racist. Blacks contend such speculations blame the victim, and that if the problem were suffered by white families, no hint of pathology would be attached.

According to Lemann, that experience persuaded Moynihan that the Left would always stymie efforts to focus on real problems, so that the best alternative was to funnel sufficient money to the poor to stave off rioting. Lemann cites a memo Moynihan wrote during the Nixon years in which he considered such payments a "subsidy," saying that a large and dependent welfare class "will come to be accepted as the normal and manageable cost of doing urban business."[22]

At Moynihan's urging, Nixon twice proposed a guaranteed annual income in the form of a Family Assistance Plan that was not much different than the negative income tax concept touted by Nixon's Democratic opponent, Senator George McGovern. The plan was voted down twice, Moynihan eventually left his post, and, during his second term, Nixon signed the order abolishing the Office of Economic Opportunity in 1974.

Not only did this signal the end of that particular effort, the public perception is that it was such a tremendous flop that it has so far effectively ended the enthusiasm for any similar efforts ever since. Even the handful of revisionists who argue that it achieved more than most people believe accept that the general unhappiness with the War on Poverty helped swing the political pendulum to the right.

Lemann cites figures that show one of the measurable benefits was that it contributed substantially to the emerging black middle class. Blacks held many of the two million new jobs created by the programs, and, by 1970, government employed 57 % of black male college graduates and 72 % of black female graduates.[23]

The turmoil of the era and the widespread disillusionment with the War on Poverty continue to frame the debate concerning what government can and should do about poverty and racism, and what implications this has on government's role in dealing with black-on-black crime. Much has changed since then, yet there are signs of encouragement – and signs of despair.

By 1988, Jesse Jackson became the first black ever to have a realistic chance at becoming the presidential candidate of a major party. Yet the Republican nominee George Bush was widely criticized for a campaign that many allege fanned racial fears by exploiting the case of Willie Horton, a convicted black murderer who brutally raped a white woman while on furlough from prison during Democractic contender

Michael Dukakis' tenure as governor of Massachusetts.

Blacks have now solidified their right to public accommodations – if they can afford them. Despite some modest gains at times, the gap in earnings between blacks and whites has steadily grown larger. The discouragingly high dropout rates for blacks and other minorities also raise concern about the future, since more and more of the unskilled jobs being created are in the low-paying service sector. Segregation may be illegal, but housing patterns continue to follow racial lines.

Though the age-old controversy about who is at fault and who must accept responsibility for answers continues to rage, concerns about a seemingly permanent Underclass are also complicated by the disproportionate representation of blacks. Many see a link between teen pregnancy, absent fathers, poverty, illiteracy, abuse and neglect, alcohol and drug abuse, easy access to guns, and the high rates of violence in Underclass neighborhoods.

The hope of economic equality in the future is also threatened in part by fears about black crime. More than ever, the United States competes in a global economy, one in which multinational corporations can choose to shop for cheap, unskilled labor in Third World countries. Optimists insist the demographics point to a shrinking pool of young workers, which will force companies to establish new plants in cities where the large number of unemployed minorities can take the jobs, thereby breaking down what many insist amounts to economic apartheid. Pessimists suggest those jobs will be exported instead, whenever possible, not only because workers in other countries will work cheaper, but because of racial fears that are inflamed further by fear of crime and drugs.

The result is that whenever we hear about a particular crime, we often look for any underlying racial subtext before commenting. To use the famous Howard Beach incident as an example, it was not enough to know this was a case where one group of boys chased another, and that one of the boys being chased was forced into traffic where he was killed by a car. To understand both the dynamics of the crime and the public reaction to it require knowing that the perpetrators were white and the victims black. Some argue we pay too much attention to race as it relates to crime; others that we pay too little. Some contend that concerns about race obscure the need to focus equal attention on other factors that can play a role – gender, class, ethnic origin, religion.

As an example, discussions about the *wilding* incident in Central Park in the spring of 1989 focused on whether race or class may have played a role, once drugs or alcohol were eliminated as contributing causes. That incident involved a "wolf pack" of middle-class black teens as young as 14, supposedly from "good" homes, who allegedly attacked joggers at random at night in Central Park, savagely beating, gang-raping, and leaving for dead a white, upper-class woman who worked as an investment banker. Yet women contend the issue should have been gender, since the most brutal attack was reserved for a defenseless female. Reportedly, one of the youths charged with the attack explained their rationale by arguing that the woman was at fault for not having a man with her and for not carrying Mace.

The fact remains that race is a prism through which we view crime. Racial bigotry can be a cause of crime. Discrimination and its link to poverty may be important root causes of crime. And everyone involved in the criminal justice system must be alert to the potential for bias to creep into the process.

What everyone agrees on is that the disproportionately high share of violent crimes committed by blacks continues to fuel racial fears. What is sometimes forgotten, however, is that the preponderance of black-on-black crime means blacks themselves have even greater reason to feel afraid. We all fear the stereotypical image that serves as a symbol of urban violence – the young black man with ropes of gold around his neck, armed with an Uzi he will use against anyone who gets in the way of his crack deals. Even if at least part of his rage stems from a sense of injustice, no one today romanticizes his crimes as political. We do not see him as a brother to the stone-throwing Palestinian youths of the *intifadeh*. He is instead a different version of Ivan Boesky, a high-roller whose greed outweighs his conscience. He is the other *yuppie* – the *Young Urban Predator*. And while he is a symbol that strikes fear in the heart of an Iowa farmer, he is much more a real and immediate threat to the black community who live where he plies his trade.

Part of the challenge white America faces is that many blacks keenly sense the pervasive white fear of violent black criminals, but not as many trust there is equal compassion for black victims. Law-abiding blacks often feel victimized twice, once by the crimes committed against them and again when society pays more attention to white citizens' concerns about crime. But since whites have more power to set society's agenda, because of their sheer numbers and greater wealth, blacks are alert to the implications of any actions that the white majority takes to protect itself from black crime, because of the consequences to the entire black community.

The sad fact is, this country's long and painful history of racism, both institutional and one-on-one, has muddied racial issues to a degree where discussing crime is often interpreted by blacks as a coded way to talk about race. Rhetoric about getting tough on crime can be viewed as a white euphemism for cracking down on blacks in general. During the 1960s, tensions ran so high the police found that the black community viewed them as the enemy. New Police/Community Relations programs and the influx of black police, prosecutors, and judges into the criminal justice system helped reduce hostility, but black activists such as the Rev. Al Sharpton can still rally followers by charging that no black can expect justice from the system. One worrisome statistic shows that a black male's chance of incarceration is six times the level for whites, which is significantly higher than the arrest rate would appear to justify.[24]

Mistrust breeds suspicion – everyone wants help from the system in fighting crime in their neighborhoods, but minorities are also sensitive to the threat of over-kill, the fear that skin color can become sufficient reason to be stopped, searched, harassed, and even harmed. And as so often happens with racial issues, people's perceptions matter as much as facts. Such complications add to the difficulty of discussing our individual and collective responses to crime.

So who can say how much of *white flight* is based on fear of crime, fear of economic loss, or fear of blacks? Are the motivations of *black flight* therefore purer? Are jewelers in Manhattan who bar black males from entering their stores behaving like bigots, or are they justified by the increased odds? If a woman on the street alone ducks into a crowded coffee shop when she sees a black man behind her, is she racist or rational – and does that depend on whether she is black or white?

What we do know for certain is that the rates of violent crime for blacks in Africa are nowhere near what they are here, so we must look for answers within cultural change, without blaming our problems on skin color. All too often we cast the debate about solutions in terms of either/or – either the white-dominated power structure must offer help or blacks must take the initiative themselves. More likely the solution requires both.

Community Policing has the virtue of addressing racial fears as a welcome by-product of delivering personalized police service to the community. As we will see later, research on the Flint experiment indicates that such efforts reduce racial tensions between the police and the black community. Community Policing's focus on using the police as the first line of defense in making communities safer holds the promise of addressing black-on-black crime in ways that can reduce overall fears.

Community Policing's expanded focus, which embraces positive social and physical changes in the community, also holds the long-term hope of addressing opportunity, by linking those who suffer poverty and discrimination to agencies and programs that can help. Unlike limited, public-relations-oriented efforts of the past, Community Policing enhances proactive efforts in the context of providing full-spectrum police service.

While it cannot be expected to provide all the answers, it may prove to be an important first step in helping to make the police response to crime color-blind, except when racism is part of the subtext. In those incidents, Community Policing's ability to generate information may help identify those cases where discrimination should be addressed – it makes a difference whether the graffitti on the wall includes racial, ethnic, or religious epithets. At the same time, Community Policing provides a sustained police presence in the community to address such problems through creative initiatives designed to address the need to reduce all forms of bigotry that arise.

Community Policing cannot be expected to provide all the answers, but it can serve as an important new force at the grass-roots, local level.

Three Types of Fear

Fear of crime covers a broad range of responses to the threat of crime that can be broken down into three basic types. First is the intense fear suffered by victims of crime, and, by extension, their family and friends. In the major study published as *The Figgie Report,* fear of crime overall was split into two basic types: *concrete fear of crime,* which means fear of specific crimes, and *formless fear of crime,* a more generalized feeling that one is simply unsafe.[25] The causes and consequences of each are different, deserving of a closer look.

Victimization

Crime victims obviously have good reason to feel afraid – their experience is not only traumatic in and of itself, but it proves to them that they are vulnerable to crime in a dramatic way they may not have been as aware of before. Quite understandably as well, it is far more traumatic to be the victim of a violent crime than a property crime, though we should not underestimate the shock of such losses, since our homes and possessions are symbolic extensions of our identity. How much resulting fear a property crime victim feels also depends on whether the victim was there at the time the crime was committed. While it is frightening to return and find your home has been burgalized, it is far worse to be there facing the burglar, knowing that the potential for violence is real.

Studies of victim and non-victim crime suffer from the difficulty in measuring and comparing the depth of fear people feel. We should remember that, when a non-victim answers yes to a question such as whether they feel afraid on the street, the feeling described may be much more benign than what the victim of a violent crime who also answers yes is experiencing. The aftermath of a violent assault often includes depression, anxiety, sleeplessness, nightmares. When we talk about fear of crime, it is important to remember that such fears can linger in victims for years – or forever – at levels non-victims rarely, if ever, experience.

The victims who suffer the greatest trauma are usually those who suffer violence at random by a stranger – made even more traumatic if the victim failed to see the threat coming. According to Silberman, when a person misreads the cues – the

COMMUNITY POLICING'S IMPACT ON FEAR OF CRIME 147

man approaching turns out not to be a panhandler but a robber who pulls a gun – many victims find it almost impossible to assess the risk in many mundane situations thereafter.[26] We all understand why *subway vigilante* Bernhard Goetz might not have been as quick to shoot the four youths who asked him for money, if he had not previously been robbed and beaten by a stranger on the street.

The physical and social consequences victims suffer also play a role in how much residual fear they feel, and those consequences tend to multiply for those on the bottom rungs of the socioeconomic ladder. A violent crime can mean doctor and hospital bills and even permanent disability, with no insurance, as well as no money to hire extra help. Or it can mean that if the TV is stolen, there is no money to buy a replacement, or that a mugging means no money for rent.

The criminal justice system's response constitutes yet another factor that can determine how much fear a victim feels. Not only does crime itself prove to victims that the system did not protect them, when they then realize that only one out of every five crimes reported results in arrest[27] – and less than one in every three arrested for a felony does time[28] – and figures for 1983 show that more than half of those released from state prisons served less than 20 months,[29] this can add to a sense of outrage and the fear that they will be victimized again.

Bertram Gross of Hunter College writes:

> While the Bill of Rights prohibits double jeopardy…, a crime victim often suffers triple jeopardy. The victim suffers at the hands of the burglar, mugger, crooked landlord, or arson profiteer; he suffers when he loses wages (or even his job) because of the time he must spend in court; and he suffers a third time if his cooperation with the authorities brings retaliation by the accused.[30] And a fourth time, psychically, if the suspect is set free.

An issue of special importance to the police concerns their role in easing victims' fears. While research shows victims overall give the police higher marks for doing the best job of anyone in the entire criminal justice system,[31] Robert B. Parks' paper on the effects of the police response noted that, if the police expended even a little more effort, they could reap tremendous rewards by improving how victims and those who know them perceive their local police.[32]

While Community Policing addresses fear of crime in other important ways to be discussed later, it can make a specific and valuable contribution in reducing the specific fears of victims – and their close friends and family, because it allows CPOs to spend that extra time. The way in which a CPO approaches people also differs from the traditional police aloofness. The CPO's job stresses communication skills and the importance of building rapport and trust.

Ideally, a crime victim should already at least know the CPO by sight, if not by name, which can make it easier to talk openly about what happened. Part of the reason Community Policing frees the CPO from the isolation of the patrol car and the never-ending demands of its radio is so that he can talk to people without the pressures and distractions that motor patrol duty implies. This promotes an atmosphere that allows victims, witnesses, and others to express their feelings as well as to relate the facts. This level of attention helps prove that the police take their victimization seriously and care about what they have suffered, and this can be important in helping them cope with the trauma – though the CPO's increased emotional involvement with people's personal suffering should alert supervisors to the danger of burnout.

Are We Too Afraid?

Though crime rates still remain higher than in the early 1960s, many experts have suggested much of today's fear is irrational, since reassuring statistics seem to show relatively few people are at any real risk. The landmark *Figgie Report* that wrapped up extensive research on fear of crime noted that UCR figures for the high-crime year of 1978 still showed that any one person's statistical likelihood of being murdered stood at a comforting 0.009 % .[33] Why then are so many people so afraid?

A truer and far more sobering picture emerges when we look at the likelihood of victimization over a lifetime. At 1987 rates, five out of every six people in this country will be victims of an attempted or completed violent crime.[34] Concerning property crime, over a 20-year span, roughly seven of 10 households will be burglarized, nine of 10 households will suffer a larceny, and two of 10 will have a vehicle stolen.[35]

While overall rates can be misleading because there are numerous factors that can make us more – or less – vulnerable, according to the *Report to the Nation on Crime and Justice:*

> Many of us will be victimized more than once. Most of us will be victims of personal larceny three times or more.[36]

Such rates make it clear that life in this country means that crime will touch almost everyone directly or harm someone we know. We can attempt to protect ourselves by reducing exposure, by installing extra locks, buying burglar alarms, even by opening ourselves up to other risks by barring our windows and buying guns, but virtually nothing we do can assure us perfect safety. Instead of questioning whether people are irrationally afraid of crime, perhaps we should ask instead why those two out of three in the Harris poll who said they felt safe on the street felt so secure.

Membership in a High-Risk Group

Part of why many people feel safe probably lies in the fact that who you are and where and how you live plays such an dramatic role in whether – and how often – you are likely to be victimized. Membership in a high-risk group increases the odds. Fear of crime is akin to fear of lightning. Under normal circumstances, you would be labelled paranoid for worrying about being killed by lightning. But if you are a golfer stranded on the fairway during an electrical storm, with tunderbolts striking all around you, you would instead be a fool not to be afraid. And many in our society are virtual lightning rods for crime.

As noted earlier, a person's race makes a dramatic difference in likelihood of victimization, but *social disadvantage* also plays a significant role, one that can overlap. As Skogan's study, noted earlier, found:

> The victims of crime are disproportionately young, black, and poor.
> The effects of age, race, and social status accumulate for those at the
> bottom of the ladder, leading to extremely high victimization rates
> for selected groups in the population.[37]

His study showed that, concerning age, 16- to 19-year olds are at greatest risk, and the threat continues to decrease with age. Males are twice as likely as females to be the victims of assault and robbery. And controlling for the effects of both race and income verified that both are independently important indicators.[38]

Women and the Elderly

What may be surprising, however, is that two groups among those that express the greatest fear of crime – women and the elderly – are not high-risk. How can their fears be justified?

Concerning women, the obvious factor that contributes to their fear of crime is the threat of rape. While homosexual rape can and does occur, and women are also arrested for rape 1 % of the time,[39] statistics show that eight of every 100 women will be raped by a man during their lifetime.[40] UCR figures, which may particularly suffer from underreporting in this case, show that women reported roughly 84,000 forcible or attempted rapes to the police in 1984, with 79 % of those forcible.[41] One of every four rapes involves two or more attackers.[42]

Part of this fear stems from assessing the threat of rape and the challenge implicit in making decisions concerning what constitutes rational – and irrational – responses to the threat. Women must be alert to the possibility that every time they allow a man into their home, they are taking a risk. Albert DeSalvo became infamous as the *Boston Strangler,* for murdering 13 women in Boston, but he also confessed to committing close to 2,000 rapes, often by posing as a repairman.[43] The increased awareness of the prevalence of date rape verifies women must also be alert to the dangers posed by men they trust.

This threat means women often do things to reduce their exposure to crime that men do not do. This alone may explain why women are robbed and attacked half as often, though their physical vulnerability would appear to make them an inviting target for robbers. While respect for the threat crime poses can serve as the impetus to exercise care, if fear inhibits a person's life so that they cannot participate fully in the culture, reducing exposure becomes a problem itself.

Now that women have jobs their mothers never dreamed of, many have their new freedom crimped in ways men's lives are not. On the road alone in a strange city, a woman is less likely to see the opportunity to explore as an adventure, but as a potential threat. Men take for granted the freedom to go into a bar alone, knowing they are better able to defend themselves if they have miscalculated. Women lead the list of groups most likely to take precautions to avoid crime,[44] an obstacle in the way of achieving true liberation, a barrier that no new law can erase.

It should also be noted that other factors can dramatically alter whether or not women fall into a high-risk group. In New York City, in 1989, a 21-year-old black woman was the most likely victim of crime.[45]

The elderly's fears are also complicated by awareness of how their age conspires to make them more vulnerable. A robber who has the choice would obviously pick a victim of advanced years rather than a young person better equipped to fight back. The elderly's relative physical fragility also makes him more likely to be injured if attacked. Should that robber shove his victim to the ground, a younger person might suffer only bruises, whereas an elderly person might be more likely to suffer broken bones.

The elderly are also often less able to cope with the economic consequences of crime. They have fewer years within which to recoup losses, and many live on a fixed income with little or nothing to spare. A younger person can take a second or part-time job, if necessary, while elderly people, many of whom are in failing health, may simply not have that option.

Like women, many of the elderly reduce their chances of becoming a victim by reducing their exposure. This is often the solution for those who find themselves trapped by what is called the *aging-in-place* phenomenon. This refers to what happens when people spend their adult lives in a relatively safe neighborhood, where they build ties that make them reluctant to leave. If the neighborhood begins to go bad, those who stay too long may find themselves economically unable to move. Their perception that they are not as safe as they used to be is therefore quite accurate. Not only is society in general less safe than in the 1950s, but elderly city dwellers may find their neighborhood has become one of the most dangerous places a person can live.

The elderly trapped in decaying neighborhoods, behind locked doors, with few friends left alive, risk becoming increasingly isolated from the world outside. As noted earlier, watching TV can contribute to that *mean world syndrome* that can make the outside world seem even more threatening than it really is. The sad reality, however, is the fear that fosters this *fortress mentality* may actually save many of the elderly from being victimized at the rates suffered by their younger neighbors who do venture out more often.

Concrete and Formless Fears

Part of the difficulty in determining changes in the overall rates of fear of crime is because no agency specifically tracks this phenomenon, in the same way we monitor crime rates. Another problem in comparing studies is that whenever you ask about fear of crime, how you pose the question can make dramatic differences in the results, which complicates comparing different studies. For example, the Harris poll cited earlier, that asked people about the fear of walking on their own streets, is measuring only one aspect of fear of crime, a particular kind of formless fear.

To get a clearer handle on the different elements that make up the entire matrix we call fear of crime, the *Figgie Report* established two barometers of fear, one for *concrete fear* and one for *formless fear.* Concrete fear, again, refers to fears about specific crimes, in this case the violent Index crimes, while formless fear relates to a diffuse feeling of being unsafe, more related to disorder. The research showed four of every 10 people felt a high level of each kind of fear, but that only 40 % overlapped and showed high degrees of both kinds of fear.[46] While rates of crime have declined overall since the Figgie study was published in 1980, what the report showed about the dynamics of fear remains valid, though we have reason to hope their overall numbers would be lower today.

The Figgie barometer of concrete fear that looked at fear of murder, rape, robbery, and assault combined also broke out results that showed 55 % of women fear being raped, 24 % of both sexes fear they will be beaten up, 23 % worry they will be robbed, and 17 % fear they will be murdered.[17]

The study also showed the five groups that exhibit the greatest concrete fear:

- people in large cities

- the young

- women

- those with more formal education

- blacks

While we expect to see the members of high-risk groups and women included, the surprise is that people with more formal education rank among those most afraid of these specific crimes. Apparently, information is the key. The assumption is that education makes people more aware of the threat crime poses, even in places where these people may not be likely to go. Any effect the media has on those who live in large cities where crime rates are highest is *washed out* by the effect made by what they see in their day-to-day life.

The Figgie research also controlled for the effects of social disadvantage and isolation, and the authors admitted surprise that people in these categories did not exhibit high levels of concrete fear. This may confirm how important access to information about crime is, since people in these two categories would probably be less likely to have access to newspapers, magazines, and books, and other sources of information.

To study formless fear, the Figgie research posed questions about six diffuse threats related to how safe people felt at home, out shopping, and in their neighborhoods, during the day and at night. The groups showing the highest rates of formless fear included:

- those with the lowest incomes

- blue-collar workers

- those with the least education

- those who do not work full time

- those who experienced a marital loss

- the elderly

To understand these findings, the researchers suggest they relate strongly to four predictors: victimization, information exposure, social disadvantage, and isolation. Of note as well is that those who showed relatively high levels of both kinds of fear are people in large cities, women, and blacks. Those who live in big cities do, in fact, have more to fear from crime, since people who live in the central city or cities with overall populations of 500,000 or more fall victim to crimes of violence roughly 1.5 times more often than people in the suburbs and twice as often as those who live in rural areas.[48]

A different study that asked people to rank their fears concerning a mix of concrete and formless threats showed that fear relates equally to the *perceived seriousness* and the *perceived risk* the person feels. Researchers Mark Warr and Mark Stafford reported:

> While murder ranks higher on perceived seriousness, it ranks only 10th in fear, and the reason is obvious: the perceived risk of murder is very low (15th rank). Indeed, respondents are more afraid of 'having strangers loiter near (their) home' than being murdered, because, despite its perceived seriousness, this event is viewed as much more likely.[49]

Such studies confirm that people are not just afraid of serious crime, but petty crime and physical and social disorder may actually outweigh serious crime as a threat to their sense of well-being. The police have often failed to realize that their own narrower definition of crime is not what people mean when they say they are afraid of crime and want the police to help.

Community Policing, Disorder, and Fear of Crime

Traditional policing can play only a limited role in addressing fear of crime. As we saw in the last chapter, the traditional police response offers little hope of preventing much crime and not much hope of interrupting crimes in progress. The bulk of the traditional response is focused on dealing with crimes after they have occurred, and petty crime and disorder are often treated as a nuisance.

What this analysis of fear of crime demonstrates is how little the traditional approach can do to reduce fear of crime. Its main potential involves handling crimes after they occur and arresting the bad guys, in the hope that doing so will reduce rates of crime in the future. This holds some promise of reducing concrete fear of crime, but it offers little if any potential to reduce formless fear of crime that is so strongly linked to neighborhood decay. By focusing on crimes after they occur, this also means that its ability to address concrete fear is limited, since it means people must suffer victimization before the traditional approach offers much help. Its theoretical ability to reduce crime rates in the future may not reduce much fear today.

The Community Policing approach not only does at least as much to address concrete fear of crime, it directly addresses formless fears in ways the traditional system cannot. By addressing property crime and so-called petty crime, Community Policing inspires confidence in people that the police take their full range of crime concerns seriously. And by expanding the police mission to embrace proactive efforts to address social and physical disorder, Community Policing directly addresses the formless fears associated with neighborhood decay.

As Skogan wrote:

> Fear of crime is higher in places where neighborhood trends point in the wrong direction; people who perceive that their communities were in decline were also more fearful.[50]

In their ground-breaking article *Broken Windows,* James Q. Wilson and George L. Kelling explained why a person's perceptions of safety depend as much on disorder as on the crime rate. As noted earlier, people express more fear of strangers loitering near their home than they do the threat of murder. What people fear most is being bothered by people they view as sinister, whether they prove to be criminals or not – panhandlers, drunks, addicts, rowdy teens, mainstreamed mental patients, the homeless. People who live engulfed by people they do not trust instinctively feel afraid – maybe that addict will rob them to buy a fix or the disheveled man raving to himself will unexpectedly turn violent.

Physical disorder is disconcerting in much the same way. Litter, abandoned buildings, potholes, broken street-lights, and wrecked cars are some of the *signs of crime* that point to a community in decline where crime can breed.

Wilson and Kelling noted that once the process of physical decay begins, its effects multiply unless some corrective action is taken. No matter whether a neighborhood is rich or poor, break one window in a building, leave it unrepaired, and soon all windows in the building will be smashed.[51] It is when a neighborhood begins sliding downhill that the prostitutes arrive, dope houses appear, and soon serious crime finds a foothold and takes over.

In their follow-up article, *Making Neighborhoods Safe,* published in February 1989, Wilson and Kelling update much of what has been learned in the intervening seven years about the direct benefits of "fixing broken windows."[52] They cite the results of research done in Newport News, Virginia, by the Police Executive Research Forum that shows refurbishing the crime-riddled New Briarfield Apartments, an aging facility built in 1942, resulted in a 35 % decline in the burglary rate. Though the apartments are ultimately scheduled to be torn down, this initiative attempted to improve the overall look of the facility until that could be accomplished – trash and abandoned vehicles were carted away, and the streets were swept and potholes filled.

Skeptics contend that such efforts do no more than displace crime, yet Wilson and Kelling suggest two factors offer hope that much of the crime will simply disappear. One reason is that many crimes are opportunistic, what Wilson and Kelling call *adventitious.* They suggest that we have focused so much attention on the role played by social forces and personal failings that we have ignored the effectiveness of addressing the immediate dynamics.

Using the bus stop example of Problem-Oriented Policing cited in Chapter 1, if you reduce the opportunity for crime to occur, by making it harder for the predators to snatch a purse from people herded behind a pipe railing and dash down the alley to escape, they may never find an equally inviting spot to commit such crimes. If the perpetrators do not give up purse snatching entirely, at least making it tougher on them offers the promise more time will elapse between attempts, fewer will succeed, and there is greater likelihood the perpetrators will be identified and apprehended.

Wilson and Kelling suggest that this is why addressing the back alleys and abandoned houses where drug users congregate can reduce the number of crimes users will commit in the area to buy drugs. Or breaking up a youth gang that terrorizes a decaying neighborhood can mean they will risk committing fewer crimes alone than they will together.

Wilson and Kelling suggest the second reason many crimes are not displaced is because most neighborhood crime is local. As the chapter on Community Policing's impact on drugs will show, Operation Pressure Point in New York's Lower East Side, a focused crackdown on drugs, did not appear to displace the problem to other neighborhoods nearby. Areas vary in their ability to resist crime. Shut down a crack house in a decaying inner-city neighborhood and chances are that the operators will not simply open shop in an upscale area next door just because it is close. Over time, they may find another site, but not only has the effort reduced or eliminated problems in the meanwhile, helping all communities to become more crime-resistant holds the promise of providing long-term solutions.

Using such tactics as part of an overall Community Policing approach also means that not only will the department address the underlying environmental dynamics of disorder that play an important role in reducing and controlling crime, but providing CPOs who maintain a sustained presence in the area, identifying problems and solutions that can change over time, gives people in the community a chance to become involved in community-based, police-supervised initiatives. The goal is not to apply problem-oriented tactics on a one-shot basis, but as part of a continuing program in the community. Only by involving CPOs as the department's outreach specialists can police departments use such tactics most effectively.

In some ways, Community Policing provides elements of *community action* and *community development,* but as part of a decentralized police approach. It addresses both people problems and problems of neighborhood decay without launching an expensive new bureaucracy, but as part of restructuring the police role. The lesson perhaps that should be learned by comparing the success of programs such as the G.I. Bill and the failure of the War on Poverty is that the greatest gains appear to be made when opportunity is enhanced as a by-product of addressing a basic need rather than as the primary goal. Redefining and expanding the police role to include social and physical disorder as part of this new way of delivering decentralized, personalized police service may be the key to addressing the role that opportunity appears to play in crime.

Yet many people both inside and outside policing continue to argue that others should handle such problems, so that the police are free to concentrate on serious crime. As Wilson and Kelling point out, however, police officers may be able to cut through the bureaucratic maze better than anyone else. They refer to John Mudd's book *Neighborhood Services,* in which he talked about dealing with a rat problem – a rat in a restaurant is a problem for public health; in an apartment, the housing authority has jurisdiction; if it is lying dead in the street, it becomes the province of public works.[53] Over time, the CPO not only learns which department to call, but who within that department will help, and the clout of being a police officer can be invaluable in forcing agencies to cooperate in solving the problem.

A shocking crime in Detroit underscores why the police have the greatest interest in attacking neighborhood decay and why such problems are so urgent that they require police intervention. The incident involves a two-year-old girl who was allegedly taken from a local park by a 15-year-old suspect who then raped the child and dumped her into a trash bin where she was later found by two men who heard her crying. The girl was assaulted in a vacant building nearby, one of many abandoned "shells" in the neighborhood.

The *Detroit Free Press* quoted a woman who lives near a shell as saying, "We've been calling about these damn houses. They told us a lie that they would get them down in three months. It made me feel so bad I wanted to hurt somebody." Another neighbor reportedly said, "Basically, the problem is these burnt-out shells. Once they get rid of these, there's no place for this kind of thing to happen."[54] The article also reported that Wayne County Social Service officials were investigating whether neglect played a role. The child's aunt defended the girl's presence in the park, saying that there were roughly 20 other youngsters there at the time, and the girl had been taught not to cross streets alone or talk to strangers.

Without in any way suggesting that the individual responsible for that horrendous act is any less culpable, this shows that people outside policing grasp that the social and physical environment plays a dramatic role in crime. Local residents cared enough about the threat posed by the abandoned buildings to phone authorities demanding action, yet apparently the promised action was not taken, at least not in time. CPOs often have the additional *muscle* required to wrest results from agencies that often appear to drag their feet the most in helping areas that suffer the greatest problems.

The sustained presence of a CPO in the community might also have identified problems with unsupervised youngsters in the park. Depending on the circumstances, a CPO who is skilled in identifying potential problems might have embarked on a program to make home visits to warn families of the dangers in leaving children unguarded. Another solution might have been to involve concerned people in the neighborhood as volunteers in a coordinated effort to provide adult supervision.

A Community Policing approach means police departments can pinpoint problems and tailor the response to fit the precise need. In Morristown, New Jersey, this meant a CPO rewarded kids who helped beautify the area with a new teddy bear, an effort that has obvious benefits beyond enhancing the physical environment. In North Miami Beach, city code enforcement was moved into the department, to work directly with CPOs on addressing the problems of physical decay. An innovative effort outside Toronto involved training young people in crime prevention techniques, then having them train the elderly in how to protect themselves, not only to prevent their victimization but to reduce their fears about the young as potential predators, directly counterbalancing the TV image of young people as marauders. A CPO faced with the twin problems of a litter-strewn lot and loitering teens solved both with one stroke by agreeing to help the youngsters establish a new baseball team if they cleaned up the lot for their ball diamond.

Because the job demands learning about the various sources of help available, CPOs can also address social disorder by linking people with emotional problems to affordable and appropriate counseling and helping the homeless find shelter. If the area is plagued by panhandlers, the CPO can tailor the response to local needs and local resources. It might mean linking people to employment opportunities in the area, with the CPO's office as a clearinghouse. In other cases, it might mean involving juveniles in after-school activities so that they have less time to harass passersby. The virtue of the Community Policing approach is that the officers understand the nature of the challenge, have the opportunity to work with people on developing new solutions, and the CPO's sustained presence provides an opportunity to monitor the results. If it does not work, the CPO can work with people on trying new ideas. If it is successful, the CPO is there to make sure that it keeps working, altering and refining the initiative to fit changing needs.

Such efforts also demonstrate to people that they can regain control of their communities, and helplessness is an important element of fear. One of the biggest challenges that a CPO faces is the apathy that too much fear can spawn. A healthy dose of fear of crime can inspire positive action, but too much can paralyze people so that they will not take part. Once initial efforts targeted at physical and social disorder begin to make a visible difference, that can galvanize more people to get involved. Community Policing can also help channel the vigilante impulse into legitimate and positive efforts.

The potential downside, however, is that even though Community Policing can make communities safer overall, that can cause the crime rate to go up. While that sounds illogical, it means that, as people feel safer, they begin participating more in daily community life. This means more exposure, which can increase the opportunities for crimes to occur.

The difficulty lies in assessing the potential trade-off, since there is no simple formula that can tell us when the gain is worth the risk. And we should also remember that an increase in crime rates may prove temporary. More crimes might occur during the transition period until rising participation in community life reaches a point where people attain the *critical mass* necessary to tip the balance to the point where they can reclaim control of their neighborhoods.

This underscores why trying to understand what is happening in a community just by looking at crime statistics may be misleading. If some of the decline in crime rates over the past few years simply means that people have cut themselves off from life by hiding behind barred doors, the solution is a problem in itself. That is also why periodic ups and downs in crime rates are not a good indicator of Community Policing's true worth. Citizen satisfaction surveys in Newark and Flint verified that people say Community Policing makes them feel safer. And while it may be easy for people to say nice things about a program, dollars speak louder than words, so the fact that Flint voters have three times assessed themselves an extra millage to pay for the program may speak loudest of all.

Though the logic sounds convoluted, Community Policing's impact on fear of crime may almost be more important in making people feel safe than would any police effort that targets crime directly. As we learned in the last chapter, there are many kinds of crime for which the police have few solutions. There are also many factors, such as poverty and employment, that probably play a greater role in the rise and fall of crime rates than what any police activity can hope to achieve. But Community Policing's ability to reduce the disorder that makes neighborhoods inviting targets for crime not only offers the hope of making those places safer but it also makes people feel safer, which is equally important in enhancing their overall quality of life.

History shows crime will always be part of any society, but we cannot let our fears overwhelm us. We live in a country where too many people do not believe the police can help, so they hide behind locked doors or lash out on their own. People who are consumed by terror are a potential danger to themselves and others. Community Policing provides people a responsible and effective way to work within the system – and the bond between people and the police helps reduce the fears of another category of victim – police officers. Research on the Flint experiment showed that CPOs felt safer than their motor patrol counterparts.

What we must also remember is that fear of crime in many urban areas is a mirror held up to the overheated climate of violence that many young people grow up in, thinking that what they see is the way the world has to be. As a society, we must find ways to provide these young people at least a glimmer of what a better life would look like. By calming the chaos and grappling with the crime and fear that are part of many young people's daily lives, Community Policing is an important step in lowering the temperature, before an indelible image of violence and decay is burned so deeply into their minds that it becomes the imprint of how they will live in the future.

NOTES

[1]*Report to the Nation on Crime and Justice,* Second Edition, U.S. Dpeartment of Justice (Washington, DC: Bureau of Justice Statistics, March 1988), p. 114.

[2]*Ibid.*

[3]Harris, Lou, *Inside America* (New York: Vintage Book, a division of Random House, May 1987), p. 185.

[4]*Report to the Nation on Crime and Justice,* p.47.

[5]*Ibid.*

[6]*Ibid,* p. 28.

[7]*Ibid.*

[8]Skogan, Wesley G., *The Victims of Crime: Some National Survey Findings* in *Criminal Behavior in Social Systems,* edited by Anthony L. Guenther (Chicago: Rand-McNally), p. 137-138.

[9]*Ibid,* p. 140.

[10]*Report to the Nation on Crime and Justice,* p.47.

[11]*Ibid.*

[12]Burnham, David, *3 of 5 Slain by Police Here Are Black, Same as Arrest Rate, New York Times* (August 25, 1973), as quoted by Silberman, p. 163, see next reference.

[13]Silberman, Charles L., *Criminal Violence, Criminal Justice* (New York: Vintage Books, a division of Random House, January 1980), p. 161.

[14]Telephone interview with Joseph Darden, Dean of Urban Affairs Programs and Professor of Geography, Michigan State University, May 4, 1989.

[15]*The United States of Lyncherdom* in *Mark Twain on the Damned Human Race,* edited by Janet Smith (Hill and Wang, 1962).

[16]Lemann, Nicholas, *The Unfinished War – Part I, The Atlantic,* December 1988.

[17]*Ibid.*

[18]*Ibid.*

[19]*Ibid.*

[20]Adams, Henry H., *Harry Hopkins* (New York: Putnam, 1977).

[21]Cleaver, Eldridge, *Soul on Ice* (New York: Mc-Graw-Hill, 1968).

[22]Lemann, Nicholas, *The Unfinished War – Part II, The Atlantic,* January 1989.

[23]*Ibid.*

[24]*Report to the Nation on Crime and Justice,* p.47.

[25]*The Figgie Report on Fear of Crime: America Afraid, Part I-III* (Willoughby, OH: Research & Forecasts, Inc, sponsored by A-T-O, Inc, 1980).

See also *Policing and the Fear of Crime* by Mark H. Moore and Robert C. Trojanowicz, *Perspectives on Policing* series No. 3, a publication of the National Institute of Justice, U.S. Department of Justice, and the Program in Criminal Justice Policy and Management, John F. Kennedy School of Government, Harvard University, June 1988.

[26]Silberman, p. 13.

[27]Lapham, Lewis, *Images of Fear, Harper's* (May 1985), p. 43.

[28]*Ibid.*

[29]*Report to the Nation on Crime and Justice,* p. 100.

[30]Gross, Bertram, *Some Anticrime Proposals for Progressives, The Nation* (February 6, 1982), p. 139.

[31]Hernon, Jolene C., and Forst, Brian, *National Institute of Justice Research Report: The Criminal Justice Response to Victim Harm* (Washington, DC: U.S. Department of Justice, National Institute of Justice, May 1984), p. 48.

[32]Parks, Robert B., *Police Response to Victimization: Effects on Attitudes and Perceptions in Same Survey of the Victims of Crime,* edited by Wesley G. Skogan (Cambridge, MA: Ballenger, 1977), p. 101.

[33]*The Figgie Report,* p. 21.

[34]*Report to the Nation on Crime and Justice,* p.29.

[35]*Ibid.*

[36]*Ibid.*

[37]Skogan, p. 137.

[38]Ibid, p. 137-138.

[39]*Report to the Nation on Crime and Justice,* p.46.

[40]*Ibid,* p. 29.

[41]*Crime in the United States 1984* (Washington, DC: FBI Law Enforcement Bulletin, September 1985), p. 14.

[42]Corliss, Richard, *"Bad" Women and Brutal Men, Time* magazine (November 21, 1988), p. 127.

[43]Leyton, Elliott, *Hunting Humans: Inside the Minds of Mass Murderers,* previously published as *Compulsive Killers* (New York: Pocket Books, a division of Simon & Schuster, 1986), p. 123.

[44]*The Figgie Report.*

[45]Journalist Pete Hamill on the MacNeil-Lehrer News Hour segment on *Wilding* on PBS, May 1, 1989.

[46]*The Figgie Report.*

[47]*Ibid.*

[48]*Report to the Nation on Crime and Justice,* p.26.

[49]Warr, Mark, and Stafford, Mark, *Fear of Victimization: A Look at the Proximate Factors, Social Forces* (Volume 61, No., 4, June 1983), p. 1038.

[50]Skogan, Wesley F., and Maxfield, Michael G., *Coping With Crime* (Beverly Hills, CA: Sage Publications, 1981), p. 121.

[51]Wilson, James Q., and Kelling, George, L., *Broken Windows, The Atlantic Monthly* (March 1982), p. 29.

See also, *Police and Communities: The Quiet Revolution* by George L. Kelling, *Perspectives on Policing* series No. 1, a publication of the National Institute of Justice, U.S. Department of Justice, and the Program in Criminal Justice Policy and Management, John F. Kennedy School of Government, Harvard University, June 1988.

[52]Wilson, James Q., and Kelling, George L., *Making Neighborhoods Safe, The Atlantic,* February 1989, p. 47.

[53]Mudd, John, *Neighborhood Services* (New Haven, CT: Yale University Press, 1984).

[54]Mathews, Lori, and Fears, Darryl, *Teen held in rape of tot left in west side trash bin, Detroit Free Press,* May 2, 1989, p. 3A & p. 10A.

SECTION THREE

WHAT THE RESEARCH SHOWS

CHAPTER 6
Methods and Measures

by David L. Carter

*The meaning of things lies not in the things
themselves but in our attitude toward them.*
—Saint-Exupery

How Do We Decide What Works?

The previous chapters have provided a fundamental understanding of the Community Policing concept. At this point, we can reasonably ask: "How did the concept develop? What factors led to its evolution? What is the basis for determining if it works? What community programs have been implemented and assessed?" These important questions lie at the foundation of the Community Policing movement.

Community Policing did not simply emerge as an independent alternative to traditional policing strategies. Instead, it is based on a solid foundation of police-service-delivery research that has been conducted over the past two decades. Community Policing was not a goal, most likely not even an idea, in the early foundation research. Rather, the findings of the early research and events created a meandering path that eventually led to this concept.

In the late 1960s, police leaders, government officials, the academic community, and society began to question whether the police were performing their job in the most effective ways possible. Police clashes with Vietnam War protesters and civil rights demonstrators prompted closer scrutiny of police practices.

The 1967 President's Commission on Law Enforcement and Administration of Justice examined various aspects of policing. The Commission noted the need for important changes in:

- the quality of police personnel

- the quality of officer preparation and training

- management structure

- how police relate to the community

- how police deliver services to the community

Specifically, the Commission recommended that the police should establish a better dialogue with the community and should attempt to be more responsive to community needs.[1]

In 1968, two additional important series of government reports addressed the relationship between law enforcement and the community. Both the National Advisory Commission on Civil Disorders (Kerner Commission) and the National Commission on the Causes and Prevention of Violence examined the riots of the 1960s and the circumstances that contributed to civil disorder. Important findings indicated that the police had paid too little attention to effective organization and deployment strategies and also to community issues and concerns. Moreover, the police had not adequately explored their internal biases, and they had not seriously considered preventive or less coercive strategies to deal with civil disorder. It was also noted that there:

> ...is an evident inability of the police, as presently organized, manned [sic], financed, equipped, and led, to meet effectively all of the demands and expectations placed on them by the public. These inadequacies are evidenced in their inability to prevent a crime; their declining record in solving crimes known to them; their sluggish response to and indifferent investigation of all but major crimes or those involving important persons, businesses, or institutions. Particularly evident is the inability to deal effectively with crime in minority-populated ghettos – for reasons which involve minority group attitudes and non-cooperation as important as police attitudes, facilities, and efficiency.[2]

The implication was clear: law enforcement must establish an open dialogue with the community, deliver comprehensive services, and re-examine the traditional police organizational structure and processes. The civil unrest of that era signalled that a change in the style of policing was neeeded to synchronize law enforcement to the social change in the country. Policing must adopt a socio-technical approach, and balance that with its traditional approach. That is, not only *high tech* but also *high touch* must be made part of the world of policing.

While the Commission reports of 1967 and 1968 drew attention to many policing issues, there was no catalyst for change until Congress passed the Omnibus Crime Control and Safe Streets Act of 1968. For the first time ever, the federal government provided assistance for local criminal justice services. Among the many facets of the act were two that proved particularly important for the Community Policing movement – the Law Enforcement Education Program (LEEP) and the National Institute for Law Enforcement and Criminal Justice (NILECJ).

LEEP was a program to stimulate criminal justice personnel to attend college. In the case of police, the belief was that better-educated law enforcement officers would provide more responsive, more comprehensive, and more insightful police service. In the long term, as college-educated officers rose into police leadership positions, they would explore new approaches, with more creativity and better planning. The evidence since then is that these efforts produced progress toward these crucial goals.[3] In addition, with the growth of criminal justice programs in higher education, research on criminal justice issues expanded among both scholars and graduate students.

While pure research is desirable, there was also a need to stimulate research that could influence social and policy change. NILECJ provided the first substantive incentive, with commensurate financial support, to allow law enforcement personnel to learn more about what works, what does not work, and what might work.

Previously, such research had been sporadic. NILECJ was a cornerstone in the criminal justice research movement that was significantly expanded by private organizations, such as the Ford Foundation, Mott Foundation, Burden Foundation, Sage Foundation, and others, that sponsored police-directed research projects. Moreover, research in policing sponsored by the National Science Foundation gave important standards for methodological controls in law enforcement research.

With significant grant support from the Ford Foundation, the Police Foundation was organized to focus scientific inquiry into policing issues. Shortly afterward, the Police Executive Research Forum (PERF) was created. Made up of college-educated police executives from major jurisdictions, PERF adopted a charter that defines its role as an organization to explore police policy research issues, with the findings debated among the nation's policing leaders.

These important milestones set the stage for an environment of scientific inquiry that would challenge traditional policing assumptions, evaluate policing strategies, and test new police-service alternatives – the essential ingredients for new law enforcement programs. In the best tradition of integrating and applying research knowledge to new programs, Community Policing has been built on the findings of this research. While many important research projects have been conducted, we will look at some of the more critical efforts related to Community Policing, to illustrate the concept's birth and maturation.

A Note on Research Methods

Research on any subject is guided by methods designed to maximize the validity and reliability of the research results.[4] An inherent part of any research is to critique a project in light of the rigor used to collect and analyze data. This is, without question, an important dimension in the research process, for it permits input and debate as a means to ensure the accuracy of the findings and it allows for exploring possible alternative explanations of the results.

In a laboratory or some other setting that permits complete control of the variables, the research protocol can be quite vigorous. However, in *real world* settings, such as police departments, research methods must take second place to pragmatic concerns, such as the responsibility to protect the public and the need to respond to calls for service. Because of the less stringent methods of this type of research, there are more points where the accuracy of the findings can be questioned.

To be sure, most research in law enforcement has been critiqued – sometimes aggressively – because all variables cannot be controlled. In the research projects discussed, there have been critics who disagree with the findings. With this *caveat* in mind, the results reported represent the findings of the project researchers and the results as generally accepted in police research literature.

The Research Foundation for Community Policing

There is a broad body of research in law enforcement that has given us insight into the nature of policing, particularly into the patrol function. Some noteworthy research warrants special attention.

- **Preventive Patrol** – Perhaps one of the most important – and controversial – research projects occurred in 1972, early in law enforcement's contemporary research history. The Kansas City (Missouri) Police Department's (KCPD) Preventive Patrol Study was designed to challenge a sacred police strategy. Essentially, the project, conducted under the auspices of the Police Foundation, asked whether marked, random police patrol truly prevented crime.

Three controlled levels of routine preventive patrol were used in the experimental areas. One area, termed *reactive,* received no preventive patrol. Officers entered the area only in response to citizen calls for assistance. This, in effect, substantially reduced police visibility in that area. In the second area, called *proactive,* police visibility was increased two to three times its usual level. In the third area, termed *control,* the normal level of patrol was maintained. Analysis of the data gathered revealed that the three areas experienced no significant differences in the level of crime, citizens' attitudes toward police services, citizens' fear of crime, police response time, or citizens' satisfaction with police response time.[5]

Basically, the study found that *preventive patrol* was not only uncommitted time, but it was also non-productive time. The findings do not imply that patrol officers are unnecessary. Rather, they suggest that traditional assumptions about the effect of random police patrol on crime and citizens' attitudes may be in error. Furthermore, they suggest that law enforcement agencies are wasting valuable resources by continuing or expanding traditional patrol procedures. Therefore, police executives should explore how police resources could be better used and what police processes may be more effective in dealing with crime problems and citizen concerns. After digesting the results of their project, KCPD researchers observed, "[W]e must now begin revising our expectations as to the police role in society."[6]

The broader implications of this research are that the isolation of the officer in the police car and enslaving the officer to the radio have resulted in less dialogue between the police and the community. Policing strategies designed to expedite the handling of calls, and therefore permit fewer officers to cover a broader area, have also made the police less responsive to – and less aware of – community needs and desires. In reviewing the research on police patrol, Kelling and Fogel wrote that studies:

> ...suggest that available evidence supports a view that the critical issue for police today is how to overcome the alienation of well-intentioned police strategies which have had the unintended consequence of alienating citizens.[7]

Preventive patrol is a well-intentioned strategy that requires reconsideration. Based on what was learned in Kansas City, Community Policing has attempted to better use uncommitted patrol time. Further, it has sought to bring the police and community closer together, thereby narrowing the distance created when a patrol car was interposed between them. Community Policing also attempts to reduce citizens' fear of crime and increase citizen satisfaction with the police – two factors that preventive patrol apparently did not improve.

- **Response Time** – Another factor examined in the KCPD Preventive Patrol Study was the effect of the patrol experiment on officer response time. Traditionally, response time was broadly defined as the amount of time it takes police officers to respond to a citizen's call for assistance. The assumption was that, the lower the response time, the greater the chance of apprehending the criminal perpetrator. It was further assumed that a faster response would indicate the police are more efficient and that this would also add to citizen satisfaction with police service.

  Using some general measures, the Preventive Patrol Study found that response time and citizen attitudes did not vary among the three experimental models. Indeed, the researchers found "that response time is a complex indicator determined not only by distance and speed, but also the attitude of officer and beat juxtaposition."[8] Despite the intuitive appearance of its value, response time obviously deserved further research.

  The response time finding continued to be debated because of the uncertain nature of its relevance and what this could mean in terms of police operations. One argument for maintaining traditional patrol was the need to have police officers available for rapid response to calls. Thus, any new patrol programs based on the preventive patrol finding was tempered by the need to make sure officers could respond rapidly to calls. These issues led to a NILECJ research grant for a new project – the Kansas City Response Time Study.

  Two fundamental questions were addressed by this study: What effect does response time have on "producing favorable crime outcomes"? What is the effect of response time on citizen satisfaction with police? On the "crime effects" issue, the Kansas City Study found:

  > First, although some patrol strategies affect police response time, a large proportion of Part I crimes are not susceptible to the impact of rapid police response. Secondly, for that proportion of crimes that can be influenced by response time, the time taken (by citizens) to report the incident largely predetermines the effect of police response time. Thirdly, the factors which produce reporting delays are primarily citizens' attitudes and voluntary actions rather than uncontrollable problems they encounter. Fourthly, if reporting time is not so long as to hamper police efforts, prompt field officer response has significant impact on certain types of crime (notably robbery) but limited impact on crime outcomes in general. Explicit in the argu-

ments for increasing or altering resources to reduce response time is the assumption that rapid response time is essential in producing favorable crime outcomes in a substantial proportion of serious crimes. However, *this assumption is dubious, given the results of this study.* (Emphasis added.)[9]

On the issue of citizen satisfaction, the analysis revealed that the primary determinant of citizen satisfaction was a citizen's perceptions and expectations concerning police response. The second most important determinant was the citizen's perception of the importance of response time in obtaining a favorable outcome. The amount of time elapsed was not, in itself, an important determinant. Rather, it was how well the actual response time matched the citizen's expectation. As expected, if the response took longer than the people expected, they were less satisfied. Similarly, those who felt a rapid response would make a positive difference were even more unhappy when the response took longer than expected.[10] Overall, the research has "shown that the difference between experienced and anticipated response time is a major determinant of citizen satisfaction."[11]

Since these findings flew in the face of the traditional wisdom, the results were widely debated. "In 1977, police managers were jolted by the results of the KCPD study of response time.... [They] were skeptical as to whether their findings would apply to [other] cities."[12]

As a result, PERF conducted a follow-up study on crime-reporting patterns of citizens in San Diego, Peoria, Rochester, and Jacksonville-Duval County (Florida). While the PERF study measured some other factors as well, the Kansas City findings were confirmed – sophisticated technology and deployment strategies to reduce response time were well-intentioned, but misguided. The PERF report concluded:

> ...police departments' resources, long focused toward rapid response to all crime calls, would have to be reallocated to other, attainable objectives.... One answer [is] to adopt a strategy of Community Policing in which the police spend more time cementing relationships with residents of neighborhoods.[13]

Since fast response time neither addressed serious crime effectively nor enhanced citizen satisfaction, this research paved the way for developing alternative police strategies. Community Policing because of its closer relationship with citizens and its strategic efforts in crime prevention and criminal apprehension, attempts to fulfill these needs.

- **Differential Police Response** – In light of the findings from the preventive patrol experiment and the response time research, a number of alternative patrol management strategies were explored, including Differential Police Response (DPR). Traditionally, police calls have been dispatched in the order they were received, except for life-threatening situations, which received immediate attention. DPR recognizes that different calls should be assigned different priorities, and it also develops alternative sources and methods for handling calls.

The National Institute of Justice conducted DPR field tests in Garden Grove (California), Greensboro (North Carolina), and Toledo (Ohio). The objectives were to:

- Reduce the number of non-emergency calls for service handled by immediate mobile response.

- Increase the number of non-emergency calls for service handled by a telephone report unit, by delayed mobile response, or by other alternative responses.

- Decrease the amount of time patrol units spent answering calls for service and increase the amount of time available for crime prevention or other activities.

- Increase the availability of patrol units to respond rapidly to emergency calls.

- Provide satisfactory explanations to citizens when they called for service about how their call would be handled.

- Provide satisfactory responses to citizens for resolving their calls for service.[14]

DPR is a resource/time management plan that matches needs to resources and expertise. It permits flexibility in handling calls and contributes both to responsiveness to community needs and efficiency in police operations. An earlier study of DPR done in Birmingham (Alabama) by PERF found that the system allowed patrol officers more time for crime-focused activities, such as investigation and prevention, as well as community service and administration.[15]

In the NIJ field test of DPR, several key findings have important implications for Community Policing:

- Police departments can achieve a sizeable reduction in the number of non-emergency calls for service handled by immediate mobile dispatch, without sacrificing citizen satisfaction.

- The results of the baseline citizen surveys showed an overall high public willingness to accept alternatives to immediate dispatch of a patrol unit for non-emergency calls.

- Three of four callers were willing to accept delays of up to an hour for non-emergency calls.

- As expected, there was a greater willingness to accept delays for calls that did not involve potential danger or threats.

- Citizen satisfaction with alternate services provided was high.

- Alternate responses are less costly than traditional mobile responses, and productivity levels are much higher for personnel using alternatives.[16]

The results imply that citizens want their problems handled when they call the police, but the response does not always have to come from a traditional police officer. The key element is the *response,* not the *method.*

The results also indicate that community education can help the public cooperate with the police on alternate problem-solving methods. Like the response-time research, the DPR evaluation found that informing the public about what would be done and how much time it would take was the key.

Since DPR is also a time-management strategy, it provides patrol officers more time for other Community Policing and problem-solving activities. Thus, DPR provides better responsiveness to citizen needs and demands, more efficient use of police resources, and greater levels of citizen satisfaction, all of which are important in a Community Policing effort.

- **Patrol Deployment** – The patrol deployment of officers has been of constant concern for police administrators. Statistics show the tremendous variability in deployment. In different places in the United States, there can be anywhere from zero to 55 officers for every 1,000 citizens – anywhere from zero (in Alaska) to 8,667 officers (in New York City) for each 100 square miles.[17] In between are distributions that vary so much that we can draw no meaningful conclusions. There is no single factor or ratio that says what the *ideal* police strength for a given area should be. The two most important variables are the resources available and the tasks officers must perform – how many officers are available for performing what functions?

Deployment decisions vary with the area, shift, and nature of the community. The types of calls and demands for police service will also influence deployment patterns. The question that must be answered is: given the number of personnel available, how can the department most effectively perform the functions the community expects?

The answer lies largely in realizing that deploying officers based on numerical demands makes no sense unless we look first at what we are trying to achieve and then figure out how to match the officers available to those needs. The goal is to balance quantity and quality – to answer calls for service, but in ways that address the community's true needs most effectively.

Research on alternate patrol deployment has explored issues such as: mathematical modelling, split-force patrol, directed patrol, and one- versus two-officer patrol cars.[18] The results substantiate several findings:

- No universal deployment tactic can be effectively applied to all law enforcement agencies, even agencies within defined size ranges.

- Different approaches can be used by multiple agencies as long as the approach is modified to meet the unique characteristics, demands, and resources of each.

- New deployment strategies should not be developed without evaluating the department's needs in terms of goals and objectives.

- Any new deployment plan should have an evaluation component and periodic assessments so it can be tailored to meet these results.

- Traditional deployment strategies, though effective in answering calls received, are inefficient when measured against citizen demands – they intervene in incidents without solving broader problems.

Though deployment research does not directly address Community Policing, the findings support the concept, and these findings can help shape Community Policing initiatives:

- *One- Versus Two-Officer Patrols* – The most comprehensive study of how many officers are optimal was the San Diego research that found that on variables such as cost, number of calls handled, arrests, response time, and handling administrative duties, one-officer units are far more efficient and clearly as effective as two-officer patrols.[19] The most controversial – at least the most emotional – issue is officer safety. The San Diego study found:

> ...both single and multiple... units had approximately equal involvement in assaults on officers. However, two-officer units were shown to have been involved in resisting arrest situations (and consequently, in total critical incidents) more frequently than were one-officer units, despite the fact that the units had equivalent exposure to potentially hazardous situations overall, and to arrest situations in particular. The groups had equivalent involvement in police vehicle accidents and had experienced equivalent exposure in terms of miles driven. ...two-officer units were found to be more frequently involved in assaults on officers, in resisting arrest situations, and in total critical incidents than were one-officer units. ...*The weight of evidence from this analysis supports the conclusion that one-officer patrol unit staffing was safer for officers.* (Emphasis added.)[20]

- *Team Policing* – This approach exhibits a wide variation in structure, responsibilities, and organizational intent:

> The common feature linking most team policing programs is their reliance on the notions of *decentralization* and *generalization.* Thus, the hypothesis underlying team policing is that effective patrol and other services can be provided in an efficient manner via a decentralized (sometimes neighborhood-based) police department consisting of officers who are generalists in the law enforcement field.[21]

    The effects of team policing projects are mixed. In many programs, the concept was well developed, but they lacked clear policy direction. Furthermore, many evaluations were methodologically weak.[22] Despite these limitations, team policing established a conceptual foundation that was ultimately strengthened and redefined in Community Policing.

- *Specialized Patrol* – These include split-force patrol (for example, in Wilmington, Delaware), directed patrol (in Kansas City), low visibility patrol (New York, Boston, Nashville, Memphis, San Francisco, Miami), high visibility patrol (Alexandria, Cleveland, San Jose), and management of demand (Wilmington).[23] The premise underlying these projects was that police productivity would improve if the two basic patrol activities – response to calls for service and general patrol – were separated, as a better way of using personnel. The evaluations consistently showed that effectiveness did not change, but efficiency improved with specialized patrol.

These successes spurred attempts to refine specialized patrol so that it would also be more effective. The Wilmington Management of Demand Project adopted alternate "response strategies" to address the unique demands placed on the police department by citizens. The result was that the police were better able to assess the demand for police services (both crime and non-crime) and respond more effectively to those demands. The concept is dynamic because the police response changes when demand changes.[24]

- **The Effect of Deployment Research** – The combined effect of the research on various aspects of deployment was to encourage departments to reassess their approach and consider new alternatives. The research highlighted the fact that the police have both crime and service responsibilities and that it may not always make sense to use two officers instead of one. Team policing emerged as a potentially important concept in putting the officer in closer contact with neighborhood problems, but one that needed stronger direction and better evaluation.

  At the same time, other departments focused on using specialized patrol to improve overall efficiency. The Wilmington Management by Demand Project refined the concept further by adding an analytic element so that police would be more responsive to citizen demands.

  Each deployment strategy added to the research foundation about patrol operations that led to experimenting with the next logical step: Community Policing.

Collateral Research in Support of Community Policing

Beyond patrol-based research, other projects have examined issues that relate to Community Policing. While most have not been conducted on Community Policing efforts, their implications are nonetheless important for understanding the application of the concept.

- **Police Staffing** – A common statistic cited in the literature is that only 10 % of a patrol officer's on-duty time is spent on crime-related activities[25] and this includes answering calls, investigation, writing reports, booking arrestees, and testifying in court. The remaining 90 % of an officer's time is spent handling service calls (though some admittedly can evolve into an arrest), traffic enforcement and control, information gathering, and uncommitted patrol time.Certainly this is, at best, an average that varies by jurisdiction, beat, time, and season. Despite the variance, it is the author's experience that even in the nation's largest cities and in the busiest patrol districts, there is a surprising amount of uncommitted patrol time. Moreover, the vast majority of calls received are non-crime or, at the most, *peripheral* crime calls. (That is, there is no immediate crime, but the situation could evolve into a crime, such as a potential assault at a domestic disturbance.)

This implies that traditional patrol operations are inefficient and perhaps misdirected – that there is a significant amount of wasted time. We can infer therefore that police officers have time to perform other duties. To neglect this implication risks decreasing both the efficiency and effectiveness of the police force, and these implications suggest that Community Policing can make better use of an officer's on-duty time.

Interestingly, research by the National Center for Community Policing (notably in Flint, Michigan; Aurora, Colorado; Alexandria, Virginia; and McAllen, Texas) indicates that while the public wants the police to respond to crimes, they have equally strong demands for order maintenance and service tasks (such as barking dogs, abandoned cars, and other quality-of-life issues). This is reinforced by citizen surveys performed by the police departments in Madison, Wisconsin, and Fort Collins, Colorado. Thus, the public demand for police response to service calls will contribute to the proportionately lower numbers of crime calls.

- **Performance Measures** – An on-going problem has been how police managers can measure police peformance. Traditional quantitative measures – numbers of arrests, reports written, calls answered, miles driven, tickets issued, etc. – do not directly address the nature of the police function and the delivery of police services. The notable advantage of such measures is that they are relatively easy to collect, document, and compare.

  Ideally, quality measures of an individual officer's performance should be collected – communication skills, how the officer relates to the public, how the officer evaluates different situations, and the quality of decisions made – all would tell us what we really want to know about the officer's effectiveness. Unfortunately, not only is this information difficult to collect, such subjective assessments might be challenged if made part of an officer's performance evaluation.

  Research suggests that police agencies should strive for a balance between qualitative and quantitative measures.[26] To do this, police administrators must first clearly establish the goals it is trying to accomplish. Then, programs must be implemented to achieve these goals, with specific officer responsibilities spelled out. Officers would then be evaluated on the criteria detailed in the program.

In some cases, evaluation methods would need to be non-traditional. It might mean meeting with the citizens the officer has contacted. It could mean reviewing the officer's plans to determine the progress made. Community Policing officers might be asked to perform self-evaluations. In traditional police patrol, there are typically no unique programs or plans on which officers may be individually evaluated. Moreover, as noted previously, using measures associated with preventive patrol or response time would be misleading. Therefore, the performance of the individual and the police organization as a whole requires comprehensive and specific new plans for officer performance measures.

Community Policing affords a wider range of variables that can be measured, and it requires that officers use initiative and creativity. Qualitative measures are particularly suitable to evaluating Community Policing responsibilities, and they can provide an important barometer of officer activity and success, as well as a measure of organizational goals.

- **Job Enrichment/Job Enlargement** – Job enrichment refers to increasing an employee's quality of life in the workplace, while job enlargement refers to allowing an employee broader responsibilities. Together they improve morale and job satisfaction, increase individual decision-making, promote innovation and power sharing, and involve subordinates in policy development and organizational plans.

  Though the literature shows that job satisfaction may not improve individual performance, it does show that it contributes to lower turnover, less absenteeism and tardiness, and fewer grievances. Other research showed high job satisfaction is a good predictor of longer life: conversely, lower satisfaction is correlated with various mental and physical illnesses. The research also indicates morale and job satisfaction are positively related to productivity, though these are mutually reciprocating variables – that is, higher productivity contributes to greater satisfaction and vice versa.[27]

  Law enforcement has traditionally meant a rigid organizational environment. Officers have not been urged to be creative or to deviate from standard procedures. Rather, they have been told to adhere strictly to custom and practice. This rigidity contributes to complacency and to occupational lethargy, if not lower job satisfaction. In comparison, Community Policing can be professionally stimulating, by providing the officers with challenges, opportunities for innovation, and rewards for creative solutions. By providing both job enrichment and job enlargement, Community Policing may contribute to lower attrition and a higher quality of occupational life.

- **Public Perceptions of the Police** – In general, people are supportive of the police. They feel that the police are fundamentally honest, generally free of corruption, do not discriminate, and do not regularly use excessive force. However, after stratifying the population into different groups, the picture changes somewhat. Of particular importance is that blacks and Hispanics are less supportive of the police in general and more likely to feel the police discriminate and use excessive force. Furthermore, blacks more often believe they receive poorer service from the police than whites do, and Hispanics feel they receive inadequate police protection.[28] It is also important to recognize that minority groups have the highest victimization rates and that the majority of police calls come from lower-income minorities, therefore, the citizens who rely most on police services also rate them the lowest. This should send a message to police administration that more attention must be given to the needs and quality of service afforded those who rely most on law enforcement agencies.

- **Citizen Demands for Police Service** – Crime analysis has – and continues – to provide important information on crime trends and therefore on police priorities. However, these sophisticated analytic techniques and computer-driven reporting methods mean that law enforcement has drifted away from communicating with average citizens. The emphasis instead is on using data from a sample of calls and reported crimes, though these can skew the perspective concerning what people really want from their police. While citizens agree that having the police respond to serious crimes is important, they also want the police to help with minor - but annoying – problems, such as abandoned cars, barking dogs, and juvenile vandalism and trespassing.

    The police must find ways to listen to people and establish a dialogue to determine the types of services they want. Then, those needs must actually be addressed and not ignored or given lip service. Preliminary research indicates that responding to community needs on these minor calls may significantly increase citizen satisfaction and confidence in their police.[29] Madison (Wisconsin), Aurora and Fort Collins (Colorado), McAllen (Texas), and Lansing (Michigan) are among the cities that have surveyed citizens to define the kinds of problems the police should address and to identify the public's perceptions about the strengths and weaknesses of police programs.

- **Police/Community Relations** – Since the genesis of the community relations movement by the National Conference of Christians and Jews and the National Institutes held at Michigan State University, there has been an on-going search to find the best means to establish effective police/community relations.[30] The approaches have included special programming, police training programs, community education, and special police units. As the concept evolved, the research pointed to the need for two major elements. First, the police must recognize that they receive their mandate from the community and are responsible to the community in the performance of their task. Second, community relations must be a product of total police operations involving all personnel – not the function of a special unit. Therefore, good relations with the community is a by-product of how the entire police department handles its tasks, and Community Policing helps in that effort. The lessons learned about culture, discrimination, citizens' perceptions of the police, and police isolation provided important direction for the evolving Community Policing movement.

- **Integrated Criminal Apprehension Program (ICAP)** - In 1975, the Law Enforcement Assistance Administration (LEAA) began funding of the Integrated Criminal Apprehension Program that eventually was implemented in more than 50 U.S. cities. ICAP represented a synthesis of the research in policing that attempted to maximize the effectiveness of the patrol function. Originally developed as the Patrol Emphasis Program (PEP), ICAP was intended to direct patrol resources toward crime problems that were identified through intensive crime analysis. It was envisioned as an operations support concept that touched on all aspects of patrol operations, based on previous research. ICAP programming relied on projects such as patrol workload management, directed patrol, managing criminal investigations, and managing patrol operations.

    The focal point of ICAP was crime analysis. Based on detailed analysis of crime trends; suspects' MOs; characteristics of trends; demographic, seasonal, and time characteristics, etc., ICAP would identify problems to be addressed by the patrol force. Relying on the previous patrol-related research, ICAP would analyze potential police responses to address the problem, select the most reasonable alternative – based on resources, potential effect, and nature of the strategy – and implement the response. Ideally, this process would utilize the best empirical knowledge related to criminal apprehension following a scientific approach to problem-solving.

    The effectiveness of ICAP was mixed. Part of this was due to the complexity of the concept. It first required skilled crime analysts with expertise (and knowledge) about variable patrol and crime apprehension strategies. Moreover, ICAP was a fluid concept that required different organizational responses to various problems. The inherent nature of the police organization - even in enlightened departments – is dogmatic and bureaucratic. These facets made the needed flexibility essential to ICAP more difficult to achieve. Another problem was the conceptual nature of ICAP. While relying on a solid foundation of research, the concept was not concrete. It was a contextual application of the research to variable situations. As such, it was simply difficult for many to grasp the breadth of the concept. While there are scientific components of ICAP, it can best be viewed as a systematic planning process designed to enhance all aspects of police service delivery.[31]

    ICAP had a direct influence on the development of Problem-Oriented Policing because of the emphasis on problem identification and response through crime analysis. Concurrently, many of the problems identified were found to be of a non-crime or peripheral crime nature, requiring the police to respond in non-traditional ways. Emerging from this desire to find non-traditional responses to solve quality of life problems was a tendency for the police to *get closer to the community.*

Summarizing the Research Related to Community Policing

The findings of these various research projects have had important implications in the development of Community Policing. Since the research shows that as little as 10 % of an officer's time may be spent on crime and a significant amount of time is spent on service calls, this has implications in patrol force programming. Furthermore, since we have learned that patrol officers spend much of their time on uncommitted patrol, which does not prevent crime, there is an obvious need to make better use of that time.

Further research showed that rapid response may not help catch criminals, yet people become dissatisfied with the police if they take longer than expected. How can this discrepancy be reconciled? Consider also how complicated it is for a police administrator to balance the need to assign officers to new programs, yet maintain enough patrol cars to provide rapid response, while making sure this does not lead to wasting more time on uncommitted patrol. The research further indicated that minority communities are the least satisfied with the police and they feel they are not responding to their demands – and their concerns appear justified.

From a management perspective, a prudent manager wants useful measures to gauge the efficiency and effectiveness of his personnel, measures that will also tell him how well the department overall is meeting its goals. At the same time, administrators must strive to enrich and enlarge the jobs they supervise, to achieve the best work environment.

Though it is not a panacea, Community Policing addresses all these needs. By reallocating the patrol officer's time, Community Policing makes better use of personnel. Furthermore, by getting close to the community and establishing a dialogue with citizens, the public develops a different – and more accurate – measure by which to gauge an officer's competence and by which to determine their satisfaction with police service. That dialogue with the community also allows people a voice in defining and prioritizing their needs. This targeted response also contributes to greater satisfaction on the part of minorities and helps establish better police/community relations.

By the same token, when an officer is given the mandate to diagnose community problems and be creative in developing solutions, he serves in many new roles – community organizer, facilitator, educator, referral resource, and law enforcement officer – and this enriches and enlarges the job.

No one argues that Community Policing is the answer to all problems the police face. Rather, Community Policing responds to many of the concerns and questions posed by the research, as it serves as the framework for new program development. Research provides an important backdrop for understanding the genesis of the Community Policing model.

Community Policing Models

The number of departments that have adopted Community Policing has grown dramatically the past few years. Perhaps the most intensively evaluated early effort, the Flint Neighborhood Foot Patrol, will be discussed in detail in the next chapter. Since then, many other program models have been developed and assessed, as noted in the work of Trojanowicz and the extensive evaluations by Rosenbaum.[32] A brief review of selected, representative projects provides a glimpse of the different structures that have been used and what the efforts have accomplished:

- **Problem-Oriented Policing: Newport News (Virginia)**

Based on the concept of problem-solving discussed by Professor Herman Goldstein,[33] experimentation with alternate means of police responses to community problems evolved. Following a pilot test of the concept,[34] the National Institute of Justice funded the comprehensively evaluated Problem-Oriented Policing (POP) program in Newport News, Virginia (see the Community Close-Up on Newport News in the back of this book).[35] POP involves looking at police responsibilities from a different perspective. The police have traditionally viewed crimes and calls for service as individual *incidents*. The police response is therefore *reactive*, and they handle the incident by investigating what happened and dealing with the components posed by the individual occurrence. In POP instead:

> ...police go beyond individual crimes and calls for service and take on the underlying problems that create them. To understand problems, police collect facts from a wide variety of sources, from outside as well as inside police agencies. To develop and implement solutions, police enlist the support of other public and private agencies and individuals. *Problem-oriented policing is a department-wide strategy aimed at solving persistent community problems. Police identify, analyze, and respond to the underlying circumstances that create incidents.*[36] (Emphasis in original.)

Thus, POP is a *proactive* strategy requiring a diagnosis of community problems and integrating the community in the response. The National Institute of Justice (NIJ) sponsored an evaluation of the program to test two premises: (1) that police officers in all assignments could use these techniques as part of their daily routine and (2) their problem-solving efforts would be effective. The evaluation found both were true. While recognizing that officers will always have to respond to incidents, the POP approach made better use of departmental resources, while increasing officer effectiveness.

The success of the Newport News experiment convinced NIJ to fund an extension of POP targeted specifically at drugs, in San Diego, Tulsa, Atlanta, and Philadelphia. The project is being conducted by PERF and no results are yet available. The hope, however, is that POP will serve as a Community Policing tool applicable to both general and directed police responsibilities.

- **Experimental Policing District: Madison (Wisconsin)**

The Madison Police Department is currently evaluating its Experimental Policing District (EPD)(see the Community Close-Up on Madison in the back of this book). In many ways, EPD is a refined, contemporarily managed team policing program, employing the program philosophy of Community Policing:

> This new organization [is] a full-service, mini-police department. The Experimental Policing District provides three functions: (1) neighborhood patrol (Community Policing), (2) around-the-clock, motorized patrol for emergency responses and traffic duties, and (3) investigative "follow-up" services. The EPD not only experiments with a service delivery strategy, it also experiments with some new concepts in work relationships and supervisory styles. The EPD organization attempts to put in place a teamwork approach to organizing work and doing the job; establishing individual professional responsibility with a minimum amount of direct supervision; a cooperative, relaxing, and enriching work atmosphere; and a commitment to achieve excellence in what we do.[37]

Beyond using the Community Policing philosophy of service delivery and community involvement, two important components of the Madison program are worthy of special note. First is the strong emphasis on the team approach and participatory management. Officers have substantive input into both operational and policy decisions. Second is the management environment. Job satisfaction, morale, individual growth, job enrichment, and job enlargement are all fundamental elements in EPD's management structure. This project is also currently being evaluated with NIJ support. While no conclusions can yet be drawn on its effectiveness, positive reactions to the management approach have been echoed by the officers involved.

● **Community Foot Patrol Officer (CFPO): Baltimore County (Maryland)**

The genesis of the Community Foot Patrol Officer (CFPO) program can be found in Balitmore County's Citizen-Oriented Police Enforcement (COPE) program (see the *Community Close-up* on Baltimore County in the back of this book). COPE was designed to use the problem-oriented policing approach to identify and reduce fear of crime.[38] COPE's success helped influence the department to organize a full Community Policing approach. The mission of the CFPO is:

> ...to gain the trust and confidence of citizens within targeted communities to identify the true origins of their fears and concerns about crime and other forms of community disorder... and to seek appropriate solutions. While some of the identified problems may call for traditional police tactics, CFPOs must also consider nontraditional approaches and to use their newly established partnerships to encourage citizen "self help" responses within the community.[39]

The department reinforces that CFPOs are full-service law enforcement officers who not only walk foot beats but also identify problems, interact with the community, diagnose potential problems, and develop solutions that use resources from both inside and outside the department. Community foot patrol officers are evaluated on three types of information:

● *Input data* – describing the community and problems targeted.

● *Activity data* – describing the tasks and activities performed by the CFPO.

● *Results data* – describing the outcomes of CFPO actions: the officer's progress in solving community problems.

Note that these factors do not rely solely on traditional quantitative measures, but on qualitative factors that reflect both effort and accomplishment.

• Neighborhood-Oriented Policing: Houston (Texas)

The Houston Community Policing plan was implemented hand-in-hand with a new department-wide decentralization plan. Similar in concept to the Madison EPD, each of four command stations in Houston will have a "team of police officers and their supervisors [who] will be responsible for planning and implementing policing strategies, with the cooperation of neighborhood residents, to address crime problems within specific neighborhood service areas."[40]

The Houston plan spells out the organization values related to Neighborhood-Oriented Policing. Among them is the recognition that crime prevention is the *primary* priority of the police department: that the police and community must work openly and cooperatively in dealing with crime problems: and that the department will use its resources in an attempt to increase the overall quality of life in Houston, rather than simply focusing on individual crimes and crime trends.

An assessment of the initial test of Houston's Community Policing approach found that the program:

> ...appears to have been successful in reducing citizens' levels of fear and in improving their perceptions of their neighborhood and their attitudes toward the police.... The lack of positive program effects for blacks and renters may be a function of their lower levels of awareness of the program. The community station relied, in part, on established civic organizations to attract residents to station programs. To the extent that blacks and renters are less likely to be members of these organizations, the program needs to rely on other means of reaching these people.[41]

With the development of the combined command station/neighborhood policing plan, these limitations have been addressed by alternate efforts that are more citizen directed, to increase citizen involvement. The problem in the test phase, where blacks and renters had not become involved, points out the importance of using broad-based, creative means to obtain the greatest participation possible.

• Foot Patrol and Fear Reduction: Newark (New Jersey)

Community Policing in Newark developed in stages, with evaluations conducted by the Police Foundation. First was the Newark Foot Patrol Experiment. After passage of the Safe and Clean Neighborhood Act, Newark used its funding to implement foot patrol:

The goal of the program [was] to develop safe neighborhoods through the use of walking police officers. Its philosophy [was] that the uniformed walking patrol officers, by being highly visible on the streets, [were] not only helping to prevent crime and enforce the laws, but at the same time [were] helping to restore confidence in citizens and... improving public relations with merchants and residents.[42]

Results showed that citizens were more aware of the police presence in foot patrol areas. Residents also felt serious crime had diminished in their neighorhoods and said they felt safer there. These findings were particularly important because there was no statistical difference in either reported crime or victimization (determined by surveys) between the foot patrol and non-foot patrol areas.[43] Thus, reduction of fear of crime and improved perceptions of safety were achieved simply by using foot patrol.

After this evaluation, the department implemented additional Community Policing strategies, as part of the NIJ-sponsored Houston-Newark Fear Reduction Program. This project employed a wider range of activities, including community newsletters and efforts to reduce the *signs of crime* – neither of which had a significant effect in reducing fear or preventing crime. However, the Coordinated Community Policing Program, designed to increase police/community information exchange and to manage both social disorder and physical deterioration, did have a significant positive impact.[44] This points to the importance of citizen involvement in Community Policing, and it provides strong evidence that one-way, proactive, community-based police strategies alone are not sufficient.

• Police Mini-Stations: Detroit (Michigan)

In the Detroit model, defined areas of the city were targeted as neighborhoods where the quality of life could be enhanced by decentralized, community-based police mini-stations. To be included, neighborhoods had to meet certain criteria:

- Evidence of crime problems.

- Predominantly residential.

- Areas where the police had received high numbers of calls for service.

- Discernible physical, social, or cultural boundaries.

The foundation of the program rested on two important concepts: (1) the officer had to become acquainted with the residents in the area and diagnose their unique crime and quality of life problems, and (2) the mini-station had to involve citizen volunteers in multiple capacities in order to develop programs that would address neighborhood problems.

Mini-stations officers were given complete responsibility for developing programs in their assigned areas. For example, the officers found office space and arranged for donations of furnishings. Not only did this force the officer to meet and talk with people in the community, but the residents immediately became involved and their donations signified their investment in the program's future success.

The Detroit program was not formally evaluated, but some internal assessments found positive results. For example, neighborhood and vertical (i.e., high-rise apartments and businesses) watch memberships increased, and participation levels were sustained. Intelligence information and crime clearances increased, while positive comments to the police department and city manager became commonplace. In addition, informal feedback from the officers involved indicated that residents told them they appreciated the program, and the improvement in the appearance of some neighborhoods was obvious. These successes spurred the expansion of the program to other portions of the city.[45]

Critiques of Community Policing Research

The early development and assessment of initiatives that ultimately led to Community Policing occurred with little consistency between the projects. In the early cases – for example, Flint, Houston, Newark, and Baltimore County – there was little coordination between the programs. The programs had conceptually similar ideas that researchers and administrators wanted tested to see if they would work.

Most criticism of Community Policing programs can be viewed from two perspectives: (1) research/evaluation design and (2) concept. In the case of the former, Greene and Taylor[46] identify several deficiences in the tested programs. These include inadequate operationalization of "community," confusion about the appropriate level of analysis, design of the experiment, defining the treatment effect, implementation of the treatment, and specification of the hypothesized outcomes of the experiments. To be sure, these methodological limitations have been present in a number of the studies.

To a large extent, these limitations have been a function of two factors. First, the programs and evaluations were of an exploratory nature. Operationalization and controls of variables were implemented to varying degrees; however, not all variables were clearly identified until the experiments were underway. This is directly related to the facets of the research that were dependent on officer initiative and citizen responses. These factors were largely unknown and unanticipated until the research exploration was under way. A second methodological problem is attempting to manipulate experimental treatment in an operational law enforcement agency. Particularly in exploratory research, when the effects and outcomes of a hypothesized concept are unknown, great care in application of the treatment must be given in order to protect the safety, security, and rights of the citizens. This is an on-going issue in all aspects of research in policing. It is apparent that functional responsibilities of the agency must take precedence over research design.

While these facets do not negate the threats to validity and reliability, they do address reasons for the limitations. Follow-up research currently being conducted by the National Center for Community Policing as well as further research on Problem-Oriented Policing by PERF are employing more rigorous methodologies in light of what was learned in the earlier research efforts.

The second perspective of criticism in Community Policing deals with concept. This is concerned with the viability of the inherent philosophy of Community Policing and its propriety within the context of police responsibilities.·⁻ It may be argued that Community Policing is a solicitous attempt by the police to get into the good graces of the community. From another perspective, it may be argued that the police should take on no responsibilities beyond those of crime control and response to emergencies. That efforts to expand police responsibilities into quality of life issues is an improper broadening of police powers that may impinge on democratic processes.

The responses to these criticisms are largely found in ideological differences. The author's experiences indicate that police executives who support the Community Policing concept view the police as a social-service agency chartered by the community to address a wide range of social ills, ranging from major crime to weedy, overgrown lots. It is a contextual difference between administrative perspectives of the police that cannot be reconciled from either a legal or empirical basis. It is an administrative prerogative of the police administrator to make a philosophical judgment about the best manner to provide police service to the community.

A Perspective

Community Policing is not the exclusive province of the United States. It has emerged somewhat independently in other countries, because of their unique social, cultural, economic, and legal needs. Despite the differences, several fundamental elements remain the same. Universally, it was developed on the basis of police research and the recognition of the need to involve the community in policing processes. Australia, Canada, Germany, Sweden, Denmark, Finland, Great Britain, Japan, and Singapore, all have Community Policing models.[48]

While not definite, a general transition process appears to emerge:

- First is the recognition that traditional police approaches have not succeeded.

- Second, attitudes about police function among administrators, line personnel, and citizens must change.

- Third, community assessments must be performed to identify new police responsibilities.

- Fourth, new organizational and operational approaches must be conceived to meet the newly defined police responsibilities.

- Fifth, the community must be enlisted to work cooperatively with the police to achieve the desired results.

- Finally, there must be a commitment both by law enforcement and the community to continue the program's growth.

Change is difficult for any organization. For police departments – which are paramilitary, bureaucratic structures with members who have been socially isolated from the community – attempts at change are particularly challenging. A common response is to resist change, to say that a new approach will not work.

This chapter has shown that many previously sacred beliefs about policing have been forced to give way after research showed they were not supported by the facts. Based on that knowledge, law enforcement leaders explored new police responsibilities and different operational tactics. Within this framework, Community Policing evolved and grew, as evaluations pointed the way. Naysayers have begun to look at the concept anew. They have witnessed how it flourishes in numerous departments, and though some still will not concede that it can work, at least they are willing to take a fresh look at the possibilities.

NOTES

[1]President's Commission on Law Enforcement and Administration of Justice, *Task Force Report: The Police* (Washington, DC: U.S. Government Printing Office, 1967). See also, Radelet, Louis, *The Police and the Community, 4th edition* (New York: MacMillan Publishing Company, 1986).

[2]National Commission on the Causes and Prevention of Violence, *Law and Order Reconsidered* (Washington, DC: U.S. Government Printing Office, 1968), p. 292.

[3]Carter, David L.; Sapp, Allen D.; and Stephens, Darrel W., *The State of Police Education: Policy Directions for the 21st Century* (Washington, DC: Police Executive Research Forum, 1989). See also: National Institute of Law Enforcement and Criminal Justice, *The National Manpower Survey of the Criminal Justice System: Law Enforcement,* Volume 2 (Washington, DC: U.S. Government Printing Office, 1978).

[4]See Kerlinger, Fred, *Foundations of Behavioral Research, Second Edition* (New York: Holt, Rinehart and Winston, 1973); Campbell, Donald, and Stanley, Julian, *Experimental and Quasi-Experimental Designs for Research* (Chicago: Rand-McNally, 1963).

[5]Kelling, George; Pate, Tony; Dieckman, Duane; and Brown, Charles E., *The Kansas City Preventive Patrol Experiment: A Summary Report* (Washington, DC: Police Foundation, 1974), p. *v.* See also, Kelling, G. *et al, The Kansas City Preventive Patrol Experiment: A Technical Report* (Washington, DC: The Police Foundation, 1974). See also Reiss, A. J., *The Police and the Public* (New Haven, CT: Yale University Press, 1971).

[6]*Ibid,* Summary Report, p. 48.

[7]Kelling, George, and Fogel, David, *Police Patrol – Some Future Directions,* in *The Future of Policing,* edited by A. W. Cohn (Beverly Hills, CA: Sage Publications, 1978), p. 177.

[8]Op. cit. Kelling et al, *Technical Report,* p. 496.

[9]Kansas City, Missouri, Police Department, *Response Time Analysis: Executive Summary* (Kansas City, MO: Board of Police Commissioners, 1977), p. 23.

[10]*Ibid,* pp. 21-22, 24.

[11]Larson, Richard C., and Cahn, Michael F., *Synthesizing and Extending the Results of Police Patrol Studies* (Washington, DC: National Institute of Justice, 1985), p. 121. See also: *Police Response Time: A Review of the Literature* by Darrel W. Stephens (Washington, DC: Unpublished paper, Police Executive Research Forum, 1985).

[12]Spelman, William, and Brown, Dale K., *Calling the Police: Citizen Reporting of Serious Crime* (Washington, DC: National Institute of Justice, 1984), p. *xi.*

[13]*Ibid,* p. vii.

[14]McEwen, J. Thomas; Connors, Edward F., III; and Cohen, Marcia I., *Evaluation of the Differential Police Response Field Test* (Washington, DC: National Institute of Justice, 1969), p. 3.

[15]Farmer, Michael T. (editor), *Differential Police Response Strategies* (Washington, DC: Police Executive Research Forum, 1981), p. 69.

[16]*Op. cit.* McEwen, Connors and Cohen, pp. 16-17.

[17]Bureau of Justice Statistics, *Report to the Nation on Crime and Justice, Second Edition* (Washington, DC: U.S. Department of Justice, 1988), p. 64.

[18]There have been projects on police patrol deployment ranging from tactical approaches to management plans. Some of the more prominent programs are discussed in:

Alfred Schwartz and Sumner Clarren, *The Cincinnati Team Policing Experiment: A Summary Report* (Washington, DC: The Urban Institute and the Police Foundation, 1977).
William Gay *et al, Issues in Team Policing: A Review of the Literature* (Washington, DC: National Institute of Law Enforcement and Criminal Justice, 1977).

William Gay, Theodore Schell, and Stephen Shack, *Improving Police Productivity: Routine Patrol* (Washington, DC: National Institute of Law Enforcement and Criminal Justice, 1977).

Stephen Shack, Theodore Schell, and William Gay, *Improving Police Productivity: Specialized Patrol* (Washington, DC: National Institute of Law Enforcement and Criminal Justice, 1977).

Kenneth Webb *et al, Specialized Patrol Projects* (Washington, DC: National Institute of Law Enforcement and Criminal Justice, 1977).

Donald Cawley and H. Jerome Miron, *Managing Patrol Operations* (Washington, DC: University Research Corporation, 1977).

Jan Chaiken et al, *Criminal Justice Models: An Overview* (Washington, DC: National Institute of Law Enforcement and Criminal Justice, 1976).

James M. Tien, James W. Simon, and Richard C. Larson, *The Wilmington Split-Force Experiment* (Washington, DC: National Institute of Law Enforcement and Criminal Justice, 1978).

John E. Boydston, Michael E. Sherry, and Nicholas P. Moelter, *Patrol Staffing in San Diego: One- or Two-Officer Units* (Washington, DC: The Police Foundation, 1977).

Tony Pate, Robert A. Bowers and Ron Parks, *Three Approaches to Criminal Apprehension in Kansas City: An Evaluation Report* (Washington, DC: The Police Foundation, 1976).

M. J. Levine and J. T. McEwan, *Patrol Deployment* (Washington, DC: National Institute of Justice, 1985).

[19]*Op. cit.* Boydston, Sherry and Moelter.

[20]*Ibid,* pp. 69-70.

[21]*Op. cit.* Larson and Cahn, p. 95.

[22]See *Op. cit.* Gay *et al.*

[23]*Op. cit.* Webb *et al;* Shack, Schell and Gay; Tien, Simon and Larson.

[24]Cahn, Michael F., and Tien, James M., *An Evaluation Report of an Alternative Approach in Police Response: The Wilmington Management of Demand Program* (Cambridge, MA: Public Systems Evaluation, Inc., 1980).

[25]See *Op. cit.* Bureau of Justice Statistics.

[26]Whitaker, Gerald P. (editor), *Understanding Police Agency Performance* (Washington, DC: National Institute of Justice, 1984); Gerald P. Whitaker et al, *Basic Issues in Police Performance* (Washington, DC: National Institute of Justice, 1982).

[27]See Swanson, Charles; Territo, Leonard; and Taylor, Robert, *Police Administration, Second Edition* (New York: MacMillan Publishing Co., 1988); see also David L. Carter, *An Overview of Research in Support of the Community Policing Concept* (Training program handout for the FBI National Academy, Quantico, VA, 1986).

[28]Carter, David L., *Hispanic Perception of Police Performance: An Empirical Assessment (Journal of Criminal Justice, Volume 13* 1985), pp. 487-500; David L. Carter, *Hispanic Interaction With the Criminal Justice System in Texas: Experiences, Attitudes, and Perceptions (Journal of Criminal Justice, Volume 11,* 1983), pp. 213-227; *Op. cit.* Radelet; Mary J. Hageman, *Police Community Relations* (Beverly Hills, CA: Sage Publications, 1985); Community Relations Service Staff, *Principles of Good Policing: Avoiding Violence Between Police and Citizens* (Washington, DC: U.S. Department of Justice, Community Relations Service, 1987).

[29]Carter, David L., *Techniques and Instruments for Assessing Community Needs* (Training program handout for the FBI National Academy, Quantico, VA, 1988).

[30]*Op. cit.* Radelet.

[31]Stephens, Darrel W., and Heck, Robert O., *ICAP Is Many Thing to Many Agencies, Law Enforcement News,* December 7, 1981, p. 1.See also Greenwood, Peter W., and Petersilia, Joan, *The Criminal Investigation Process – Volume 1: Summary and Policy Implications* (Santa Monica, CA: Rand Corporation, 1975).

[32]See also Trojanowicz, Robert C., *An Evaluation of the Neighborhood Foot Patrol Program in Flint, Michigan* (East Lansing, MI: National Neighborhood Foot Patrol Center, Michigan State University, 1980). A good assessment of other programming can be found in Rosenbaum, Dennis R. (Ed.), *Community Crime Prevention: Does It Work?* (Beverly Hills, CA: Sage Publications, 1986).

[33]Goldstein, Herman, *Improving Policing: A Problem-Oriented Approach, Crime and Delinquency,* 25:236-258, 1979.

[34]Goldstein, Herman, and Susmilch, Charles, *Experimenting With the Problem-Oriented Approach to Improving Police Service: A Report and Some Reflections on Two Case Studies* (Madison, WI: Law School, University of Wisconsin, 1982).

[35]Eck, John E., and Spelman, William, *Problem Solving: Problem-Oriented Policing in Newport News* (Washington, DC: Police Executive Research Forum and the National Institute of Justice, 1987). See also John Eck and William Spelman, *Problem-Oriented Policing* (Washington, DC: National Institute of Justice/Research in Brief, 1987).

[36]*Op. cit.* Eck and Spelman, Problem Solving, p. *xv.*

[37]Madison, Wisconsin, Police Departent, *Planning Report for the Experimental Police District* (Madison, WI: Madison Police Department, 1988), p. 13f.

[38]Higdon, Richard K. and Huber, Phillip G., *How To Fight Fear: The Citizen Oriented Police Enforcement Program Package* (Washington, DC: Police Executive Research Forum and Baltimore County, Maryland, Police Department, 1987), p. 3.

[39]Baltimore County Field Operations Bureau, *Community Foot Patrol Officer Guidelines and Procedures* (Towson, MD: Baltimore County Police Department, 1988), p. 3.

[40]Whitmire, Kathryn J. and Brown, Lee P., *City of Houston Police Department Command Station/Neighborhood Oriented Policing Overview* (Houston, TX: Houston Police Department, undated), p. 2.

[41]Skogan, Wesley G. and Wycoff, Mary Ann, *Storefront Police Officers: The Houston Field Test,* in Dennis P. Rosenbaum (editor), *Community Crime Prevention: Does It Work?* (Beverly Hils, CA: Sage Publications, 1986).

[42]Utne, Mary *et al, A Description of Foot Patrol In New Jersey: The Safe and Clean Neighborhoods Program,* p. 22.

[43]Kelling, George L., *Conclusions from the Newark Foot Patrol Experiment in The Newark Foot Patrol Experiment* (Washington, DC: The Police Foundation, 1981), p. 122.

[44]Pate, Antony M. et al, *Reducing Fear of Crime in Houston and Newark: A Summary Report* (Washington, DC: The Police Foundation and National Institute of Justice, 1986).

[45]Information for the Detroit Mini-Station Program was gained through review of department documents on the program, site visits at the stations, and conversations with the Mini-Station Commander, Inspector Lawrence Holland. See also: Jerome H. Skolnick and David Bayley, *The New Blue Line* (New York: The Free Press, 1986), pp. 50-80.

[46]Greene, Jack, and Taylor, Ralph, *Community Based Policing and Foot Patrol: Issues of Theory and Evaluation,* in Jack Greene and Stephen Mastrofski (Eds.), *Community Policing: Rhetoric or Reality?* (New York: Praeger, 1988), pp. 216-219.

[47]See Manning, Peter, *Community Policing as Drama of Control,* in Jack Greene and Stephen Mastrofski (Eds.), *Community Policing: Rhetoric or Reality?* (New York: Praeger, 1988).

⁴⁸See Skolnick, Jerome H., and Bayley, David, *Community Policing: Issues and Practices Around the World* (Washington, DC: National Institute of Justice, 1988); David M. Kennedy, *Neighborhood Policing: The London Metropolitan Police Force,* Case Program: John F. Kennedy School of Government (Cambridge, MA: Harvard University, 1986); John Brown, *Neighborhood Policing in West Berlin* (Police Studies, Volume 5, No. 4, Winter 1983), pp. 29-32; David Brown and Susan Iles, Community Constables: A Study of a Policing Initiative (Washington, DC: National Institute of Justice/International Summaries, 1986).

CHAPTER 7
The Flint Experience

*What you have in the City of Flint is about 10
years of a generation that has never been
employed, never held a job. You're talking
about very high drug usage. Eighty percent
of our theft and violent crimes are drug and/
or alcohol related.*

— Robert Weiss
Genesee County Prosecutor (1988)

Why Focus on Flint?

The first question that must be addressed is why the Flint experience deserves
its own chapter. Some dismiss the Flint experience as ancient history, an early effort
that has been eclipsed now that those foot patrol experiments of the late 1970s and
early 1980s have evolved into a nationwide Community Policing revolution. Others
avoid Flint because they see it as a tragedy – an impressive effort that failed to survive
intact, providing ammunition to critics who say that Community Policing sounds
good in theory, but that it can falter in the real world.

As the continuing controversy attests, the Flint experiment provides many useful lessons about Community Policing – how the concept was born, how it developed, and what it can achieve – and also about the pitfalls it faces. In that regard, the
Flint effort would deserve special attention if only because it remains the most extensively and exhaustively researched and evaluated effort of its kind so far.

But beyond the research, important as that is, Flint also offers a cautionary tale
about the pressures Community Policing faces, many of which any new effort must
contend with, at least to some degree. Even those elements particular to the Flint
situation tell an important story about the ways any new effort must be tailored to the
prevailing political and economic challenges in the local area. The story can also be

read as a *who dunnit,* though instead of trying to figure out *who* tried to kill off the program, this mystery looks at *what* kinds of forces tend to conspire against Community Policing's survival. The Flint experience also provides a chance to capture the flavor of Community Policing, by allowing us to see the real people behind the numbers and statistics.

The Flint Environment

When people outside the state think of Michigan, they usually think first of Detroit, synonymous in most people's minds with two things – the auto industry and violence. Those inside the state see Flint as a mini-Detroit, a more intense micro-version of the macro-problems a turbulent city faces when its economy is dominated by an industry in transition.

An analysis of the 1987 FBI figures for the eight most serious (Index) crimes showed that Flint actually ranked as the sixth most dangerous city in the United States, while Detroit placed 16th. The crime rate for these Part I crimes of homicide, rape, robbery, assault, burglary, larceny, motor vehicle theft, and arson was 15,795 per 100,000 for Flint, compared to 12,824 for Detroit (and only 4,836 for the upscale Detroit suburb of Sterling Heights).

Detroit led the nation in homicides, at 62 per 100,000 population, yet Flint was close behind, in sixth place with a rate of 35 per 100,000. Perhaps a more telling comparison comes from looking at how Flint, now down below 150,000 people, stacks up to the Capitol city of Lansing, roughly 70 miles away, which claims roughly 125,000 people. Lansing ranked 141st among this country's cities on the basis of its homicide rate, yet its six homicides per 100,000 rate was up 32.6% from the year before. In comparison, Flint's rate had declined 12.5% during the same period, yet it still ranked as one of the top 10 most murderous cities in the nation, though it is not much larger than relatively safe cities nearby.[1]

It was Flint, not Detroit, that was the actual birthplace of both General Motors and the union movement (dating from the famous sit-down strike of 1937). And both have continued to shape the city in ways beyond what this brief analysis can detail. Flint stands as the model of a prototypical northern, industrial, blue-collar city, a rough-and-tumble town, with the good and bad that description implies.

Flint's dependence on the auto industry fostered a certain schizophrenic attitude toward its main benefactor. As the auto industry continued to grow and prosper, no Flint resident could deny the benefit of all those industry dollars rippling through the local economy. Many also appreciated their good fortune in finding a job at an auto plant, where someone without even a high-school diploma could outearn a college professor. For many in Flint, the American dream translated into owning a home, with at least one new car, a snowmobile, and a boat in the driveway.

At the same time, many union workers, especially those who could remember the movement's early days, keenly understood the toll in sweat and sometimes blood exacted to wrest concessions from management. Whenever the locals referred to GM by its nickname of Generous Motors, you could hear both the sarcasm and the respect, mirroring the ambivalence that universally dominates a company town.

The auto industry further shaped Flint because those excellent wages and bene-fits served as a magnet for southern, rural blacks, who flocked to northern cities, in numbers that exceeeded the migration of immigrants from Europe after the turn of the century, dramatically changing the racial mix of the city. By the middle of the 20th century, the continued growth of the auto industry seemed to promise an ever-expanding prosperity. In 1970, Flint's population stood at slightly more than 193,000, with unemployment in the single-digit range.

Flint was still, in some important ways, a modern-day frontier town, whose underlying problems and tensions were masked by the wealth created by the Gold Rush of the auto industry. There had long been growing friction between *haves* and *have-nots,* between working people and welfare recipients, and between the mana-gerial and professional class, who often looked down on, but barely outearned, the auto worker – a pecking order based on whether your paycheck depended on brains or brawn. Smoldering racial and class tensions increased when the new expressway system made it easier for upper- and middle-class workers to flee to the suburbs after work, allowing them to escape the city's tradition of violence.

Beginning in the early 1970s, economic and social changes plunged Flint into a decline from which it may never fully recover. The first sign that autoworkers were vulnerable to new economic forces appeared when it became evident that ever-increasing automation spelled fewer jobs on the line. Before the unions could find a way to cope with the ominous implications, the energy crunch hit, accelerating the shift to smaller, foreign-made cars, which in turn caused the bottom to drop out of the domestic car market.

American car companies had resisted downsizing, for reasons that continue to be debated. Some argue that no one could have foreseen the oil-price hikes and their devastating impact on car sales, while others contend management arrogantly ignored obvious warning signs. The auto industry slump helped lead the entire coun-try into recession (paraphrasing the adage: when General Motors catches cold, the country risks pneumonia).

In this escalating climate of blame, one thing remains clear, which is that the recession hit Flint the hardest of any American city. Unemployment reached 25 %, the highest in the nation, a rate unequalled anywhere since the Depression. At the same time, even before cocaine and crack made things worse, drugs were a serious problem in the city. By the time the Flint Neighborhood Foot Patrol Program (NFPP) was launched in 1979, one-fourth of Flint's citizens had moved away, leaving slightly fewer than 160,000 residents, 41.5 % black and 56.2 % white, in a city riddled with violent crime, racial tension, and seemingly endless recriminations about what had happened to its once-promising future – a daunting environment for a new policing venture.

Yet it is appropriate, perhaps prophetic, that Flint, so hard hit by the energy crisis, served as one of the cradles of the Community Policing movement. In 1977, science and science fiction writer Isaac Asimov wrote an essay envisioning what the country would look like in ten years if we would find ourselves confronting *The Nightmare Life Without Fuel*:

> Against most predictions, the crime rate has dropped. With the police car too expensive (and too easy a target), police are back on their beats. More importantly, the streets are full. Legs are king in the cities of 1987, and people walk everywhere far into the night. Even the parks are full, and there is mutual protection in crowds.[2]

The good news is that the nightmare of an escalating energy crisis did not happen, but the bad news is that the dream of safer cities achieved by putting officers back in the community has been blighted in one of the cities that served as a model for others nationwide.

The Birth of Flint Foot Patrol

The Charles Stewart Mott Foundation of Flint has sponsored a number of efforts in the city that have helped make it a more inviting place to live. Since the death of C.S. Mott in 1973, new president William White has continued to refine the foundation's mission, which is to be both a good neighbor to the city and to play a role in effecting positive social change at the national level. The foundation has long enjoyed a supportive relationship with the Flint Police Department, such as providing a start-up grant for the Police/School Liaison Program.

As the grant for that program was expiring, then-Mayor James Rutherford (who had been Flint's police chief for many years), Coordinator of Community Schools Jerry Zerbe, and Frank Rutherford, the mayor's brother and a former police officer, planned to approach Mott about funding an expanded police effort to reach beyond the schools.

"Police Chief Max Durbin expressed concern that the police needed to do more than have patrol officers riding in cars, especially in neighborhoods with high concentrations of single-parent heads of households," says Marilyn Steele, the program officer for Mott who has shepherded the foundation's involvement in Community Policing since those earliest days. "Particularly following the civil unrest and campus riots of the late sixties, the police had acquired a hostile image among the general public. Especially among the poor and those who live in highly impacted neighborhoods, the police were not seen as the protector of the people, but as an enemy."

Three unfortunate incidents added urgency to exploring new solutions. The case that made headlines nationwide involved an altercation between two motor patrol officers, a white male and black female, who began arguing behind the police station about which one would drive the car, as other officers gathered around. The official investigation later verified that the woman opened fire, some of the other officers began firing back, and of the 14 shots fired, one wounded the black, female officer. Both the sex and race of the officers were noted in many media accounts of the incident – and many also made fun of the shooting skills of officers in the department.

The second incident that increased public concern was when Flint officers fired buckshot at a 15-year-old black youngster as he tried to flee by going over a fence, and an errant pellet hit a vital spot and killed him. Adding to the tension between the police and the black community, initial newspaper accounts ran a photo of the boy when he was much younger, which left the impression that police had fired on a small child.

The third incident occurred during a mock shakedown conducted jointly by the Flint Police Department and the Michigan State Police. The goal of staging these public shakedowns was to allow undercover officers to make inroads with onlookers, but one attempt ended tragically when a white Flint officer's firearm accidentally discharged, killing a black trooper involved in the sting.

The racial component in these three incidents heightened the tensions between the police and the black community to an unprecedented degree. There was public clamor for the police to make changes in how they delivered police service to the community.

Chief Durbin had a vision for a new kind of police officer, whom he had dubbed the "Neighborhood House Husband." He saw this as a way for police officers to become involved in high-risk, single-parent households in poor neighborhoods. The name would have made it an extremely tough sell within any police department, but it conveyed the kernel of an idea about what a new decentralized and more personalized form of policing could achieve.

Durbin approached the International Association of Chiefs of Police (IACP) about conducting a study of where and how such a program might work. Mott provided $50,000, and the City of Flint contracted for the study, but Steele says, "It ended up being a canned survey that showed there was supposedly no fear of crime in the community, and it made management recommendations on that basis."

General uphappiness with the recommendations prompted Joe Wilson, sheriff of Genesee County but then a deputy chief of the Flint department, to make another attempt to develop an administrative model. Wilson hosted a number of meetings with community residents around the city in 1977 and 1978, and the concept of the Flint Neighborhood Foot Patrol Program grew out of this collaboration between the people and the police. The effort culminated in a large meeting at the Municipal Building, where representatives from the neighborhoods met to commit themselves to the new program. The people not only endorsed the plan for a new decentralized police approach, they also agreed to participate directly themselves in helping to make it work.

The plan targeted 14 neighborhoods, selected not only because of crime concerns, but because they exhibited a strong base of citizen support considered essential for success. In January 1979, the Mott Foundation provided a $2.6-million, three-year grant to put 22 foot patrol officers into base stations (many in schools) within those 14 neighborhoods that collectively contained roughly 20 % of the city's total population. The effort would augment existing efforts, which consisted primarily of motor patrols, as well as crime prevention and undercover operations.

The meetings had identified three distinct underlying problems: (1) lack of comprehensive neighborhood organizations and services, (2) lack of citizen involvement in crime prevention, and (3) depersonalization of interactions between officers and residents. Input from community residents in the initial experimental beat areas targeted seven basic goals:

- To decrease the amount of actual or perceived criminal activity.

- To increase the citizens' perceptions of personal safety.

- To deliver to Flint residents a type of law enforcement consistent with community needs and the ideals of modern police practice.

- To create a community awareness of crime problems and methods of increasing law enforcement's ability to deal with actual or potential criminal activity effectively.

- To develop citizen volunteer action in support of and under the direction of the police department aimed at various target crimes.

- To eliminate citizen apathy about reporting crimes to police.

- To increase protection for women, children, and the aged.

A Strong Commitment to Evaluation

Within a month after the program started, Steele contacted the School of Criminal Justice at Michigan State University. "From the outset, we also supported the notion of evaluative research on the experimental program," says Steele. "Michigan State University is our neighbor, widely renowned for its School of Criminal Justice." Mott provided funding for four years of research, and George Felkenes, then the director of the school, suggested Robert Trojanowicz to head the project.

Trojanowicz understood the potential problems inherent in social science research, the result of his prior experience singlehandedly surveying and interviewing all 270 officers in the Lansing Police Department during a six-month sabbatical. He therefore developed an evaluation plan that he calls a *self-correcting research model.* He also conscripted a dozen talented people of diverse skills to serve as the research team to administer, conduct, and evaluate the research.

Not wanting to make the mistake of developing a system relying just on formal questionnaires or informal exchanges of information, Trojanowicz opted for a multifaceted, two-pronged approach, consisting of conventional surveys and meetings with everyone involved, in the police department and in the community, as well as face-to-face visits with both motor and foot patrol officers in their own environment. The research model focused on comparing foot patrol's effects in the 14 target areas against controls in other parts of the city, with built-in flexibility to adjust for any changes.

The challenge was to synthesize and cross check the information gleaned from the more than 2,000 surveys, to be conducted on average citizens, the police, community leaders, school officials, religious leaders, and business people, with the feedback from personal observations made walking beats with the officers and talking to them "at local watering holes." The research convinced Trojanowicz that a forced-answer survey can intimidate officers into thinking they should try to pick the answer they think management wants to hear. He believed that there was a need to follow up with informal discussions to build the rapport required to persuade people to trust you and to open up.

Trojanowicz hired Robert Baldwin, who was then a detective with the Ingham County Sheriff's Department outside Lansing, to spearhead the police research because of his police experience, his ability to see the big picture, and because Baldwin could be trusted to do the best job possible.

Trojanowicz selected Jesse Thompson, now director of Personnel and Labor Relations for the City of Flint, as Baldwin's community counterpart. Thompson was highly recommended and turned out to be tremendous in developing rapport with people from all walks of life. Baldwin and Thompson quickly developed a working relationship that allowed them to approach the research challenge as partners.

Foot Patrol in Action

Baldwin's first task was to become familiar with the officers involved in the new foot patrol program, which meant walking the beat with them twice a week for a total of 16 hours, in addition to his full-time job. "It was especially tough for many of these officers to get a handle on the job at first because roughly a third of them had come straight from the academy," says Baldwin. "Here we had a new program, with no past experience to fall back on, and many officers weren't sure what was really expected of them, even though they had received special training. My biggest surprise was seeing how quickly many of them earned the trust of the people in their beat areas. I would walk with an officer during his first few weeks on the job, then come back three months later and be shocked to see the difference. With a good foot patrol officer, people would roll down car windows to say hello, calling the officer by name. And women would drop off cakes and cookies at the office, maybe to show appreciation for something the officer had done with their kids. You could always tell when a foot officer wasn't doing the job, by the way people treated them like a stranger."

On one occasion, Baldwin was walking the afternoon beat with a rookie who didn't know Baldwin was himself a fellow officer. The young man had not yet mastered the knack of monitoring his radio as he talked, so when Baldwin picked out the message that an armed man fleeing a domestic dispute might be headed to their area, he kept scanning the area as they walked. When Baldwin spotted the suspect hiding in the weeds of a vacant lot they were approaching, he had to alert his "partner." "Helping him make his first felony bust earned me his trust," says Baldwin.

Of the seven rookies who were part of the initial effort, five transferred out. "I think it's a mistake to use officers with no experience in any Community Policing effort," says Baldwin. "They need time on the road, if only to get the red-light-and-siren syndrome out of their systems. And they need to work with a seasoned officer who can show them the ropes." The two who remained in foot patrol had both been schoolteachers before joining the police department. Trojanowicz credits their success to their communication skills and experience in working with people in an educational role.

As time went on, Baldwin could see that foot patrol officers with a feel for the job benefited from the freedom to experiment with new ideas. By allowing the officers to "own" their own piece of the city, where they could operate as the chief of their own area, the program overall began to take shape. Some officers concentrated first on the physical appearance of their neighborhoods, often employing strategies to involve local people in the process. Others found the people in their area first wanted help in dealing with juveniles.

In essence, this was the genesis of a new problem-solving approach to community problems related to crime and disorder. Freed from the patrol car and the police radio, the Flint foot officers began to make the shift from responding to incidents to focusing on addressing the underlying dynamics, without formally articulating what the philosophical shift entailed. In Flint, the approach was limited to the foot officers who acted as community problem-solving specialists. Later, in other places such as Baltimore County and Newport News (see Chapter 6), it evolved beyond being a tactic that special units could use to a shift in attitude within the entire department.

An idea that struck Baldwin as a great way to accomplish many goals involved having the foot patrol officer recruit kids for Saturday morning expeditions during which the kids would offer to paint the scuffed-up front doors on people's houses. It helped make the houses look better, challenged people to do even more, offered an opportunity for positive interaction between young and old, and provided the officer an opportunity to get to know the area and the kids and residents better.

Thompson says he was especially struck by the program's impact on the elderly. "I was shocked at how much fear they felt when I first interviewed them, before the program got going. It was personally gratifying to see how their perceptions of safety improved." Baldwin was encouraged to see the program's impact on race relations. "When you see people from the community physically hugging their officers, regardless of race, you know the program is doing something right," he says. He also notes many officers trusted the community so much they relied on them as unofficial backup if they found themselves in trouble.

Thompson's only concern was that the program's success made many people think their officers could work miracles. "When people began to see how much good the officers were doing in the community, some began to think that foot patrol could wipe out all crime. Foot patrol officers can indirectly help with a problem like a domestic assault, by linking people to appropriate services, but they cannot guarantee that such violence will not occur again or even escalate to murder. Yet some people got to the point where they tried to put this responsibility – this burden – onto the officers."

As Steele notes, "The police see their role as crook catchers. But what people want is prevention – they want the police to prevent them from being victimized. They appreciate the help the police provide after the fact, but Community Policing addresses the need to help people avoid being the target of crime in the first place."

One Officer's Initiatives

Because the Flint experiment was among the first of such efforts, there were few models for officers to rely on, which intimidated some, while it provided others the freedom to develop initiatives that have been adopted and adapted elsewhere. Not only rookies, but black, female officers were also over-represented in foot patrol, as compared to the make-up of the Flint Police Department overall. Baldwin says many of them became the program's stars, and among the brightest lights was Jowanne Barnes-Coney, who has since been promoted to sergeant in charge of the aforementioned Police/School Liaison Program. As a foot patrol officer, Barnes-Coney walked a beat in a high-crime public housing area "down the hill" from her apartment. "Even that short distance implied a big difference in quality of life," she says. "If you lived on the hill, they viewed you as someone who had made it."

A firm believer that you attract the parents by involving their kids, Barnes-Coney spent her first few shifts making friends with two young people who acted as her emissaries to meet others. She decided to focus first on teen pregnancy, by involving agencies that could help young mothers learn how to care for their babies and also by talking to young girls about the responsibility that having sex implies. "Schoolteachers aren't allowed to talk to them about birth control, but I could," she notes.

Barnes-Coney also felt that she could make a difference by discouraging kids from hanging out on the streets all night. She organized a curfew incentive program, in which parents set the deadlines. "It didn't matter what the curfew law was – it mattered when your mother said you had to be home," she says. The parents would report to her each month whether their kids were home by curfew every night – one miss and no payoff. "One reward was what I called 'Discover Flint.' We had an old school bus we could use, so I would take the kids on an excursion to see the city. Many of the kids had literally never been out of their own neighborhoods. I felt it was very important for them to see what the city had to offer and how other people live."

Barnes-Coney inaugurated or adopted numerous programs, concentrating on those that made the area look better, but especially on those that targeted kids. She established Teen Esteem Clubs, designed to help kids avoid destructive habits through peer support and role modeling. Operation ID identified kids who aspired to drug dealing or other illegal activities. She would warn parents that their kids appeared to be at risk, then offer to link them to appropriate counseling or other suitable sources of help. She also promoted drug-free rallies, where kids received free t-shirts for participating, as a way of making them want to *just say no*. T.I.P.S. is a cable TV show she has been involved in that features crime prevention tips for kids, using law enforcement talent such as a Blues Band, so called because of their uniforms as well as their music.

In addition to numerous other efforts, she also launched a Teen Boys Entrepreneur program in her beat area, as well as the Coney's Boys and Girls Prep Club.

Barnes-Coney got tremendous mileage from using a videocam to make tapes of activities with "her" kids that were aired on Saturday mornings for all to see. Officer Charles Reynolds, an officer from North Miami Beach, walked the beat with her in Flint during a training session on Community Policing. He was looking for some way to break the ice with kids in the beat area he would be assigned to as part of the department's new program. He did not have a videocam, so he instead decided to write and record a rap tune – called the Reynolds Rap – and he played it over and over on his boom box as he first walked his new beat, until he looked like the Pied Piper with an army of kids behind him – an example of how officers often borrow and then transform ideas from other programs.

Not all the new ideas tried panned out, of course. Some efforts bordered on outright disaster. A well-meaning officer in Flint rewarded kids in his beat area with a trip to the mall to see the movie *Pinocchio*. The school bus acted up on the way, so after the officer saw the kids to the theater, he went back to the parking lot to make repairs. Later, calls to the department from irate parents let him know that he had deposited the kids at an X-rated version of the fairy tale.

Administration, Supervision, and Accountability

Fortunately for all involved, Deputy Chief Wilson, who was then in charge of the program, accepted blunders as a necessary part of the process. A flamboyant idea man who favored a freewheeling approach, Wilson promoted experimentation – far more than Bruce Benson, who was then a lieutenant at the department, felt necessary. Benson did not transfer in because he was a fan of foot patrol. He had enjoyed his stint in Homicide, but when he returned from training at the FBI Academy, he found he had been transferred to Internal Affairs, which he loathed enough that it made foot patrol look good in comparison. "My attitude back then was that foot patrol was a waste of resources that would have better been used to focus on serious crime in Flint," he remembers.

Benson recalls attending his first foot patrol roll call. He knew that Wilson's commitment to freedom included allowing officers to wear street clothes, but he was stunned to find one officer dressed as Rags the Clown and another, clad in a red track suit, sporting a hat festooned with Viking horns. When someone zinged Benson with a spitball, he decided his mission was to contribute the structure he felt was sorely lacking.

Though he had to lobby hard to make changes, Benson succeeded in promoting a shift back to uniforms, unless the officers could demonstrate the need to dress otherwise. He also increased the number of roll calls and introduced management by objectives (MBO). He required foot officers to identify three community problems and the tactics they intended to use during the next month to work toward making a positive impact. The goals were not typically related to crime incidents. A goal might be as general as increasing contact with the community, followed by three specific efforts the officer would make within a specified period of time. This helped the officers focus on results, at the same time it provided supervisors some way to assess performance.

Benson also reviewed current efforts to see which were – and were not – accomplishing the program's stated goals. He saw his challenge as adding structure and accountability without stifling initiative. One popular program that met the test used a bus to take the elderly to the bank and then shopping each month after Social Security checks arrived. Having an armed officer protecting seniors may or may not have prevented their actual victimization, but it dramatically helped ease their fears. However, Benson ultimately axed using the bus to take schoolteachers shopping at an upscale mall near Detroit. The teachers loved the expeditions, and the program undeniably won foot patrol their support, but Benson drew the line, saying that it was improper use of scarce resources.

Benson said that incident highlights one of the challenges in Community Policing, what he calls the "galloping psychology of entitlement." He only found out about those excursions that took teachers to the shopping mall when one of the teachers called to ask him what he was going to do about their scheduled shopping trip, since the bus was being repaired. Much to Benson's surprise, instead of being appreciative about past trips, the teacher began haranguing him about how he should rent a bus to ensure they could go as planned.

Over time, Benson became a convert, especially when he saw the effect Community Policing can make on juveniles and on drugs (detailed in the section *Special People/Special Problems)*. Foot patrol's impact on kids was driven home in a uniquely personal way on the day his daughter's bike was stolen. "She never thought to call the department and ask for me. Instead she spent hours tracking down Officer Jeff, the foot patrol officer who had an office in her school, because he was her pal."

His commitment to the concept added to his determination to help the program succeed. "Enthusiastic and effective officers will do a good job no matter what kind of supervisory system is in place, and officers who aren't cut out for it cannot be saved by any new set of guidelines," says Benson. "But we needed to draw lines, to sharpen the focus of the program, not only to help make it more effective, but to promote respect within the department as a whole."

It is important to remember that all involved were inventing a new wheel for which there was no blueprint. No one really knew what such a program should look like and what problems it would face. What became obvious early on, however, was that internal hostility toward the program was a serious threat, exacerbated by a number of factors beyond the impression made by clown costumes and spitballs – though those did not help.

As Baldwin notes, "They did a great job of educating the community and the officers involved in the program, but they forgot to include motor patrol in the educational process." Traditional officers not only felt neglected but insulted, laying the groundwork for hostility between the two units. Efforts intended to heal the breach spanned the gamut from those that helped (such as rotating in motor patrol officers who could see for themselves what the program could do so that they could later carry word back to their peers), to those that failed miserably (such as the ill-fated "Take a Motor Patrol Officer to Lunch" scheme).

Adjustments in the Evaluation Process

Trojanowicz and Baldwin realized early on that one supervisor either failed to understand the approach or refused to implement it as ordered. While the Community Policing philosophy rests on having the officer act as a full-fledged law enforcement officer, this sergeant instead told his officers not to make arrests – his rationale was that this was a better way to earn the community's support. This situation typifies the variety of unexpected ethical and moral dilemmas that social science researchers in the field can face. In the "hard" sciences, "pure" research supposedly demands absolute objectivity, and evaluators are expected to stand back, as uninvolved observers, no matter what happens. Yet Trojanowicz cites the recent case where medical researchers abandoned their trials on a new drug for AIDS, when the Food and Drug Administration decided it would be unethical to withhold such promising treatment from the control group, as an example of how researchers must always weigh means against ends.

In this unusual situation, Trojanowicz had to wrestle with a number of complex issues. If he did nothing, he risked evaluating a program that would bear little resemblance to the one that the top police officials and the Mott Foundation thought they were implementing. Yet, if he involved himself in the internal workings of the department, that could be construed as violating his observer status. Also of concern was that any interference might label him as someone who would "snitch" to top brass – a threat to the evaluation team's credibility with line officers. Fortunately, rumors about the problem had already reached the top, so Trojanowicz was simply asked to confirm their decision to replace the man with someone more attuned to implementing the program as outlined.

This was not the only kind of pressure with which the researchers had to cope.

Though initial research results confirmed the new program had obvious merit, Trojanowicz could not ethically shift gears and become a cheerleader for the cause. On occasion, when the program was threatened, he was asked to do things to help save it. But he remained vigilant about the need to limit his role to answering questions about what the evaluation showed, if asked. He rejected entreaties to take action to promote the positive findings the research continued to verify.

In addition, the researchers had to keep updating their research model. As noted earlier, Trojanowicz developed an evaluation scheme with built-in options to adjust for changes, the self-correcting research model. The first jolt hit when the programs took off so well in the experimental areas that the mayor and the police chief decided to expand it to more beats any time new money could be found to do so.

By the time Benson joined the program, a year after its inception, it had already grown so that it covered all but one-third of the city; at one point it climbed to 44 officers, in 44 beats, then back down to 36 officers in 36 beats. Eventually, foot patrol covered the entire city.

This rapid expansion caused headaches for the program and for the researchers. The original plan allocated 22 officers to the 14 beats, so that two-person teams, with overlapping morning and afternoon shifts, could cover high-density, high-crime areas. The luxury of doubling up officers quickly disappeared, and further expansion caused many officers to complain they were being stretched too thin. Many beats expanded, so that it was increasingly difficult for one officer to cover so much more territory or so many more people. In addition, Benson said all new funding went into adding new officers without increasing the supervisory staff, which further strained the seams.

Meanwhile, the evaluation staff watched the control beats shrink and then vanish, as the boundaries and staffing for experimental beats continued to shift and change. To complete their analysis of crime rates, the researchers found they had to read all 37,000 complaints, processing them by hand, to ensure they could tell precisely where and when each crime had occurred and whether the area was or was not then covered by foot patrol.

Mott initially agreed to fund foot patrol for three years, the evaluation for four. Though the foundation extended its commitment, eventually foot patrol would have to become self-supporting. The city ultimately made the decision to ask the voters to approve a special millage to fund foot patrol citywide. That meant that foot patrol officers who had a vested interest in protecting their jobs realized early on that they had to lobby their constituents for support. The researchers had to remain alert to how such pressures might skew certain findings.

A Program Under Siege

The effort faced enormous economic and political pressures during and after the experimental and research phases. As the Flint economy soured, tax revenues plunged, which translated into drastic cuts in the city budget, including funds for the police department. Benson remembers, "At one point, they closed the City Jail rather than lay off officers, so it was not a good time to try to find any extra funds for a new program, and it made the foot patrol budget an attractive target for politicians who needed to find new revenue."

By the time the Flint project was launched, the number of sworn officers in the Flint Police Department had declined substantially from levels enjoyed in the affluent 1960s to no more than 300 officers in total. Benson, who kept tabs on the numbers for many years, said that despite the fact that the grant money was supposed to be used exclusively to pay for new foot patrol officers, above and beyond existing staffing, the number of officers in the department as a whole never really grew.

This is not to suggest anyone "cooked the books," but it is easy to see that city government faced incredible pressure trying to maintain city services with declining revenues. Therefore, perhaps when a motor patrol officer retired or quit, it made sense to leave the job unfilled and use grant money to hire a new foot patrol officer instead. Quite obviously, the bottom line was that the money saved by not using the new funds to increase total numbers helped cover shortfalls elsewhere in the system.

While the motivation was understandable, and the economic pressures intense, the fact remained that the police department had launched an ambitious, ever-expanding, and widely popular effort with no ultimate increase in staffing. It also meant the chief had to "rob" Peter, who in this case was motor patrol, to "pay" for the Paul of the new foot patrol initiative, further fueling internal dissent and straining both kinds of patrols to the breaking point.

Many hoped and expected that overall numbers could be increased over time, if foot patrol could be continued once the extended Mott funding ran out. The vote slated for August 1982 asking voters to pay a special millage for three years to fund foot patrol was therefore a referendum on the existing program, as well as an expression of faith in a better future. Though that millage proposal passed, Flint's economic problems persisted, which meant staffing levels remained stagnant, despite the new pressures caused by the cocaine problem that hit the city shortly thereafter, soon to be followed by a crack "epidemic."

In 1984, Flint voters elected a new mayor, James Sharp, the first black mayor since the city switched to a strong-mayor system. Sharp replaced Chief Durbin. After an interim chief served six months, the new mayor hired William Lyght, Jr., to serve as the city's first black police chief. Mayor Rutherford, coming as he did from the ranks of police, established the precedent of involving the mayor in the police department, a practice Sharp continued, though he had no direct expertise in police work. Sharp told voters he was committed to foot patrol, though he soon found how hard it was to increase budgets in the midst of economic chaos.

Prior to the second millage vote, slated for the summer of 1985, concerned voters asked the new mayor to clarify whether he would commit himself to using the millage funds exclusively earmarked for foot patrol as intended. Benson says the mayor assured him the millage would go to foot patrol. The millage passed again, by an even wider margin than before, but Benson's number crunching showed little if any resulting improvement in staffing.

Adding to the program's woes, lack of continuity at the top in the police department again became a serious problem. The outspoken Police Chief Lyght had been openly critical of the mayor's interference in police matters, and the mayor replaced him, citing his alleged lack of management skills. (Many believe Lyght was vindicated when he was later hired by the International Association of Chiefs of Police to evaluate management strategies in departments nationwide.)

Foot patrol came under siege from a new quarter when a Flint City Council member, Melvin McCree, asked the city to hire an outside management consulting firm to study the police department, since the company said it could help cities save money on their police departments or at least allow them to make the most of dwindling resources.

Steele says the Mott Foundation was approached about providing the $100,000 fee, but that the foundation rejected the proposal. She had grave concerns about the potential negative impact on foot patrol by the consulting firm, since she had talked with police personnel in Dade County (Florida), foundation personnel in St. Louis (Missouri), and Chief Richard Gleason of the Lansing Police Department. Gleason told her that he had been unhappy with the recommendations that the same firm had made after doing a study of his department.

Gleason complained to her and others that he felt the researchers put too much stock in efficiency measures, such as response time, and too little in citizen satisfaction. Steele knew foot patrol's virtues cannot be measured by yardsticks developed to assess motor patrol, so she worried about what such a study would recommend.

Her fears were confirmed when the city commissioned the study and Mayor Sharp cited its recommendations when he announced, in April 1987, that he was putting all Flint police officers back in their cars. He said the spirit of the foot patrol program would be maintained by having officers "park and walk" when they were on free patrol. Some foot patrol advocates considered filing suit to prevent the mayor from spending the millage money for a program different from the one the voters had approved.

Steele says that "park and walk" degenerated into "park and watch," as officers found themselves again tied to their radios. She took two personal days off work to look around the city herself to see what was happening, and she says her "windshield survey," conducted while driving around the city, showed her there were more kids delivering newspapers and more mail carriers than police, even police in their cars.

In the fall of 1987, Steele said, "I look around Flint today, and I read the newspaper about the kinds of crimes taking place and the amount of crime we have, and it's very clear the police have limited impact on crime. The officers aren't out walking and talking with people anymore. They aren't there to help the shopkeeper close up at night, so that he knows that he and his income are safe for the day, because of the presence of a foot patrol officer. I think of the relationships that were developed between the foot patrol officers and the Flint people in the neighborhoods and how that's been lost, and that's very sad."

In November 1987, Mayor Sharp lost his bid for re-election, and some suggest that many voters used that opportunity as a referendum on his dismantling of foot patrol. Flint voters instead elected 29-year-old Matt Collier, a white West Point graduate, who eventually chose Fay Peek III as police chief, which meant the department had had six chiefs in less than five years.

The third vote to fund a special millage for foot patrol, this time for four years, was slated for August 1988. Even foot patrol's staunchest supporters, who admitted they were surprised when the measure was approved the second time, held out little hope it would pass again. After all, many voters felt betrayed that their extra taxes never resulted in extra officers for foot patrol. Now they found themselves assessed an extra tax that was being used to pay for a program different from the one they had voted for. Yet Flint voters resoundingly approved the millage the third time, again by a new record margin, with 68 % voting yes.

Robert McFadden, a lieutenant in the department who has seen almost all these changes firsthand, says that the department under Peek is now trying to revive Community Policing, in a new form. Every officer has now received training in Neighborhood Policing, a program where all officers will be in cars taking radio calls, but they are encouraged to maintain contacts with residents in their beat areas. It is too early to tell how well the program will fare, he says, because they are still too short-staffed to allow much time for informal interaction.

"Yesterday (December 14, 1988) was a cold Wednesday, the middle of the week, yet we had 350 calls for service – calls we responded to, not total calls – so that means we are working hard just to keep up," he says. The department plans to add 40 new officers in the spring of 1989, with rumors of another 25 after that. "I don't mean to sound overly optimistic or overly pessimistic, but I don't think we will be able to tell for another year after we have those new officers whether the Neighborhood Policing concept is working."

Steele says, however, that the people of Flint are frustrated that it has taken so long for concrete action. "The people spoke when they elected our new mayor a year ago and when they passed the millage for a third time, yet we are still waiting to see more officers on the street."

The Flint Legacy

In the years since the final Flint evaluation was published, Trojanowicz, Baldwin, and Thompson have made more than 40 technical assistance visits, usually as a team, to departments in the United States and Canada that have asked the trio to help set up new Community Policing efforts based on what was learned from Flint.

Freed years ago from his obligation to act solely as a neutral observer, Trojanowicz has now assumed the role of advocate for Community Policing. Looking back, he says the Flint experience dramatically highlights Community Policing's promise and potential pitfalls. The positive research results, in particular those on fear of crime within the community and the officer's perceptions of personal safety and job satisfaction, have been replicated in important studies that have since been done on Community Policing in New York, Baltimore County (Maryland), and Houston. It must be remembered that just because a new idea demonstrates its merit, that is no guarantee that it will prevail.

Community Policing means change, and change is threatening, especially to those with a vested interest in the status quo. Some threats are internal and some are external. The police in general are conservative and therefore slow to adopt change. Some police officials still do not understand or accept what Comunity Policing can accomplish – and many say and even think they have Community Policing, though they do not. This program also demands strong support from the top, and any new Community Policing effort must do all it can to reduce the potential for hostility from motor patrol.

There are also forces in the community that can threaten its survival. Most city governments are struggling to find ways to do more with less, an economic climate far from conducive to launching a new labor-intensive program. Special interests can also feel threatened. Elected politicians, such as city council members, often worry about their support eroding when they see their constituents begin to turn to their CPOs for the kinds of help they once provided. Business people can resent a new program that focuses on residential areas, especially if their level of service therefore declines. Taxpayers, in particular middle-class homeowners who must work very hard for their money, can resent seeing their taxes go up to fund programs that seem to benefit the neighborhoods and people who contribute less. You can never ignore the role that politics and economics play in the delivery of police service.

Benson says that Flint serves as a lesson that Community Policing must never be funded separately, by a special pot of money. "Even government employee retirement funds have become an inviting target for politicians who face tremendous pressure to find new sources of funding," he says. "In many communities, people have demonstrated that they are willing to tax themselves more to pay for improved and expanded police service, but there is obvious danger in putting those funds in a special account where it can become a temptation." Benson also worries about the potential for corrupting officers, if they must pander to voters to save their jobs.

Many problems stemmed from the fact that Flint foot patrol was an add-on, a separately funded unit, instead of being part of a department-wide shift to what has now come to be called the Community Policing philosophy, with its structural changes that include using CPOs as community outreach specialists. Of course, at the time of the Flint experiment, no one expected that this effort would evolve into a revolutionary new way of policing. Flint was originally conceived as a pilot project to see what a focused foot patrol program could and could not achieve. Yet once out on those beats, without a rigid agenda and with the mandate to innovate, the possibilities concerning what this kind of approach could achieve began to coalesce into a vision of how the police could function as community problem-solvers, serving as the catalyst for short- and long-term positive change.

Baldwin says Flint serves as a cautionary tale for those who are launching new efforts, because it proves the importance of enlisting the support of motor patrol officers in the planning process. Benson concurs, suggesting that Community Team Policing, which will be discussed in the last section, may be the most pragmatic new way of forestalling internal tensions that can threaten Community Policing from within.

Steele, recently returned from the Executive Sessions on Policing at Harvard University's Kennedy School of Government that Mott helped to fund, says, "I have spent many years involved in making grants for social change. The adoption of Community Policing has been as fast as any social change I've seen. The challenge is to provide workable models and the information to allow police departments to understand this new philosophy and how it can be made to work."

While some advocates worried that Flint's checkered history might be held against the Community Policing concept, those familiar with the details of what happened there grant that Flint faced a uniquely intense series of economic and political crises. As noted earlier, its history is not a story filled with villains who were intent on killing foot patrol. Rather, it shows that even people who thought they were helping often ended up causing damage. Edmonton (Canada) Police Superintendent Chris Braiden may have summed it up best when he said, "Perhaps Flint had to throw itself on the barbed wire so that others could go over the top."

The Flint Results

Results of the research on the Flint experimental program were published as *An Evaluation of the Neighborhood Foot Patrol Program in Flint, Michigan**. The evaluation analyzed the research data in terms of the program goals, which were developed before the researchers came on board.

The findings were based on data from many sources. To determine the impact of the program on the community, random citizens were sampled each year, with those findings compared and contrasted with a survey of a panel of area residents. Block club leaders in the experimental areas were also surveyed, along with association leaders from around the city. To complete the picture of the community, the reseachers queried business people, the clergy, and social service agencies.

Research on the police included surveys and informal interviews with some motor patrol officers and all foot patrol officers, as well as their respective supervisors. The research team also analyzed data from crime complaints, daily-weekly-monthly reports, foot officers' flex-time records, juvenile booking sheets, and articles from four area newspapers.

Highlights as they relate to the program goals include:

Goal Number One – To decrease the amount of actual or perceived criminal activity:

• **Crime Rates** – Though it sounds logical to assess any new police program on how well it impacts on crime rates, this approach automatically has problems, because external factors such as unemployment can affect crime and because relying on crime statistics ignores the large number of crimes that go unreported.

In the case of Community Policing, the problem is compounded further, because, as noted before, reported crime may actually increase as a result, at least temporarily, for two reasons. First, a successful Community Policing effort should

---

*A limited number of copies are available free of charge. See details in the Notes of this chapter.

boost confidence in the police, which can mean people trust them enough to begin reporting a greater share of the crimes that typically go unreported. The second reason relates to increased exposure. As people feel safer, they are more likely to venture out, which can mean more opportunities for people to be victimized, resulting in at least a temporary rise in certain kinds of crime.

Critics suggest that this means Community Policing deludes people into thinking they are safer, when, in fact, they are not. Supporters contend the potential risk of a small increase in individual victimization may be a collective price worth paying, if this also means many more people begin to participate more freely in community life. If it occurs, this may also prove to be a transitional phase, until people reach the *critical mass* necessary to regain control of their neighborhoods from predators.

In Flint, such concerns were irrelevant, because the research showed that target crimes in the experimental areas decreased during the three-year period. The crimes monitored included burglary, automobile theft, assault, vandalism, robbery, criminal sexual assault, and larceny from a home, a person, or a vehicle. These crimes were selected as those most likely to be committed by juveniles, the most crime-prone age group and a group targeted for special attention by foot patrol officers.

The research team found that 4,085 of these crimes were committed in the experimental area in 1978, and the number declined to 3,731 in 1981 at the end of the study, an overall decrease of 8.7%. In the city as a whole, crime generally increased during this same period.

Breaking the figures down further, of the nine crimes analyzed, all except burglary and robbery declined over the three years, with criminal sexual conduct down most (46%). If burglary and robbery are subtracted from the total, the rate for the remaining seven crimes dropped 21.8% during the experiment. (It should also be noted that the two crimes that increased typically occur during nighttime hours, when the foot patrol officers were not on duty.)

Analyzing those statistics by beat shows that these crimes declined in 10 of the experimental beat areas, remained the same in one, and rose in three. Keep in mind, however, that both the geographic area and the number of people covered in each beat increased substantially during the three-year period. For example, the beat area where crime rates remained the same was 20 times larger at the end of the study compared to the beginning. The three beats where crime rates rose had also expanded significantly compared to their original size.

While proponents of Community Policing have been reluctant to claim that it has any enhanced ability to reduce the amount of crimes committed, the Flint results appeared encouraging. Research on other initiatives has failed to confirm these optimistic findings, but it should be remembered that the Flint experiment involved a higher level of saturation of foot patrol officers than most other efforts have enjoyed.

• **Calls for Service** – The typical wisdom is that Community Policing efforts will spur a jump in calls for service, as people turn to the police for help more often than in the past. The startling result in Flint was that calls for service decreased dramatically instead, down 43.4 % during the three-year period, from 678 calls in 1978 to 384 in 1981. The researchers speculated that foot patrol encouraged people to deal with many nagging but relatively minor problems informally. Instead of calling the police about that barking dog, they would wait to talk it over with their foot patrol officer the next time they crossed paths, or they learned to confront their neighbors directly without involving the police.

• **Citizen Perceptions** – To monitor how community residents perceived foot patrol during the first year of foot patrol, the research team selected 84 residents at random from the 14 beat areas to serve as a panel that could be surveyed extensively about their attitudes toward various concerns. At the end of the second year, only 48 panel members could be located and surveyed, so the team augmented those findings by surveying an additional 320 residents at random with a shortened form of the questionnaire. At the end of the third year, the panel consisted of 44 people from the foot patrol areas, who were surveyed in depth. In addition, 280 residents chosen at random from people in the experimental areas were surveyed the third year using the shortened form. (In this wrap-up, the term *panel* refers to the smaller group surveyed in depth all three years, while *survey* refers to the larger group that was asked the shortened form of the questionnaire in years two and three of the study.)

   The survey of residents conducted at the end of the three-year period showed that almost half (48 %) said foot patrol had reduced crime in their areas. (Fewer than 15 % said it had not, while the remaining 37 % had no opinion.) Over the three-year period, there was a progressive increase in the number of people who said foot patrol did, in fact, deter crime.

   This corresponded with a decrease in actual victimizations for daytime crime among panel residents, best viewed as anecdotal, given the small numbers involved. In the first year of the study, panel members reported being the victims of five daytime crimes in the past year. By the third year, only one panel member reported being victimized during morning and afternoon hours, the period when foot patrol officers were on duty.

Goal Number Two – To increase the citizens' perception of personal safety:

• **Citizen Perceptions** – At the end of the third year, roughly 70 % of those surveyed reported feeling safer as a result of foot patrol, though many qualified their response by saying they felt especially safe when their foot patrol officer was well known and highly visible. This perception of safety increased each year during the three years of the experiment, despite the progressive expansion and increased turnover among foot officers, the result of layoffs and excessive rotation.

When the people surveyed the third year were asked if they felt crime was a more serious problem in their neighborhoods, compared to other neighborhoods, only 14% said this was true. Roughly half (49%) said their area had fewer crime problems, while another 26% rated the crime problem in their area as average. People identified burglary as the crime they feared most.

Goal Number Three – To deliver to Flint residents the type of law enforcement service consistent with community needs and the ideals of modern police practice:

- **Citizen Perceptions** – The purpose of this goal was to direct foot patrol's energies toward the greatest community need, which meant the program should encourage a high degree of input from residents. Of the 280 people surveyed in year three, 42% said they knew what foot patrol's duties were, and they listed patrolling, working with neighborhood groups, taking complaints, and working with young people. Many also said foot patrol officers should function as general problem-solvers in the community. When asked what they expected from foot patrol officers, 27% said protection, 19% patrolling, 12% high visibility and availability, and 6% taking complaints.

  In year three, 64% expressed satisfaction with the program (18% were not satisfied, and the same percentage had no opinion), up from 58% the previous year (when dissatisfaction stood at 27%). Almost half (48%) had ideas about how the program could be improved, and, of those, 48% said more foot officers were needed. A significant number also said the foot patrol beat areas were too large.

- **Officer Perceptions** – During all three years of the study, both motor and foot patrol officers said they were doing a job the department wanted done. Though the vast majority of foot officers continued to say each year that they felt they were doing a job the department valued, their numbers declined slightly each year. In contrast, foot patrol supervisors did not feel they were doing a job the department valued highly, though this improved a bit each year.

  The study also showed that foot patrol supervisors felt increasingly isolated from the rest of the department. Foot officers felt most isolated the second year, the least during the last year.

  It also appears that foot officers learned to value their independence. In the first year, both foot and motor patrol officers agreed that police officers should be held accountable to their peers. Motor officers continued to hold this belief, but, over time, foot officers began to worry less about pleasing their fellow officers and more about pleasing the community. Foot officers more often than motor patrol officers said they improved community relations as a result of the job.

Foot officers, far more than motor officers, also felt that knowing community residents and teaching them to report crime were important police goals. The study showed that motor officers placed more importance on professional detachment, while foot officers valued their involvement in counseling, reassuring, and helping people in the community. Of note is how the foot officer's feelings about maintaining control changed over the course of the study. Foot officers ranked maintaining control very highly during the first and third years of the study, but lower during the second year. When they were new on the job, this seemed important, but as the program settled in, they began to feel more secure. By year three, however, the rapid expansion again appeared to add to their insecurity.

Foot officers also considered enforcing the law and maintaining public acceptance as top priorities. Neither foot nor motor patrol officers rated moving up in the department as an important goal. Where they differed was in the importance of helping victims, with foot patrol officers consistently rating that as a more important goal than their motor patrol counterparts.

Enthusiasm for the job of foot patrol declined during the three years, resulting in part from the expansion and other changes. Many also cited the added emotional strain implicit in the job, a problem supervisors should be made aware of because of the danger of burnout.

Goal Number Four – To create a community awareness of crime problems and methods of increasing law enforcement's ability to deal with actual or potential criminal activity effectively:

- **Unreported Crime** – Any community crime prevention effort must contend with the problem of unreported crime, so the researchers surveyed people in the target areas about this issue. In the third year, fewer than 12 % said they knew of any unreported crime. Most people surveyed said that people report crime, especially serious crime. Sixty-two percent said their foot officers encouraged them to report crime (only 5 % said the officer was indifferent, while the remaining had no opinion).

- **Victimization** – 27 % said they had been a victim of crime within the past three years. More than half (56 %) of those who had been victimized said they had reported the crime to the police. Keep in mind, however, that many unreported crimes were relatively minor – broken windows, stolen bikes. Panel participants reported that their victimization rate was cut in half by the end of the third year of foot patrol (it had been even better at the end of year two).

- **Officer Perceptions** – When the foot officers were surveyed, most said people were more likely to report crimes. They also noted neighborhood associations were playing less of a role in keeping citizens informed about crime. That answer reflected in part the fact that foot officers were playing a greater role in keeping people informed, but it may also reflect that, by the third year, foot officers were stretched so thin that they had less contact with association leaders and therefore knew less about their activities.

Goal Number Five – **To develop citizen volunteer action in support of and under the direction of the police department aimed at various target crimes:**

- **Citizen Interaction** – Meeting this goal depended on promoting interaction among citizens, and the survey showed that 44 % said they had talked to neighbors about crime prevention and about the foot patrol program (all but 1 % said their comments about foot patrol were favorable). People who lived in areas that were not covered by foot patrol were far less likely to discuss crime prevention with neighbors.

  People in the experimental areas were also asked if they knew about programs their foot patrol officers had helped initiate, and 30 % did, citing block club meetings, safety and crime prevention programs, and efforts targeted at schools and kids. In addition, 29 % could provide at least one name of a community leader who was influential in local affairs.

Goal Number Six – **To eliminate citizen apathy about reporting crime to police:** (see Goal Number Four)

Goal Number Seven – **To increase protection for women, children, and the aged:**

- **Target Populations** – In the third year, when people were asked if foot patrol enhanced the safety and well-being of these three target groups, 61 % said that it did (8 % said no, while the remaining 31 % had no opinion), up significantly from the year before when only 47 % felt this was true. When asked how protection for women, children, and the elderly could be improved, 19 % cited more help in teaching self-protection. One in five said adding more foot officers would help.

Goal Number Eight – To monitor the activities of the foot patrol officers:

- **Citizen Perceptions** – More than 90 % of the people in target areas surveyed the third year said they were aware of the program – 38 % had seen a foot patrol officer, 29 % had personal contact, and 11 % learned of the program from media coverage. This means 67 % had either seen or had personal contact with a foot officer. How often people saw their foot officer varied widely – some saw them only occasionally, while others said they saw them several times a week. More than a third knew the officer by name.

- **Officer Involvement** – The researchers examined the foot officers' daily, weekly, and monthly reports, as well as their flex-time schedules, to determine their level of involvement with the people in their area. Because of the way records were kept, however, it was difficult to establish a meaningful way of counting specific community contacts. The research did show that foot officers spent more time each succeeding year in counseling victims, and that they produced articles about crime prevention for school, community, and church publications. Documentary evidence of juvenile contact was sketchy, but the researchers who spent time one-on-one with foot officers in their beat areas confirmed extensive time was spent working with juveniles. As noted in the wrap-up on the Flint experiment, many programs also targeted the elderly. Foot patrol officers were particularly concerned about rape, so many tried to find ways to teach women self-protection, both individually and in groups.

Goal Number Nine – To measure the interface between foot patrol officers and other units of the Flint Police Department as well as referrals to other agencies:

- **Citizen Perceptions** – The resident survey asked people which kind of officer – foot or motor – was more effective in terms of six important police activities. By large margins, people saw foot officers as more effective in preventing crime, encouraging citizen self-protection, working with juveniles, and following up complaints. Motor officers were viewed as superior in responding to complaints and investigating the circumstances of crime.

  A closer look shows that people in eight of the 14 experimental areas actually rated foot patrol officers higher on investigation, but not by enough to overcome results from other areas. Motor patrol's edge in the category of responding to complaints no doubt related to their ability to respond rapidly. Surveys of business people, block club leaders, and religious leaders showed all gave foot patrol the nod in all six categories.

- **Police Perceptions** – When officers were asked the same questions, results showed that foot patrol officers rated themselves higher in all six areas, while motor patrol officers saw little difference between the two kinds of patrol. The survey of foot officers also showed their contacts with social service agencies, elementary schools, employers, and programs for the elderly rose each year. Part of the reason was because budget problems forced Flint to abandon neighborhood service representatives, which meant foot officers had to become more directly involved in making referrals. Attempts to quantify referrals were complicated by lack of an adequate data retrieval system.

    Since lack of cooperation between foot patrol and motor patrol had been cited as a problem, the research staff surveyed supervisors of both kinds of officers on 14 questions to clarify areas of agreement and disagreement:

- **Supervisory Contact** – Supervisors for both kinds of units agreed it was easier for a supervisor to contact a motor patrol officer than a foot officer.

- **Supervisory Control** – Both also agreed it was harder to monitor foot officers.

- **Developing Rapport** – This question generated disagreement. One group said the competence and demeanor of the individual supervisor was the most critical factor, while others felt foot patrol's looser approach fostered greater rapport.

- **Supervisory Problems** – Both groups felt a foot patrol officer intent on shirking his duty could hide this from a superior more easily than a motor patrol officer, and that there was also a danger foot officers could choose to spend time with just a few residents in their area.

- **Supervisory Respect** – The broad consensus was that the supervisor's competence was the crucial issue in winning respect. However, motor patrol supervisors said that being in dangerous situations with the officers under them provided them more opportunities to earn respect. Foot patrol supervisors, on the other hand, believed that the informal contact promoted within foot patrol was a decided advantage.

- **Roll Call** – All supervisors agreed that instituting regular roll calls for foot patrol was a good idea that would specifically improve accountability.

- **Pressure on Supervisors** – Both groups agree that foot patrol supervisors were more likely to receive extra pressure from upper police administration, other supervisors, and local politicians. Foot patrol supervisors said their motor counterparts did not appreciate the complexity of the foot patrol supervisor's job, the political sensitivity involved, and the difficulties in supervising officers in a less structured environment. Motor patrol supervisors, on the other hand, said the kinds of decisions a motor patrol supervisor had to make and the hours they had to work made their job the more difficult one.

- **Supervisory Promotions** – Individual competence was again cited as the major determinant, though some felt motor patrol supervisors had an edge because of the variety of situations they face.

- **Supervisory Motivation** – Some said they chose supervision of foot patrol because of the variety of work and the excitement of being involved in a new community-based effort. A more cynical view was that foot patrol supervisors chose the assignment because there was no night duty and to avoid many of the uglier and more dangerous aspects of traditional police work.

- **Supervisory Advantages** – Each kind of supervisory job had its own advantages and disadvantages. Foot patrol supervisors worked better hours and had more opportunity for individual initiative. They also enjoyed the special prestige that comes from being part of a new program aimed at people in the community. The job also had its own set of pressures, in particular the demands involved in keeping track of foot officers. Supervisors of motor patrol officers benefited from the fact their officers had a more clearly defined job and less interference from inside and outside the department. The disadvantages included a rigid routine, nighttime hours, and less room for creativity.

- **Supervisory Authority** – Both groups of supervisors felt they had the same amount of authority, but that their responsibilities were very different.

- **Supervisory Evaluation** – Both agreed that each job should have its own set of criteria for evaluation. There was consensus that foot patrol supervisors should have superior communications skills and a sound sense of how society actually operates. Motor patrol officers need to know the law and its applications in greater depth, and they must be able to make quick decisions in life-threatening situations.

- **Future of Foot Patrol** – Most believed the program was good for Flint and that it should be supported. However, all felt economics would ultimately determine whether it would be continued, and in what form. There was general agreement that the program would be greatly reduced if it had to be supported solely by city funds.

Goal Number Ten – To evaluate the impact of training on the performance of foot patrol officers:

- **Officer Training** – A total of three training sessions were held during the course of the experiment. The first was a two-week program at the Flint Police Academy in 1978, just before the program was launched. Topics included: problems of aging, voluntary action, neighborhood block clubs, human relations, and juvenile and departmental procedures.

  The second session was held at Michigan State University roughly a year later. Topics covered during the four-day session: organization and structure of foot patrol, working with the community, interpersonal communications and conflict resolution, the role of foot versus motor officers, stress in policing, dealing with juveniles inside and outside the court, using supervision, city ordinances, and police/community relations.

  The third session, three days' long, was held in November 1981 to wrap up the first two years of the evaluation and to provide additional training. Topics included: working with juveniles, obtaining community input, the objectives of foot patrol, procedures and paperwork, arrests and appearance tickets, abandoned cars, block clubs, newsletters, referrals to other agencies, the elderly, working with other Flint Police Department units, public presentations, city ordinances, city code enforcement, neighborhood complaints, the image of foot patrol, and the role of creativity, input, and discipline.

  As this wrap-up shows, officers in the program helped shape the training as the experiment progressed. Officers were repeatedly asked to make suggestions about what the sessions should cover. In addition to these regular training opportunities, one-on-one consultation and training were provided as needed to improve individual performance. Efforts were also made to train new officers as they came on board.

  Foot officers consistently said that practical police experience was the best education, but that training in interpersonal and communications skills was also important. Foot officers placed a greater value on training than their supervisors.

Other Important Findings

The Mott Foundation funded the foot patrol experiment in Flint to help the city cope with its crime problems, but the foundation's other stated goal is to influence social change at the national level. When the research confirmed the success of the

Flint pilot project, the foundation then supported efforts to inform people nationwide about what Community Policing can accomplish. As part of that continuing effort, Mott approved funding to establish the National Neighborhood Foot Patrol Center (now called the National Center for Community Policing) at Michigan State University.

The purpose of the center was to disseminate information and research on Community Policing to police administrators, government officials, and community leaders nationwide. In that regard, the center has distributed many publications (including 16 booklets, the Community Policing Series) about Community Policing issues. As many as 7,500 copies at one time have been mailed free to interested individuals and organizations worldwide. A brief synopsis of some topics covered in the series that relate directly to the Flint research follows:

- **Perceptions of Safety: A Comparison of Foot Patrol Versus Motor Patrol Officers** – The Flint research team queried both foot and motor patrol officers on five questions related to how safe they felt after a year on the job and again in 1984. Both studies showed that foot officers, to a statistically significant degree, felt safer than their motor patrol counterparts on all five measures. The findings were consistent regardless of age, race, gender, and any prior police or military experience.

    When asked to explain their feelings of security, foot patrol officers most frequently cited their familiarity with both the people and places in their beats. In essence, they felt they could tell the bad guys from the good guys, and they knew which places were safe to enter and which meant trouble. They also felt confident that they knew when they would need to call for backup, and they felt equally secure that community residents would help them, if needed.

    This does not mean that foot officers promoted vigilantism. The kind of help people offered is exemplified by what happened when a foot officer was being harassed by a group of teenagers after dark. People who saw the problem unfolding dashed to their phones and called neighbors, urging them to turn on their porch lights. When all those lights flicked on, the kids fled.

    In the 1984 study, foot officers also said their patrol areas were safer than the rest of the city, mainly because they "owned" that portion of the city and had done things to make the area safer. The study also showed foot officers conducted fewer *pat-downs,* since they only frisked strangers and others they did not trust.

- **Job Satisfaction: A Comparison of Foot Patrol Versus Motor Patrol Officers** – Questions about job satisfaction were not part of the 1981 study, done two years after foot patrol had been in operation, but they were a major focus in the 1984 research. Again, to a statistically significant degree, more foot than motor patrol officers felt they were:

- doing an important job in the department

- doing an important job in their patrol area

- keeping up with problems in their patrol area

- doing a job the department sees as important

- working as part of a police team

Both foot and motor officers agree that, though foot officers had more difficulty communicating with headquarters and other police units, motor officers had more difficulty maintaining high morale and job satisfaction. Foot officers were also more enthusiastic about their current job compared to when they joined the department, though as noted earlier, dissatisfaction with changes made in the foot patrol effort meant that they were increasingly less enthusiastic about the way it was implemented. It should also be noted that most foot officers had volunteered for foot patrol duty, whereas motor patrol officers did not typically have the option of selecting their assignment.

Foot patrol officers also felt that being part of foot patrol did not have a negative impact on advancement. The main job satisfaction scale where there was no difference between the two units concerned whether they would re-enter police work if they could start over again, with roughly seven of 10 in both groups saying they would.

- **The Impact of Foot Patrol on Black and White Perceptions of Policing** – National Crime Surveys in the 1970s consistently showed that blacks rated the police less favorably than whites. The 1979 survey of Flint residents reflected this pattern, with blacks roughly 20 % more likely to view police performance negatively. This disparity dropped dramatically when a sample of Flint residents of both races was asked to rate foot patrol, in studies done in 1981, 1982, and 1983. The overwhelming majority of all Flint residents expressed satisfaction with the program, with variations between blacks and whites ranging from 0.7 % (in 1982) to 3.5 % (in 1981). By 1983, whites were 2.2 % more likely to express dissatisfaction with motor patrol than blacks.

  As noted earlier, foot patrol officers were less likely to frisk people than motor patrol officers, at least in part because foot patrol officers knew many people in the beat area well enough to determine whether they were a threat or not. Blacks have often contended they are routinely frisked, simply because of race, so this may be part of the reason that the black community did not perceive foot patrol as negatively as whites.

- **Community Policing: A Taxpayer's Perspective** – Among the many findings discussed in this in-depth analysis of the information gleaned from the community surveys was the erosion of the program's overall effectiveness as the rapid expansion began to dilute foot patrol's impact. By 1985, 17 % fewer people said they felt safer compared to figures for 1981. Satisfaction with foot patrol officers also declined 13 % over the same period. In addition, the number of people who said yes when asked whether foot patrol lowered crime in their neighborhoods declined 11 % over the intervening four years.

  The 1985 citizen survey added three new questions that had not been asked before. When asked whether the program had changed, precisely half of those who were surveyed said it had changed for the worse. When asked whether their expectations for the program had changed, now that it would funded by tax dollars, three of four said their attitude had not changed, though one in four said their expectations were now higher. When asked whether the program should be continued (and under what conditions), roughly nine of 10 said it should be maintained, with almost one-fourth saying that officers should be more visible. Comparing people's expectations for the program, the 1981 study showed one in four mentioned visibility, rising to almost half in 1985. Despite the obvious disillusionment, remember that the special millage for foot patrol has now passed three times, each time by a record-setting margin of approval.

  As this analysis shows, the research confirms that the foot patrol effort in Flint was a remarkable success. Yet the full story of what happened to foot patrol in Flint also shows how political and economic pressures can mean the operation was a success, but the patient died, though many continue to hope it will be reborn even stronger.

NOTES

If you would like a free copy of *An Evaluation of the Neighborhood Foot Patrol Program in Flint*, write to:

> The National Center for Community Policing
> Michigan State University
> School of Criminal Justice – 560 Baker Hall
> East Lansing, MI 48824-1118

Please let us know your affiliation or interest. We will make this offer available as long as supplies last.

[1] *Homicide Rate for Detroit Leads the Nation,* Detroit Free Press, July 10, 1988, p. 15A.

[2] Asimov, Isaac, *The Nightmare Life Without Fuel,* an essay first published in *Time* magazine that appeared in *The Prose Reader,* edited by Kim Flachmann and Michael Flachmann (Englewood Cliffs, NJ: Prentice-Hall), 1987.

The section of this chapter detailing the story of the Flint experiment was the result of in-person and telephone interviews with the main participants quoted. Since Robert Trojanowicz is not only co-author of this book, but he also headed the research evaluation, his information regarding that era is handled the same as the other interviewees. Names and dates of the interviews follow in alphabetical order:

Robert Baldwin – He was part of the Michigan State University research team, in addition to full-time duties as a detective with the Ingham County Sheriff's Department. He is now with Lansing Community College's criminal justice program. Interviewed December 5, 1988.

Jowanne Barnes-Coney – She was among the first foot patrol officers on the beat in Flint, and she is now a sergeant in charge of supervising the Flint Police Department's Police/School Liaison Program.

Bruce Benson – He was a lieutenant supervising the Flint foot patrol officers beginning approximately one year after the program was launched. Benson was deputy chief when he retired from the Flint Police Department and is now director of Public Safety at Michigan State University. Interviewed November 21, 1988.

Chris Braiden – Superintendent with the Edmonton (Canada) Police Department, from remarks made at the training sessions on community policing hosted by the National Neighborhood Foot Patrol Center at Michigan State University in April 1987.

Richard Gleason – Retired as chief of the Lansing Police Department in 1988. Interviewed twice at his office during March 1986.

Robert McFadden – A lieutenant in the Flint Police Department who was still involved in the Community Policing effort at the time he was interviewed on December 15, 1988.

Marilyn Steele – Program officer for the C.S. Mott Foundation in Flint, Michigan, who was interviewed numerous times, including in-person and telephone interviews in the fall of 1987, as well as telephone interviews during December 1988.

Jesse Thompson – Part of the MSU research team, in charge of surveying the community and now director of Personnel and Labor Relations for the City of Flint. Interviewed December 13, 1988.

Information included in the section called *The Flint Results* was condensed from *An Evaluation of the Neighborhood Foot Patrol Program in Flint,* by Robert Trojanowicz (East Lansing, MI: National Neighborhood Foot Patrol Center, Michigan State University), 1982.

Information included in the section called *Other Important Findings* was extracted from various booklets in the Community Policing Series, published by the National Neighborhood Foot Patrol

Center, located at Michigan State University, East Lansing, MI:

Perceptions of Safety: A Comparison of Foot Patrol Versus Motor Patrol Officers, by Robert C. Trojanowicz and Dennis W. Banas, Community Policing Series No. 1, published in 1985.

Job Satisfaction: A Comparison of Foot Patrol Versus Motor Patrol Officers, by Robert C. Trojanowicz and Dennis W. Banas, Community Policing Series No. 2, published in 1985.

The Impact of Foot Patrol on Black and White Perceptions of Policing, by Robert C. Trojanowicz and Dennis W. Banas, Community Policing Series No. 4, published in 1985.

Performance Profiles of Foot Versus Motor Officers, by Dennis M. Payne and Robert C. Trojanowicz, Community Policing Series No. 6, published in 1985.

Community Policing: A Taxpayer's Perspective, by Robert Trojanowicz, Marilyn Steele, and Susan Trojanowicz, Community Policing Series No. 7, published in 1986.

Other titles in the series:

The Status of Contemporary Community Policing Programs
Uniform Crime Reporting and Community Policing: An Historical Perspective
Implementing a Community Policing Model for Work With Juveniles: An Exploratory Study
Community Policing: Training Issues
Community Policing Programs: A Twenty-Year View
The Foot Patrol Officer, the Community and the School: A Coalition Against Crime
Foot Patrol: Some Problem Areas
Community Policing: The Line Officer's Perspective
Community Policing: Community Input Into Police Policy-Making
The Philosophy and Role of Community Policing
Community Policing: University Input Into Campus Police Policy-Making
The Meaning of Community in Community Policing
Community Policing: Would You Know It If You Saw It?

SECTION FOUR

SPECIAL PEOPLE/
SPECIAL PROBLEMS

CHAPTER 8
How Community Policing
Addresses Special Populations

Human nature is the same everywhere; the
modes only are different.
— *Lord Chesterfield*

By counterbalancing the traditional system's emphasis on reacting to calls for service with a proactive focus on solving community problems, Community Policing addresses many needs that would otherwise be left unmet. At the same time, this also implies extending personalized police service to many groups whose concerns can easily be overlooked in the existing system. Traditional policing tends to limit the department's response to crimes and those who commit them, especially those crimes where someone calls the police. Community Policing broadens the police mission, sending CPOs into the community as outreach specialists, so that they can learn about community problems related to crime, fear of crime, and disorder.

Even as early as the Flint experiment, special groups (in that case women, juveniles, and the elderly) were singled out for special attention. Since then, as the concept has continued to evolve, experience in other communities has demonstrated Community Policing's unique ability to reach out to many other diverse groups with personalized police service. As this chapter will show, Community Policing provides a new organizational model that allows the police to address the problems of groups who have not routinely turned to the police for help, for various reasons.

Critics of the Community Policing movement have argued that this new form of power-sharing between the police and people is unnecessary – and even dangerous. They contend that the existing system allows people input, through the political process, and that further involvement risks interference.

The first issue this ignores is that the reform movement in policing helped insu-

231

late the police from political pressure, though admittedly this can vary from locale to locale. While the police are never totally immune to political pressure – and complete isolation implies new risks, the existing system affords the police a greater measure of autonomy. Even though voters can express their will through the ballot box, people vote for city officials because of their positions on a number of issues, not just police service. The second flaw in that reasoning is that a simple yes or no vote can convey any meaningful information about the particular kinds of changes people want. Priorities shift and change, so that reaching a meaningful consensus on what the police agenda should be depends on encouraging constant dialogue between the police and average citizens.

The third and most important issue is that many groups, often those who suffer the highest rates of victimization, are literally or figuratively *disenfranchised* – the homeless cannot register because they have no fixed address, juveniles are too young, immigrants and undocumented aliens have no vote, and residents of many of the highest-crime areas are also among the groups least likely to exercise their franchise. Many such groups also fail to organize, they lack the money to lobby for their concerns, and their relative lack of social standing means they are unlikely to gain formal and informal access to those who hold power. Their lack of political clout may be part of why their priorities can be ignored, which may be part of why their problems persist.

Yet many contend the existing system is completely democratic, because everyone has the opportunity to trigger action from the police just by placing a phone call. However, many groups fail to call the police, for economic or cultural reasons. A mother on welfare may not have a telephone. A Mexican national living illegally in the United States may fear being deported. Legal immigrants may also be reluctant to call the police if their experience in their home countries makes them fearful of anyone in uniform.

Another worrisome trend is that the police response to a call for service may vary depending on where the call comes from. An article in the spring of 1989 in the *U.S. News & World Report* that calls some drug-infested hot spots *Little Beiruts,* says that "overburdened war-zone police districts apply triage to crime reports, focusing mainly on murders and shootings and ignoring burglaries. Implicitly, if not explicitly, many have adopted a policy of crime containment rather than prevention."[1]

Community Policing's ability to involve the disenfranchised in the police process and to reach out to other groups who are reluctant to contact the police offers everyone in the community grass-roots input into the police process. The following is a partial list of specific groups who are likely to benefit from a Community Policing approach. Though some applications are speculative, this list provides a blueprint concerning how Community Policing is used today and how it can be of even greater benefit tomorrow:

• **Juveniles** – Community Policing's potential impact on juveniles is one of its major strengths. As noted before, kids commit a disproportionate share of reported crime, and they are also at high risk of being victimized. Roughly 42 % of all persons arrested for the most serious Index violent and property crimes in 1985 were under 20 years old; almost four-fifths were male.[2] The age group with the highest victimization rates for both violent and property crimes were young people 16 through 19 years old.[3] Obviously as well, there is the potential for overlap, especially with minor offenses – the youngster who shoplifts a shirt from a store today is a perpetrator, but he becomes a victim if a classmate steals something from his gym locker tomorrow.

As a society, we recognize the need to handle juvenile offenders differently, because we hope they are more pliable than adults, more responsive to rehabilitation. We also expect that the exuberance of youth, coupled with an adolescent's need to test limits as a means of learning how to function in the adult world, tempts good kids to experiment with bad behavior. We have therefore attempted to fashion a juvenile justice system that will encourage development of internal controls, because no external system can ever be as effective in curbing misconduct as a strong individual and collective conscience. The goal is to find ways to teach young people that there are negative consequences for breaking the law, but without branding them as criminals or imposing sanctions that might inhibit their future growth.

This poses an obvious challenge for law enforcement. Police officers must be allowed discretion in dealing with juveniles, but how can any officer know if that seemingly chastened youngster is really taking that stern warning seriously – or laughing behind the officer's back? Many budding sociopaths are skillful manipulators who know how to exploit the potential weaknesses in any system. Many adult criminals exploit youngsters because their virtual immunity from harsh sanctions makes them useful pawns. If it does nothing else, Community Policing offers the police the opportunity, over time, to know the kids in their beats well enough to make informed decisions about how each should be handled.

A corollary danger in the existing system is that the traditional police response may depend too much on the behavior of the parents and too little on the needs of the individual youngster. Using shoplifting as an example, if the young offender is marched into the station house by his concerned parents, the police are expected to "play along." They may threaten dire consequences, but with no real intention of involving the formal system. In this case, the police role is to support the parents, because they offer the best hope of making a long-term, positive impact on their child.

The question becomes what happens if that youngster's parents are too busy or self-absorbed to notice the problem – or they simply do not care? If the police are instead called by the aggrieved shopkeeper and especially if the parents then appear indifferent, it may be far more likely the police will engage the formal system, in essence as a substitute for the parents' apparent failure to control their child. The unanswered question is whether formal action will be more likely to help or hurt and how Community Policing can help officers make wise judgment calls.

It is quite possible that a youngster from a troubled home, who may therefore already suffer low self-esteem, would have his already damaged opinion of himself lowered even more by being thrown into the formal juvenile justice system. That result may also invite further abuse from parents who have already helped persuade him that he is *bad, stupid,* or a *troublemaker.* This may be part of the key concerning why some youngsters respond positively to formal sanctions while others career further out of control. Community Policing allows officers the time and opportunity to focus on the youngster, rather than to allow the parents to control the police agenda. The existing system often means that the decision whether the blunder should be viewed as a "prank" or as a "crime" depends on the parents' behavior rather than the child's.

The greatest danger is that the existing system can degenerate into outright bias. It can mean that kids from *good* homes (white, middle-and upper-class, two-parent families) are more often treated with greater sensitivity and concern than kids from *high-risk* homes (minorities, low-income or Underclass, single-parent families). To show how use of discretion risks becoming abuse, a police administrator explained what he considered proper use of discretion in dealing with a young student suspected of committing a string of sexual assaults on young coeds. The chief met with the young man's parents, who were well-connected, well-respected, and affluent members of the community, and together all agreed that the best solution was for the family to remove the young man from school and enroll him in extensive and expensive private counseling, in exchange for which the police would leave the file open, but they would not pursue the case to arrest unless the rapes persisted.

This situation raises a number of important issues, not the least of which is whether the police official in charge had any faith in the juvenile justice system's ability to cope with the problem. It also raises concerns about the factors that tipped the scales – did the decision have anything to do with the young man, or did it have more to do with the apparently sincere concern expressed by the parents or their assurances about the efficacy of private help? The obvious question, of course, was whether the decision to allow the young man to remain free was unduly influenced by the parents' money, race, and social standing.

While that particular incident reeks of abuse, it highlights the tendency toward two-track justice. We must guard against a system where the sons and daughters of the affluent both expect and receive special treatment, because the parents engender respect, they know how to gain access at the top, and they can persuasively articulate and fund expensive alternatives to the formal system. Allowing anyone to make a judgment call means that some mistakes will be made, but limiting that power to those at the top, to the police officials who are least accountable to oversight within the department, appears misguided.

In that sense, because Community Policing profoundly restructures the police, by extending personalized police service to social classes previously excluded, it provides a way for line officers to use informed discretion to provide support to youngsters and their families who might otherwise never gain access to decision-makers in the traditional system. While critics might argue that simply allows more people to make more mistakes, it not only promotes a fairer system, but one where CPOs have an enhanced opportunity to make reasoned judgments based on greater knowledge of the juvenile's potential for rehabilitation, with oversight provided by supervisors. Community Policing should at least allow the line officer more information on which to decide whether that shoplifter deserves a break or not. It also helps counterbalance the concern that the existing system allows privileged youngsters to go free, even if they have committed serious crimes, while youngsters from less fortunate families more often find themselves enmeshed in the system for lesser crimes.

In the role of community liaison, a CPO can also link families to public and private agencies who can help, whether that is in the form of affordable counseling for the juvenile or perhaps a substance abuse program for the parents. The CPO's intense involvement with the community allows him to reach out to families who need assistance, at the same time it increases the likelihood that people will trust him enough to ask for help.

Though we often stress that Community Policing reaches out to law-abiding people in the community, we must also remember people do not fall into neatly defined categories. There are now more than 2.6 million adults under some form of correctional care, custody, or supervision,[4] and many are the fathers and mothers – or brothers and sisters – of impressionable youngsters struggling to define values in which to believe. In some homes, young people are taught that the police are the enemies, and that the law is a joke that only suckers obey. Community Policing can counterbalance those views, by allowing youngsters to see officers in a different light, as people who work hard to help others.

The only direct exposure to the police these children might have otherwise is when uniformed strangers arrive to take their loved ones away. Community Policing cannot be expected to work miracles, but it offers the police an important new way to challenge the strong anti-police sentiments brewing in the young people who may set the tone for their neighborhoods in the future.

While many in this era tend to romanticize the virtues of the family, we must also recognize that troubled families can wreak incalculable damage on their young. Domestic violence is an obvious concern, and a very conservative estimate places such incidents at more than a half-million a year.[5] As noted before, the American Humane Society found more than 1.7 million cases of child abuse had been reported to authorities in 1984.[6] Experts estimate that 60% to 70% of children raised in violent homes become abusers themselves as adults.[7]

Parents with alcohol or drug problems can also poison young lives. Membership in Alcoholics Anonymous has grown from 96,000 in 1950 to 775,000 by 1989.[8] A study of 155,000 pregnant women nationwide showed 11% admitted taking an illegal drug during their pregnancy, with cocaine cited most often. This is of great concern because evidence is emerging that the fetus or breast-fed newborn can suffer when the mother takes even one toke on a crack pipe. The resulting damage can include reduced head and brain size.[9]

Nearly two million young people run away from home every year, and one in five of those is a *throwaway,* forced out of their homes because of hardship or conflict.[10] Of those who end up homeless, 80% report being the victim of sexual abuse at home.[11] Mounting evidence also suggests a link between childhood sexual victimization and adult sex offenses. Of the 255 sex offenders in the Massachusetts Treatment Center, 90% reported they were sexually abused as children.[12]

While we will discuss later Community Policing's specific role in broadening the police's opportunity to cope with illegal drugs, the approach's ability to help youngsters master their lives and build self-esteem offers direct help to kids who do daily battle against a variety of oppressive family problems and pressures. Many such children are too embarrassed or afraid to talk about their problems with adult outsiders, yet many CPOs report that they have been able to establish sufficient trust so that young people talk openly to them.

Though critics contend this should be the province of social workers and not police officers, today's centralized welfare system typically does not put social workers into the community where they can interact directly with troubled kids. While CPOs, by default, often become the primary social agents who regularly interact with young people, they may also be the best choice, because of the broad array of options at their disposal. Sometimes the best solution might be simply to provide a sympathetic ear, other times to assist in securing professional help, and even on occasion to make an arrest, a necessity in some cases of child abuse.

The CPO can also serve as one of the few positive role models in low-income, high-crime areas. In many such communities, the only people left who make good money are pimps and drug dealers, because everyone else who can afford to has moved away. Children grow up with little or no exposure to people with college degrees and people who hold down interesting, creative, and productive jobs.

Instead they are surrounded by people whose idleness and poverty breed a host of other problems. The CPO who takes kids to the zoo, organizes softball teams, and also arrests wrongdoers offers a potent alternative to criminals whose thick bankroll, fashionable clothes, and fancy cars otherwise seem to spell success. And who better than a CPO to show young people firsthand the personal satisfaction that comes from working hard at a challenging job that will never make you rich?

Distorted or overly confining sexual roles also appear to contribute to violence in some neighborhoods, particularly in Underclass areas. Though experts continue to debate where responsibility lies and the relative role of each, lack of jobs and lack of a strong work ethic conspire to reduce the likelihood that young people in Underclass neighborhoods learn to seek their sexual identity in work. In middle class families, being a man means working to support a family. Being female either means staying home to raise the children, or increasingly, it means working part-time or full-time to help support the household.

On the mean streets in many cities, a different ethic prevails, because fewer people work, and even among those who do, unemployment is often a chronic problem. In those neighborhoods, being a man often means being willing to use violence – male macho behavior. Their female counterparts derive their sexual identity by having babies, often before they have completed high school and before marriage. Though rarely touched upon, there is good reason to suppose that the macho image of the tough cop fostered in many police departments contributes to the overall climiate of violence, verifying that *real* men are willing to play rough, and reinforcing that fists and guns are the most virile way to solve problems.

The police uniform implies power, as do the badge and gun, so substituting the symbol of the CPO in uniform, an officer who relies on brains, not brawn, someone who openly demonstrates care and concern, offers both sexes a far healthier role model. CPOs of both sexes send important messages to members of their own sex and their opposites, though it is the violence associated with males that causes the most potentially lethal problems. Male CPOs function as healthy role models for males, men who use force as a last resort, and also as a reminder to young women of virtues that they should seek in a mate. This, in turn, can put additional pressure on young males to abandon macho strutting as a way to win female approval.

Female CPOs allow young women growing up to see a woman in an authoritative and productive role, a woman who is independent and in charge of her life. A female CPO also teaches young males that power derives from respect and not gender, and that being a woman does not mean being subservient. This is not to suggest that traditional officers who do not succumb to the macho myth cannot also serve as role models, but that the expanded mission and constant presence of CPOs offer them more opportunities to make an impact.

No one can design a research study to prove or disprove that Community Policing's primary long-range effect is that it can deter a certain percentage of high-risk youngsters from embarking on a life of crime. How can we measure the long-term effect of the officer in Flint who incorporated his love of fishing into his job by inaugurating an annual Fishing Derby, where each youngster who participated won a trophy? Is that any less cost effective than using sworn officers to guard parade routes, protect politicians, or make drug education speeches in schools? Even solely in terms of self-protection, does it not make sense to suppose that years down the road, an officer ordered to shut down an after-hours *blind pig* or illegal gambling game would be safer doing so in a community that had benefited from years of Community Policing?

Community Policing provides full-fledged law enforcement in a more comprehensive way than traditional efforts. The tragic flaw in existing police efforts is that officers waste too much time on free patrol, accomplishing little or nothing, waiting for that rare call where a quick response can make a valid difference. This reflects the prevailing wisdom throughout the criminal justice system that scarce resources are best allocated according to the severity of the crime.

That may seem like a wise budget strategy, but the drawback is that it translates into a system that sends a dangerous message to young people, because children learn more from what we do than from what we say. Youngsters, especially those in high-crime areas, quickly learn that only the most violent offenders serve much time behind bars. As a society, we may say that we abhor burglars, thieves, and dope dealers, but in many communities, young people see that those offenders are often right back on the street. This proves to them that this society either does not care much about such crimes, that the system has no teeth, or that we do not care enough to put our money where our mouth is.

Young people do not launch long-term criminal careers with a daring bank robbery, an elaborate kidnapping scheme, or a million-dollar dope deal. Yet the traditional police delivery system does not want officers "wasting" much time tracking down the kid who may have thrown rocks through a few windows at school. Narcotics officers on their way to bust Mr. Big at the dope house cruise right by those fleet-footed 10-year-old lookouts. And a call about a botched attempt by a youngster to hotwire a car would not be much of a priority, especially in neighborhoods where far more serious crimes occur every day.

Community Policing not only addresses the fact these crimes serve as a youngster's training wheels, but it encourages officers to consider them a priority and to develop short- and long-term programs to intervene. Unless we make institutional changes that free officers to take *petty* juvenile infractions seriously – and allow them to own a piece of the city so that they can identify youngsters at risk – we are telling kids they are free to hone criminal skills until the day they cross the line so dramatically that we can no longer ignore them. In the meanwhile, however, our collective failure risks permitting that first successful experiment to be repeated often enough to become a habit – sometimes a lifelong habit.

As Bruce Benson of the Flint experiment noted, we do not have any obvious means of turning around a hardened career criminal – the 40-year-old burglar. This makes it vitally important to provide CPOs so that we can catch that 12-year-old when he commits his first burglary. The police must never stop telling kids that breaking the law is wrong, but we must invest more in efforts that prove to them that we mean it.

- **Youth Gangs** – The police have long had concerns about the link between youth gangs and juvenile delinquency. Movies such as *Blackboard Jungle* and *West Side Story* focused public attention on the problem decades ago, but we are now reaping the legacy of our failure to deal with the threat before those youngsters exchanged their *zip guns* for Uzi's and Mac-10's.

What is also different today is that some youth gangs have become lucrative, self-supporting crime syndicates through drug dealing. According to Carl Taylor, a Michigan State University professor who has spent years studying gangs in Detroit, youth gangs now break down into two distinct types, what he calls the *scavenger gangs* and the organized *corporate gangs*. Scavengers fit the old *West Side Story/ Blackboard Jungle* mold, where members band together to socialize and for mutual protection, while the emerging corporate gangs model themselves more closely on organized crime.

Taylor's research showed important differences between the two types of gangs. Scavenger gang members said they had no desire to work unless they could land a high-paying job, highly unlikely since their school attendance was usually low and many admitted to using alcohol and illicit drugs. Scavenger gang members also reported committing criminal acts at random, and they viewed violence as a way of life, but they considered delinquent acts as wrong. In contrast, corporate gang members saw criminal activity as their way to share in the American dream of "big money," with violence as a tool useful in achieving that goal. Criminal acts were planned, as part of doing business, and almost all saw nothing wrong with what they were doing and felt no remorse. Unlike their scavenger counterparts, most corporate gang members attend school fairly regularly, and less than half said they used alcohol recreationally. And while their business was dealing drugs, gang rules meant they never dared use the illicit substances they were selling.[13]

This frightening phenomenon harkens back to Prohibition, when bootlegging syndicates opened fire with sub-machine guns in battles on city streets, killing innocent bystanders; gang members who broke the rules were tortured and killed; and kids were used as lookouts and to make low-level deliveries. What is new with crack gangs is that the *Cosa Nostra* code of honor has been abandoned in favor of using wholesale slaughter of entire families to enforce discipline and frighten competitors.

Repeal of the Volstead Act ended the escalating open reign of terror on city streets caused by gang warfare – one reason that even teetotallers had reason to oppose Prohibition – and some gangs survived, by adopting a lower profile and moving into new legal and illegal ventures, while others faded away. Though decriminalization has now become part of the public debate about how to solve today's drug problems, there is virtually no chance drugs like heroin and cocaine (and its cheap and highly addictive form, crack) will be legalized in the foreseeable future. Alcohol has always been a mainstream drug. While alcohol blights the lives of many people and results in staggering carnage on the nation's highways, people do not see someone who enjoys a beer now and then as a potential threat in the same way as someone who takes a hit from a crack pipe.

Though we will deal in the next chapter specifically with Community Policing's role in coping with illegal drugs, its potential role in dealing with both kinds of youth gangs deserves special mention. The police have always supported youth clubs and Police Athletic Leagues as a social outlet for kids as an alternative to joining gangs. Yet as Harvard policy analyst Mark A.R. Kleiman and his associate Kerry D. Smith noted in a recent paper, "Gangs also serve (and help create) the need among kids in tough neighborhoods for simple physical protection. In some Los Angeles neighborhoods, being a Blood is safer than not being a Blood, because it offers protection both from the Bloods themselves and from random bullying and theft."[14]

Regardless of what kind of gang is involved, this offers the police a hook to at least prevent marginal members – the hangers-on who join out of concern for their personal safety – from becoming hard-core gang members. As Kleiman and Smith have argued, providing young people "protection against assault and theft, by threatening assailants and thieves with arrest and punishment, is what the police are all about."[15] They wrote that we may have made a serious mistake in social policy by taking robbery, extortion, and aggravated assault less seriously when adolescents are involved than when the perpetrators and victims are adults.

Quite obviously, CPOs would be the most logical choice for the job. Traditional motor patrol officers could never provide kids the same high level of protection that gang membership affords. Only CPOs are there in the same community every day. A concerted Community Policing effort also breaks down the barriers between the police and young people, so that the police are no longer viewed as the enemy, but as people kids can trust. This potential niche is one that should obviously be fully explored, since there is no indication that gang violence will subside. Indeed, one of the unpleasant side effects of stepping up efforts to arrest high-level dealers can be that this triggers bloody new battles over lucrative drug turf.

- **The Homeless** – More than 2.5 million units of low-income housing have disappeared since 1980, according to Jacob V. Lamar in a *Time* magazine essay on this growing problem. This means that today more than two million people will find themselves without a place to stay at some time during the year. What is also new is that more than one-third of the homeless are now families with children. One-fourth are people who have jobs – the working poor.[16] These relative newcomers swelled the already growing ranks of the homeless created by closing large mental institutions, in favor of providing more community-based care – which never materialized. Lamar reported that the number of mental patients in institutions declined from a peak of 560,000 to only 143,000 by 1988, explaining why the mentally ill constitute roughly one-third of the homeless, though all figures relating to this phenomenon are difficult to verify.[17]

  The homeless constitute a two-fold problem for police. As discussed in the chapter on fear of crime, people are more afraid of potentially menacing strangers loitering nearby than they are of being murdered. Even though no figures exist concerning how many homeless people commit crimes, their desperate straits make people uneasy that they will resort to crime for sheer survival. Anyone who has walked past the ragged, homeless people who dot the tunnels in New York City's subways knows that they inspire an anguished mix of feelings that include fear, guilt, revulsion, and shame. Their hand-lettered signs detailing real or embellished horror stories about why they have been reduced to begging constitute a grim litany of modern problems – AIDS, Vietnam vets who cannot find work, pregnant women with nowhere to go.

  The constant barrage of unrelenting misery also threatens to spawn a backlash. Major newspapers and magazines in late 1988 often seemed to devote more ink to questioning the ethics of giving handouts than to offering concrete solutions. What this suggests is not that our society has become heartless, but that we risk becoming numb. And public apathy is part of the dilemma the police face in attempting to gain the upper hand against predators.

  The second concern is the alarming rates of victimization that the homeless suffer. There is growing awareness that the children in shelters for the homeless are targets of sexual abuse. A study of the elderly homeless in Detroit showed that more than half had been beaten, robbed, or raped the preceding year, and many report they do not stay in shelters because of the fear of victimization.[18] These are people whose lack of a permanent address already robs them of their right to vote, which effectively muzzles them from having a direct say in the political process.

The homeless cannot simply pick up a phone to call the police when they are threatened, yet traditional policing depends on a call for service as the primary impetus for taking action. Community Policing, in contrast, "goes looking for trouble" before problems erupt into a crisis. Just because the homeless have no votes, no PAC money, and no telephones should not mean they are excluded from police priorities. Their complex dilemma requires more than crisis intervention, and this is yet another niche where Community Policing offers unique opportunities to make a positive difference.

In the role of community liaison, CPOs can help link homeless people to public and private agencies that can help. CPOs are also the logical candidates to enlist and work with community volunteers on improving security in shelters and on the street. The police response must include more than rousting the homeless whenever their unnerving presence inflames taxpayers to demand visual relief or arresting those homeless people who take over abandoned, federally-owned houses. In New York City, the Transit Authority officers have had to balance the rights of the homeless with the rights of the general public. This means protecting the homeless' right to take shelter in the public subway tunnels, free from harm. At the same time it means people must be allowed unobstructed access to the system, and they must be protected from harassment. It took years to create the current crisis, so even a concerted and well-funded effort will no doubt take years to undo. This is an obvious area where Community Policing can help.

- **Minorities** – Race is a volatile criminal justice issue because of:

    - the alarming rates of victimization many minority groups endure

    - the disproportionate number of minorities arrested and incarcerated

    - the debate about how best to promote minority hiring and promotion in police departments

    - the role of race as a common factor in police brutality

    - the concern that racially motivated incidents and attacks are on the rise

    - the worrisome emergence and growth of new militant groups, such as the Skinheads, who openly advocate violence against minorities

The police will no doubt face even greater pressure to deal with these issues as the racial balance in the United States continues to shift. According to a recent report by the Census Bureau, America will become dramatically less white over the next century. In a study projecting population trends 100 years into the future, the Census Bureau projected that by 2080, white, non-Hispanic Americans will be close to losing majority status to today's three major minority groups – blacks, Asians, and Hispanics (precise figures for Hispanics are not calculated because Hispanics are not considered a race).[19]

As Hubert Williams and Patrick V. Murphy have written, blacks in particular among minorities were long excluded completely from political power. When the reform era substituted the law for politics as the source of police power, this made a difference for the white mainstream, but not for blacks. "For those who lacked both political power and equal protection under the law, however, such a transformation could have little significance."[20] The concern even now is that the politically powerful will influence the allocation of police resources so that Community Policing will be implemented in strong communities where community or business organizations have access to the political leadership, rather than to disintegrating minority neighborhoods with less political clout.

While Community Policing is no panacea that can erase all minority concerns, it can make valuable contributions toward easing racial tensions and addressing minority crime concerns. Not only does Community Policing differ from traditional policing because it takes all crime and disorder problems seriously, it does so in ways that empower rather than alienate the law-abiding members of the community, including minorities who have often felt their needs and concerns did not receive the priority they deserved. By improving police/community relations as a by-product of delivering personalized police service, instead of as its primary focus, Community Policing does not suffer from any taint of condescension or pandering. It also offers an opportunity for the police to gather broad, in-depth information about racial incidents and the possible arrival and activities of troublesome groups, such as the new breed of white supremacists.

Because Community Policing broadens the scope of the police, it not only addresses the concerns of blacks, but other minorities as well. Research currently under way on new Community Policing efforts in McAllen, Texas, with its substantial Hispanic population, and in Aurora, Colorado, with Asian enclaves made up primarily of Koreans, should provide useful information on how Community Policing meets the particular needs of those minority groups. In Boston, Community Disorder Units carefully screen complaints, particularly for crimes such as vandalism and assault, for underlying signs of racial or ethnic elements that might otherwise be missed. In many departments, the existing system can mask problems, such as when a call about problems with graffitti then uncovers the fact that swastikas were painted on the walls.

Community Policing can trace its history to the Police/Community Relations programs that sprang up after the race riots of the late 1960s and early 1970s, as a response to those incidents and the minority allegations of unfair treatment at the hands of the police. Unfortunately, two incidents in January 1989 underscore the concern that such problems are still smoldering, and that Community Policing offers the best hope of real solutions.

Concerning the issue of police brutality, the first incident involved how officers from the Long Beach (California) Police Department appeared to mistreat civil rights activist Don Jackson, a police sergeant on leave from his department. Jackson, a member of the Police Misconduct Lawyer Referral Service who had received more than 50 complaints about the department, enlisted a local TV news crew to help him stage a *sting*. Though controversy continues to swirl about what Jackson said during the exchange after officers stopped his car, the dramatic footage aired on the national TV news caused widespread concern. The tape showed the police pull Jackson's car over for no apparent reason and later an officer smashed Jackson's head through a storefront window.[21]

Less than a month later, another incident of alleged excessive force triggered rioting in Miami during Super Bowl week. In that case, an officer heard a call on the radio about a motorcyclist who had refused to stop after committing a traffic violation. When the unarmed black man drove by, the officer shot and killed him, and the man's companion riding in back died later.[22]

Race may not have been a factor in either situation, and questions about the use of excessive force are not exclusively a minority concern. However, Miami served as a grim reminder that when minorities fear that race plays a role in possible police misconduct, this can serve as the tinder that allows a suspicious incident to spark violent riots that can quickly burn out of control.

Reforms such as Police/Community Relations obviously have not solved the problem. Such deep, longstanding concerns appear to demand institutional rather than superficial, cosmetic change. Community Policing is a dramatic way to provide full-fledged law enforcement in a new and highly personalized form. It offers the promise of directly addressing racially motivated police brutality and excessive use of force by breaking down the *us against them* mindset – a profound shift in the way the police and the public interact.

As noted in Chapter 4, black-on-black and minority crime is a pernicious and complex problem, one that the police cannot solve alone. Yet the alienation fostered by the existing system that isolates police officers in patrol cars no doubt contributes to a siege mentality. Officers can begin to lose proper perspective and start to associate minority status with criminality, generalizing the misbehavior of the law-breaking few to the law-abiding many. And just as cultural acceptance of macho behavior within segments of some minority sub-cultures can contribute to perpetuating violence, the same can hold true within traditional police departments. Left unchecked, this attitude can blur the line between tough and fair enforcement of the law and abuse of police power.

As violence begets more violence, this vicious cycle can contribute to escalating violence between the police and minorities, thereby blocking future communication. In a marriage, communication is the key to allowing the couple to work together as a team, so that they can accomplish more than either could alone. When communication breaks down between the police and the community, the predators gain the upper hand. As crime rates escalate and citizens refuse to cooperate, that can perpetuate the misperception among police that everyone in minority communities condones crime. Traditional policing therefore risks causing as many problems as it can ever solve in minority communities, because it does not offer enough opportunity for the police to develop the rapport required to open up lines of communication.

Community Policing has been attacked as being too much a social work approach, yet quite obviously the far greater danger is that the existing approach fails to offer enough opportunities for meaningful dialogue with people in minority communities and this risks mutual alienation and hostility. This is the unfortunate but logical result of a system where minorities often feel the existing structure prevents them from making any contribution to the police process and which fails to allow them some voice in setting police priorities.

Outsiders often naively believe that curbing police excess is a simple matter of having the chief issue a directive. But experience shows that in departments with serious, longstanding problems, orders from above are an important first step, but not a total solution. Hiring more minority officers also helps, but the macho culture in some police departments can overwhelm individuals to the point where it obliterates their sensitivity to their own race's concerns.

The Flint research provided dramatic evidence that a Community Policing effort can ease racial tensions and improve relations between the police and the community, but more research is needed to confirm that this kind of structural change will work in other situations. Not only is the issue of particular concern to minorities, but it is a serious challenge that the police must face because it threatens to tarnish their image overall, and it can contribute to the climate of violence that blackens our national reputation worldwide.

- **Undocumented Aliens** – Precise figures are obviously difficult to come by, but the Immigration and Naturalization Service (INS) in 1987 estimated close to four million undocumented aliens would attempt to apply for citizenship under the amnesty program.[23] In addition, an untold number would try to remain without applying, because they were ineligible or they were too afraid to risk rejection. Within the ranks of new arrivals are those who have some hope of remaining legally, if they can prove they fled political repression and face retaliation if returned home. Those who left their homes because of economic problems are routinely deported, and Mexican nationals automatically fall into this category, as do Canadians and citizens of most European and Asian countries. Haitians have also had notable difficulty in establishing political grounds.

Undocumented aliens pose a difficult challenge for police, because fear of deportation often makes them reluctant to report crimes committed against them – which also makes them easy prey. They can also fall victim to crimes related to their vulnerability – scams include extortion, fees for phony documentation, supposed bribes to judges, and other creative cons. Without legal status, many take jobs in the *grey economy,* and employers often exploit their status by underpaying them or refusing to pay them at all. Because so many arrive with little or no money and have difficulty making a living, undocumented aliens often cluster in low-income, high-crime areas.

Mexican nationals have been targeted for special attention by the new Community Policing effort in McAllen, Texas. Chief Alex Longoria has expressed concern that the illegal status of undocumented aliens makes them fearful of cooperating with police. The decision was made that local police priorities must override concerns about status. Basically, this means the police will leave the job of assessing the person's immigration status to INS, since that is their job, while the police concentrate on their crime and disorder concerns. Only in cases where the perpetrators prove to be undocumented aliens will the individual's immigration status become an issue.

Research is currently being conducted to see whether Community Policing can make inroads in building cooperation with the substantial number of Hispanics, particularly Mexican nationals, who continue to flow into this border town.

- **Students** – Michigan State University was the first major university in the United States to institute a Community Policing approach on the entire campus, under the direction of Bruce Benson, the director of the Department of Public Safety (DPS) who had previously been involved in the Flint experiment (see Chapter 7). Planning for the new effort began in the fall of 1986, when Benson sent six DPS officers (line and supervision) to Flint to walk the beat for two days with foot patrol officers. The following March, the Flint research evaluation team of Robert Trojanowicz, Robert Baldwin, and Jesse Thompson made a technical assistance visit, and shortly afterward, sworn and non-sworn members of the department were sent to the Community Policing training sessions held on campus through what was then called the National Neighborhood Foot Patrol Center (now the National Center for Community Policing).

Before launching the program in the spring of 1987, Benson held round-table discussions with his personnel, to shape the final plan. In the beginning, the entire campus was divided into three districts, with a supervisor and 12 officers assigned to each. One of the officers was designated as the Community Policing Specialist (CPS), modelled after the Flint foot patrol officer.

As discussed in the final chapter, Benson hoped that using the CPS as part of a *community team policing* approach would reduce internal dissent. Each CPS operated from an office in a residence hall, which had been outfitted with a telephone answering machine. All the officers *owned* their district, and they were encouraged to use the office as a check-in.

The CPS made a special effort to walk the beat – one took a dog with him – so that they could learn about their territory and begin to talk to the students. On occasion, they would use a car or ride a bicycle, but the goal was not only to establish a visible presence but to begin to involve students in the police process.

Students are a unique community – a group of strangers who are thrown together for a few years. "They are all renters - none own property, and most are between 18 and 22 years old, though we have more older students on campus than ever before," says Benson. All the problems associated with making the shift from dependent child to autonomous adult occur during that period, so the typical problems campus police face include theft, pranks such as false fire alarms, and behavior problems associated with drinking and drugs. Michigan State University also averages 12 rapes a year, almost all of which tend to be date rapes.

Michigan State University has the largest number of student residents on campus of any university in the country, but while it might seem the population is so homogeneous that there would be no need to tailor Community Policing district to district, it soon became obvious that different areas had different needs. The CPS stationed in a large residence hall on the north campus organized a Neighborhood Watch in the dorm, and they invented the *Gotcha Card,* which could be left anywhere they uncovered a condition that provided an opportunity for crime. This meant students might come back to their rooms and find a card in an unlocked door, a reminder that if it had not been the Watch group who put it there, they might have found their stereo or money gone. Another CPS developed a comic book on the adventures of *Captain Freedom,* a superhero who battles against drugs, a useful tool in conveying an anti-drug message to the children whose parents attend classes on campus.

"Our program continues to evolve, and we always face budget pressures," Benson says. Part of the funding to launch the new effort came from eliminating the Crime Prevention position. "We don't need one officer who is the 'good' guy who talks about prevention, while everyone else is the 'bad' guy who does enforcement," he says. The number of districts was scaled back from three to two (sharing three CPOs) to provide officers more flexibility in scheduling, since they can only exchange shift assignments with others in their district. Now that a fourth CPS will be added, Benson may expand again to three districts, and he has yet to decide whether to place that new CPS in a large residence hall or in married housing. "I am quite concerned about the problem of child abuse and neglect," says Benson. While that is not a problem many people think about in relation to college students, Benson notes that many such families face intense economic and emotional pressures.

Benson also faces a new threat because drug dealers from Detroit, less than two hours away, have begun to use the campus as a "vacation resort." The information he has gathered convinces him that many dealers view having a Michigan State University coed for a girlfriend as a status symbol, and he's concerned this phenomenon played a role in two shootings, one fatal, that occurred on campus in 1988. Benson says the rapport engendered by the community team policing effort allows the department to learn about potential problems quickly. The University of Michigan, 70 miles away in Ann Arbor, has recently been plagued with racially motivated altercations, some involving Skinheads. Benson hopes that Community Policing can help the department anticipate such problems before they escalate.

Research on the program is being conducted, though results are not yet available. Benson is encouraged by informal feedback from the officers, students, and the administration, faculty, and staff. The apparent success persuaded him to share information on the Community Policing's applications on campus at a recent meeting of police chiefs from "Big 10" universities. Benson said many expressed interest in starting their own efforts.[24]

- **Tourists and Transients** – Many summer and winter resort communities face problems because of the influx of tourists and part-time residents who swell the population at different seasons of the year. An obvious concern is that people who have no long- range stake in the community adopt the conventioneer syndrome, where they behave away from home in ways they would never risk at where people know them – public drunkenness, vandalism, skipping out on bills.

  The McAllen (Texas) Police Department has targeted "winter Texans" for special attention as part of their new Community Policing effort,[25] and North Miami Beach and Clearwater[26] in Florida have also initiated efforts targeted at tourists. The challenge is to maintain order without oppressive tactics that drive tourist dollars somewhere else. In Clearwater, for example, the new Beach Patrol District employs CPOs dressed in shorts and short-sleeved shirts, and they communicate by radio with civilian volunteers who have also been trained to defuse problems by appealing to people to cooperate, rather than by authoritarian confrontation. Beach patrol officers also visit local business owners to ensure their needs are met.[27]

This chapter cannot explore all the potential benefits that particular groups may derive from a Community Policing approach, but this was designed to show the basic ways in which the effort can address specific groups and the particular situations they face. Because Community Policing is a philosophical change in the delivery of police service, rather than a precise strategy or tactic, it can be adapted to changing conditions.

As noted before, from its earliest days, Community Policing has also targeted *women* and the *elderly* for special attention. Now that more and more women are entering the work force and raising families alone, this increases their exposure to crime — from white-collar fraud to muggings to rape. We can expect that women will therefore become an even greater focus of Community Policing efforts in the future.

The elderly, who are among those most fearful of crime, will begin to dominate the culture over time. As the number of Baby Boomers reach retirement age, the ranks of the elderly will swell from roughly 30 million today, to 39 million by 2010 – 66 million by 2030.[28] As graduate student Michael J. Hanna, a captain in the Flint Police Department, wrote in a paper on future trends in policing, there is little doubt that when the people that Tom Wolfe targeted as the "Me Generation" reach old age,[29] they will demand effective protection, and Community Policing's ability to reduce fear of crime will become even more important.

At the same time, crime rates will likely decline as births begin to drop sharply, from 3.7 million in 1990 to 3.4 million in 2005 and 3 million in 2080.[30] After a lag, this should mean that there are fewer young people overall in their most crime-prone years and that they will constitute a smaller share of the overall population. Community Policing's ability to work with juveniles should benefit from even greater support from the broader culture.

No one can foresee what the world of the future will look like and all the challenges it will mean for police. No doubt new technological advances, far beyond the exotic techniques such as DNA mapping that show great promise, will make it easier for the police to identify the guilty. But Community Policing, whose hallmarks are flexibility and creativity, will allow the police a new way to approach the changing and shifting needs within various communities. Technological advances have always outstripped progress in addressing social problems. Perhaps Community Policing provides the proper balance, by tempering reliance on technology with a new commitment to the human touch.

NOTES

[1]*Dead Zones, U.S. News & World Report,* April 10, 1989, p. 22.

[2]*Report to the Nation on Crime and Justice,* Second Edition, U.S. Department of Justice (Washington, DC: Bureau of Justice Statistics, March 1988), p. 41.

[3]*Ibid,* p. 27.

[4]*Ibid,* p. 102.

[5]*Ibid,* p. 33.

[6]*Ibid.*

[7]Lannon, Linnea, *Battered Lives,* Detroit Free Press, August 9, 1987.

[8]*Addiction in America: An Introduction, Lear's,* Jan.-Feb. 1989, p. 59.

[9]Langone, John, *Crack Comes to the Nursery, Time,* September 19, 1988.

[10]*Runaway and Homeless Youth* issued by the Michigan Network for Runaway and Homeless Youth, from State Representative Bob Emerson, (Lansing, MI: Office of Rep. Bob Emerson, State Capitol)(undated).

[11]*Facts on Runaway and Homeless Youth,* handout from the Michigan Network for Runaway and Homeless Youth (Lansing, MI)(undated).

[12]Brand, David, *In Massachusetts: Theater Therapy, American Scene, Time,* November 9, 1987.

[13]Taylor, Carl-Spencer, *Black Urban Youth Gangs: Analysis of Contemporary Issues,* prepared for the American Society of Criminology, October 29, 1986, pp. 3-6.

[14]Kleiman, Mark A.R., and Smith, Kerry D., *State and Local Drug Enforcement: In Search of a Strategy – Working Paper #89-01-14* (Cambridge, MA: Program in Criminal Justice Policy and Management, John F. Kennedy School of Government) (undated), p. 25.

[15]*Ibid.*

[16]Lamar, Jacob V., *The Homeless: Brick by Brick, Time,* October 24, 1988, pp. 34-38.

[17]*Ibid.*

[18]Chandler, Michele, *'Disturbing' Plight of Homeless Elderly Studied, Detroit Free Press,* December 22, 1988.

[19]Scanlan, Christopher, *An Older, Less White America Predicted, Detroit Free Press,* February 1, 1989.

[20]Williams, Hubert, and Murphy, Patrick V., *The Evolving Strategy of Police: A Minority View,* June 7, 1988, revised August 3, 1988 (unattributed but available from – Washington, DC: The Police Foundation).

[21]Wagner, Michael G., *Police Brutality: The Ugly Issue Returns, Detroit Free Press,* January 22, 1989.

[22]*Ibid.*

[23]Hackett, George, with Brooks, Hugh, and McKillop, Peter, *Ripping Off Immigrants, Newsweek,* September 7, 1987, p. 21.

[24]Benson, Bruce, director of Michigan State University Department of Public Safety, interview conducted at his office, December 27, 1988.

[25]Longoria, Alex, *Community Policing: A Policy Statement* (McAllen, TX: McAllen Police Department).

[26]Bucqueroux, Bonnie, *Footprint Focus,* Footprints (East Lansing, MI: National Neighborhood Foot Patrol Center, Michigan State University).

[27]*Ibid.*

[28]Scanlan.

[29]Hanna, Michael J. *The Aging of America: Implications for Law Enforcement* (East Lansing, MI: School of Criminal Justice, Michigan State University) (unpublished).

[30]Scanlan.

SPECIAL PEOPLE/ SPECIAL PROBLEMS:

THE SPECIAL CHALLENGE OF DRUGS

CHAPTER 9
A Country Hooked on Drugs

The inhabitants of the earth spend more money on illegal drugs than they spend on food. More than they spend on housing, clothes, education, medical care, or any other product or service.

—*James Mills*
The Underground Empire

The Scope of the Drug Problem

Drugs, both legal and illegal, cause problems for which there are no easy answers. In the United States, most people *just say yes* to a dizzying array of chemicals. We take drugs when we are sick and when we are healthy. We take drugs to ease real or imagined physical or psychic pain. We pop diet pills to slim us down and steroids to pump us up. We take drugs to escape, to celebrate and to mourn, to rev us up and slow us down, to help us sleep and keep us awake.

We take drugs when we are afraid, angry, happy, sad – or just plain bored. We take drugs to steady our nerves, to feel brave, to fit in, to enhance romance, to feel secure, to find ourselves, to lose ourselves, to have fun – and to commit suicide. We take drugs to solve problems – then many of us take even more drugs to cope with the problems that taking drugs can cause, whether that means the "hair of the dog" hangover cure or uppers to counteract the downers (and vice versa).

The first drug we take is usually an aspirin that Mother gives us when we have a fever – a "magic bullet" that miraculously makes us feel better. We first experiment on our own with a *gateway drug* – a beer, some wine or liquor, a cigarette, maybe even a puff of marijuana. Sometimes it is our parents who introduce us to such substances, but most kids find extra excitement in sneaking something forbidden.

We expect to feel a thrill – or at least to feel more grown up. Instead, that first taste almost always makes us cough, gag, wince, or even throw up – can this be what

255

adults call fun? For some, that first time is also the last, but others persist – no one knows for certain why. Millions of dollars have been spent researching what constitutes an "addictive personality," but so far the only factor that all abusers appear to share in common is use of the drug.[1]

For those who persist long enough and often enough, the drug can at least become a bad habit. In the case of some drugs, taken by some people, that bad habit becomes addiction – physical or psychological, or both. Some drugs are so powerful that anyone who takes enough of them for long enough risks becoming hooked. And a growing number of people end up abusing a virtual pharmacopia of various substances. Of the people who seek treatment for substance abuse today, 40% to 75% are now multi-drug abusers.[2]

Different people, different drugs, different effects, different timetables – and different penalties. Our collective concern about ingesting natural and manufactured substances to change how we act and feel has resulted in a confusing and shifting maze of formal and informal sanctions. We vacillate about where to place the line between use and abuse – and about whether such a line exists at all for certain drugs. On the issue of drugs, our heartfelt devotion to the ideal of individual freedom runs headlong into our equally strong belief that laws should be used to promote the common good and protect the innocent. We struggle to balance the rights of adults to make personal choices with the need to shield children from harm. The end result is that our society's response to drugs consists of an often paradoxical and ever-changing thicket of customs, laws, and regulations that are constantly being debated and tested, as problems with new drugs emerge and the dangers of existing drugs are re-evaluated.

Controlling Legal Drugs

At one extreme is a totally unregulated drug such as caffeine, which millions of Americans consume in coffee, tea, colas, over-the-counter medications – and even chocolate. We have no laws requiring anyone to show proof of age to buy caffeine, and while we might look askance at serving a six-year-old a cup of black coffee, we often worry more about the sugar than the caffeine if the child ingests a soft drink or candy bar. In the case of this drug, we rely exclusively on custom to enforce distinctions between what we collectively consider proper and improper use, regardless of any concern about possible problems related to addiction, hyperactivity, and the role it may play in diseases.

At the next level are legal but restricted drugs like alcohol and tobacco. We have long had laws to restrict sale to minors and against drunk driving, and we have also levied so-called *sin* taxes on both drugs as a way of controlling and reducing their use. But growing awareness of the toll they exact on society has spawned efforts to use the law as a way to discourage use even more and to protect others from the dangers such drugs can pose to non-users.

One in three Americans drinks alcohol, and almost 100,000 people die each year from alcohol poisoning and alcohol-related diseases and accidents – roughly half the fatal accidents on the nation's highways involve drinking.[3] The economic costs associated with alcohol cost this country roughly $128 billion a year, added to the toll of alcohol's role in family violence, child abuse and neglect, and crime.[4] Almost half of all convicted felons admit using alcohol just before they committed the crime.[5]

More than one in four people in this country smokes, and Surgeon General C. Everett Koop announced in late 1988 that tobacco kills even more people than previously suspected – as many as 390,000 deaths each year are attributable to smoking-related illnesses, on top of the unknown number of people who die each year in fires caused by careless smoking.[6] Medical costs and lost productivity associated with smoking constitute a hidden tax of $65 billion each year,[7] and evidence continues to mount that passive, or *slipstream smoke,* endangers the health of non-smokers as well.[8]

Non-profit groups such as MADD (Mothers Against Drunk Driving) and ASH (Association for Smoking and Health) have helped to spearhead recent efforts to use the law as a way to protect the rights of non-users at risk. The trend toward criminalizing alcohol and tobacco that began with successful campaigns to regulate TV advertising has now led to laws mandating smoke-free airline flights and the controversial use of alcohol check lanes on the highway. With smoking in particular, increasing regulation has created a "crazy-quilt" of local ordinances, so that smoking can be legal in an office or restaurant on one side of the street but not the other.

When Licit Becomes Illicit

Pharmaceuticals and medicinals constitute a particularly gray area, where many new drugs initially hailed as a panacea ultimately show their dark side. When cocaine first appeared in the United States during the 1880's, it was hailed as a cure-all. According to Yale historian David Musto, Thomas Edison regularly imbibed cocaine-laced wine, which may explain how he got by on so little sleep. By 1890, cocaine crystals for sniffing were sold by mail order for $5 an ounce, and the American Hay Fever Association then named the drug its official remedy. By 1900, every bottle of Coca-Cola contained one-third to one-half a *line* of coke – a competitive drink also manufactured in Atlanta was aptly and simply called *Dope.*[9]

At the other end of the spectrum are medicinals such as aspirin that have always been available without prescription, though teenagers for many years abused the drug by dropping it into a Coke to get "high." Over-the-counter cold remedies pose a risk because of the drowsiness they cause, and coroners suggest they probably rank second behind alcohol as the drug most frequently involved in fatal accidents.[10]

Musto and others note that many drugs require 20 to 30 years to go from being touted as a miracle to being damned as an evil, a history lesson we have often been doomed to repeat. Early tranquilizers like Miltown first became popular in the 1950s. By 1981, doctors wrote 57 million prescriptions just for Valium in that one year.[11] By then it was becoming increasingly apparent that the drug fostered dependency.

A similar progression occurred with amphetamines – *speed* – which masks fatigue and suppresses appetite. Benzedrine inhalers were once sold over the counter, and amphetamines were often prescribed for allergies. By the 1970s, diet pills had been immortalized as *Mother's Little Helper* in the song by the Rolling Stones, and posters appeared bearing the warning *Speed Kills,* as injecting the drug grew in popularity. By the 1980s, one doctor in Detroit had procured 2.5 million amphetamine tablets over a five-year period before he was arrested.[12]

PCP and quaaludes are two other obvious examples of drugs that once appeared to have bona fide medical uses, until their potential for abuse overshadowed whatever benefits they may have had. More recently, a coterie of mental health professionals fought to save MDMA, also known as *Ecstasy,* but it was banned and not just regulated because of concerns about street sales and abuse.

Potent painkillers, for example codeine, morphine, demerol, Dilaudid, Percodan, and Talwin, pose an even greater challenge, because of their value in health care – the problem is not the drug, but how it is used. The morphine shot that eases a terminal cancer patient's pain is a blessing, but it is a curse if it ends up in the arm of a surgeon on his way into the operating room. Our fears have resulted in a complete ban on heroin, creating the anomaly where terminal patients are denied access to its pain-killing properties, while half-a-million addicts have little trouble finding a ready supply. We often have great difficulty determining proper use. Recent experiments using lollipops impregnated with fentanyl as a less threatening and stressful way to anesthetize children for surgery no doubt stemmed from good intentions, but some have attacked the technique for teaching children to equate drugs with candy.[13]

To maintain access to a supply of regulated pharmaceuticals, abusers will beg leftovers from friends, feign symptoms to trick physicians, or buy them on the black market. Naive or opportunistic physicians sometimes collude in the process, and others with access to the drugs anywhere along the route from manufacture to retail sale have found ways to divert licit drugs into illicit channels for a profit. Avaricious or addicted health-care workers pilfer drugs on the job, while other addicts and entrepreneurs outside the system rob doctors' offices and pharmacies.

Some clandestine labs specialize in making drugs almost indistinguishable from the real thing, though the conditions under which the drugs are made are far from hygienic and *quality control* is usually a foreign concept. There are also overseas drug companies that produce drugs in bulk that smugglers then press into pills. Other creative chemists exploited a niche by changing a molecule or two in a banned substance, producing a *new* product that could be sold without serious penalty until the laws had the time to catch up. These so-called designer drugs were sometimes found to cause horrendous side effects when "tested" in the uncontrolled lab of the streets. Another wrinkle involves labs that make *lookalikes,* pills and capsules that contain legal substances, often caffein, marketed in ways that dupe buyers into thinking that they are buying something more exotic.

Street Drugs

Once we cross the line from legal or regulated drugs to illegal street drugs, precise numbers become harder to determine. Though surveys that rely on self-reporting probably err on the low side, the 1985 National Household Survey showed that 36.9% of the population will use an illicit substance at least once in their lifetime (70.39 million people). A total of 19.3% or 36.79 million reported doing so during the past year; 12% or 22.98 million within the past month.[14] As a frame of reference, there were approximately 56 million current smokers in the United States in 1989.[15] Best estimates suggest that 20 million Americans smoke marijuana, six million use cocaine, half-a-million take heroin.[16] Smaller numbers of people indulge in opium, hashish, and hash oil. Hallucinogens such as LSD, peyote, psyllocybin, and mescaline appear less popular than during the "psychedelic" 1960s, but occasional big busts show a lucrative market remains, and then there are all the other banned or regulated substances that people take for non-medical reasons.

No more than 6,000 people die each year from heroin and cocaine overdoses combined.[17] While that figure seems low compared to the staggering number of deaths linked to alcohol and tobacco, remember that these figures are only for overdoses – no one knows how many deaths may be caused by illnesses or accidents related to using these two drugs. Indeed this highlights how little we know about the additional health risks posed by street drugs, especially since many are polluted with questionable adulterants, ranging from the herbicides the government sprays on marijuana to substances including laxatives and strychnine that dealers use to *step on* the drug or give it an extra boost.

Cocaine is often sold at 85% purity, while the purity of heroin on the street usually ranges from 1% to 6%. If cocaine purity falls much lower, customers will often switch dealers.[18] To enhance profit margins, dealers have also been known to substitute methamphetamine, which is cheaper, for part of the cocaine. Doctors face great difficulty in treating cocaine overdoses because there is no effective antidote. Heroin purity constitutes a different problem because users can overdose if the purity is dangerously stronger than anticipated.

In the case of pills in particular, dealers often claim to be selling one drug when it is actually another – often because they were duped by someone higher up the line. Hard-core multi-drug abusers often seem to care little what kind of pills they take, and they routinely mix and match with little concern about what the synergistic effects might be, greatly complicating treatment if they end up in the emergency room. Part of the difficulty in calculating how many overdose deaths are caused by drug abuse stems from the number of people who intentionally over-dose to commit suicide.

One thing we do know is that intravenous (IV) drug users constitute the second-largest pool of AIDS victims.[19] More than half the IV drug users in New York City tested positive for AIDS at the beginning of 1989,[20] and the federal government now projects that 450,000 Americans will be diagnosed with the disease by 1993.[21] While most of the media attention has been focused on the link between IV drug use and AIDS, equally of concern is the connection to hepatitis-B. A 1983 study which calcu-lated that illicit drug use costs society almost $60 billion[22] did not include an amount for the percentage of such illnesses attributable to IV drug use.

While half of that $60 billion figure relates to lost productivity, this includes no figure for the social costs linked to youngsters who have not yet entered the work force, though an early deficit in education can have long-term career consequences. While the findings may at least partially confuse cause and effect, research shows that drug use often coincides with a decline in school performance.[23] Studies also show that high-school seniors who are heavy drug users are more than three times as likely to skip school,[24] and four of five dropouts were regular drug users (though we do not know rates for their peers who stay in school).[25] Of concern as well is that schools awash in drugs are not an environment in which learning flourishes.

Drug trafficking exacts a toll in both money and blood. The unintended and unfortunate by-product of making a drug illegal is that this adds to its market value. A *Dilaudid* on the street often costs 100 times what a pharmacy would charge for the same pill. It takes $75 worth of chemicals to make $45,000 worth of methampheta-mines in a clandestine lab.[26] The annual sales of illicit drugs in Detroit alone were expected to top $1 billion by 1990.[27] People in the United States consume more illegal drugs per-capita than anywhere else in the world, and, though no one can possibly know the true figure and government figures are often considered inflated, officials allege that illegal drug profits amount to $100 billion a year[28] – tax free.

More difficult to assess but equally as worrisome as those uncollected taxes are the other less obvious ripple effect on the national economy. Statistics on the U.S. trade deficit do not include the dollars flowing out of the country to foreign suppliers for drugs like cocaine. Growers, manufacturers, and dealers inside this country also find it difficult to funnel their proceeds into banks or other legitimate enterprises. Many times those dollars simply sit in stacks in a dealer's home or apartment, still retaining their potential value as money, but as removed from the national economy as if they had been sucked down a black hole in space. Much of this money never gets to banks or other financial institutions where it could be loaned as capital for investments that create jobs.

Though the Federal Reserve can always print dollars to replace those that simply "disappear," dollars that sit idle in the hands of drug dealers simply stop churning through the economy, short-circuiting their ability to spread the wealth so that they enrich others as they flow through other people's hand. The dollars spent on drugs by users might otherwise be spent in ways that would do more to boost the local economy – at area stores, on debts. Instead the businesses and homes in areas plagued by dealing lose value, often selling for far less than even the cost of the materials required to build them, creating pockets of recession wherever the drug dealing spreads.

No one knows the actual cost in blood. According to the National Institute of Justice, several cities report at least one-fourth of all homicides are drug-related.[29] Jamaican and Haitian drug gangs may be notorious for their viciousness in protecting their profits, but home-grown drug gangs such as the *Crips* and the *Bloods* appear willing to mow down innocent bystanders in their never-ending war over what has now become lucrative drug turf. A study done by the New York County Lawyers' Association estimated 750 such gang-war murders each year.[30]

The huge profits involved in drug dealing also raise concern about corruption at all levels. Police officers in cities such as Miami, New York, and Detroit have been arrested for taking bribes, stealing drugs for their own use or resale, feeding crack to a suspect, and some have even been accused of murdering their competitors in the drug trade.[31] In late November 1988, three former DEA agents were charged with laundering drug money (and were suspected of tipping off dealers and involvement in the loss of more than five pounds of heroin in DEA custody). It would also be naive to assume that all politicians, prosecutors, and judges are immune.

Another layer of corruption stems from the tremendous problem major dealers face in laundering drug money. Lawyers and tax accountants have been arrested for colluding with dealers in setting up off-shore corporations to launder drug money. Bank officers have also been arrested for knowingly circumventing the reporting laws designed to uncover drug proceeds.[32] Beyond that relatively small circle are the local car dealers, real estate agents, developers, business people, and entrepreneurs who look the other way when clients and investors pay in cash that they know could not have been earned any other way.

Users also exact a toll in many ways, first because of their behavior under the influence of drugs. Long-term cocaine use, for example, notoriously inspires paranoia, which is why many officers say that even traffic stops are no longer routine, since they never know when someone might feel threatened enough to pull a gun. Worst of all may be people on PCP, which deadens pain so much that many police have been injured trying to subdue them.

Private citizens, of course, can also find themselves facing an unknown threat posed by someone high on drugs, including the danger they pose on the highway and on the job. Calculating the true cost of drugs to society should therefore include some figure for the deaths, medical costs, disability payments, and lost productivity of those who have been killed or injured because someone else was high on drugs. And no one can put a dollar value on the physical and emotional damage inflicted on spouses and children in homes where drugs are the top priority.

Users of illicit drugs, in particular addictive drugs like heroin and cocaine, are also linked to violent crimes and property crimes committed to make up for the shortfall if their habit prevents them from holding a job and to pay for the exorbitant cost of the drug itself. Only a handful of celebrities and others could make enough money to afford a *modest* $100-a-day cocaine or heroin habit. Many become at least part-time dealers, con artists, prostitutes, burglars, robbers, and thieves. No one knows the actual dollar value of the white-collar and street crimes directly or indirectly linked to drug abuse, but the average heroin addict in New York City must somehow generate $33,000 in cash or goods each year to buy the drug.[33] Equally staggering is the discount on stolen property that society absorbs whenever a $400 TV is fenced for a few dollars, and logic dictates that some personal and business bankruptcies have their roots in someone's addiction.

Adding to concerns about the link between drugs and crime are the initial results of the NIJ's Drug Use Forecasting (DUF) program, gathered from January through March 1988. Lab testing of urine samples from arrestees in selected cities nationwide showed unexpectedly high rates of illicit drug use. The highest overall was in New York City, where 82 % of male arrestees tested positive for at least one illegal drug – 80 % when marijuana was excluded. (Lowest was 58 % in New Orleans – 41 % without marijuana.) While this does not establish direct cause and effect, it raises obvious red flags, especially since a drug like cocaine had to be ingested within 48 hours of arrest to show up. The DUF study showed 73 % of male arrestees in New York City tested positive for cocaine (compared to 32 % in New Orleans, with the lowest at 29 % in Phoenix).[34]

Of particular concern is the role drugs may play in crimes committed by juveniles. A study funded by NIJ examined a group of youngsters who had committed robberies and felony assaults. The results showed that a small handful of these youngsters, roughly 3 %, were habitual offenders who accounted for three-fourths of the burglaries and half the felony assaults. A closer look also showed these were youths who used pills, cocaine, or heroin.[35]

Addiction also exacts a cost that cannot be expressed in dollars – the loss of self-respect. Therapists at treatment centers explain the difference between alcoholics and drug addicts by saying that an alcoholic will steal your money – but an addict will steal it and then help you look for it. Fewer and fewer people today can escape first- or second-hand knowledge of the horror stories that stem from addiction. We all know about someone such as the public relations officer for a local hospital who hid her heroin addiction for decades until a dirty needle caused the heart infection that almost killed her. Or the bright young man who wrote so many bad checks on his dying mother's bank account to fund his addiction that she spent her final days struggling to get by.

The Crack Epidemic

In the midst of the hysteria and confusion surrounding the issue of drugs comes what may well be the ultimate challenge – crack, a drug that threatens to make the cocaine "blizzard" of the late 1970s look like a flurry. Crack may well be the nightmare drug that tests both our ability to avert disaster and our commitment to democratic principles.

As one writer put it, "Crack is the logical development of the selling of cocaine in America – the mass-produced, mass-distributed model-T versus the once unaffordable horseless carriage."[36] Cocaine's high price tag was once part of its cachet among the affluent. The joke was that cocaine was nature's way of telling you that you made too much money. A gram of cocaine in 1981 cost about $120,[37] which translated into a $1,000-a-day habit for addicts like rock star John Phillips, who graduated from sniffing to injecting the drug.[38]

Another famous cocaine casualty, comedian Richard Pryor, made freebasing famous. Pryor set himself ablaze while igniting the ether in a crack pipe to burn off the cocaine alkaloid as smoke, a process that allows the concentrated essence of the drug to enter the bloodstream more quickly and directly.[39] Some of the drug is lost in the process, but freebasing becomes increasingly expensive because of the user's escalating desire to use more and more.

Cocaine smoke's ability to attract users fast was not lost on the unknown drug entrepreneur who first figured out how to mix cocaine crystals with ammonia or baking soda, cook it into a paste, and chop it into *rocks* that could be smoked in a pipe with less risk of becoming a human torch than with freebasing. Though, again, some cocaine is also lost in the process of making crack, the opportunity to sell rocks for as little as $5 each opened up vast new markets, specifically the young and the poor.[40]

According to Harvard University's Mark A.R. Kleiman, crack users are not addicts in the classic sense, like heroin addicts. Crack quickly becomes a compulsion, and the compulsion to do more and more begins with the first dose of the day. While it can take 10 to 20 years to become a full-blown alcoholic[41] and sniffing cocaine requires months of frequent, heavy use before a fierce compulsion sets in, crack customers become hard-core repeaters within weeks.[42]

Crack also emerged at a time when cocaine traffickers were eager to find a solution to the glut of cocaine on the market in the early 1980s. The cocaine craze of the late 1970s had encouraged coca growers in Latin America to expand cultivation – the number of acres devoted to coca production in Peru, a major supplier, have expanded sixfold in the past decade.[43] The Drug Enforcement Administration (DEA) had primary responsibility for efforts targeted at keeping drugs like cocaine from coming into the United States, but they have never been able to interdict more than an estimated 10 % of the illegal drugs flowing in.[44]

Controversy also swirls around concerns that U.S. foreign policy often placed a higher priority on a country's anti-communist efforts rather than its anti-drug efforts. U.S. aid and assistance continued to flow to countries such as Panama, a major transshipment point for cocaine produced and distributed by Colombia's Medellin Cartel. This earned Panamanian General Manuel Noriega titles such as *narcomilitarist* or *narcoterrorist,* new terms coined to describe officials in a regime who use their power to protect their profits from the illegal drug trade. A report issued by Senator John Kerry, as well as a lawsuit filed by the Christic Institute and books such as *Out of Control,* also raise questions about whether some current or former government officials may have tolerated or ignored drug-running in their zeal to re-supply the contras fighting the Sandinistas in Nicaragua.[45] DEA's pleas for more help in fighting cocaine also came at a time when the U.S. cocaine craze appeared to be levelling off, as people re-learned the lesson that the drug is far from benign.

The result was that crack was invented at a time when cocaine wholesalers were desperately trying to prop up profits. By the mid-1980s, a kilogram of cocaine that once sold for as much as $30,000 could be purchased for as little as $15,000 a year later.[46] From its surreptitious introduction in the middle of the decade, crack use exploded in the inner cities, where many other serious problems converge and magnify. Cocaine in crystal form had become the drug of choice for the idle rich; cocaine as crack became the drug of the idle poor. Though police had to worry about parties in trendy areas of New York and L.A. where heaping bowls of cocaine were passed, at least those upscale users were not likely to rob a liquor store on the way home to buy more of the drug. What many middle-class families in between worried about was that this new cheaper form of the drug would explode out of the ghetto straight into the schools their kids attend.

As late as June 1985, police in New York City had yet to make a single crack arrest – by the end of just the first 10 months of 1988, they had already made 19,074.[47] When Mayor Coleman Young launched Detroit's War on Crack at the close of 1987, he estimated 10,000 crack houses were then operating in the city.[48] The increase in hospital emergency room admissions for cocaine monitored through DAWN (Drug Abuse Warning Network) jumped 86% between 1986 and 1987.[49]

Since the days of the movie *Reefer Madness,* critics have scoffed at how quickly we announce a crisis that later appears overblown – and the risk that poses to overall credibility concerning drug issues. Even as recently as the spring of 1988, delegates meeting in Washington on a new drug data collection effort only reluctantly agreed to start monitoring crack as a separate category, in the hope it might follow the PCP model. PCP – angel dust – initially spawned a spate of ugly stories similar to those about crack, yet it never became the nationwide menace that many had feared. Though some isolated areas, such as Washington, D.C., still appear to have significant problems with PCP, it did not run rife through society, maybe because not that many people found the high enticing, or its dangers were too well known, the profit margin was too low, the distribution system had problems – or because crack better fit the niche.

As months go by, crack threatens to become the country's most serious drug problem. Almost overnight, drug gangs have spun a network capable of supplying all major cities, and they appear eager to franchise into every smaller city, suburb, and town. At the 1989 Governors' Conference, even the governor of Iowa reported that two people each week in his state die from cocaine.[50] With crack has come the dramatic emergence of "the other Yuppie" – the Young Urban Predator – as a key player. As greedy as Wall Street's Ivan Boesky, the other yuppie's Mac is not a computer but a Mac-10 automatic. He has traded Boesky's trademark red suspenders for gold chains. *Crips* and *Bloods* also take great care in wearing blue or red, since being caught in the wrong place with the wrong color can prove fatal.

The other yuppie can be white, as "White Boy" Rick Wershe in Detroit proved. More often, however, he is black, like alleged kingpin "Maserati" Rick Carter, famous for being buried in a coffin fashioned from a Mercedes after he was gunned down in his Detroit hospital room.[51]

As columnist Jimmy Breslin notes, crack has allowed blacks to own their own crime for the first time in their history in this country.[52] Though Breslin hopes that serves as a rite of passage to allow all blacks full participation, both crack dealing and crack use no doubt cause more problems than they solve. Overall cocaine use in Michigan stood at 64 users for every 100,000 people in 1986, yet the rate among minority males stood at an alarming 492 per 100,000- and rising.[53] Part of the rationale for that may be found in the words of Louis "Satchmo" Armstrong, when he explained that he smoked pot every day "because it makes you feel good, man, makes you forget all the bad things that happen to a Negro."[54]

Inner-city crack addicts desperate for cash are picking clean areas already stripped bare by previous predators, further destroying what little property value still remains in their neighborhoods. Grisly stories abound, such as the case of a man who stabbed his grandfather and aunt 53 times, then stole money from the dead man's pockets to buy crack.[55] Stories about single mothers held prisoner in their apartments by crack dealers who want to use them as a dope house have almost become routine.

Areas dominated by wraith-like addicts and the murderous violence that erupts when dealers clash over turf scare even the bravest potential investors looking for a bargain. Despite the inducement of tax abatements, cheap property, and a pool of unemployed workers, drugs and drug crime frighten off companies that could provide needed jobs, compounding the hopelessness and despair, especially among young people. Some give up and give in, while others turn to vigilantism. Frustrated Detroiters fed up with a crack house nearby admitted burning it down, yet the jury acquitted them, saying that though they did not condone the action, they could understand it.[56]

The spectre of inner cities as places where dealers and addicts rule the streets confounds agencies trying to help, and it also saps the enthusiasm of many middle-class taxpayers asked to pay even more to help people they view as unwilling to do their share by *just saying no*. Nor are politicians immune. As *Detroit Free Press* columnist Hugh McDiarmid wrote, "Probably half or more of the Michigan Legislature doesn't give a damn what happens in Detroit so long as its residents, when they shoot, shoot each other."[57] Black drug gangs and drug addicts also provide ammunition to racists, always on the lookout for evidence they can twist to imply a cause-and-effect link between skin color and crime and drugs.

Blacks themselves are divided by the drug issue. On the one hand, Baltimore mayor Kurt Schmoke, a former prosecutor, says it is time to debate legalizing drugs as a way to wring the profit from drug trafficking, as Repeal of Prohibition did with bootlegging.[58] On the other side is gang expert Carl Taylor who says decriminalizing drugs is the "moral equivalent of suicide" for our inner cities.[59] In between are black activists who fear that focusing so much attention on crack provides an easy way to make blacks the scapegoat for all of society's drug problems. Some see the attention paid to crack as part of a larger conspiracy by whites to send more black men to prison, while whites with drug problems receive treatment instead.

In the middle of the debate swirling around them are the beleaguered law-abiding residents of neighborhoods crumbling even further under the burden of violence and addiction that crack imposes. Alongside them are the police, society's front line in the War on Drugs, attempting to fashion an effective response with scarce resources. And coming next may be new wars over *crank* – methamphetamine, also called crystal or crystal meth – which is having a dramatic resurgence in popularity in cities such as San Diego as a competitor to crack, because the high reportedly lasts longer, which makes it even cheaper.

Funding the War on Drugs

The ultimate purpose behind making a drug illegal is to reduce its sale and use. But just as passing a law against murder does not stop the crime, the same holds true for drugs. In 1985, more than 800,000 Americans were arrested by state and local authorities for drug offenses.[60] Obviously, the more realistic goal is that drug laws should provide a strong deterrent – a means of preventing, reducing, and controlling society's complex drug problems.

As drugs have become a bigger priority, more of the almost $50 billion of federal, state, and local tax dollars spent on criminal justice efforts annually are devoted to drug offenses and drug-related crime. Of the estimated $4 billion spent by the federal government each year fighting drugs, three-fourths is targeted at eliminating supplies coming in.[61] The federal criminal justice share also includes the entire 1989 budget of $535 million for DEA (augmented by its $37 million portion of the $270 million asset forfeiture fund administered by the Department of Justice).[62] Added to that are substantial portions of the budgets for the U.S. Customs Service, Federal Bureau of Investigation (FBI), U.S. Attorney's Offices, federal courts, and various agencies of the Department of Justice. In addition as well is the expense of keeping the 8 % of those admitted to federal prisons for drug offenses behind bars.[63]

Increasing involvement of the military in efforts to stop illegal drugs from coming into the country adds to the bill. Writer R. Richard Banks estimated that the Air Force spent more than $45 million and the Navy more than $37 million in 1987 on military efforts related to catching drug smugglers. His tally showed the Air Force made two busts and the Navy seized 20 vessels carrying drugs as a result of that investment.[64]

For each dollar the federal government spends on criminal justice efforts overall, state and local governments combined spend almost seven times more. Determining how much of the almost $45 billion spent on state and local law enforcement efforts should be considered as part of the War on Drugs proves difficult.[65] Keeping drug offenders behind bars becomes increasing costly as their numbers rise. The most obvious expenditures within police departments are for narcotics squads, but as noted earlier, drugs are linked to a host of violent and property crimes, so an unknown portion of the money allocated to such efforts is at least indirectly aimed at drugs.

Tabulating the total amount also becomes complicated because of the increasing use of forfeiture as a way to make anti-drug criminal justice efforts more self-funding. In 1983, the federal government seized cash and property (excluding drugs) in excess of $100 million from narcotics traffickers. Just six years later, that figure was expected to reach $1 billion for 1989.[66] Tom McWeenie of the DEA's budget office in Washington, D.C., said that past experience shows that 40% to 50% of the total is cash or other liquid instruments that can go directly into the federal fund. The remaining portion is property that typically nets 10% to 20% of its retail dollar value. In fiscal year 1988, the Department of Justice returned $79 million of the previous year's total back to the states, earmarked for their anti-drug efforts.[67]

Many states have also taken a lesson from DEA's example. Laws vary state to state, but many states have been able to beef up their criminal and civil forfeiture laws to confiscate valuables purchased with the proceeds of drug sales. Many have also made sure the laws return the proceeds for future anti-drug efforts, as a crucial inducement for those within the system to do the work involved to make aggressive use of this tool. Not only does forfeiture raise needed funds – and allow agents to drive expensive cars when they impersonate dealers, it can help wring some of the profits out of drug dealing. Without forfeiture, many dealers can emerge from incarceration with their fortunes intact, which sends a message, especially to kids, that drug crime pays. The danger, however, is that some of the assets seized, such as failing factories, have proved to be money losers. And there is the case of the valuable racehorse seized by DEA, which the agents in charge unknowingly overfed so much that it died.

While the sums listed above may seem enormous, they have obviously been inadequate to the task. Police especially feel they are outspent and outgunned by drug dealers. The $100 billion in profits earned annually in the drug trade is more than double what this country spends for its entire federal, state, and local criminal justice system. Many expected that the highly touted War on Drugs would mean substantial increases, especially during a presidential election year. Voters listed drugs as their top priority and concern, even ahead of national defense, for which the budget is approaching half-a-trillion dollars. A total of 245 of the 1099 bills before the U.S. House of Representatives in 1988 dealt with drugs.[68]

Yet when it came time to set the budget for fiscal year 1989 under the Anti-Drug Abuse Act (passed in 1986 as a way to provide federal dollars for state and local drug education, treatment, and criminal justice efforts), funding was cut from the previous year's $225 million to $150 million.[69] Many in the field also worried that the criminal justice slice of this dwindling pie would erode even further over time, in favor of spending an ever-greater share on education and treatment.

The literal bottom line is that we are spending roughly 10 times as much defending our country against foreign threats as we spend on our internal security against the domestic threat posed by all crime. This is especially troubling in view of the relative casualties, since the true terrorists claiming lives on city streets are not foreigners motivated by politics, but fellow citizens driven by greed. It is little wonder that many who have been asked to serve in the trenches of the War on Drugs say that they have barely been given enough to engage in occasional skirmishes with the enemy.

The Criminal Justice Dilemma

The enormity and complexity of the drug problem in the United States defies easy answers. We ban substances because we want to rid society of them, yet making a drug illegal instead allows it to become big business. Much of our collective problem also stems from our difficulty in deciding how we view people who take drugs. It seemed a simpler world in the 1950s, when overall numbers of users were smaller – then anyone who took drugs automatically became a "dope fiend." The explosion of drug use during the 1960s, however, caused us to re-evaluate, not only because of sheer numbers, but because many who experimented were college students, the sons and daughters of the mainstream.

As the first wave of Baby Boomers approached adulthood, many of those otherwise normal kids shucked convention and rallied to the cry of *sex and drugs and rock 'n' roll*. Using drugs such as marijuana and psychedelics also became a symbol of defiance to the war in Vietnam and the draft. The tremendous number of "nice" young people experimenting with "bad" drugs led to a watermark shift in blame from the drug user to the drug itself.

Where previously as well society had viewed all drugs as a monolithic evil, the era also forced a reappraisal of the threat that each individual drug posed. The dangers of marijuana in particular had been overrated, in part no doubt because of a desire to scare kids away. Yet when the drug failed to live up to its reputation as being on par with heroin, this made all official pronouncements about drugs suspect. Some marijuana users did become casualties, but most grew up to become respected citizens – in 1988 more than one presidential candidate and a Supreme Court nominee admitted trying marijuana. Though many today have already forgotten the climate of the times, even as recently as the late 1970s, many reputable experts, including officials of the Carter administration, suggested that warnings about cocaine's addictive properties were a hoax akin to the myths propagated about marijuana.

Since those times, society has had great difficulty in determining its response to the *demand* side of the drug equation. We vent our righteous anger and disgust at the *supply* side, the dealers, ignoring that they would quickly be out of business if users did *just say no*. This ambivalence toward users means we have never answered clearly, as one voice, whether addicts are victims, who therefore deserve unreserved compassion and help – or criminals who exercised free will when they made choices for which they should pay the penalty. And what about the casual user who does not fit neatly into the definition of an addict?

Our collective uneasiness becomes even more apparent in the criminal justice response, because putting laws on paper forces us to move from ambiguous gray to harsh black-and-white. The new federal drug law allowing the death penalty for *drug kingpins* is a symbol of our frustration. Dealers are *them,* people who are not at all like us, people who ignore the damage they do because of greed.

We reserve our compassion for users, because we see them as vastly different than dealers. In many cases, users are us. More than one in three Americans will use an illegal drug over their lifetime – or that figure embraces children, friends, and people with whom we can identify. No death penalty for users here, as the government did in China to eliminate demand. Instead we expect harsh laws aimed at dealers to send the message that we will no longer tolerate a society where drug gangs open fire on the streets; where addicts kill, maim, and steal from us; and especially where innocent kids can be lured into lifelong addiction because our schools are often supermarkets for drugs.

Though nobly intended, such simple solutions often founder on the rocks of reality. The problem we face is that we aim our laws and the bulk of law enforcement at Mr. Big – but he is never the one actually selling drugs to kids at school or to the addicts on the street who are robbing us and stealing from us. That dealer at school is far more likely to be another youngster, who sells his friend part of his marijuana (or pills or cocaine) – at cost, for enough to indulge himself for free, or for a profit.

And the dealer on the street these days might be someone like the 14-year-old in the District of Columbia who had been dealing crack part-time for two months. He openly told a CBS reporter interviewing him that so far he had made about $800 a night,[70] undoubtedly more than the adult camera operator filming the sequence. This is no drug kingpin, but a teenager too young even to apply for a job at a fast-food restaurant for minimum wage, who can expect to clear $200,000 a year, tax-free, if he is ambitious enough to go full-time five nights a week.

Even if the police invest the time to catch either youngster, the juvenile justice system will typically shield him from adult penalties. Often the best that the police can hope for is that the child will be frightened enough to "narc" on his supplier (potentially exposing the child to consequences far beyond what the authorized system can apply).

By doing the same thing ever upward along the chain of supply, eventually perhaps the police will reach Mr. Big. Yet even though new laws make the penalties even higher, the profits available at the top of the drug pyramid are so great that if Mr. Big is finally arrested, another Mr. Big will quickly appear, with little or no significant interruption or reduction of frustrating schoolyard – and street-level – sales, and its low-level buys for which addicts commit crimes. Also of concern is that the law of unintended consequences can mean that arresting Mr. Big simply sparks a new round of inter- and intra-gang warfare that can spill onto the streets, as verified by the spurt in the murder rate in more than one big city after the police succeeded in putting the major players away.

This is not meant to suggest that the police should ignore Mr. Big. Not only is putting him away the morally right thing to do, one can only shudder at the thought of what would happen if dealers thought they could operate without penalty. But this demonstrates the constraints under which the police operate and the complexity of grappling with the drug problem effectively.

What we have failed to address is the need to interrupt that sale when the drug changes hands from dealer to seller, not just when the profits ultimately spiral upward to Mr. Big. He is part of our problem, but not the serious and immediate problem that both youngsters pose. The 14-year-old selling part of his own drug supply to friends believes he is doing them a favor, a proselytizer sharing something with pals that he himself enjoys.

His counterpart selling crack in the inner city may or may not be a user, but he is addicted to that six-figure annual income, even if there is a risk. After all, he can already see that he is living in a war zone, whether he is dealing or not. Ask either of them about the ethics of dealing death and misery to others, and the kid at school selling some of his marijuana argues that what he is selling does not kill people like booze. Both will ask why you do not talk instead to that "greedy" liquor store owner respectable enough to join the Chamber of Commerce or maybe a vice-president at a tobacco company. The only logical argument left is that the drugs they are selling are illegal, but where we fail is when they point out at their level the law has often become a joke – no one seems to care.

Until or unless we commit the police to the task of making it clear to these youngsters – and their adult counterparts – that low-level dealing is against the law, and that society will invest the manpower and time to stop them, such sales will not end. No wonder that the failure of the criminal justice system to control drugs at their most visible level, on the streets and in the schools, has spawned outrage. No one denies the police have tried hard to make a difference, but the problem is not going away. Appeals to conscience will not stop the dealers at any level, nor can drug education be expected to eliminate all demand. Efforts to target Mr. Big as the key will ultimately fail as long as those sales in the schools and on the street keep churning dollars upwards to someone willing to kill anyone, including the police, for a chance to make millions.

More and more people now propose draconian solutions that would sacrifice civil rights in favor of results. In a letter to the editor written in response to a *New York* magazine article on crack, the reader urged the government to lace random batches of street drugs with fatal poison and then distribute them nationwide, to send a message to users.[71] Los Angeles Police Chief Daryl Gates, who is also an ardent supporter of drug education, made a speech at the 1988 Washington, D.C. conference on the DUF findings in which he argued for tattooing *addict* permanently on the forehead of anyone caught with any illicit substance – and take away any government-sanctioned licenses that the person may hold as well.[72]

On the other side are an increasing number of people urging legalization of all drugs, as a way to wring the profit from drug trafficking. While this would likely eliminate or at least reduce gang warfare and the number of crimes committed to feed a habit, it also risks thousands, perhaps millions, of new users, who would bring with them the additional health and social costs of their drug problems. The unanswerable question as well is how many new addicts would prove unable to hold jobs, especially since legalization would no doubt spur increased drug testing. Would those whose addiction cost them a way to make an honest living resort to crime? If so, how many addicts and how much crime could we afford before the economic and social losses would outstrip any gains?

Chances are, there is little point in the police wasting much time debating the wisdom of options at either extreme. Politicians do not get elected talking about how intractable and complex a problem is, but by proposing easy answers. The most likely future will be one in which the police are asked to do more, with little chance of a dramatic increase in resources. Instead of looking for leadership and support from outside, the police must look within. The most appropriate question therefore becomes whether the police can make changes that will allow them to do a better job with what they already have. To understand the crucial (and as-yet not fully explored) role that Community Policing can play first requires examining and critiquing the overall police response. The obvious niche that must be filled is one that realistically and affordably addresses the challenge posed by street-level sales, and there is where Community Policing may make its most dramatic contribution. If nothing else, it may be the best way for the police to remind both 14-year-olds and their associates that not only will the police no longer ignore what they are doing, but that they will enlist their parents, neighbors, and friends in efforts to stop them.

NOTES

[1]Blume, Sheila, director of treatment programs, South Oaks Hospital, Amityville, NY, as quoted in *The Struggle of Kitty Dukakis, Time,* by Aratastia Toufexis, February 20, 1989, p. 79.

[2]Toufexis, above.

[3]The *Bottom Line on Alcohol in Society, 1986 Statistical Review,* edited by Robert L. Hammond, Alcohol Research Information Service, Lansing, MI, Vol. 8, Number 3, Fall 1987.

[4]*Ibid.*

[5]*Ibid.*

[6]Telephone interview with the Lansing Chapter of the American Lung Association, March 7, 1989.

[7]*Ibid.*

[8]*Ibid.*

[9]Musto, David, as quoted in *A Yale Historian Sniffs Something Familiar in Today's Cocaine Craze,* interview by Maria Wilhelm, in *People* Magazine, November 24, 1986, about his book, *The American Disease,* Oxford University Press, 1987.

[10]*Michigan Drug Strategy – 1986,* from the Michigan Office of Criminal Justice, Department of Management and Budget, prepared for Governor James B. Blanchard (estimate came from Wayne County Coroner's Office and Michigan Crime Lab personnel).

[11]Drummond, Hugh, M.D., *A Spirited Guide to Health Care in a Dying Empire* (New York: Grove Press, 1980).

[12]Calkins.

[13]*Group seeks to halt study of drug in form of lollipop, New York Times,* February 23, 1989.

[14]*National Household Survey on Drug Abuse: Main Findings, 1985,* National Institute of Drug Abuse, U.S. Department of Health and Human Services, Washington, DC.

[15]From the Lansing Chapter of the America Lung Association, public information section.

[16]Figures provided by DEA and FBI at national drug strategy sessions, Washington, D.C., based on rough estimates from the *National Household Survey* above.

[17]Widely quoted in the popular press, apparently an extrapolation of DAWN (Drug Abuse Warning Network) data, but the ACLU's Loren Siegel puts the figure for deaths from all illegal deaths as being no higher than 3,652 (*Playboy Forum* below), while figures from the National Institute of Drug Abuse provided to *Newsweek* for a profile of Dr. William Bennett (April 10, 1989), puts the number of cocaine deaths at 1,582 for 1988 (measured from July to June of the previous year), compared to only 470 for 1984. Precise figures are obviously unknowable.

[18]Calkins.

[19]Shilts, Randy, *Are We Talking AIDS to Death?, Esquire,* March 1989.

[20]New York State Division of Substance Abuse.

[21]Shilts.

[22]*Report to the Nation on Crime and Justice – Second Edition,* U.S. Department of Justice (Washington, D.C.: Bureau of Justice Statistics, March 1988).

[23]*(What Works) Schools Without Drugs,* United States Department of Education, Washington, DC, 1986.

[24]*Ibid.*

[25]*Ibid.*

[26]DEA slide presentation at the Drug Data Collection Consortium Workshop, Denver, Colorado, May 1988.

[27]Gilliam, Joel, Detroit Police Department inspector, as quoted in *Detroit puts cocaine sales at nearing $1 billion,* by Brenda J. Gilchrist, Detroit Free Press, October 20, 1987.

[28]Estimate used by FBI/DEA.

[29]Gropper, Bernard A., *Probing the Links Between Drugs and Crime, Research in Brief,* National Institute of Justice, Washington, DC, February 1985.

[30]*Decriminalize Drugs Now, Playboy Forum, Playboy* magazine, January 1989.

[31]Morganthau, Tom, with Miami bureau assistance, *Miami, Newsweek,* January 25, 1988.

Daly, Michael, *The Crack in the Shield, New York Magazine,* December 8, 1986.

Flanigan, Brian; Kresnak, Jack; and Trimer, Margaret, *2 police officers held in robberies, Detroit Free Press,* August 17, 1988.

[32]Castro, Janice, *The Cash Cleaners, Time,* October 24, 1988.

[33]See *Playboy Forum* above.

[34]*Drug Use Forecasting (DUF),* a program of the National Institute of Justice, co-founded by the Bureau of Justice Assistance, issued May 1988.

[35]Gropper.

[36]Cole, Lewis, *Prisoners of Crack, Rolling Stone,* February 9, 1989.

[37]*Ibid.*

[38]Phillips, John, *Papa John, An Autobiography* (New York, NY: Dell Books, 1986).

[39]Cole.

[40]*Ibid.*

[41]*The Bottom Line on Alcohol,* above.

[42]Cole.

[43]McConahay, Mary Jo, and Kirk, Robin, *Over There, Mother Jones,* Vol. 14, No. 2, February/March 1989.

[44]Mills, James, *The Underground Empire – Where Crime and Governments Embrace* (Garden City, NY: Doubleday, 1986.)

[45]*Drugs, Law Enforcement, and Foreign Policy,* Senate Sub-Committee on Terrorism, Narcotics, and International Operations, Senate Foreign Relations Committee, Washington, DC, 1989, available from the office of Senator John Kerry of Massachusetts.

Out of Control, Leslie Cockburn (New York: Atlantic Monthly Press, 1987).

[46]Cole.

[47]Hackett, George, with New York Bureau Assistance, *(Hour by Hour) Crack, Newsweek,* November 28, 1988.

[48]*Michigan Drug Strategy – 1987,* from the Michigan Officer of Criminal Justice, Department of Management and Budget, prepared for Governor James B. Blanchard.

[49]Hackett.

[50]As reported by the CBS Evening News with Dan Rather.

[51]McGraw, Bill: Kaplan, Deborah; and Gilchrist, Brenda J., *Recovering Man Killed in Hospital, Detroit Free Press,* September 13, 1988.

[52]Breslin, Jimmy, as quoted in *Who Really Counts?, New York Magazine,* April 25, 1988.

[53]Calkins.

[54]Giddings, Gary, *Satchmo* (New York, NY: Dolphin/Doubleday, 1989).

[55]Swickard, Joe, *Man Confesses to Killing Kin, Robbing Grandfather, Detroit Free Press,* August 1, 1987.

[56]Swickard, Joe, and Trimer, Margaret, *Jury Acquits 2 Vigilantes of Burning Down House, Detroit Free Press,* November 7, 1988.

[57]McDiarmid, Hugh, *Gun Control Help: Now That's a Laugh, Detroit Free Press,* February 29, 1989.

[58]Hamill, Pete, *Facing Up to Drugs, New York Magazine,* August 15, 1988.

[59]Carl-Spencer Taylor of Michigan State University, during an interview in his office, March 14, 1989.

[60]Telephone query to National Institute of Justice Statistical Services Division, Washington, DC.

[61]McConahay and Kirk.

[62]Telephone interview with Tom McWeenie, Drug Enforcement Administration, Washington, D.C., February 23, 1989.

[63]*Report to the Nation on Crime and Justice – Second Edition.*

[64]*Playboy Forum.*

[65]*Report to the Nation on Crime and Justice – Second Edition.*

[66]McWeenie/DEA.

[67]*Ibid.*

[68]*Playboy Forum.*

[69]Telephone interview with Patricia Cuza, Michigan Office of Criminal Justice, Department of Management and Budget, Lansing, MI, April 26, 1989.

[70]CBS *48 Hours, Murder Capital,* aired nationwide March 9, 1989.

[71]Malina, Fred, Mount Kisco, NY, in *Letters* section of *New York Magazine,* August 29, 1989, in response to the previous article by Pete Hamill (see above).

[72]Speaking at the National Institute of Justice conference annoucing the May 1988 DUF data.

CHAPTER 10
Community Policing and Drugs

Stabilizing a neighborhood requires a strategy that creates community cohesion; a strategy which can be extended, with limited resources, citywide.

—*Chief Anthony Bouza*
Minneapolis

The Police Response: The Military Model & the War on Drugs

The police have adapted the military model as the most logical structure to confront the domestic threats of crime and civil disorder. While that makes obvious sense, it also means the police can risk falling victim to the same kinds of pitfalls the military faces. One obvious problem is the potential for duplication of effort and lack of coordination among the branches of the armed forces. Left unaddressed, such problems can cause confusion and leave gaping holes that any enemy could penetrate and exploit, and the system would invite waste and fraud.

To minimize the dangers, the Joint Chiefs of Staff meet regularly to discuss and develop an overall strategy – and also in the hope that focusing on common goals will keep territorialism and jealousy to a minimum. The Joint Chiefs also individually and collectively use intelligence to formulate scenarios about the the broadest possible range of problems that might arise. This allows them to analyze and test various options, make adjustments, and update their strategies as conditions change.

While that system is obviously far from perfect, the federal, state, and local criminal justice response suffer from all the drawbacks of the military model, with few of its saving graces. The three main actors in the criminal justice system are not co-equals in the same way as the Army, Navy, and Air Force. Federal, state, and local police agencies are not a hierarchy as much as a loose aggregation of entities, separately funded, with few urgent reasons or opportunities to interact. This makes it difficult for them to coordinate efforts as if they were part of the same unified team.

Appeals to the common good can carry weight, but money and power often matter more. In the War on Drugs, for example, the federal funds available to state and local departments are contingent on demonstrating cooperation and coordination. The regulations also require that the states write a drug strategy each year, which must mesh with the federal drug strategy. But the relatively small amounts of money involved have caused numerous problems, not the least of which is whether it is worth the investment in time and money for many local agencies to apply for the grants and do the paperwork required to verify performance. Another problem the states face is that they cannot possibly stretch the federal funds to cover all the worthwhile efforts that seek assistance, which means losing an opportunity to involve those agencies in the process. Lack of coordination has also been complicated by the situation where some major cities have been able to circumvent state government, by applying directly for federal funds.

The challenge for the police is to decide how any additional dollars they receive should be spent. The goal is to reduce supply (importation, manufacture, production, distribution, and sale of drugs) and demand (purchase, possession, and use). For the most part, the traditional police response has been to focus on arresting dealers, in the belief that arresting enough dealers will ultimately remove enough drugs to dry up demand. The problem when the police focus on making more and more arrests, however, is that this risks creating bottlenecks elsewhere in the criminal justice system. Ultimately, generating more arrests without considering and coping with the potential backlog can cause as many problems as it solves, since overloading the crime labs, prosecutors, courts, or corrections risks undermining the effectiveness and credibility of the entire system.

While federal funding allocated for the War on Drugs urged states to integrate the new money in ways that would not cause bottlenecks, the available funds could only be stretched so far. The unevenness of federal funding year-to-year also complicates intelligent long-term planning, and some states have grave concerns about starting new efforts only to find future funding may disappear, leaving states no options other than abandoning the initiatives or finding ways to fund them themselves.

This underscores the different kinds of problems that can plague well-meaning efforts to encourage agencies at various levels to work together. The DEA, for example, has been able to use the lure of sharing forfeiture money as a way to involve other agencies in joint operations. As more states develop tougher criminal and civil forfeiture laws of their own, however, state and local agencies can choose to go it alone. Though the increasing use of forfeiture provides a way to wring profits out of drug trafficking, the competition among various agencies for forfeiture risks undermining cooperation, and it can spawn new opportunities for abuse.

The reality is that various agencies face different drug problems, have different strategies, and they also have good reason to guard their autonomy. Competition, mistrust, and jealousy among police agencies erodes cooperation, and there is often no formal system to coerce – or even encourage – communication. In many areas, the municipal police stereotype the county sheriff's department as their inferior, and both dismiss the state police as arrogant and aloof. In one state, an organized crime task force refuses to alert anyone in a certain big-city police department about an upcoming raid, because past experience raised concerns about corruption and tipoffs. Instead of providing a seamless web that drug dealers cannot penetrate, the result is all too often a patchwork quilt dotted with gaping holes.

Outsiders often see the police as one big team. They see the DEA and FBI at the top, working with other federal agencies to keep drugs from flowing in and on efforts aimed at distributors and major dealers inside the country. They assume all state and local agencies are linked to the top of this pyramid, with information flowing smoothly up and down, top to bottom.

People also assume that those at the federal and state level concentrate on Mr. Big, freeing local agencies to concentrate on drug problems at the community level. While it is true that the increasing use of multi-agency task forces offers the promise of improved cooperation, the desire to bag Mr. Big can often prove too seductive for even the smallest agencies to abandon.

Catching Mr. Big means great press coverage – an opportunity for the chief, the mayor, and perhaps even the officers involved to appear on TV in front of stacks of money and drugs. It often means glory, promotions, and verification that the police can match wits with the shrewdest drug kingpins and beat them at their own game. Increasingly as well, arresting Mr. Big means forfeiture money – money that need not be shared if the agency achieved the coup on its own.

In contrast, the seemingly endless hassling of street-level dealing in crumbling neighborhoods is never glamorous – and no forfeiture money. An occasional sweep to keep low-level dealers and addicts off the streets, especially when visiting conventioneers or foreign dignitaries are due, may be a necessary evil. But many police officials see this tactic as pointless, and they worry that allowing officers to get too close invites corruption and abuse. Most officers have little reason to lobby for such efforts, since most have reason not to be enthusiastic about spending much time dealing with such a sad and frustrating group.

Yet lacking most of all perhaps is a coordinated think-tank approach that allows the police to assess and re-assess their drug strategies, to see whether they are – or even whether they can – achieve the desired goals. The danger in trying to solve any problem is that preconceptions can cloud our ability to see clearly. Particularly in the case of drugs, many police departments have simply become reactors, so overwhelmed that they have little time to think through whether simply doing more of the same is the best answer. Within agencies and departments, let alone across jurisdictional lines, few policymakers can afford to stand back from the fray, evaluate the available research, gather information on local priorities, debate the merits and ramifications of various options, and then implement the overall strategy, with a system in place to evaluate the results and make appropriate changes.

The problem is often that many departments think that they are being rigorously logical in their approach, but they tend to measure results in arrests made rather than on whether the drug problem is getting better or worse. All too often, the department has no system that allows them to anticipate and plan for new drug problems in the future, because they are too busy fighting the good fight today. The result is that people in the community see the system breaking down, yet the police seem to offer few, if any, fresh ideas.

Whether they live there or not, people nationwide are outraged that there are virtual drug bazaars in many major cities, where dealers brazenly hawk their wares. Drug-ridden areas of major cities have become the laboratories for uncontrolled experiments that produce new drugs and new drug problems. Crack did not find a toehold in the suburbs or rural areas and flow into the cities – it emerged in the inner city where problems with hard drugs have festered for years. Harvard University's George Kelling says that organized sweeps and focused crackdowns prove that the police "can take the beach," but what is less clear is if they have an affordable and effective strategy to "hold the beach."[1]

The police who work the crack-infested inner-city hot spots "are finding themselves outgunned and outmanned by crack traders brazenly willing to unload military-assault weapons on anyone in their way."[2] The fear is that drugs and drug violence will spread. Embattled police in many cities have instituted *de facto* decriminalization of marijuana use, since they cannot keep up with efforts targeted at hard drugs. Police in suburban or rural areas may have the luxury of worrying about someone selling lookalikes at schools, but metro police in many cities must first contend with the 12-year-olds experimenting with crack, as the age of first use of cocaine continues to drop.[3]

Not only do people have reason to fear that the intense problems of the inner city will spread, but Americans are inherently offended at the notion that we can tolerate the law being applied unequally place to place. By tolerating a level of lawlessness in drug-infested neighborhoods to persist, we perpetuate an environment likely to cause even more problems over time. Parents who try to raise children in the urban equivalent of a war zone need support in their struggle to instill proper values in their youngsters. They face enough obstacles without the additional burden of trying to undo the obvious message on the streets, which is that the criminal justice system is on the verge of impotence in the face of drugs.

The police cannot do the job alone, and there is some optimism that drug education may be helping to reduce demand, as evidenced by the decline in drug use by high-school seniors for the second year in a row.[4] The concern, however, is that drug education works best where education works best. The dropout rate in many inner-city schools exceeds 40 % , and achievement scores often fall below statewide norms. Of concern as well is whether these modest gains in reduced demand will continue to hold up over time, and whether these improvements will soon translate into visible relief on the streets, where dealers have stepped up their hard-sell marketing aimed at the young.

As the turn of the century approaches, the police have no way to know whether the chilling drug problems in major cities will recede, stabilize, or continue to spill into the areas where the system had previously worked fairly well. Drug education and treatment can make valid long-term contributions, but the police are increasingly being asked to put their lives on the line today, with little relief in sight. Of increasing concern as well is whether aggressive police anti-drug efforts might inadvertently trigger a new wave of urban riots. The so-called "Super Bowl riot" in Miami occurred when a Hispanic officer shot and killed a black motorcycle rider, and the companion riding in back died as well. In the months following the riot, some Hispanic officers reported being hit with rocks in black neighborhoods, highlighting the tensions that persist.[5] A *Newsweek* article in 1989 focused on the pressures that drug enforcement places on the police, the "stress of fighting a war they can't seem to win."[6]

No one claims to have all the answers, but the problem is obviously so complex that it demands a problem-solving approach that focuses on understanding the underlying dynamics. Otherwise the law of unintended consequences can mean that well-meaning efforts inadvertently produce new problems that risk making the situation even worse.

Research on Police Strategies Aimed at Drugs

Harvard policy analyst Mark H. Moore and his colleague Mark A.R. Kleiman of the John F. Kennedy School of Government have separately and together examined the goals the police hope to accomplish with their anti-drug efforts as well as the strategies they can and do use to achieve those ends.* Both have arrived at compatible but not identical conclusions, and both agree that departments can fail to see that the strategies they have developed are not achieving the results they expect.

At the top of Moore's list of what police departments target as their primary goals is eliminating or reducing the violence associated with drug trafficking, in particular the violence in the crack trade, which can involve youth gangs. The second

---

*To avoid the clutter of footnotes, only direct quotes are referenced by number, but a list of pertinent publications by both men can be found in the Notes for this chapter.

goal is to reduce user crime. Moore also wrote that "drug trafficking threatens the civility of city life and undermines parenting,"[7] so he ranked police efforts targeted at improving those conditions third. In addition, any strategy the police employ must take into account potential bottlenecks elsewhere in the criminal justice system. And finally, administrators must also acknowledge the importance of controlling police corruption and abuse of power. Kleiman's list of primary police goals includes: drug abuse control, crime control, neighborhood protection, and organized crime control.

Though Moore and Kleiman arrange the strategies and tactics that the police can use to achieve those goals into different *strategic bundles,* together they break down into three general kinds of approaches: those that look upward toward top dealers, those that focus downward at street level, and those that target juveniles, including both drug trafficking by youth gangs and juvenile drug abuse.

High-Level Enforcement

Both Moore and Kleiman concur that police departments that adopt the DEA/FBI strategy of *Targeting Mr. Big* (high-level enforcement) as their sole or primary approach are often unwittingly buying into its limitations and drawbacks. Ideally, of course, arresting Mr. Big should help take drugs off the street, and penalizing him should deter others from dealing.

The economics of supply and demand dictate that anything that substantially reduces supply should result in a price increase. The price of coffee in the United States jumped dramatically a few years ago when drought in Colombia reduced the supply. If either nature or man had interfered sufficiently with the amount of Colombian cocaine reaching city streets, we would expect to see a similar rise in price. As Kleiman writes, "The theory predicts a price rise, other things being equal, if enforcement activity per unit of drug sales rises. But it [price] hasn't been rising. The theory that high-level enforcement raises prices is thus untested (and probably weakly true)."[8] Even though a price increase might have benefits, such as discouraging first-time or casual users, it could also mean those who persist in using the drug simply have to commit more crimes to pay the higher price.

Kleiman also noted the possibility of another unfortunate consequence of high-level enforcement, which is that the Mr. Bigs the police catch may well be the sloppiest or weakest, so that law enforcement is inadvertently "toughen[ing] the breed...."[9] Of concern as well is that, since one of the primary goals of any police strategy is to reduce the violence associated with drug trafficking, arresting Mr. Big risks triggering a new round of violence, as pretenders battle for the vacated throne. While cynics argue that anything that encourages dealers to kill each other is desirable, crack dealers in particular are notorious for wiping out whole families and innocent bystanders as well. This escalating climate of violence risks undermining people's faith in the system overall.

There is also reason to believe that Mr. Big is clever enough to understand the virtue of finding ways to eliminate the competition without violence, if possible, since that fuels public outrage and draws increased attention of the police. No doubt some of the information about dealers that a department receives comes from a competing Mr. Big who hopes the police will do his dirty work for him for free.

Moore suggests why one of the best outcomes of any drug strategy is what he calls "increased search time," which encompasses the non-monetary costs addicts face in securing a supply of their drug of choice. Any police action that forces addicts to look longer means less of the drug is sold and used, therefore overall profits to dealers go down. If addicts spend less money overall on drugs, theoretically they need not commit as many crimes to pay for their habits. Increasing search time also offers the promise that frustrated buyers will be more inclined to seek treatment. Making it harder for the casual or first-time user also has the obvious virtue of providing hope of reducing the number of new addicts in the future.

While a Mr. Big strategy seems to offer the hope of eliminating or interrupting the supply flowing to retail level enough to increase search time, Kleiman failed to find a single documented instance where one or more high-level busts resulted in a significant reduction in drug consumption.

Retail-Level Enforcement

If police strategies that aim upward in the chain have failed, what about those that look downward, toward street level? Retail-level enforcement strategies attempt to reduce "discreet" and "indiscreet" drug dealing, with the latter more susceptible to control. Indiscreet drug dealing includes open street dealing, as well as the dope houses and shooting galleries used exclusively to sell drugs to large numbers of customers. Transactions that take place in people's homes, offices, nightclubs, and other locations where drug dealing is not the facility's sole reason for being are therefore considered relatively discreet.

Tactics such as "street-sweeping" and "focused crackdowns" target indiscreet dealing in the hope that this will at least drive it underground. If nothing else, that should increase search time, which should reduce the total amount of drugs sold and the number of crimes committed to buy the drugs. It may also reduce the overall pool of users, by frustrating some enough to seek treatment and making it less likely that casual and first-time users can become hard-core abusers. These benefits can also improve the quality of life in the community, and there is also obvious virtue in reducing or eliminating open dealing, since it sends the message that lawlessness prevails, a particular concern with young people.

As Kleiman explains, though the targets are retail, the tactics are wholesale. The primary focus remains dealers, but low-level dealers (though users present at the time are often picked up as well). The danger here, of course, is that mass arrests often cause bottlenecks further up the line. Street-sweeping has been used extensively in Washington, D.C., yet a RAND study showed that from 1981 to 1986, despite the fact drug felony arrests went up tenfold and aggregate sentences twentyfold as a result, there was no notable decrease in drug abuse.[10]

Focused crackdowns involve using officers to maintain pressure on open dealing by repeatedly sweeping problem areas and making a bigger investment in gathering intelligence and enlisting community cooperation, if only by providing *hotline* telephone numbers where callers can circumvent the switchboard and talk directly to the crackdown's command center. Research on three different focused crackdowns that targeted heroin resulted in two success stories and one partial flop.

The Kleiman, Holland, and Hayes study of the effort in Lynn, Massachusetts, showed a reduction in crimes that are often drug related. During the first year of operation of the Lynn Drug Task Force, the number of robberies reported declined 18.5%, burglaries 37.5%, and crimes against persons 66%. Kleiman's research on New York City's Operation Pressure Point I, which saturated the notorious Alphabet City area of Manhattan, showed robberies down 47%, burglaries down 37%, and homicides down 62% at the end of the first year. This operation not only disrupted drug markets and improved the quality of life, but fears about displacement proved groundless; the study also showed that crime rates nearby either stayed the same or declined.

The apparent failure was in Lawrence, Massachusetts, where a focused crackdown on heroin did not produce reductions in target crimes – in fact, the rates rose somewhat, though not significantly so. Apparently, the major problem was that a flourishing heroin market in nearby Lowell offered addicts an easy alternative source of supply, and addicts continued to commit crimes near home to pay for the drug. At the time as well, Lawrence also faced an escalating cocaine problem, so the new crimes committed to pay for cocaine may have overwhelmed any reduction in crimes committed to buy heroin. In addition, the department was forced to divert resources from the heroin crackdown to efforts aimed at cocaine. Kleiman noted, however, that people in the heroin-infested neighborhoods appreciated the reduction in open trafficking.

Reactions to the Lawrence experiment deserve a closer look because of the important issues raised. Scholar Arnold Barnett of the Massachusetts Institute of

Technology was more pessimistic than Kleiman, both about the Lynn success and the Lawrence failure. His primary concerns centered on whether there was true long-term change in Lynn, and whether the example of Lowell should raise questions about whether the supposed Lynn success may have only displaced the problem elsewhere.

Police Chief Anthony Bouza had many reservations – indeed his conclusion is that retail-level enforcement is appealing but that the "only real problem is that it doesn't work."[11] Among his many concerns were displacement, potential abuse of police authority, clogging of the criminal justice system, and inefficient use of scarce resources. The latter was of particular concern to Bouza, who noted that, once started, such efforts often prove hard to abandon because they are so popular with voters (as the discussion later of Pressure Point I in New York City illustrates). His assessment is that aiming at high-level dealers is the answer to interdicting drugs, to control the supply side, while education about the dangers of drug abuse helps reduce demand. As the quote introducing this chapter shows, he also notes that stabilizing a neighborhood requires a "strategy that creates community cohesion; a strategy which can be extended, with limited resources, citywide."[12]

On the other hand, prosecutor Kevin M. Burke of Essex County, who established and directed both the Lynn and Lawrence efforts, was more sanguine about the results, in particular the alleged failure in Lawrence. He contended that even though addicts could purchase drugs elsewhere, so they still had reason to commit crimes near home, the Lawrence success lay in the improved quality of life in targeted neighborhoods and the removal of heroin dealers as visible role models in the community.

Moore has proposed that city-wide, or at least neighborhood-based, street-level enforcement would address many of these concerns, which will be explored further as part of Community Policing's contribution.

Efforts Aimed at Juveniles

Both Moore and Kleiman note that the police also place a high priority on efforts they hope will address juveniles, both as part of strategies aimed at drug gangs like the *Crips* and *Bloods* and those that target young people in the hope preventing a new generation of adult addicts. Not only does the latter goal spring from a humanitarian impulse, but young addicts constitute a potential pool of lifelong criminals, with many years left to commit crimes that will plague both society and its police in the future. Toward that goal, various federal and state laws provide higher penalties for sales to minors and sales made close to schools.

In some areas, officers work directly in the schools, though Kleiman noted the potential for clashes over control. "[A] principal enthusiastic about having a chronic troublemaker arrested for selling crack may still want to avoid having his valedicto-rian busted for possession of a joint," he wrote.[13]

Involving police officers in drug education is also becoming more common, and many departments have adopted the model provided by the D.A.R.E. project in Los Angeles, spearheaded by Chief Daryl Gates. The rationale behind D.A.R.E. is that police officers have more credibility and expertise on drug issues than most teachers, so that they can make a lasting impact on children's future behavior. More compre-hensive than simply urging kids to *just say no,* the program is based on the assump-tion that most kids experiment with drugs because of an inability to withstand peer pressure, problems with low self-esteem, and lack of training in values clarification.

Research on results after the first year of the program in Los Angeles showed that youngsters in the program demonstrated a statistically significant (though not dramatic) reduction in illicit drug use, but it is too early to tell whether those gains will persist as the children mature. One concern is that D.A.R.E. overlooks adoles-cent rebellion against adult authority as a root cause of experimentation, which might mean police officers are not the best choice for such efforts, of concern espe-cially because police pay scales often make them an expensive choice as well.

The Real Police World

Equally as important as theorizing about what the police can and should do about drugs is examining what they are doing. To that end, Kleiman looked at the drug strategies of three big-city police departments – New York, Los Angeles, and Detroit:

• **New York** – The Narcotics Division, with more than 2,000 sworn officers, is roughly two-thirds the size of the DEA, with which it cooperates, sharing the DEA's commit-ment to the Mr. Big strategy. Kleiman also discovered that the Narcotics Division remains particularly sensitive about scandals of the past, which means the administra-tion has grave reservations about involving uniformed officers in street-level enforce-ment. Even so, as mentioned earlier, Operation Pressure Point I in Alphabet City, the largest and longest-running focused drug crackdown in the country, uses sworn offi-cers in a program operated jointly by the Narcotics Division and Manhattan South.

The difficulty of extricating officers from such operations once started has caused concern within the department. Kleiman said that the Narcotics Division's Tactical Narcotics Team (TNT) street-level unit was used and then pulled from an effort in southeast Queens – and drug trafficking sprang back full force once the officers were removed. The problem, however, is that efforts such as Operation Pressure Point I can work only if the officers stay, but this raises the concern that they are left there with little to do.

Though pressure from Mayor Edward Koch's office meant that 700 new narcotics officers were added in 1988, both Police Commissioner Benjamin Ward and narcotics commanders remain skeptical that expanding TNT will dramatically reduce drug dealing citywide. Many in the department compare the situation to the losing effort in Vietnam, according to Kleiman.

- **Los Angeles** – While New York was forced to build upward, Los Angeles sprawled outward, and Kleiman found that the Los Angeles Police Department and the Los Angeles County Sheriff's Department that share primary responsibility for drug enforcement in the county have far fewer officers to do the job than in New York, both on a per-capita and per-square-mile basis. Unlike New York, Los Angeles makes little effort to compete with the federal efforts aimed at Mr. Big, assigning only 100 officers to anything that could be considered high-level enforcement. Kleiman found that most of L.A. effort is targeted at the middlemen between importers and gang-affiliated retailers.

  Echoing the chief, L.A. officers insist that "the current generation of drug users is lost," so their short-term efforts focus on gangs and street-level enforcement and their long-term efforts on drug education. The CRASH unit, initially named for a local project, has been expanded into a citywide effort to control youth gangs, which have roughly 70,000 members, according to the chief. The good cop/bad cop approach embraced by CRASH was portrayed in the movie *Colors* by the two main characters, and though far from a documentary, the film captured this elite unit's sense of dedication to the cause.

  The retail-enforcement strategy consists of having undercover officers make buys from both gang members and independent operations. The education effort commits 90 officers to D.A.R.E. full time. These officers receive special training and then spend all their time in schools teaching the classes, and they make no arrests.

  Kleiman says the department considers this three-pronged effort a unified strategy, but he wondered if it might instead be three independent programs in search of a common theme.

- **Detroit** – Though the District of Columbia edged out Detroit as having the highest murder rate in 1988, many people think of Motown as Murder City. Detroit still suffered a rate of 58 murders per 100,000 population in 1988,[14] many of which are no doubt drug-related. Scholars like Kleiman and a number of journalists are often amazed that the department does not reveal figures that other departments would consider part of the public record, but Kleiman was able to find out that "more than

200" of the department's 4,800 officers are assigned to narcotics, with most targeted at street-level enforcement, through the Narcotics Enforcement Units (NEUs) at precinct level.

In December 1987, the division launched Operation Maximum Effort, which the mayor calls the War on Crack. It has reportedly resulted in one or two raids a day at crack houses, usually initiated by tips received on the 24-hour DOPE hotline. After its first six months of operation, the figures showed a 300 % increase in arrests and a 75 % reduction in calls to the hotline.

While these figures sound encouraging, Kleiman's associate Kerry Smith discovered that morale in the department was low, in part because officers resented what they considered pointless activity and pressure to generate numbers. They also expressed unhappiness with leaving efforts aimed at suppliers and top-level dealers to federal authorities. Concerns outside the department relate to rumors of corruption, including high-level corruption, and allegations of excessive force and harassment. Detroit police officers have been arrested and charged with stealing drugs, and both Detroit newspapers have also carried stories about people who said they were unfairly harassed.

As these examples demonstrate, different departments have adopted different strategies, in part because of the particular problems in the area and also because of divergent beliefs held by different department policymakers. Yet difficulties arise in determining what is and is not working, because there is not yet sufficient experience or research to offer much guidance. It is impossible to tell, for instance, whether the decline in the murder rate in Detroit can in part be attributed to police efforts aimed at drugs – or whether instead that means the drug gangs operating in the city are so entrenched that fewer and fewer newcomers dare challenge their power. Michigan State Supreme Court Justice Dennis Archer, speaking at Governor James J. Blanchard's Conference on the Violent Young Offender in December 1988, said that West Coast drug gangs eager to franchise into new markets avoid Detroit, because the cost in blood would be too high. What is clear is that the public appreciates the efforts of the police, but they are worried that they appear unable to bring drugs under control, especially open dealing on the streets.

The Community Policing Contribution

The purpose in devoting so much space to the discussion of the overall scope and complexity of the drug problems facing the United States is to show that the police cannot be expected to do the job alone. A three-pronged approach, involving law enforcement, drug education, and drug treatment, appears to hold the best promise of making a short- and long-term difference, but it also implies a tug-of-war among the three for scarce resources. While it is vital to educate young people about the threats drugs pose and help them learn how to resist temptation, and it seems tantamount to scandal that many who seek drug treatment must wait months before it is available, people are beginning to question whether the police have an equally clear vision of success.

In the District of Columbia, where lawmakers who control the federal purse-strings go to work every day, there are now three times as many open drug markets as there are supermarkets.[15] People are increasingly concerned that the police seem unable to do more. If average citizens see open dealing on the street, on their way to and from work, why can't the police shut them down? The visible scourge of open drug dealing intensifies the fear that nothing works.

Those who can afford to do so have the option to seek private help. In New York City, at least one neighborhood association has hired a private firm to patrol their streets as a way to reduce open dealing.[16] As we will discuss in detail in the last chapter, the public police have reason to worry about competition from the private sector. There is also a growing clamor to send the military into areas where the police appear unequal to the task of bringing open dealing under control.

If public policing as we now know it is to survive to the end of the 21st Century, some say its future may hinge on its ability to control drugs, the primary law-and-order issue of our times. While that may overstate the case, it is safe to say that a failure to make a valid and visible contribution risks a two-track system, where those who want and can afford more protection buy it from private sources, leaving the public police the frustrating task of policing everyone else, particularly the poor neighborhoods in our inner cities where the greatest problems tend to congregate.

As the number of people behind bars begins to approach one million, does the best criminal justice contribution lie in making more and more arrests? Many have criticized the criminal justice approach for being far costlier than drug education and drug treatment. Arrest is usually just the beginning of the increasingly expensive process of putting drug offenders away. The number of new drug cases threatens to overwhelm the existing system, which leads to the perception that the criminal justice system acts like a revolving door that spits dealers back onto the street, where they work even harder to sell more drugs to pay for their legal fees. An estimated 97% of the drug arrests in New York City in 1989 will be plea bargained because of the crush, particularly worrisome because it is often the most successful and powerful dealers who have the money for bail and for top lawyers skilled in keeping their clients out of prison.[17]

People outside police circles do not always appreciate the magnitude of the expense for personnel and facilities beyond arrest. Few appreciate the costs involved in confirming the kind of drugs seized, so that the courts will consider the evidence as valid. Add to that the tax dollars for prosecutors and public defenders to prepare the case and confer about plea bargaining options. Those costs rise dramatically if the case goes to trial, and victory for the prosecution often means more money will be spent incarcerating or otherwise monitoring the convicted drug offender. Voters often demonstrate a greater willingness to support giving drug offenders longer terms behind bars than to tax themselves to pay for new jail and prison space. Many jurisdictions that want to explore expanded drug testing of suspects out on bond before trial and after conviction as part of probation or parole face additional expense.

Most people think of the police contribution as being limited to arrest – a view held by many police officers as well. The dynamics underlying the distinct problems loosely called this nation's drug problem stem from many root causes often deemed far beyond the scope of the police – the factors that impel a suburban teenager to sample marijuana may be vastly different from those that spark an inner-city teenager to start *rolling*. Though ultimately part of the same cocaine chain, the young woman sniffing coke in a Manhattan club does not pose the same threat of violence as the drug-free gang enforcer whose job is to maim and kill competitors – and do the same to those in the gang who disobey. The police face a different challenge in uncovering and closing down a clandestine lab making crank than they do in controlling open crack dealing on city streets.

It may well prove to be a mistake for the police to treat drugs as the exclusive province of a special division within the department. Perhaps an important lesson to be learned from the DUF data, which showed that drugs are involved in as many as four of every five people arrested in some cities, is that drugs are deeply woven into the total fabric of police work, from child abuse to gangland-style executions, from muggings to traffic accidents. Though drugs are not the cause of all the problems the police face, the DUF data shows that they play some immediate role in the lives of the vast majority of people arrested in our major cities.

This could mean that delegating efforts aimed at drugs to a special Narcotics Unit makes as little sense as referring property crimes to a Greed and Poverty Squad, the only difference being that greed and poverty are not themselves illegal. What is clear is that new ways must be found to involve the entire department and its sworn officers in efforts aimed at drugs and the problems they spawn.

Harvard's Mark Moore suggests that neighborhood or citywide street-level enforcement offers a unique opportunity for departments to address the retail drug dealing that has made urban life in many areas a nightmare. Not only does the dealing itself erode the environment and provide odious role models for future generations, the variety of crimes it spawns threatens to overwhelm the police, whether it's gun-toting gangs locked in armed struggle or addicts snatching purses and stealing TVs. Yet many police administrators resist committing the patrol officers necessary to fight a targeted or citywide war aimed at the streets, for fear they will be tempted into corruption or abuse, or because people demand that they stay, even if the officers are then left idle once the crisis subsides.

What has been so often overlooked is the unique contribution that Community Policing can make – and how it might be used even more effectively in the future. Because of the vast number of different kinds of problems that drugs create, a community problem-solving approach obviously makes better sense than simply responding to individual incidents. Community Policing also allows the department to fashion responses tailored to local problems and needs, without focusing exclusively on arrest, which often engages the rest of the expensive criminal justice system to little effect.

As the department's community outreach specialists, CPOs have a particularly vital role to play in improving relations between the department and the community, to prepare people to accept new anti-drug initiatives with less risk of a backlash or riots. As these suggestions demonstrate, CPOs can play an important role in helping to bring the current drug crisis under control, then they can continue to focus on developing longer-term proactive initiatives that offer the prospect of making communities more drug-resistant in the future.

The current applications and theoretical possibilities concerning how Community Policing can help reduce society's drug problems has yet to be fully explored. The following should be considered a partial list of what Community Policing is doing now and a blueprint for how it might be used to accomplish more in the future:

- **Community Policing directly addresses the problems of discreet and indiscreet retail-level drug dealing.** If the police are to maintain public confidence, they must find new ways to address retail drug dealing, because this is the dealing that occurs where people live, the dealing that directly threatens their children and that leaves dazed, erratic, and potentially criminal addicts in its wake, destroying community life. A sense of fairness would seem to dictate that both indiscreet and discreet dealing would receive equal police attention, but open dealing is even more pernicious because it reinforces the public perception that drugs have careened out of control, a singularly dangerous message to send to young people. Open dealing also makes it too easy for casual and first-time users as well as addicts to find a ready supply, which adds to the current and future profits of this illicit industry and which supports an expanding pool of addicts who threaten to spiral the rates of other drug-related crime.

  Community Policing can provide the department's first line of defense against both indiscreet and discreet dealing. The shift from focusing on responding to calls and making arrests to solving community problems reorders overall department priorities to a proper emphasis on helping people feel safer from the threat drugs pose. Through its CPOs, Community Policing provides a permanent, citywide, neighborhood-based approach to drug problems. By allowing CPOs to *own* their beat areas, they can build bridges to the people in the community whose support and participation are crucial in bringing retail-level dealing under control.

Enlisting CPOs directly in attacking retail-level dealing may require a shift in thinking or a change in policy, and CPOs might benefit from additional training in useful anti-drug techniques, but experience shows that Community Policing is already making a remarkable contribution in controlling open dealing in ways that do not focus exclusively on arrest.

In North Miami Beach, Florida, CPO Charles Reynolds was assigned to a low-income, primarily black neighborhood notorious as a supermarket for drugs. Once Reynolds had gained the trust of the people in his beat area, he bravely tackled the problem in person, by individually warning low-level dealers that he would make it his business to arrest them if they persisted – but that if they wanted help in finding a job, he would provide that as well. Reynolds then proceeded to back up both his threat and his promise. He made cases against those who failed to heed his warning, but he also provided individualized and broad-based assistance to help people find work.

As part of that effort, each week Reynolds posted a list in his office of the jobs available in the community, and he referred specific people to companies that he knew were hiring people with their skills. Reynolds also worked with business and professional leaders to host a Job Fair in the Community Policing office. That event provided classes on everything from how to dress for an interview to how to write a resume, and it involved people in role-playing so that they could assess their performance in mock job interviews. By tailoring the police response to community needs, Reynolds was able to bring open dealing under control without the mass arrests that might have done little more than clog the system to dubious effect.

In Lansing, Michigan, Lt. James Rapp reported success with using foot patrol officers to make repeated visits each day to knock on the door of known dope houses – sometimes they just stood outside. Home visits are part of a CPO's routine tasks, but having the officer appear in front of a dope house meant that the operators inside routinely flushed any drugs on the premises each time, never knowing when the officer's arrival might signal a bust. The officer's visible presence also helped drive customers away, which reduced profits even further. Though such tactics raise concern about displacement, Rapp said that the real mistake lies in leaving dealers somewhere to hide.

In major metropolitan areas plagued by open dealing, the department could use its CPOs to prepare communities to accept aggressive tactics such as coordinated sweeps and focused crackdowns, by enlisting their cooperation and support. In some cases, one or more sweeps might be enough to disrupt and reduce open dealing sufficiently so that the CPOs community-based efforts would be enough to maintain control. In other cases, it might prove necessary to increase the overall number of CPOs, so that enough could be freed to pay undivided attention to the areas with the most severe drug problems. Not only would they be able to sustain gains made by coordinating their efforts with periodic sweeps, but they would not be left idle, but free to pursue new initiatives aimed at a broad range of community concerns, including crime, fear of crime, social and physical disorder and neighborhood decay.

The problem with relying on sweeps and focused crackdowns that are not part of a Community Policing approach is that these tactics reinforce the perception that the answer to controlling open dealing is the sole responsibility of the police. Community Policing recognizes that law-abiding people must accept their responsibility to become involved in efforts to save their own neighborhoods, and that the police are a resource that can help – not the total cure.

In a notoriously drug-infested area of the District of Columbia, members of the Nation of Islam (formerly called the Black Muslims) have achieved notable success by working with residents directly to develop initiatives to eliminate open dealing. Their success demonstrates what a relatively small but dedicated group can do with grassroots community support. The goal of the police should be to use CPOs as the initiators and supervisors in community-based efforts, not only because this model offers the opportunity for success, but because the CPO's involvement provides additional assurance against potential corruption, abuse, and vigilantism.

Once the immediate priority of controlling open dealing has been achieved, Community Policing can then address indiscreet dealing in new ways. An example reported in *New York* magazine shows how a sustained Community Policing effort can help turn an area around. A single mother of two sons who was studying at Hunter College moved into a housing project on the Lower East Side and found that the complex was dominated by a major crack and marijuana dealer operating from one apartment. Although no fan of the police, the woman felt she had no choice but to ask for their help, so she contacted the Community Patrol Officer Program (CPOP) team in her area. Together they developed a strategy that included making *vertical patrols* of the apartment building; offering to escort customers inside (which scared many away); and making arrests (and getting convictions) on a variety of charges, including disorderly conduct. The sustained pressure ultimately caused the dealer to make a slip that allowed the police to make a good arrest.

The woman was quoted as saying, "[Police Commissioner] Ben Ward should come down here and give these men a big kiss. They did the police job with decency, sensitivity, and integrity. No one can believe the quality of police care this building was given – they say, "You talking about the *New York City* Police Department?"[18] The success of this effort has encouraged the residents and their CPOP team to orchestrate efforts targeted at other problems in the community, ranging from a brothel, to a youth posse, to dealers in empty apartments. Community Policing allows the department to build on and expand initial success in ways that limited sweeps and focused crackdowns cannot.

• **Community Policing can often gather more and better information about retail-level and even high-level drug dealing with less danger and expense than traditional undercover operations.** It bears repeating that two groups of people have information about crime – the criminals themselves and the law-abiding citizens who know what they are doing. Traditional police efforts focus on the former, though they have the greatest reason to guard their secrets – sometimes with guns. Community Policing instead works on developing the trust required so that law-abiding people will tell what they know, and experience in the field shows that CPOs often generate intelligence about drug dealing beyond what any other approach can achieve.

In the Flint experiment, then-lieutenant Bruce Benson said that the narcotics officers were routinely frustrated because people would call with a tip, but they rarely provided more than an address before hanging up. The officers would try to follow up, but often found little to go on, yet the caller would call again to complain the police were not doing their job.

Once the Flint foot patrol program got underway, instead what often happened was that a person near a dope house would tell the officer in person about the operation – not just the address, but the names or license plate numbers of the dealers and customers, hours of operation, kinds of drugs sold, a physical description of the layout. Even if the people did not know the details, they were often willing to work with the officer to find out what the police needed to know. The foot officer would then transmit the information to the narcotics squad, so that they had enough information to launch the process of securing a warrant to make a successful bust.

Flint was not an isolated case. When a new Community Policing effort was launched in Morristown, New Jersey, the officers and the administration were amazed at how much information about drug dealing people would pass on during routine visits on other matters. One woman was able to provide police enough detailed information to break up a broad-based drug dealing ring shortly after the new program started, the result of an unrelated home visit.

CPOs say that the answer often lies in finding the neighborhood *busybody*, often a retired person who keeps track of everything going on, including the neighborhood's drug problems. The inherent drawback in the traditional approach is that a motor patrol officer rarely has the time or opportunity to develop the level of trust necessary for that person to divulge what they know, or the officer is there for other reasons and does not want to waste time listening to *worthless gossip*.

Another reason that Community Policing often elicits information that other police will never get stems from the fact that home visits and chats on the street are routine, so that people are not targeted for revenge as they might be if dealers saw a patrol car parked outside. Cost concerns have persuaded some departments that they cannot afford to free CPOs completely from patrol cars, yet this may hamper their effectiveness in gathering information, especially information on drugs. A CPO on foot (or on a bike or even a horse) is more approachable. And when people see their CPO walking the same streets they do, they know that the officer has good reason to care about what goes on at street level. This can also inspire people to venture out themselves, and part of the answer in reclaiming streets from the drug dealers may lie in those who do not approve of coming forth in sufficient numbers to drive them away.

In Tulsa, Oklahoma, a Community Policing effort put officers assigned to a public housing complex on horseback, so that the horse could act as an icebreaker, especially with kids. This allowed both adults and children the excuse of petting the horse as an opportunity for them to tell the CPOs about problems, including drug dealing, without drawing undue attention to themselves. In one dramatic episode, the officers were able to rescue a single mother literally held captive by cocaine dealers who had taken over her apartment.

- **Community Policing attacks street-level dealing in ways that need not always engage or overwhelm the rest of the criminal justice system.** In the past two years in the District of Columbia, police sweeps have succeeded in arresting roughly 45,000 people without making any dents in the gang-related violence or the amount of open dealing visible on the streets. Meanwhile, the rest of the system has been overwhelmed – prison costs alone have soared 400 % over the past eight years.[19]

  The tally on Detroit's War on Crack reported by the *Detroit Free Press* shows that 144 of the 1,041 people arrested on felony drug charges during the first three months never appeared after they had been released on bond or freed because of jail overcrowding. A report prepared by Detroit Recorder's Court seeking more funds to add more judges said that 86.7 % of all people arrested on drug charges go free on bond because of backlogged dockets and jail overcrowding.[20]

  Instead of sending the message that the system has the teeth to put dealers away, the criminal justice response instead seems to ensure that the dealer arrested today will be back in business tomorrow – hustling even harder to pay for legal fees. Community Policing approaches the overall problem from a different perspective, by employing arrest as only one of the tools in its arsenal. The traditional police response to a problem often stresses the number of arrests made as a measure of success, but particularly with the problem of open dealing, this yardstick may not always be the best solution, if it clogs the rest of the system to little effect and pressuring the officers to generate numbers promotes abuse of authority.

The account of the CPOP efforts in New York City highlights the importance of solving the problem without focusing on felony drug busts as the primary goal. In that case, using midsdemeanor disorderly conduct charges discouraged addicts from making buys, as did having CPOs and tenants offer to escort them inside. In Wisconsin, an enterprising Neighborhood Watch group boldly held its meetings across the street from open dealing, thereby driving customers and eventually the dealers away.

CPOs are full-fledged law enforcement officers who make arrests, but they understand that the real goal is to solve the problem, which might or might not include making arrests. The hallmark of the Community Policing approach is its ability to generate creative, new, community-based, police-supervised approaches. It recognizes that generating arrests beyond what the rest of the criminal justice system can handle risks creating bottlenecks that can undermine confidence in the entire system. Community Policing shifts the focus from arrest as the primary means of achieving solutions to one that recognizes that arrest is an expensive and time-consuming option that plays an important role in addressing community problems, but a tool that must be used wisely for maximum effect.

Even in areas where new jails and prisons are under construction and additional funds are being made available to ease the squeeze drug enforcement puts on all the other elements of the criminal justice system, there is concern that there will never be enough dollars to do much more than play catch-up. Frustration has tempted those involved to overload the system with arrests as a way of calling attention to the shortages elsewhere in the system, yet that ignores the obvious dangers in such tactics. Community Policing's problem-solving orientation promotes developing drug strategies that take constraints in the overall system into account.

- **Community Policing can make the best use of visual harassment as a tactic to reduce open dealing.** One way for the police to address open dealing without always engaging the rest of the criminal justice system involves the judicious and lawful use of visual harassment. A neighborhood group, with a CPO in the lead, making periodic sweeps of streets infested with open drug dealing can have the same effect as those vertical sweeps floor-by-floor that the CPOP officers used in apartment houses.

Creative CPOs and neighborhood residents working together can also employ a host of other tactics to make dealers nervous enough to dispose of their drugs and drive customers away, such as visibly taking down license plate numbers of potential buyers or clicking cameras (without film) at people making dope deals on the street. The purpose is not to assemble lists, which could raise concerns about violation of civil rights, but to make buyers and sellers think that they are under surveillance. One CPO even posted signs in his beat area saying that drug dealing would not be tolerated. The goal is to turn up the heat as much as possible, so that the police and people together demonstrate that they will not let up. As Moore's analysis hypothesized, anything that increases a user's search time has numerous short- and long-term benefits.

- **Community Policing develops and bolsters community participation in anti-drug efforts.** Areas overwhelmed with drug problems promote apathy and despair because people feel there is nothing they can do that will make a difference. With Community Policing, sometimes it takes only one committed person to spark an effort that can achieve some success, and that, in turn, can help recruit others for new efforts. The CPO's job is to be a motivator, so that the momentum is not allowed to die even if the initial goal of curtailing street dealing is accomplished.

    If a focused crackdown achieves success, but the officers are then removed, only to have the drug dealers return, people can rightfully feel abandoned and betrayed. Many people have expressed concern that traditional efforts ignore them – their needs and concerns and their potential support and participation as well. Community Policing pays attention to average citizens, allowing them a voice in setting priorities and fashioning solutions tailored to their concerns. The Community Policing alternative to flooding an area with a lot of police for a short time is to substitute a smaller number of CPOs who are stationed in the community permanently, so that they can recruit people in the community to help themselves.

    Most often, the first goal in many areas is to reduce open dealing, to stabilize the neighborhood, then focus on indiscreet dealing to maintain the pressure. As the area begins to improve, the CPO can brainstorm with people in the community about new ways to address the broader spectrum of drug problems. This might mean linking addicts to proper treatment. Or it could include working with area businesses to provide jobs for recovering addicts. Community Policing provides a way for the police to link arms with all other law-abiding people who understand that they must become part of the answer if drug problems are to be brought under control.

- **Community Policing can harness the vigilante impulse and channel it in positive directions.** If the police fail to find a way to tap into and control the frustration people feel when they are inundated with drug problems in their neighborhoods, this positive energy can erupt into corrosive vigilantism, which only serves to undermine respect for the law even further. The jury that acquitted the self-admitted arsonists in Detroit who burned down a crack house signified the danger in ignoring people's desire to do something concrete about their concerns.

One major problem with traditional police efforts is that the officers do not have an opportunity to spend enough time in the community talking to people in depth, so that they can identify and work with people whose energies can be harnessed to the task. CPOs can work with people on developing effective and *lawful* ways for them to address the problem together, not just today, but over time. An effective CPO can transmute the dangerous impulse to vigilantism into efforts that maintain respect for the law, efforts that do not endanger either the civil rights or physical safety of innocent bystanders. Again, because CPOs are stationed permanently in their beat areas, they provide continuous and personalized supervision of citizen participation in efforts that might otherwise cross the line.

- **Community Policing provides the best way to involve the entire department in anti-drug efforts with the least risk of corruption and abuse of authority.** Much of the reluctance of many police departments to involve line officers in street-level anti-drug initiatives stems from the unwarranted fear that this will promote corruption and abuse. As Kleiman noted, the irony is that virtually all of the most scandalous incidents where drugs and drug money have spawned widespread corruption involved narcotics officers, not patrol personnel.

There will always be the occasional "dirty cop" who crosses the line, but the dynamic most likely to promote widespread corruption and abuse appears to be when an elite unit is put on the task, especially a unit cloaked in secrecy. A system that also focuses on the number of arrests as the sole or primary measure of success can also pressure police to cross the into abuse, entrapment, and fraud. The structure can promote an "if you can't beat 'em, join 'em" mindset. The officers involved in the drug corruption scandal in the 77th Precinct in New York, where narcotics officers allegedly robbed dealers and resold the drugs, apparently thought of themselves as modern-day equivalents of Robin Hood even after they were exposed.

Yet police administrators still worry that putting an officer into a beat in a drug-riddled neighborhood invites corruption or abuse of authority. No doubt this stems from concern that when officers band together and begin to see themselves as part of a cohesive brotherhood, they can also adopt an unofficial code of silence that demands that they refuse to report a fellow officer's transgressions. This bonding is why departments plagued by problems with officers using excessive force often find the situation difficult to reverse.

Ironically, one Community Policing's supposed drawbacks may actually be one of its greatest strengths. Because CPOs spend so much time with average citizens rather than with their fellow officers, they are more likely to identify with the needs of the people they serve rather than their fellow officers. CPOs are less likely to adopt the traditional police mindset of *us* (the police) against *them* (everybody else). Being out of the loop in the department often means CPOs are viewed as breed apart by their traditional fellow officers. While that can cause problems of internal dissension, it also makes CPOs less likely than their traditional counterparts to indulge in abuse of authority out on the street.

CPOs also have an additional check on their performance beyond police supervisors, since the people they serve are more likely to complain if they stray. Most people have so little contact with traditional officers that they could not comment knowledgeably about what they do on the job. The intense, personal relationship between CPOs and their constituents involves average citizens in the police process, so not only are they better able to assess performance, but experience shows they are quite quick to complain to higher-ups if they do not like what they see.

- **Community Policing can help reduce the overall profitability of drug dealing in ways that do not increase user crime.** As explained before, strategies that target Mr. Big, if they worked well, should eventually cause the price of drugs to increase, since one of the few laws that drugs cannot break is the law of supply and demand. By focusing the bulk of its attention at disrupting and reducing retail-level dealing, Community Policing reduces the overall profits of the drug trade in ways that do not threaten a price increase, so addicts need not commit more crimes to pay for the drugs. Street-level enforcement instead increases search time, which means addicts spend less on drugs, so they may not need to commit as many crimes to earn the money to spend on their drugs.

- **Community Policing enlists the direct cooperation of credible informants.** One of the most frustrating problems that narcotics officers face is that they must often rely on "turning" addicts or low-level dealers to build cases against higher-level dealers. The problem, however, is that when the cases go to court, the questionable character and dubious veracity of such informants can result in acquittal. Jurors can find it hard to believe testimony from addicts and drug dealers, especially when they have concerns about possible entrapment or that the person may be lying about others to secure a deal for himself.

Bruce Benson, the former lieutenant in the Flint experiment, said one of the biggest surprises was that foot patrol officers recruited many people with impeccable reputations who volunteered to help the police build cases against dope dealers, even at great personal risk. One local business owner felt so personally frustrated by the city's growing drug problem that he agreed many times to make undercover buys and then testify in court. Benson said that the man's credibility helped them win cases.

The Flint experiment showed that foot officers could develop a roster of credible informants who would never have been reached by traditional efforts.

- **Community Policing can best employ problem-solving tactics aimed at drug-dealing and drug-related crime.** Problem-Oriented Policing (also called Problem-Solving Policing) has become a hot buzzword in police circles. As discussed in Chapter 1, it basically asks officers to use their heads, to look beyond individual incidents to the underlying patterns and dynamics. The purpose is to identify possible pressure points where a police intervention can make an impact on solving the problem, whether or not that involves arrest. CPOs, because of their intense and sustained community involvement, are often the best candidates to identify, launch, and supervise problem-solving initiatives, adjusting them as needed based on their evaluation of the results.

    Low-level dealing and user crime can both lend themselves to problem-solving techniques. Perhaps it means having the CPO persuade the city to install high-intensity streetlights in areas where open dealing takes place at night. In North Miami Beach, Florida, the city officials in charge of code enforcement have actually been moved into the department, in part because of the hope that CPOs can work with them to use the regulations as a means to close dope houses. In some communities, it could mean enlisting area businesses and parents in efforts to turn a vacant lot used for dealing into a baseball diamond where kids could play softball instead.

    These tactics can also prove useful in addressing addict crime. As the research discussed earlier indicated, drug users often commit crimes near home. This could mean CPOs working with residents in drug-infested housing complexes on strategies to reduce robberies, by improving outdoor lighting and clipping back bushes where muggers can hide. It could mean working with the manager on a system to issue identification cards and visitor passes, to discourage outsiders from coming in to make buys – and robbing residents to pay for the drugs. Problem-solving techniques may also discover that a rash of burglaries can be traced to the opening of a new dope house in the area, so that closing it down brings the number of those crimes down. The beauty of a community problem-solving approach is that no one can ever anticipate all the forms it will take, because imaginative new strategies are being tested each day.

- **Community Policing can target youth gangs for special attention.** As discussed in Chapter 8 on special populations, the police have the opportunity to play an expanded role in addressing the problem of youth gangs, not only in targeting existing gangs for special attention, but by providing lawful alternatives. The problem with many youth gangs today is that they have discovered the potential profits available in drug dealing and laws aimed at protecting juveniles can also inadvertently serve as a shield to protect young operatives from harsh penalties. Community Policing can play a unique and important role in working with youth gangs, to reduce open warfare, to gather intelligence, and to help prevent hangers-on or potential recruits from becoming hard-core *gangbangers.*

The example of the Blackstone Rangers in Chicago demonstrates why the police must be involved in continuing efforts. In the 1960s, members of this gang were hailed by many people in the community as their protectors. Then their agenda changed, so that by the time the gang became known as the El Rukyns of the 1980s, its members were charged with drug dealing and for conspiring to accept payoffs from Libya to conduct terrorist activity in the United States.

As Kleiman noted as well, kids join gangs for identity, for the recreational activities they provide, and for protection – including protection from the gangs themselves. Community Policing targets juveniles for special attention, an important part of its overall mandate, and many CPOs have been instrumental in working with individuals and business people to organize alternative activities for young people. Involving CPOs in youth clubs and sports and recreational activities for young people also adds that vital element of protection, and CPOs can also enlist adults willing to provide additional security for youngsters who need a lawful alternative. With additional guidance, Community Policing offers an opportunity to do more in this regard.

- **Community Policing can target juveniles, particularly high-risk youngsters, with efforts to reduce the likelihood they will become drug abusers or drug dealers.** Because Community Policing does not focus on arrest as its primary rationale for existence, CPOs are free to look at old problems in new ways. For a traditional officer to intervene with a juvenile flirting with drug dealing, the officer is trained to look for a hook that would allow for an arrest. In contrast, Community Policing can employ a wide variety of approaches aimed at the problem without narrowing to those that focus on arrest as the primary goal.

  In Flint, for example, foot patrol officer Jowanne Barnes-Coney took the proactive approach of trying to identify high-risk youngsters, so that she could bring pressure to bear on them in many ways, to discourage them from experimenting with or selling drugs. Her rapport with the youngsters in her beat area allowed her to gather a list of young people at risk – those kids whose friends said they worried about them because they were either dabbling in drug use or they had talked about wanting to become a dealer someday. Barnes-Coney first visited the parents of these youngsters potentially at risk, explaining her concerns and offering to work with them on ways to intervene, including involving teachers in the effort.

  In the role of community liaison, Barnes-Coney was also able to help link families to appropriate and affordable counseling help, as needed. Her program that rewarded young people for arriving home by the curfew set by their parents was another way of supporting overall anti-drug efforts, by reducing their exposure to temptation. She also worked with people in the community to host broad-based efforts, such as the drug-free rally, where each child who participated received a t-shirt.

The police have an important role to play in drug education, and the Community Policing approach can go beyond programs like D.A.R.E., by reaching out beyond schools, to the truants and dropouts who may well be at greatest risk. CPOs make presentations in classrooms, and many work within schools. But they also initiate community-based initiatives and activities designed to include youngsters in positive activities as an alternative to drug use. Because they have the opportunity to work with youngsters over time, CPOs can develop informal, one-on-one relationships with youngsters who need special attention. They can also reinforce the anti-drug message in group activities, whether that includes a summer softball league or classes on child care for teen mothers. Barnes-Coney became persuaded that many of the youngsters she saw turn to drugs did so because they did not feel good about themselves. As a result, she organized teen self-esteem clubs designed to boost a positive self-image.

The problem with many well-meaning educational approaches is that they find their warmest acceptance among those at least risk, whereas the challenge lies in developing a wide range of approaches in the hope of reaching a broad spectrum of young people with different problems and needs. CPOs have the opportunity to serve as positive role models themselves in a variety of initiatives aimed at young people, so that they can transmit and reinforce the anti-drug message directly and indirectly. Though they remain adult authority figures, their personal relationship with the juveniles in their beat areas holds some promise that CPOs can breach the problem of teenage rebellion against what grown-ups say. Their sustained presence in the community as a trusted adult also allows them to identify new drugs coming in, before they become the latest "fashion," in the hope of launching efforts so that they never become a fad or a persistent problem.

- **Community Policing maintains a pro-family focus in dealing with drug problems.** As the example above demonstrates, Community Policing allows the police to employ proactive strategies designed to support families in their anti-drug efforts. All too often, the only time that many families see the traditional police is when they arrive as adversaries, seeking information or making an arrest. Community Policing allows youngsters to enjoy positive interactions with the police, so that they are not simply authority figures who "will take you away if you are bad."

This important shift allows young people to talk openly to their CPOs, which is what allowed Barnes-Coney to generate the trust necessary so that young people would talk honestly to her about what they and their friends were thinking and doing. An important element in her approach was to involve the parents in the process whenever possible, allowing the family and the police to work together to provide each other mutual support.

A hotly debated new law in Los Angeles has already led to the arrest of a mother who was charged with failing to stop her son from involvement in gang activity. Parental responsibility is an important issue in juvenile drug abuse and drug dealing, but it is vitally important that the police not only focus on sanctions, but also on providing families the law enforcement support they need in efforts to control their youngsters. Parents often need help from the police to counteract the message many young people receive from their peers, which is that adult authority can be ignored. This message is reinforced in areas where serious crime has demanded so much attention that many youngsters have good reason to believe that anything less than a serious transgression will be ignored. By taking juveniles and their misdeeds seriously, CPOs can provide families the assistance they need in proving that laws must be obeyed.

There has also been growing concern about so-called *mercenary* parents, those who look the other way – or applaud – when their children make money from drug trafficking. Community Policing can find and work with these families, and they can initiate community-based efforts designed to put pressure on them to change. In essence, this is a form of child abuse that the police must find new ways to confront.

Another problem the police must begin to contend with more directly is drug abuse within families. This is a problem where special training might allow CPOs the opportunity to do more. CPOs can link families to appropriate help, and they can work to initiate community-based efforts to provide support to troubled families. This might mean organizing people who would be willing to take a child into their homes overnight when a parent comes home high – and abusive. Perhaps it could mean recruiting retirees to babysit on occasion for the children of a recovering addict who would benefit from a break, to make it easier for the addict to focus on rehabilitation and to resist temptation.

- **Community Policing can serve as the link to public and private agencies that can help.** Estimates vary, but the best guess is that if all drug abusers asked for treatment today, the existing system could handle only one of 10. Those who can afford the substantial expense of private care can usually enter treatment more quickly than those who must rely on public services – and those who have no insurance or money to pay themselves are often least able to thread their way through the bureaucratic maze to find the help that they need.

Another problem is helping people find the right kind of help. Some may have serious drug problems that require residential detoxification, but others may fare better with the free help available through groups such as Alcoholics Anonymous, Narcotics Anonymous, or Cocaine Anonymous. Even then, local chapters may differ in their willingness to accept multi-substance abusers. CPOs already play an important role as the community's liaison to public and private agencies that can help with problems ranging from potholes in the street to job counseling, so many are already know about local drug treatment options available, or they could be encouraged to do so. CPOs could also assist by using their special clout, when appropriate, to lobby for priority status for emergency cases, especially those where domestic violence or child neglect is a serious concern.

CPOs can also serve as facilitators to provide recovering addicts useful information, since the consequences of addiction can include homelessness, unemployment, and other health concerns. Community Policing demonstrates that the police are not just there to arrest people, but to offer help to those trying to live within the law.

- **Community Policing can tackle some of the root causes of drug abuse in new ways.** The long-term, proactive focus provided by Community Policing can provide a way for the police to grapple with some of the underlying dynamics that foster drug abuse in certain neighborhoods. People take drugs for many reasons, but the serious drug problems that cluster in the inner city often serve as symptoms of deeper problems. People with too much time on their hands, trapped in decaying neighborhoods, may find taking a chemical *trip* is the only vacation they can afford – at first. By addressing the problems of social and physical decay in afflicted neighborhoods, Community Policing might be able to shore up a community's ability to be more *drug-resistant* overall.

Dealers have good reason to set up shop in run-down neighborhoods, because such areas send a non-verbal but deafening message that the people who live there are not organized and that they do not seem to care. As Community Policing begins to stabilize the neighborhood, it can encourage people to organize and participate in more community activities, reversing the downward cycle where open dealing drives people into their homes, which encourages even more dealers to move in.

A person with a lucrative and interesting job, who owns an attractive home in a good neighborhood – with a steep mortgage – can still fall victim to drugs, and they often find they must go to the inner city to buy drugs, since open dealing would not be tolerated in areas where they live. The bigger risk of addiction – and the more profitable market for a dealer – is among those who have too much time on their hands and little to lose, conditions all too common in decaying areas. Retail-level drug dealers have learned to perfect the hard sell. Neighborhoods visibly on the decline act as a magnet for their aggressive merchandising, so Community Policing's ability to address all forms of disorder, whether that means graffitti, open begging, or abandoned cars and buildings, may play an important but often overlooked role in providing longer-range answers to the problems of drug abuse and drug dealing.

• **Community Policing provides a logical mechanism for disseminating information on AIDS and other diseases related to IV drug use.** Failure to involve the police in efforts to reduce the potential number of AIDS victims is short-sighted. Not only are the police one of the most logical candidates for the job, because they come in contact with many IV drug users, it is in their enlightened self-interest to do all they can to reduce the spread of these disease, since AIDS victims in particular threaten to put a tremendous strain on all local resources, the pie for which the police must compete to receive their slice.

Of increasing concern as well is the growing legion of AIDS victims whose disease has left them destitute. The police have good reason to worry about a population that may well turn to crime for the money to support themselves, especially when these are desperate people who have reason to believe that they have already received a death sentence.

In addition to overall public health efforts, CPOs can be encouraged to use their local offices as a clearinghouse for information on preventing AIDS and other diseases such as hepatitis-B caused by sharing needles. They can also enlist community support in informational efforts, such as how to use bleach to clean needles. CPOs can also disseminate information about agencies that offer assistance to those already afflicted. Educating the community about the threat of AIDS can also enlist cooperation and support for efforts aimed at closing down so-called *shooting galleries,* where addicts often share infected needles.

• **Community Policing adds both scope and continuity to the overall police effort, providing sustained, citywide retail-drug enforcement without underutilizing scarce resources.** By using CPOs as the backbone of the department's anti-drug efforts, police departments automatically extend their anti-drug efforts beyond what any special unit, such as a narcotics division, can provide. In essence, considering – and further exploiting – the ability of Community Policing to fashion short- and long-term solutions to the entire spectrum of problems associated with drugs that the police must face is a way to make drugs the top police priority overall, as it is in the minds of most voters.

The mistake in talking about the drug crisis is that the traditional police response to a crisis is to look for ways to make massive, short-term interventions to bring the emergency under control, but without any coordinated follow-up – or prevention. It can be argued that drugs have reached emergency status, in part, because because of the failure to provide sustained, proactive police efforts in the past. Street-sweeps and focused crackdowns allow the police to put their finger in the dike, but the problem floods back once they remove their collective fingers.

Even Chief Bouza, whose comments demonstrated he was no fan of retail-level enforcement, said that stabilizing neighborhoods depends on efforts that promote "community cohesion" and that what is needed is an effort that can be instituted and maintained citywide, with limited resources. That is an important prescription that Community Policing fills best, because it is not a single-purpose approach, a special unit with new budget demands, but a different and creative way of providing basic police services.

No matter what the problem is, whether it's drug dealing or potholes in the street, Community Policing provides a problem-solving approach, with CPOs in place to listen to people and respond to their input and ideas. Community Policing is not a tactic the police employ until they achieve a goal, and then they pull the officers for use elsewhere. Instead it allows the police to deliver permanent, decentralized, and personalized police service. Only by multiplying the police presence, by involving the people in the community who do not use drugs in the police process, can departments hope to bring drugs under control. Traditional efforts focus on the drug dealers and users, but Community Policing recognizes that those who do not want to see drugs sold and used in their neighborhoods hold an important key in solving this society's drug problems.

Perhaps the most remarkable benefit of the Community Policing approach is that once a specific goal, such as open drug dealing, has been accomplished, the CPO is not left idle, but a CPO can then focus on the full range of crime and disorder problems the community faces, problems that the community can help identify and prioritize. CPOs are far more likely to suffer burnout than boredom.

- **Community Policing allows departments to anticipate new drug problems and also to plan efforts to repel them.** In the past few years, many police departments knew that crack would eventually reach them, but few were able to do much more than brace for the assault. Because of Community Policing's superior ability to generate information, it can serve as the *early warning system* to call attention to the problem at the first sign of trouble. There is also some hope that by mobilizing the community in advance, neighborhoods can resist being overrun by new dealers and new drugs. The time for the police to address drug problems is before the dealers are supplying an entrenched pool of users eager to buy their wares. By alerting the department as soon as new problems emerge and by strengthening communities through efforts aimed at eliminating neighborhood decay, Community Policing may be able to make communities more drug-resistant.

- **Community Policing may help reduce the risk of civil disturbances and rioting that could be triggered by aggressive anti-drug initiatives.** Frustration with open dealing has increased the pressure to take drastic action, such as sending the National Guard or state militia into areas that appear to be out of control. There is obvious danger that troops who are not properly trained for such assignments could inadvertently spark civil disturbances or urban rioting.

    A Community Policing approach deserves the opportunity to have its potential explored before we risk causing more problems than we may solve. Establishing CPOs in the community can help reduce tensions between the police department and the community, particularly race relations, and this can help establish the authority within the community that they need to take an aggressive anti-drug stance. CPOs can also provide the sustained police presence in the community that offers the opportunity for the department to maintain the gains that aggressive action, such as street-sweeps and focused crackdowns, can achieve.

    When ABC newsman Ted Koppel held an expanded *Nightline* segment on drugs (March 9, 1989), following his prime-time special that focused on inner-city drug problems, a number of District of Columbia residents who spoke talked about the role of racism. Much to mainstream America's obvious surprise, as least as evidenced in articles written later about that program, many blacks expressed sincere concern that inner-city drug problems and the police response might constitute a conspiracy aimed at what one participant called black genocide. Without debating the merits of their arguments, their vehemence made it clear that many have serious concerns that draconian, anti-drug initiatives pose a particular threat to the black community. Police departments must remember the lesson of the turbulent late 1960s and early 1970s, which is that police departments must reach out to minority communities, to enlist their support in efforts to make their neighborhoods safer. Ignoring history could doom us to repeat past mistakes, and Community Policing provides a coordinated and creative way for departments to encourage participation and support, without inciting further paranoia.

- **Community Policing provides an important new element in a department's approach to drugs that offers the hope of allowing them to develop an effective and affordable drug strategy.** As the analysis of existing drug strategies in various police departments demonstrates, the element that has been lacking is an effective and affordable citywide effort that can help stabilize neighborhoods. If departments with Community Policing considered the approach as their first-line of defense, and other communities without it understood how it can work, they could begin to fashion an overall drug strategy that holds greater promise of making short- and long-term improvements on many fronts. With additional funding, for more officers and specialized training, Community Policing could well achieve far more than it already does in providing both immediate solutions and long-term prevention.

Community Policing makes an important contribution to the three main areas that an intelligent drug strategy must address. It focuses its energies toward street level each day, at the transactions where supply and demand meet. It has also demonstrated the ability to generate large amounts of high-quality intelligence about local dealing patterns that aim upwards at Mr. Big. Community Policing has always been known for its ability to target juveniles for special attention, which has great potential to address both young gangs and juvenile drug abuse. If police departments think of Community Policing as an essential and integral part of their overall drug strategy, the War on Drugs may see some important new victories.

An Intelligent and Effective Response

It also seems increasingly urgent to explore what Community Policing can offer, since mounting frustration with society's collective inability to bring drugs under control carries the risk we will overreact and embrace extreme solutions. Despite the increasing attention paid to decriminalization, on one extreme, the reality is that the political mood of the country makes it more likely that people will instead more likely support increasingly draconian measures.

The danger is not only that such solutions threaten our cherished civil rights, but they rarely work as intended. Consider, for example, the get-tough proposal to throw all drug users out of public housing. At first glance, it sounds like the right thing to do – after all, taxpayers have good reason to balk at subsidizing drug abuse. Yet a closer looks shows that, given the lack of treatment slots available, the end result might well be that this would simply add these people to the growing pool of homeless addicts already on the streets – a far less appealing prospect than we may have supposed.

At the National Institute of Justice Conference in Washington, D.C., on the DUF results, a respected police chief on the program openly advocated what he called draconian solutions. One involved revoking all licenses held by drug users – driver's licenses, cosmetician and barber's licenses, licenses to practice medicine and the law. He also supported permanently tattooing *ADDICT* on all convicted users' foreheads. While his outrage at the casual acceptance – and even glorification – of drug use in this society is easily understandable, it raises questions about whether we are losing perspective. Drugs are a scourge, but are drug users a bigger threat than murderers, child molesters, rapists, or even drunk drivers? Responsible organizations would not devote time to a serious discussion about tattooing those words on people's foreheads, yet the criminal justice system's frustration with drugs mirrors the growing public clamor to *do something.*

Before we risk doing the wrong things just to demonstrate our will to do something, Community Policing deserves a chance to demonstrate whether it can achieve some badly needed victories in the War on Drugs. Doing more of the same old things offers little likelihood of success, and there is obvious danger in experimenting with extremes. Community Policing is a fresh and imaginative approach, but it is not exotic, dramatic – or easily conveyed in a catchy slogan. Perhaps we should consider that most realistic solutions are often more likely to sound sensible, not sensational. Community Policing is a subtle but bold new way for the police to focus their energies on solving many of the serious problems that drugs pose. It allows police departments to get tough on drugs, while maintaining respect for civil rights, by harnessing the creative energies of the people and the police working together.

NOTES

[1] Kelling, George L., telephone interview at his office at Harvard University, May 15, 1989.

[2] Hackett, George (with bureau assistance), *On the Firing Line,* Newsweek, May 29, 1989. p. 32.

[3] Calkins, Richard, *Drug Abuse Trends 1986,* Office of Substance Abuse Services - Data Evaluation, Michigan Department of Public Health, Lansing, MI.

[4] Johnston, Lloyd D., *Drug Use Among American High School Students,* University of Michigan, School of Social Research, Ann Arbor, MI.

[5] Wagner, Michael G., *Police Brutality: the Ugly Issue Returns,* Detroit Free Press, January 22, 1989, p. 1 and p. 6.

[6] Hackett.

[7] Relevant publications - Mark A.R. Kleiman:

Kleiman, Mark A.R., and Smith, Kerry D., *State and Local Drug Enforcement: In Search of a Strategy,* Working Paper #89-01-14, cited with permission of author, Harvard University, John F. Kennedy School of Government, Program in Criminal Justice Policy and Management, Cambridge, MA.

Kleiman, Mark A.R., Barnett, Arnold, Bouza, Anthony V., and Burke, Kevin M., *Street Level Drug Enforcement: Examining the Issues,* edited by Marcia R. Chaiken, National Institute of Justice, Issues and Practices, U.S. Department of Justice, Washington, DC, August 1988.

Kleiman, Mark A.R., *Drug Abuse Control Policy,* Working Paper #88-01-12, Harvard University, John F. Kennedy School of Government, Program in Criminal Justice Policy and Management, Cambridge, MA.

Kleiman, Mark A.R., *Making and Evaluating Drug Abuse Policies,* Harvard University, John F. Kennedy School of Government, Program in Criminal Justice Policy and Management, Cambridge, MA, June 1, 1987.

Relevant publications - Mark H. Moore:

Moore, Mark H., *Policies to Achieve Discrimination in the Effective Price of Heroin, American Economic Review,* May 1973.

Moore, Mark H., *Buy or Bust: The Effective Regulation of an Illicit Market in Heroin* (Lexington, MA: D.C. Health Co., 1976).

Moore, Mark H., *Limiting the Supplies of Drugs to Illicit Markets, Journal of Drug Issues.* Spring 1979.

Moore, Mark H., *The Police and Drugs, Perspectives on Policing,* National Institute of Justice, Washington, DC, forthcoming.

[8] From the letter to the authors from A.R. Kleiman.

[9] Kleiman & Smith, *State and Local Drug Enforcement: In Search of a Strategy.*

[10] Reuter, Peter; Haaga, John; Murphy, Patrick; and Praskac, Amy, *Drug Use and Drug Programs in the Washington Metropolitan Area,* The RAND Corporation, R-3655-GWRC, July 1988.

[11] Bouza, in *Street-Level Drug Enforcement: Examining the Issues.*

[12] *Ibid.*

[13] Kleiman & Smith.

[14] Morganthau, Tom, with bureau assistance, *Murder Wave in the Capital,* Newsweek, March 13, 1989.

[15] Koppel, Ted, introducing the ABC Television *Nightline* segment on drug violence in Washington, DC, March 9, 1989.

[16] Pooley, Eric, *Fighting Back Against Crack, New York Magazine,* January 12, 1989, p. 39.

[17] Turque, Bill (with bureau assistance), *Why Justice Can't Be Done, Newsweek,* May 29, 1989.

[18] Pooley.

[19] Turque.

[20] Castine, John, and Lowery, Mark, *Many caught; few jailed, Detroit Free Press,* April 3, 1988.

SECTION FIVE

THE FUTURE OF COMMUNITY POLICING

CHAPTER 11
Toward a New Breed
of Police Officer

*Every society gets the kind of criminal it
deserves. What is equally true is that every
community gets the kind of law enforcement
it insists on.*

—*Robert F. Kennedy*

Images and Impressions

What image comes to mind when someone says police officer? Some people conjure up the Norman Rockwellesque vision of the friendly cop offering a lost child an ice cream cone at the station house. For others, it is Dirty Harry looking down the barrel of his .357 begging some scumbag to "make my day." Some of us grew up being told that police officers are our friends, someone to turn to whenever we are in trouble. Others were raised with the warning to be good or "the police will take you away." Many of us remember the disturbing TV images of the police decades ago loosing dogs and firehoses on civil rights protestors, then a few years later clubbing protestors outside the Democratic Convention in Chicago. Younger generations are more likely to conjure up graphic scenes of police officers battling for their lives against drug gangs or trying to protect school children under siege from gun-wielding lunatics. Maybe our most vivid memory is the police officer who personally saved our lives – or the officer who gave us a speeding ticket.

Police officers, peace officers, law enforcement officers, cops. No matter what term we attach to the job, most people have a vivid, if not always accurate, image of what police work entails, one that often blends awe, respect, and a touch of fear. Our personalized picture is the end result of our cumulative exposure to the police in real life and reel life – the officers we have met, the ones we have seen in the theater, and the ones we learn about from the news. As one writer put it, "A vague uneasiness:

the police. It's like when you suddenly understand you have to undress in front of the doctor."[1]

In a democratic society, where there is great tension between our desire to allow the police the power to protect us and, at the same time, our fear that we must circumscribe their role to protect our civil rights, the police have always played an ambiguous role. In *Policing in a Free Society,* Herman Goldstein wrote about the "basic pervasive conflict between crime-fighting and constitutional due process which is inherent in the police function in a free society."[2] In 1962, before the explosion of serious crime in our society, Michigan Harrington wrote in *The Other America,* "For the middle class, the police protect property, give directions, and help old ladies. For the urban poor, the police are those who arrest you."[3]

While Harrington's view may seem somewhat dated today, it underscores our lingering ambivalence. The police have the power to "put us away." The police are also the only agents of domestic social control with the right to use force, including deadly force. Though bounded by the law and department procedures, police officers can do things that others cannot. By emphasizing their role as crime-fighters, we see them as the *thin blue line* protecting the forces of light from the powers of evil. At the end of roll call on the popular TV show *Hill Street Blues,* the late actor Michael Conrad used to admonish his fellow officers to "do it to them before they do it to us."[4]

Not only does this narrow view ignore the importance of the service component in policing, it reinforces the perception of society as divided into the Good Guys in the White Hats versus a a smaller pool of Bad Guys in Black Hats. Though it provides a convenient shorthand when referring to crime situations to divide the world into the law-abiding people who must remain vigilant against predators, the real world is blessed with only a handful of saints above reproach and an equally small number of unregenerate monsters. In between is the vast majority of people who struggle to live by the Golden Rule that says we should do unto others as we would want them to do unto us, though, on any given day, any given individual may fall closer to or wider of the mark.

The danger in oversimplification is that we can fall victim to the temptation to *demonize* those who break the law, thereby robbing them of their humanity. We are fortunate to live in a country with a high standard of living and many social safety nets that protect us from being unduly tested, yet how many of us can say with absolute certainty where we would draw the line, if we had a sick, hungry child and no money?

We must also remember that many people who would never think of committing crimes as adults wince at things they did when they were younger. As a society, we believe strongly in redemption of the young, because many youngsters who threw a rock through a window at school, shoplifted something from a store, or even went joyriding in a "borrowed" car grew up to become valuable members of society. The line between law-abiding and law-breaking can shift and change at different times and in different circumstances. While there is great nobility in the notion that the police provide a thin blue line of uniformed officers who can protect good people from evil, real life also requires confronting shifting shades of gray.

As we become increasingly sophisticated about how people behave, individually and collectively, we begin to recognize the importance of the police role as catalysts who can promote good and lawful behavior, while discouraging the bad. The police must always stand ready to do all they can to protect us from a Ted Bundy, a "gangbanger" who opens fire with an Uzi, and the teenagers who went on a *wilding* rampage in Central Park. But fortunately for all of us, the police included, only a miniscule number of people ever commit such horrors. Without diminishing in any way the tremendous responsibility the police face as society's first line of defense against those who would harm the innocent, we must also look more closely at what the job entails outside these relatively rare incidents.

The goal in this chapter is to examine the police role, to separate myth from reality, to see what it takes to have "the right stuff" for the real job of policing. We will begin by exploring what the job involves in a traditional department, to see the kind of people who are attracted to this career field, and what they find once they are on the job. We will also explore the implications now that police departments are hiring more and more candidates with at least some college education. Then we will look at what a shift to a Community Policing approach portends. Does it mean departments must find ways to attract and hire candidates with different qualities, skills, and abilities? Does the job of being a CPO require attributes that differ from what we have traditionally associated with being a police officer? Do we need a new breed of police officer to handle the challenges of the job as we approach the 21st century?

Policing in a Traditional Department

Motor patrol officers are the backbone of the traditional police approach. They are the *grunts* in the trenches, the individuals in the department who must deal directly with the community every day. In that sense, they are the traditional department's bridge to the saints, sinners, and average citizens who constitute the real world. Therefore, to understand what the real job of policing entails in a traditional department, it is important to explore what incoming candidates expect from the job – and what they find.

Most candidates say that they are drawn to police work as a career because of a desire to help others. As Alvin F. Alcuri wrote, the police "see themselves as a bulwark against fear and crime" and their role is "helping people on an individual level and protecting society at large."[5] While police departments must always be alert to the danger that some people will be attracted to the job because of an unhealthy desire to wield power over others, most of the men and women who seek careers in policing are inspired by idealism and altruism. They view the unique power conferred on police officers as a tool they can use to make a valid contribution in making society a safer and better place to live. It is an activist role, one that Alcuri says allows them to "take a deep pride in contributing to the quality of life."[6]

If these idealistic candidates succeed in becoming motor patrol officers, many are often surprised to find much of the job involves waiting for something to happen rather than making something happen. As the Flint research attests, motor patrol officers spend most of their time on patrol, waiting for a call.[7] While cruising around on patrol, the officers are, in essence, waiting to spot some sign of trouble, whether it's a traffic violation or some suspicious activity on the street. The opportunities to initiate positive action are limited by the need to remain available to handle the next call.

The basic rationale for deploying the bulk of the force in patrol cars is to ensure a quick response – the system focuses on ensuring that officers can arrive quickly when that all-important call comes in. And, to be worthy of the name, a police department must be able to send officers immediately should a call involve a situation where someone is firing an assault weapon at children in a schoolyard or there is a bank robbery under way. Most motor patrol officers will retire without ever having to face such a call, but part of the stress in policing relates to the uncertainty in the job, because motor patrol officers can never know for certain whether the next call will put their lives on the line.

The secondary rationale behind deploying so much of the force on motor patrol duty is that the sight of a police car patrolling the streets should help deter crime. Yet as the Kansas City Preventive Patrol Study indicated, there is concern that preventive patrol may have little, if any, impact on reducing crime. Many motor patrol officers talk about the nagging suspicion that predators simply wait to act until they see the patrol car's taillights disappear around the corner. Indeed, it is often the smartest and shrewdest who know best how to elude the police, and, especially today, urban dope dealers have even further corrupted the young, by hiring them as lookouts to warn them whenever a patrol car is approaching.

The second most time-consuming aspect of the job is handling *complaints* – and that term can seem particularly apt, since one of the surprises many fledgling officers face is realizing the amount of friction with the community that they encounter on the job. As James Q. Wilson noted, we often equate crime-fighters with fire-fighters, as if the jobs were pretty much alike. Yet police officers often feel far more alienated from the community, because they are far more likely to find themselves in adversarial situations where they are perceived as the antagonist. About the police role, Wilson wrote, "...he issues summonses, makes arrests, conducts inquiries, searches homes, stops cars, testifies in court, and keeps a jail."[8]

That feeling of being separate and apart from society at large explains why police officers so often band together for mutual support. The job contains an undeniable element of danger, which means officers must rely on each other for their mutual safety. But, in addition, the isolation and antagonism inherent in the job also encourages them to pull together into a separate subculture of their own. Even the uniform, badge, and gun serve as symbols of being different from the "civilian" on the street.

That sense of being separate and apart from the rest of society is also heightened by the fact that police officers see things that other people do not see. Most people are spared the sight of mangled bodies crushed in cars, battered children, women who have been raped, decaying corpses, yet this is part of what police work entails. The job also requires peeking into people's private lives in ways no other job does, which means the police tend to see people at their worst, not their best. People do not call the police to come share their triumphs and joys, but when they are hurt, angry, frightened, and upset.

The need to pull together is also reinforced in traditional departments where those at the bottom of the police pyramid can feel thwarted by the restrictions imposed by working in a paramilitary bureaucracy. Those altruistic candidates who chose police work so that they could make a positive difference can feel frustrated at finding themselves inhibited by a structure where the emphasis on avoiding mistakes seems to overshadow the opportunities to take creative action. Police work has been called the most unprofessional profession, because traditional departments often seem to expend more energy in defining the limits of the job than in supporting autonomy and innovation. As one researcher discovered, even those officers who otherwise enjoyed the job often bitterly accused the police leadership of being "unfair, rigid, and archaic."[9]

Negative Pressures in the Traditional System

Critics can use these elements to paint a dark picture of the traditional police role. They begin by noting that the power of the police can serve as an uhealthy lure for those who want to dominate and abuse others. Yet even the most altrustic candidates can find the job both dangerous and tedious, one in which they see the horrors that people inflict on each other, horrors they often appear powerless to prevent.

Much of their time is spent on random patrol, which produces random results. Most of the rest of their time is spent handling calls that may require a burst of frenzied activity – or a *nuisance* calls that can seem terribly trivial compared to the horrific sights that they have witnessed.

Many find themselves trapped in a system where they receive little support from superiors for taking any initiative. In some departments, turning to their peers for support requires embracing a macho ethic that puts the highest premium on acting tough and aggressive, regardless of the situation. No matter how well their education and prior experience may have prepared them to understand the full range of human dynamics that impel people to act as they do, that knowledge can be *washed out* by the combination of the ugliness they see and the callous indifference that their seasoned peers insist is the only way to survive the rigors of the job. Thwarted idealists may struggle against becoming cynics, but cynicism toward the general public and toward the police hierarchy may be so potent that few can resist.

Left unchallenged and unaddressed, such pressures can make motor patrol officers feel that their superiors use them as pawns in a cat-and-mouse game in which they must follow rules, but their opponents do not. Especially today, with the growing menace posed by drugs, motor patrol officers can see themselves as outmanned, outgunned, underpaid, and bound by rigid rules that the predators exploit. The intellectual and emotional leap required to adopt the view that police officers are trapped between an ungrateful public and unthinking superiors can seem small, especially when your peers insist that it is emotional suicide to do otherwise.

Yet, in most cases, this bleak scenario is a gross distortion of reality. While there have always been a few, isolated departments where such attitudes are permitted to run rampant, most departments strive to do the best job they can to encourage motor patrol officers to focus on protecting and helping the people they are sworn to serve. The more important concern, however, is whether they do so because of the traditional system – or despite it.

The Impact of Education

While we have focused on the external pressures that prompted re-thinking the overall police role, perhaps the strongest internal impetus to change has been the tremendous increase in the number of college-educated officers in police departments during the past two decades. According to noted police executive Patrick Murphy, who headed departments in New York, Detroit, and Washington, D.C., the overall educational level of the police has continued to rise. In his foreword to a Police Executive Research Forum (PERF) study on *The State of Police Education,* fully

55% of the 124,000 officers embraced by the study had at least two years of college, compared to only 15% of police officers in 1970.[10]

The PERF study also verified the perception that college-educated officers bring different qualities to the job of policing. The report included both a review of previous research and the results of the PERF survey of police managers. Quoting directly from the study, the literature review suggested that:

- College-educated officers perform the tasks of policing better than their non-college-educated counterparts.

- College-educated officers are generally better communicators, whether with a citizen, in court, or as part of a written police report.

- The college-educated officer is more flexible in dealing with difficult situations and in dealing with persons of diverse cultures, lifestyles, races, and ethnicity.

- Officers with higher education are more *professional* and more dedicated to policing as a career rather than as a job.

- Educated officers adapt better to organizational change and are more responsive to alternative approaches to policing.

- College-educated officers are more likely to see the broader picture of the criminal justice system than to view police more provincially as an exclusive group.[11]

The PERF survey of police managers also identified a list of qualities attributed to college-educated officers:

- better communication skills, both written and verbal

- more sensitive to racial and cultural differences and more understanding of people's social and cultural concerns

- better rounded, more developed socially and professionally

- more flexible, more open-minded

- more goal-oriented and career minded

- more knowledgeable, more competent

- better able to organize and make logical decisions[12]

When asked how college-educated officers fared against a list of traits, police managers strongly agreed with the statement that college-educated officers communicate better with the community, and they strongly disagreed with the statement that they receive more citizen complaints. The study also showed that even if the department did not require any college-education, most police managers looked favorably at candidates who had attended college. The prevailing sentiment among police managers seemed to be that there are still many cases where the best officers in the department may not have had any college education – and conversely as well, there are officers with degrees who perform poorly – but that police departments overall will benefit from the expansion of college-educated officers within the ranks.

One of the few negatives associated with college-educated officers is that a number of police managers had concerns about attracting and holding onto them. Though salaries for police officers have increasingly become comparable with other fields that also demand degrees (a recent Census Bureau study showed law enforcement officers outearn degree holders in biology, journalism, psychology, education, and nursing[13]), a number of police managers said it was difficult to retain police officers who were tempted by *greener pastures* elsewhere.

The implications in these findings suggest that there has been tremendous internal pressure for change within departments. College-educated officers are perceived as different from their peers who did not attend college, and those differences overall tend to relate to a more professional attitude about the job; enhanced skills, particularly in communication; and a greater sensitivity to people in the community. Now that college-educated officers are no longer the minority, but the majority, within many police departments, this has obvious implications concerning the directions in which they are taking the job. The findings also imply that money alone is not the deciding factor in attracting and retaining college-educated officers, but that departments must find ways to enhance job satisfaction if they want to lure the best and the brightest into police work – and keep them once they are on the job.

It requires no great leap of imagination to suggest that the traditional approach tends to squelch college-educated officers. While all idealists risk being disillusioned to find that the real world of work is different from what they had hoped, a hidebound and rigid police department can be a forbidding environment to educated altruists who expect to function as respected professionals. One of the unnamed police managers who participated in the PERF study cited a half-dozen attributes that could be ascribed to college-educated officers, and this list raises concern that traditional departments may not make the best use of these attributes:

- officer recognizes the need for growth, development, etc.

- officer demonstrates ability to organize his time, effort, etc.

- officer shows flexibility and willingness to put forth effort

- exposes officer to positive environment to offset negative aspects of police work

- provides mental relief, new ideas, different perspectives

- enhances the overall skills and abilities of the *police profession*[14]

The emergence of the college-educated officer as the norm may well be part of the reason that many departments have been able to resist the negative pressures that can cause problems with the traditional approach. At the same time as well, there has been a tremendous influx of minorities and women into the ranks. In the PERF study, 12 % of the officers covered by the survey were black, 6 % Hispanic, and 1 % other, with 12 % female.[15]

Without succumbing to the temptation to engage in racial, ethnic, or sexual stereotyping, it is still fair to say that the diversity within modern police departments has also contributed to the department's overall responsiveness to a broader range of people within the community. It should also be noted that the PERF study showed that more minorities had undergraduate and graduate college credits compared to their white male counterparts, and that women were even somewhat more likely to have had undergraduate and graduate degree credits compared to males.[16] While women continue to be dramatically underrepresented, these figures for blacks and Hispanics reflect their relative distribution within the culture at large, which suggests that police departments are becoming a more accurate mirror of the society they serve.

It also means that racial, ethnic, or sexual stereotyping within departments is less likely to go unchallenged than it might have been in the past. That "shootout at the OK corral" that occurred in Flint where the two motor patrol officers began blazing away at each other may have had as much or more to do with sexual, rather than racial, friction within the department. The increase in the percentage of women who hold jobs as police officers automatically challenges male dominance of the field.

Dramatically altering the educational, cultural, racial, ethnic, and sexual mix of the police officers within police departments implies a tremendous change, even if there has been no change in the organizational structure. It means that modern police departments are no longer dominated almost exclusively by white males, as many were in the past. Not only does this militate against the danger that the department will adopt an ethnocentric, macho ethic, the influx of college-educated officers also implies that the officers will demand greater autonomy and flexibility. The job has long attracted idealists who want to make a positive difference, but now that the job increasingly attracts college-educated candidates armed with the values and skills of professionals, this increases the pressure on police managers to allow them to function more as professionals within the community.

Yet there are limits inherent in the traditional approach that no doubt have contributed to the concern that the police risk losing these most valued employees to other careers. In a traditional department, the system can only be bent so much before it risks falling apart entirely. There are inherent limits on how much freedom officers can be given, considering the restrictions of the traditional mandate as crime-fighters and the reliance on a speedy response by motor patrol officers as the best means of achieving that mission.

Many traditional departments have responded to the challenge posed by these dramatic changes in the overall make-up of their line officers by making at least tentative steps toward broadening the police mandate from crime-fighting to community problem-solving. Officially and unofficially, police officers have been exploring ways to employ problem-solving techniques. Many departments still restrict their application primarily to crime incidents, insisting that other problems are beyond the proper purview of the police. Others have broadened their mandate to include involving officers in efforts to combat social and physical disorder, but often without allowing officers the time and the sustained presence in one area to develop a feel for the underlying dynamics and the continued presence in the community that may be required to enhance the likelihood of success.

Even so, there has been increasing pressure from below on police officials to grant line officers greater professional autonomy, responsibility, and authority. Those idealistic candidates seeking to change society for the better through a career in policing have been a major force in promoting experimentation with new ideas. Basically, they are more likely to reject the simplistic notion that communities can become safer and better places to live if line officers embrace an unwritten code that the solution lies in tough cops cracking more heads and making more arrests. Such officers are obviously more likely to think that brains are even more important than brawn and bullets in most situations. The police will always have to exercise the use of force in discharging their duty, but college-educated officers probably tend to generate fewer citizen complaints because they may be more likely to explore other options first, whenever possible. In general as well, these officers have a greater grasp of the complexity and diversity in the real world, which implies a greater appreciation of those shifting shades of gray.

Part of the problem college-educated officers face on the job in a traditional department stems from the reality that the traditional model attempts to make sense of the world and make the officer's job *easier* by casting the police in the role of the tough cops who protect the forces of light from the forces of evil – that thin blue line. Sophisticated and educated police officers often do not find that narrow view comforting, but confining. Instead of being overwhelmed or frustrated by the ambiguities of the real world, they are more likely to find the challenge a stimulating opportunity to see how much they can achieve. This can make the limitations and periods of inactivity that are often part of the traditional approach seem like obstacles that prevent them from accomplishing the goal of making communities safer and better places to live.

What Community Policing Offers

While there may be other theoretical models that might do a better job of capitalizing on some of the attributes, talents, and aspirations of this new breed of police officer who is beginning to dominate the ranks of departments nationwide, Community Policing comprehensively addresses all of the important issues raised. By broadening the police mandate and making substantive changes that provide organizational support and encouragement for innovation, Community Policing provides all officers within the department the philosophical and structural underpinnings necessary to do more toward that altruistic and idealistic goal of improving the overall quality of life in the community.

By expanding police work to include addressing the full range of community concerns, including crime, fear of crime, social and physical disorder, and community decay, Community Policing gives police officers an expanded agenda that allows fuller expression of their full range of talents, skills, and abilities. And by making that all-important shift from seeing the police officer primarily as a crime-fighter to enlarging their role to that of community problem-solver, this not only opens up the scope of the job, but it changes the basic nature of the police response from an emphasis on dealing with individual crime incidents to attacking the underlying dynamics that detract from the overall quality of life in the community.

If this new breed of college-educated officers is perceived as being more professional, better able to grasp *the big picture,* and more attuned to community needs, they should therefore be more likely to thrive in a system that grants them more freedom and autonomy to explore proactive solutions to community problems. Just as the U.S. automakers learned that their most talented and valuable line workers chafed in a system that tended to undervalue their potential contribution in the mistaken belief that mechanical repetition was a hedge against mistakes, the police have faced tremendous pressure from college-educated officers to grant them additional responsibility and authority. To attract and retain the best candidates for the job required re-thinking a system that focused more on ensuring control than supporting innovation.

A New Career Option

Not only does Community Policing reinvigorate the motor patrol officer's job, it also offers college-educated idealists attracted to police work an entirely new career option that never existed before, as the department's community outreach specialist, the CPO. To understand the differences and distinctions between being a motor patrol officer and a CPO, it again pays to take a closer look at the results of the Flint research that compared motor patrol and foot patrol officers, as well as the research done there on overall job satisfaction.[17]

In addition to the results concerning differences in time and activity components of each job discussed earlier, the Flint research also showed that foot patrol officers self-initiated action far more often than their motor patrol counterparts. This meant making business and home visits and security checks, attending meetings, make speeches, and developing efforts aimed at juveniles. In essence, the job allowed the officers one-on-one and group opportunities to interact with people outside situations triggered by a call for service. In contrast, the motor patrol officer's interactions with people tended to be reactive; action results because someone or some situation triggered the response.

Comparing the number of community contacts that each kind of officer had is complicated by the fact that foot patrol officers often spoke to groups. Does that count as one contact, or should some consideration be given to the number of people the officer reached through that one occasion? More important than the respective numbers of people reached is the concern about the quality of the contacts and what was accomplished. As noted before, nine of every 10 contacts between a foot patrol officer and the general public were considered non-adversarial, while precisely the reverse proved true for motor patrol officers. Obviously, because motor patrol officers spent much of their day responding to problems, the job automatically entailed more instances when they were pursuing possible suspects, seeking information from possible witnesses, or trying to resolve conflicts between people – situations where the job tended to require that they tell people what to do.

However, the Flint research also suggested that motor patrol officers had opportunities to initiate positive interactions with the community during their free patrol time, but that few motor patrol officers took advantage of the chance to do so as often as they might have. Perhaps this plays a role in why the Flint research also showed that foot patrol officers felt they were far more effective in doing an important job in their patrol areas and in keeping up with problems there than their motor patrol counterparts did. Roughly one in every five motor patrol officers said they felt they were not at all effective in doing an important job in their patrol area, while none of the foot officers said they felt that way. In addition, more than half the foot officers said they were effective "to a very great extent," while only one in four motor patrol officers said that described how they felt about their job. The findings were roughly the same for how both kinds of officers felt about their effectiveness in keeping up with the problems in their beat areas.

Important as well is that all but one of the foot patrol officers in Flint said that the job allowed them to be effective in improving police/community relations, but 11 of the 50 motor patrol officers said that their job did not. It should also be noted that the research controlled for other factors, such as age, gender, race, military experience, and years of police experience, yet the research showed that it was the job and not these other factors that made the difference in overall job satisfaction. "The Flint foot patrol officers clearly sustained a higher level of enthusiasm for their work than did motor officers. They exhibited less evidence of dissatisfaction or disaffection than motor officers," according to the researchers.[18]

The evaluation team also said that this satisfaction appeared strongly linked to the fact that foot officers had a clear set of objectives that helped them structure their day, while motor officers suffered demoralizing bouts of inactivity. In contrast as well, foot officers viewed the job as allowing them to be the chief of their beat areas in ways the motor patrol officer's job did not. In addition to all the other actions the job allowed them to self-initiate, the foot officer's increased opportunities to give speeches and write articles for publication also seemed to enhance their perception of themselves as true professionals.

As this analysis suggests, the CPO's job is qualitatively different from motor patrol duty. Though there is no research to confirm or deny his assertions, Robert Baldwin, the member of the Flint evaluation team who spent the most time with the foot officers, including walking their beats with them, said that he began to find there was one indicator that seemed to predict who would succeed and who would fail in the job. Baldwin said that if the foot officer was gregarious, outgoing, and talked easily and openly with the people he met while walking the beat, the person proved well suited for the job. Conversely, if the person hung back, appeared ill at ease, or had difficulty approaching different kinds of people and initiating conversation, the officer inevitably proved ill-suited to the challenge.[19]

As noted earlier, police officers who had formerly taught school also proved very well suited to the foot patrol officer's job in Flint, though their numbers were too small to consider them a valid sample. Yet in addition to being college educated, which school teachers obviously must be, the traits attributed to people who would also be drawn to a career in education would seem to overlap the proactive role that CPOs play.

Baldwin also noted that women overall did extraordinarily well as foot patrol officers. Whether the imperative is biological, cultural, or both, women have historically been credited with exhibiting greater skill in nurturing the young. With its emphasis on working directly with juveniles, one-on-one and in groups, CPOs who have the ability to work well with youngsters can make an important contribution that the traditional approach rarely allows. Indeed many dedicated officers often volunteer their off duty time to work directly with juveniles, because the job shows them how important that can be. What Community Policing provides is a way for the police to become the formal catalyst to inspire new and imaginative initiatives that directly meet local needs.

Implications for the Future

Putting all the pieces together, it appears that the Community Policing approach overall, and the CPO's job in particular, demands a new breed of police officer. It means that police departments must recruit a broad mix of individuals so that they can more closely mirror the sexual, racial, and ethnic composition of the communities they serve, and it also means those candidates should be sensitive to, and tolerant of, diversity.

In particular as well, the focus on community problem-solving that is an integral part of all officers' jobs in a department that has adopted Community Policing demands recruiting candidates who can think for themselves. Because the Community Policing philosophy means a shift from focusing on individual crime incidents to exploring creative ways to address the underlying dynamics that create an environment where problems can persist, the best candidates must also be creative and innovative.

Because Community Policing grants more freedom and autonomy to line officers, the best candidates will be individuals who can function as true professionals. This means they must be able to act responsibly, without constant supervision, and they must be able to exercise good judgment, consistent with the values and goals of the profession. This also implies the ability to develop and execute plans aimed at accomplishing realistic and achievable goals. To be professional also implies the capacity to use time wisely and to exercise self-discipline.

The new job of CPO in particular requires all this and more. It appears that the most critical determinant of future success as a CPO is superior communication skills. A good CPO must be able to communicate well with people from all walks of life, one-on-one and in groups. The ability to prepare and deliver speeches and write articles for publication is another obvious plus.

And because the research tends to show that the officers who function in this capacity tend to internalize the orientation and goals of the people they serve, rather than to turn to their fellow officers for guidance and approval, the job perhaps demands an even higher degree of professionalism than almost any other police role. While this is part of the reason for friction between motor patrol officers and CPOs, it is also part of the key in resisting the tendency of the traditional system to foster an internal climate dominated by the macho ethic of the tough cop.

The day-to-day job of being a CPO also means the best officers will strive to stay abreast of all the various kinds of help that public and private agencies can provide. This implies that the best candidates have experience in seeking out new information, individuals who know how to find what they need on their own.

Meeting the Challenge of the 21st Century

As even this cursory analysis verifies, Community Policing demands a new breed of police officer, one who possesses specific attributes, qualities, and skills. As this analysis also shows, the college-educated men and women of diverse ethnic and racial backgrounds (who make up an increasingly greater share of the officers who have been hired) have the "right stuff" for the job. In essence, the new breed of police officer that Community Policing demands are already on board.

The major problem that police managers have had to contend with was how to hold onto these most highly prized new employees. Not only did such candidates tend to chafe under the restrictions and narrowness implicit in the police officer's role in the traditional system, they usually had other options available to them to enter jobs where their attributes and skills might be allowed fuller expression – and where, in addition, the monetary rewards are greater.

Yet true professionals worry as much or more about their opportunity to make a valid contribution through their work as they do about the size of their income. The idealists attracted to police work because of the altruistic desire to make communities better and safer places in which to live and work find the Community Policing approach offers more opportunities for job enrichment, job enhancement, job enlargement, and overall job satisfaction.

In particular, the new position as the department's outreach specialist, the CPO, not only provides the best candidates a worthwhile new option, but the job provides the autonomy and freedom to allow the most talented individuals a new and unique opportunity to make the most of themselves. The job challenges individuals to see how much they can accomplish, because the boundaries of what can be achieved have yet to be fully defined. Each day, CPOs are discovering and developing new ways to make a positive difference, and the standard of excellence goes up yet another notch as creative and innovative officers find out how they can do even more.

The shift also has implications concerning how criminal justice education must change to meet these new demands. As the PERF study showed, many police managers suggest that future candidates for police work should be encouraged to take college classes beyond those that directly relate to the "nuts-and-bolts" of police work.[20] A curriculum that emphasizes exposure to the social sciences – psychology, sociology, anthropology – as well as disciplines such as economics and business administration would enhance an individual's overall knowledge about how the real world works, at the same time it would provide future police officers skills in areas that are becoming increasingly important in the job.

The new breed of police officer whose emergence into the field has already changed the composition of police departments nationwide will help shape the future of Community Policing. The basic job description emphasizes the ability to think, act, and communicate. No one knows for sure precisely how Community Policing will evolve in years to come. What is clear, however, is that the officers who capitalize on the flexibility and autonomy that are the hallmarks of this new approach will help define and refine what it can and cannot do in practice. Not only will they be able to help police departments find new ways to meet the challenge of helping communities cope with the problems that they face as they approach the 21st century, this new breed of officer, armed with those enhanced communication skills, will be able to tell us what it will take to do the job well.

NOTES

[1] Betti, Ugo, *The Inquiry,* edited by Gino Rizzi (1944-45), I.10, in *The International Thesaurus of Quotations,* compiled by Rhoda Thomas Tripp (New York: Harper & Row/Perennial Library, 1970), p. 483.

[2] Goldstein, Herman, *Policing in a Free Society* (Cambridge, MA: Ballinger Publishing Co., 1977), p. 3.

[3] Harrington, Michael, *The Other America* (1962), I.2, in *The International Thesaurus of Quotations* (see above).

[4] From the television series *Hill Street Blues* aired on the NBC Television Network, written and produced by Stephen Bochco.

[5] Alcuri, Alan F., *Police Pride and Self-Esteem: Indications of Future Occupational Changes, Journal of Police Science and Administration* (Vol. 4, No. 4), p. 441.

[6] *Ibid.*

[7] Payne, Dennis M., and Trojanowicz, Robert C., *Performance Profiles of Foot Versus Motor Officers*, *Community Policing Series No. 6* (East Lansing, MI: National Neighborhood Foot Patrol Center, Michigan State University, 1985).

[8] Wilson, James Q., *The Police and Their Problems: A Theory in Arthur Neiderhoffer and Abraham S. Blumberg, eds., The Ambivalent Force: Perspectives on the Police* (Waltham, MA: Ginn and Company Publishers, 1970), p. 294.

[9] Alcuri, Alan F., p. 444, see also Kirchoff, Judith Johnson, and Roberg, Roy R., *Management Trauma in a Small City Police Department: A Case Study, Journal of Police Science and Administration* (Vol. 9, 1981), and Slovak, Jeffrey S., *Work Satisfaction and Municipal Police Officers, Journal of Police Science and Administration* (Vol. 6, 1978).

[10] Carter, David L.; Sapp, Allen D.; and Stephens, Darrel W., *The State of Police Education: Policy Direction for the 21st Century* (Washington, DC: Police Executive Research Forum, 1989).

[11] *Ibid.*

[12] *Ibid.*

[13] Information provided by U.S. Census Bureau Public Information Service by telephone from Washington, DC.

[14] Carter, et al.

[15] *Ibid.*

[16] *Ibid.*

[17] Publications referred to in this section are part of the Community Policing Series issued by the National Neighborhood Foot Patrol Center, Michigan State University, East Lansing, MI. For ease of reading, only direct quotes are footnoted, as indicated.

> *Job Satisfaction: A Comparison of Foot Patrol Versus Motor Patrol Officers* by Robert C. Trojanowicz and Dennis W. Banas, 1985. *Performance Profiles of Foot Versus Motor Officers* by Dennis M. Payne and Robert C. Trojanowicz, 1985. *Perceptions of Safety: A Comparison of Foot Patrol Versus Motor Patrol Officers* by Robert C. Trojanowicz and Dennis We. Banas, 1985. *Community Policing: Training Issues* by Robert Trojanowicz and Joanne Belknap, 1986.

> See also, Christian, Kenneth, *Supervisory Promotional Practices* in Robert C. Trojanowicz' *The Environment of the First Line Police Supervisor* (Englewood Cliffs, NJ: Prentice Hall, 1980).

[18] See Trojanowicz and Banas, *Job Satisfaction,* above.

[19] Baldwin, Bob, interview on December 5, 1988.

[20] Carter, *et al.*

CHAPTER 12
Building Support for New Community Policing Efforts

Bad administration, to be sure, can destroy good policy; but good administration can never save bad policy.

—*Adlai Stevenson*

When External Pressures Prompt Change

To understand fully the issues and challenges involved in shifting to Community Policing requires taking yet another look at the past, to understand the forces that spawned the Community Policing movement and the structural changes the concept entails. Much of the residual resistance to Community Policing stems from the fact that the impetus to change came primarily from outside police departments, rather than from within.

Like any other conservative institution, police departments are, by nature, slow to embrace change. Yet ever since the reform era of the 1930's, the police had little reason to re-examine their basic mission. The FBI's J. Edgar Hoover helped set the tone for modern policing, by repositioning the police from peacekeepers to crime-fighters, and police departments had good reason to identify themselves with that noble mission, especially since it seemed they continued to make progress toward that worthy goal. Some police departments might have to battle the occasional *crime wave,* but there was general optimism that improved police procedures, new crime-fighting technologies, and the continued rise in the overall standard of living might someday mean that the scourge of crime, like polio, would ultimately be conquered.

In the early 1960s, mainstream America still expressed overwhelming optimism that progress ensured an unbroken march toward utopia. There were still problems to be conquered. Racial integration and equality had not yet been achieved, but Dr.

Martin Luther King Jr.'s non-violent approach offered hope of peaceful progress toward that goal. The war in Vietnam continued to escalate, but military leaders assured the country of victory and that they could see light at end of the tunnel. After all, just like in World War II, we were the good guys destined to win.

Then that rosy view of an increasingly brighter future was shattered, almost overnight. The police soon found themselves under assault on three fronts. On college campuses nationwide, students and other anti-war protestors screamed at the police across the barricades, calling them *pigs,* sometimes spitting on them or hurling rocks. In inner-city black neighborhoods, where the police were *honkies,* officers battled for their lives during the frightening series of race riots that seemed to erupt each summer. And especially in major cities, the rates of serious crime exploded, tarnishing the image of the police as efficient and effective crime-fighters. Something seemed to have gone terribly wrong with the American dream, and the visible presence of the police on the front lines of the battles taking place on all three fronts made them the symbol – some would say the scapegoat – of society's frustration with the escalating domestic upheaval that seemed unstoppable.

The emergence of the concept of the CPO as community outreach specialist had its roots in the early foot patrol experiments in Flint and Newark that were launched as a response to concerns about rising crime and the volatility of police/community relations. Rates of serious crime, particularly violent crime, had risen to levels virtually unthinkable a decade before, and people worried that there appeared to be no relief in sight. Newark had suffered a devastating riot, and the Flint Police Department experienced a series of disturbing incidents with racial overtones. There was an overall crisis of confidence that American society could pull itself back from the brink of anarchy portended by the rising tide of violence. There was tremendous pressure on the police to do more, to do something different, and, most of all, to do something that would help.

Though controversial, the Kerner Commission report focused on the need for the police to build better relations with the community, particularly in minority neighborhoods. The experiment in Newark stationed foot officers in the community, but it provided them little if any concrete direction on what their new role would entail other than providing a visible police presence. In Flint, a serious effort was made to do more. The department held meetings with people all over the city, asking them what they needed and wanted, and this input became part of a comprehensive new plan of action. The Flint foot patrol officers were trained in many of the areas that are now considered basics in the CPO's job description.

Though the initial impetus in both cases stemmed from the urgent need to explore ways to reduce crime and improve police/community relations, it became increasingly apparent to those involved in evaluating these experiments that both

Flint and Newark were sending important messages, but perhaps not quite the ones envisioned. Harvard's George Kelling, who studied the Newark effort, said that the experiment verified that the police had to do more than just put officers on foot in the community like the beat cops of old. In some ways, Newark served as the unofficial control experiment for Flint, by showing the merit in giving the foot officers more direction and support in becoming community problem-solvers.

The research on Flint seemed to indicate that this new kind of foot patrol could achieve the two major goals of controlling crime and improving race relations. The Flint study did show a significant improvement in the perception of the police in the black community, and it also showed that target crimes likely to be influenced by the new foot patrol effort dropped substantially in the experimental areas.

Yet there was good news and bad news in those positive Flint results. The good news was that this new approach seemed to offer a way to help heal the breach between the police and the black community, and Flint residents obviously benefited from the decrease in those target crimes. But the bad news was that crime reduction quickly became the primary measure of success or failure. Not only was reducing serious crime an urgent goal, but it also fit best with the traditional view of police officers as society's crime-fighters – and it was also relatively easy to measure without expensive research. However, that meant that when other similar experiments failed to confirm that they reduced target crimes, it seemed that this novel idea sounded better in theory than it worked in practice. Perhaps Flint had simply been a fluke.

Yet those involved felt they had come upon a promising new concept, that delivering decentralized and personalized police service to the community produced benefits not fully understood. Even if crime rates failed to verify that people were, in fact, safer, people in both Newark and Flint said they *felt* safer. Thoughtful and concerned critics worried that could be dangerous. Making people feel safer without actually making them safer risked encouraging them to increase exposure, which could mean even more people would be victimized.

Over time, however, there was growing awareness that the police faced almost as big a challenge in coping with fear of crime as crime itself. Reducing fear of crime through what came to be called a Community Policing approach improved the quality of life for people in the community, and it encouraged, empowered, and emboldened them to cooperate and participate more with the police in efforts to improve their actual safety.

It also took time to understand fully the merits of involving officers directly in efforts to reduce social and physical disorder and reverse neighborhood decay. While it was obvious that neighborhoods in chronic disarray were also places where crime flourished, the idea that attacking disorder would contribute to controlling crime was not. If there was a direct cause-and-effect link, many people supposed that crime spawned decay, and even if the reverse were also true, that only crime, not decay, was the police department's concern.

So it took more time for theory and experience to converge in demonstrating that the police not only had the time, but good reason, to consider broadening their focus from crime-fighting to community problem-solving. Making the philosophical shift required understanding that the traditional approach devotes tremendous resources to random – or preventive – patrol, yet research raised serious questions about whether it produced a valid return on the investment. The police had focused on ensuring there were enough officers on random patrol so that they could send an officer to the scene as quickly as possible, even though there are relatively few times that speed makes any significant difference in the outcome.

It required a leap of imagination to suggest that if the department reordered patrol deployment, so that dispatchers explained to people why non-emergency calls did not receieve the speediest response, some line officers could be freed from motor patrol duty to serve as community outreach specialists, CPOs, who would operate much like their precursors on foot patrol in Flint. Until it became clear that Community Policing was a new way for the entire police department to focus on community problem-solving, the effort was routinely attacked as being an expensive add-on, one that detracted from a proper focus on serious crime.

After it became clear that Community Policing's community problem-solving focus must be integrated into every job within the department – and that many departments could at least begin to deploy CPOs by shifting existing resources – much of the resistance to the new approach within police circles subsided. Yet there are still reasons that people inside and outside policing will never become fans. Some resistance stems from a general reluctance to embrace change, no matter how positive. Others have philosophical concerns that have led them to reach an honest difference of opinion. Those who think they fare better under the existing system also have reason to resist change. But perhaps most of the resistance stems from people inside and outside the department who have not been exposed to what Community Policing can do for them directly.

Before addressing ways that police departments can address and possibly defuse internal and external resistance, yet another look backward can help identify the dynamics that must be understood. As we did with the Medical Model in Chapter 1, we will now explore how the auto industry provides a useful model to help clarify the issues that the police have faced in making the change to Community Policing.

The Auto Industry Model

It is especially apt that Flint not only served as one of the early cradles for what is now the Community Policing movement, but for the auto industry as well. To grasp the significance of the resistance that ensues when change is thrust upon a conservative organization from outside, the identity crisis that the automobile industry endured during roughly that same era offers important insights.

The U.S. auto industry was plunged into a wrenching re-assessment of its relationship to the public by a succession of punches in the late 1960s and early 1970s that threatened to deliver a knockout blow. In retrospect, it is easy to see how these companies had become complacent, but it is also easy to see why their past achievements allowed them to assume they knew best how to run their business.

Since the early days of the invention of the automobile, the U.S. auto industry had achieved an unparalleled record of success. Certainly, the shakeout during the early years meant that many small car companies failed, but by the 1960s, American cars had become the standard for engineering excellence. Henry Ford's dream of transforming the automobile from a luxury reserved for the very rich to a necessity enjoyed by all Americans had been achieved.

Like any conservative organization, car companies suffered from creeping bureaucratization, with its red tape and paperwork. Critics also warned that top executives were becoming increasingly insulated and isolated from both the general public and the workers on the line by a top-heavy management system. They pointed to the danger of allowing layer upon layer of yes-men to tell the bosses what they wanted to hear, rather than what they should hear. Yet for many years, those at the top always had the last laugh, since they could consistently point to that black bottom line as proof that they were doing things right. Even when profits started to erode, as more and more customers switched to smaller, more fuel-efficient foreign imports, the auto industry scorned this as a meaningless, temporary – and even silly – fad. No one of authority inside the system dared suggest that the fad was fast becoming a trend.

By the time that the continued assault on corporate profits became too worrisome to ignore any longer, the entire country was reeled at the impact when the OPEC nations turned off the tap and oil prices worldwide skyrocketed overnight. The U.S. economy staggered from the blow, but no industry suffered more than U.S. carmakers, who could not re-tool quickly enough to prevent a glut of gas-guzzlers from stacking up unsold on dealer lots. To stanch the red ink hemorrhaging onto the bottom line, the Big Three threw thousands of autoworkers out of their jobs, and the ripple effect in the rest of the economy undeniably added to both the length and severity of the recession in the mid-1970s.

That painful lesson forced a dramatic re-thinking about how the prevailing system must change. The challenge was to move quickly beyond dwelling on past mistakes, to look for new solutions. The first problem to be solved was how to lure the customers back, which required admitting that the companies had lost touch with the consumer. Success had spawned complacency, even arrogance, so the companies faced a tremendous obstacle in convincing consumers that they were sincere when they said they would listen to their wants and needs.

To get the message out, they launched an aggressive outreach program, marketing their new openness to the car-buying public. Most visibly, Chrysler Corporation's chairman Lee Iacocca appealed directly to customers, asking them to trust him personally and tell him what they thought – a far cry from the immediate past when auto executives made it clear that they felt they knew best what people needed.

What their customers told them was that they had turned to imports because they cared more about fuel-efficiency, safety, and quality workmanship than about minor styling changes in the chrome and fins. In essence, this also forced the companies to reassess their mission, a subtle but perceptible shift from selling products on the basis of styling and image to a new emphasis on content and substance.

The economic threat posed by foreign competition also promoted internal changes within the corporations. The turbulent history of management/labor relations had pitted both sides against each other, but faced with the common threat, they were now forced to find common ground. Threatened with further layoffs, the unions agreed to wage and benefit concessions in exchange for job protection. Management borrowed ideas from its Japanese competitors and experimented with ways to involve workers in decision-making. Allowing workers a say in how cars were built not only offered the promise of improving the final product, but it had the added benefit of improving worker satisfaction.

The parallels to policing are obvious. The police were stunned at the degree of hostility they faced from college students and minorities, but they were perhaps most shocked at criticism levelled at them from the primary *consumers* of police services, the taxpayers upon whom they depend.

Yet because the police are publicly funded institutions, many police departments initially tried to ignore the mounting pressures to change, dismissing taxpayers concerns because, after all, they could not shop for service elsewhere, as those disgruntled automobile buyers had. The surprising passage of the Jarvis Amendment in California, that cut property taxes in half overnight, sent a brutal message to all government institutions that the people paying bills could revolt if they were asked to pay more for what they perceived as less. The police also began to see the burgeoning growth in the private security industry as a growing threat, an ominous indication that people who could afford to pay more to feel safer were turning to the private, not the public, sector for help.

These upheavals prompted the era of increased funding for research on and experimentation in policing detailed in Chapter 6. Fears that strained race relations could mean new riots meant much of the attention focused on ways the police could reach out to minorities. Many departments faced increasing pressure to adopt civilian review boards as a way to address allegations of abuse of authority. While minorities often viewed a department's willingness to accept such proposals as a bellwether of its sincerity in addressing their concerns, many police chiefs resisted them, arguing that they allowed people who did not understand policing unwarranted intrusion in determining police policy and procedures.

As an alternative, police departments often agreed to institute some form of Police/Community Relations program. Typically this was a unit consisting of one or more staff officers who met periodically with community leaders. Many were sincere, well-meaning outreach efforts, but others were, at best, half-hearted gestures that aimed primarily at deflecting criticism and not on making substantive changes – tantamount to American carmakers' fiddling with the chrome trim instead of re-designing the total product.

What has now come to be called Community Policing constitutes a total re-tooling. It has evolved over time into what is now a revolutionary departure from the past, a new and distinctly different way of delivering expanded police service to the community. It recognizes that crime, like poverty, is a problem that has so far defied easy answers, and that despite their valiant and best efforts, the police will never be able to control it alone. What the police can do is make better use of their resources, so that they can do a better job of reducing and controlling crime, by focusing more attention on the underlying dynamics that allow crimes to occur. A Community Policing approach also allows the police to expand beyond a narrow focus on crime, to address a broader spectrum of community concerns, such as fear of crime, social and physical disorder, and neighborhood decay.

To continue the metaphor, Community Policing often means departments downsize the number of motor patrol officers on free patrol at any given time. While that usually means a less speedy response to non-emergency calls, it allows the department to get greater mileage out of its line officers, by retreading some as CPOs, a brand-new model of police officers who acts as the department's community outreach specialist. As the cornerstone of providing decentralized, personalized police service to the community, CPOs assist the department in improving overall race relations, but as a by-product of delivering enhanced police service, not as the primary goal. Through its CPOs, the department can reach out directly to the consumers of police service, allowing their input to ensure the department does not lose touch with their wants and needs.

By paying more direct attention to the consumers of police services and allowing them input into the police agenda, the police also enlist their direct cooperation and support, including their individual and collective participation in new community-based initiatives designed to make the communities safer and improve the quality of life in the community long term. CPOs also act as the people's ombudsman to other government agencies and serve as the community's direct link to area agencies, private and public, that offer needed help.

While what happened in policing sounds much like what happened in the auto industry, the big difference is that only three CEOs set policy for the Big Three automakers, yet there are individual chiefs in each of the more than 14,000 municipal, county, and township police departments nationwide.[1] Like Lee Iacocca, Houston's Lee Brown became a highly visible spokesperson for Community Policing, and his credibility, as well as that of other prominent and respected chiefs who adopted the new approach, has helped the movement gain acceptance.

Yet conversion to Community Policing is a revolution in slow motion. Many departments were far quicker to adopt a problem-solving approach than to make the structural changes required to put CPOs directly in the community. Yet as they see the direct benefits that a problem-solving orientation produces, many also realize that it works best when CPOs are part of the process, because they know the people and their turf so well. They can identify and even anticipate problems, and they grasp the underlying dynamics so that they know how to fashion a logical response. Their continued presence in the community allows them to monitor the results and make adjustments, and it also means they can embark on long-term proactive efforts that required a sustained police presence as supervisors.

Just as car companies were forced to recognize that they had been ignoring the contribution that their line workers can make, Community Policing accords new respect to all line officers, encouraging them to take the initiative to find new ways to address old problems and thereby increasing worker satisfaction. By considering arrest as only one tool that police officers can use, police officers are being challenged to look beyond individual crime incidents, to see if an initiative that alters the environment that allows the crimes to occur can help. By granting line officers the autonomy to act as community problem-solvers, they have an opportunity to do more to enhance overall productivity than simply respond to calls for service.

Important as well is the lesson that the impetus for Community Policing came from unavoidable pressures from outside the system more than because insiders were eager to explore new ideas. In fact, the unwillingness of police departments to respond to changing needs and changing times is what allowed them to be caught off-guard, just as the auto industry was staggered by its losses. It is also fair to say that advance planning might have spared both institutions some – but not all – of the grief they faced. The auto industry was beginning to respond to the threat of foreign competition when it was blind-sided by the oil price hike. Police departments were also beginning to struggle with need to address minority concerns and they were bracing for the anticipated rise in crime as those Baby Boomers started to hit their most crime-prone years. But they were shocked to find themselves literally and figuratively under fire from so many groups at the same time.

So it is fair to say that part of the resistance to Community Policing stems from the fact that change has been thrust upon the institution of policing from outside. U.S. automakers talk about how glad they are now that they were forced to learn to listen to their customers – how thankful they are that foreign competitors help keep them on their toes. Yet the horrendous losses those companies and their stockholders suffered offered little cause for celebration. It was a bitter and traumatic transition for both the U.S. auto industry and the police. Within both organizations are many traditionalists who still feel they were insulted and betrayed by an ungrateful public that chose to exaggerate their failures and ignore their achievements. It is important to understand the climate of the past, as well as the prevailing mood of today, to grasp why the long, painful, and difficult birth of the Community Policing movement has left scars that have not completely healed, and why that can play a role in resistance to new efforts launched today.

Assessing the Climate for Change

Community Policing will likely find its warmest reception in progressive police departments, ones where the administration has demonstrated its openness to new ideas and the importance of keeping pace with changing times. The problem in assessing how well any particular department measures up to this standard is complicated by the difficulty in knowing what yardstick to use. Crime trends, arrest and clearance rates, and efficiency measures such as response time offer little guidance about the department's responsiveness to the people it serves. To paraphrase organizational analyst Peter Drucker, the greatest danger lies in doing well that which should not be done at all.

People who live in the community often have an instinctive feel for whether their police department is doing a good job or not, but the challenge lies in being able to identify how to make improvements. The following dozen items are offered as a way to ask meaningful questions about the department, to produce a clearer picture of how likely it is to meet changing needs. This can prove a useful tool for people to use to assess the department they already work for, or that job candidates can use to see whether the department is likely to be one where they will be happy. Government officials, community leaders, journalists, and interested citizens can also use these measures to determine where improvements could be made.

- **The Police Chief** – Effective leadership begins at the top. The first challenge is to choose the best, the next is to give the chief the autonomy necessary to do a good job. When a new chief is hired, is there a professional interviewing process that involves the community? Or is the chief appointed by a local politician or board that can be pressured by special-interest groups? Is the goal to find a qualified, strong, and visionary leader – or a person whose real job is to do the politicians' bidding, to make them look good or be fired? How much security does the chief have? Is the chief given a contract or civil service protection? Can the chief be removed without cause?

- **Top Command** – Again, the first question is whether the selection process has been stripped of favoritism and cronyism. The best departments use competitive exams, oral boards, or, as is increasingly common, sophisticated assessment centers to make sure the best are promoted. A system based on personality or politics invites corruption and stagnation. When promotions are a reward for keeping superiors happy and not for serving the entire community, fear of making mistakes instead of striving for excellence can permeate the entire department. Asking anyone promoted to submit an undated letter of resignation is a regrettable tactic that some departments still employ – the message is clear: Don't make waves.

- **Middle Managers and Line Officers** – What kind of people are being selected as police officers? Are assignments and promotions made on the basis of education, skills, training, experience, and interest? Do supervisors encourage line officers to do their best – or paralyze initiative by worrying more about preventing mistakes? Is the emphasis on how quickly the officers arrive after taking a call or on what they achieve once they are there? Are officers rated exclusively on easily quantifiable measures – calls answered, speed of response, arrests made, tickets issued – or do performance assessments attempt to make more fundamental assessments of their effectiveness in the community? Are line officers accorded the autonomy and respect of professionals? Morale is often a good indicator of whether the system is forward-thinking and fair. Is the department considered a good place to work?

- **Deployment of Officers** – Deciding where to deploy officers shows where the department puts its priorities. Something is askew when there are too many officers visible in business districts or affluent areas and not enough in high-crime neighborhoods plagued with drug dealing and violence. Some departments assign too many officers to guard local politicians, leaving too few officers on the street. Morale also suffers if top command uses plum assignments and overtime to play favorites.

- **Inter-Agency Cooperation** – If the department has a reputation for refusing to cooperate with other local, state, and federal law enforcement agencies, it is important to know why. Do officers in other agencies trust and respect the department? Does the department cooperate effectively with other agencies in the criminal justice system – the prosecutor's officer, crime lab, and the courts?

- **Management/Union Relations** – Heated exchanges during negotiations are a normal part of the process, but once an agreement is reached, do both sides focus on common objectives? Is too much energy wasted on hostile debates that have little to do with providing the best possible police service? Have both sides set up back-channels of communication to address mutual goals?

- **Internal Affairs Division** – This division should operate as the internal equivalent of a special prosecutor, an independent unit whose mission is to ferret out bad apples. How are personnel selected? Are they insulated from pressure from special-interest groups? Is the department open to investigating complaints against officers, and is it willing and able to investigate itself?

- **Lawsuits** – In today's litigious society, no department can completely avoid lawsuits, but how many does the department win, and why? Is the department open to constructive criticism? Does it face problems squarely and make adjustments as needed?

- **Media Relations** – The government and the press have traditionally had an adversarial relationship, but it should be based on mutual respect and honesty. If the department appears reluctant to talk to the media, is that because of justifiable concerns about confidentiality – or is it the fear that they will expose mistakes or problems? Who speaks for the department – only politicians or those they designate? Does the chief or his representative talk openly to the press? Does the department trust its officers enough to allow them to answer questions from reporters? Does the political structure try to manage the police news?

- **Access to Information** – Data on crime rates, victim information, and arrest statistics are tax-paid, public information. All departments should be willing to share this information or they violate the public trust. While the impulse to tout good news and downplay the bad is only human, the best departments understand that the price of credibility may require taking lumps when they are deserved, otherwise people will not trust them when they trumpet their triumphs. Honesty and openness are essential in promoting informed community feedback.

- **Citizen Input** – As in any business or profession, the executives in charge can begin to think they have all the answers. The *consumers* of police service, the people who live and work in the community, deserve a voice in setting the police agenda. Community Policing obviously provides the best integrated and most responsive system to allow people input into the police process. Assigning an officer or unit to build bridges to the community may demonstrate good intentions, but this kind of limited tactic is far less likely to produce substantive results.

- **Community Commitment** – Departments with top-flight leadership instill a sense of dedication within the ranks that extends beyond work hours. Do officers volunteer for such off-duty activities as Big Brother/Big Sister and local athletic leagues or clubs for kids? Does the department demonstrate a sincere concern for the quality of life in the community?

No police department is perfect, and this listing was not meant as a bludgeon for anyone to attack a department's failings. It was offered as a blueprint for excellence, so that police departments and the people they serve can help identify areas of improvement. While there has never been any structured research to determine that Community Policing will fare better in a department that scores well on these measures, it stands to reason that those that rate well against this yardstick would probably have fewer problems in starting a successful effort.

Winners and Losers in the Community

Though much of the pressure to find a new way of policing equal to the challenges in contemporary society came, for the most part, from outside police departments, this does not mean that everyone in the community should be expected to cheerlead for Community Policing. Many individuals and groups outside policing are not fully aware of what the new movement can do, and some who do understand how it works have sincere reservations about its methods and effectiveness. But Community Policing also implies that current winners and losers under the traditional system may trade places after the shift. Efforts to reduce resistance depend on identifying likely winners and losers and understanding their concerns, to anticipate the reasons for their resistance and find ways to show them why Community Policing will ultimately benefit them as well.

Those outside the department who may have the most to fear from Community Policing are the local politicians – the mayor, city manager, or municipal, county and township officials – who can see CPOs as a threat to their power base. Experience shows that CPOs, in the role of community ombudsman, often solve problems for individuals or groups who might well have turned to their politicians for help in the past. This kind of direct assistance is the grease that oils the wheels of local politics, since it allows incumbents to solidify their support in the community. In addition, even those politicians who embrace and support a shift to Community Policing have good reason to worry they also face being ridiculed by embarrassing mistakes or spectacular failures, a problem that will be discussed further when we look at the risk this new concept poses to the chief.

The traditional police system also benefits the movers-and-shakers in the community, since they typically have the greatest access to police officials, a distinct advantage in a top-down, hierarchical system where decision-making resides among those at the top. Business owners, corporate executives, community leaders, and the affluent can often make their wishes known through formal and informal contacts. A busy police chief cannot make time for every private citizen who might call for an appointment, but most will try to make time to meet with the president of a major corporation or the elected leader of a powerful community group.

The traditional system also discourages average citizens from asking for a formal appointment, especially unless they have a pressing concern. In contrast, the power brokers in the community often interact informally or socialize with police officials, at meetings, at luncheons, or as friends. This not only gives them the chance to air specific concerns, but also to share opinions and general impressions. Because the top command in the department often shares much in common with other successful people in the community, in terms of education, values, and current lifestyle, they often reinforce each other's perceptions – and biases. While the paranoid view is that this means the power brokers at the top ignore the little guy when they make policy and set priorities, it more likely means that people at the top rarely have much exposure to dissenting views.

Community Policing turns that equation upside down, by allowing the line officers and average citizens on the street the power to set immediate priorities and launch new initiatives. In essence, this means new ideas may bubble up to the top as often as they trickle down. A powerful business owner may want the police to do something about the homeless who scare customers away from the front of his store. A Community Policing focus might reduce the number of patrols in the business district, to free CPOs for new initiatives, which might include a new effort to protect the homeless from victimization, which is not what the business owner had in mind.

A shift to Community Policing often means a shift in the services provided. The police might no longer help people who are locked out of their homes and cars, and they might ask people to drive to the department to report minor traffic accidents. A shift to Community Policing also means the police will probably respond more slowly to non-emergency calls than they did in the past. People who feel cheated by these changes can put pressure on the chief to abandon the effort, especially the first time a new CPO makes a highly visible mistake.

Some may see this as an overly cynical portrait of the traditional system. The fact is, however, that enlightened police administrators who want to serve the entire community often find they must do so in spite of the constraints in the traditional system. Community Policing helps balance power, shifting some to the base of the pyramid, to the line officers and the people on the street. CPOs and the people they serve are the obvious winners, but the challenge in promoting this change lies in showing why that will ultimately benefit everyone in the community, top to bottom.

Reducing Opposition in the Community

When a police chief commits to exploring a shift to Community Policing, the first step should be to educate the community about what the approach can and cannot do, so that both the winners and losers understand the rationale for the change. Many departments precede the launch by hosting a series of meetings open to everyone in the community, which often draw many people who have never been heard before. While it might seem that politicians and power brokers already benefit from access, a wise chief will take care to lobby them, formally and informally, since their support can prove crucial. And though stressing the approach's increased opportunity to produce failures or mistakes and its shift in the power relationship can prove threatening to the groups who may think they benefit more from the status quo, the best bet is to meet potential resistance honestly and openly.

The point the chief must stress is that the overall quality of life in the community is at stake, and that everyone's safety is important. It is also in the enlightened self-interest of politicians and power brokers to support a movement that holds the promise of preventing problems in the future. As the riots in Miami during the 1980s certify, racial unrest remains a problem, one that Community Policing addresses directly. The approach also offers promise of controlling or reducing the epidemic of drug dealing and drug-related violence and crime that can engulf entire communities. And Community Policing also addresses crime, fear of crime, and disorder in new ways that can help improve the quality of community life over time.

Chief Gary Leonard of Alexandria, Virginia, defuses complaints about cuts in service by asking people whether they really care about having an officer dash to the "crime scene" moments after someone finds their lawnmower gone. About all the officer can do is look at the spot on the lawn where it was and commiserate – "So *that's* where it was." Then Leonard explains how, by reordering priorities so that speed of response is not perceived as a crucial measure of police performance, the department can now have CPOs gathering information about drug dealing that it might never get any other way.

The danger, of course, is that this kind of advance work may simply allow those who oppose the change an opportunity to derail the plan. This is an undeniable risk, yet the chances are that the worst time for these groups to find out that Community Policing may threaten their values, their power, or the current levels of service they enjoy is before the chief has the opportunity to explain how it can help.

By involving these individuals and groups in the planning process, the chief may also benefit from their input. In some circumstances, it may be possible to compromise. In a specific situation, politicians might want to volunteer to work with their CPOs on nagging problems their constituents face. Politicians must be made to understand that working with CPOs can enhance their visibility and credibility with voters, whereas opposing a popular effort only risks costing them more votes. Perhaps the chief might want to consider some mechanism to keep local politicians informed directly about Community Policing initiatives in their areas, so that they would not feel left out of the process.

Police officials might also try approaching business leaders about becoming sponsors for new community-based activities, or they could encourage them to donate goods and services as a form of goodwill. Handled properly, just paying special attention to their concerns can help defuse potential problems.

Winners and Losers Within the Department

Part of the internal resistance to a new Community Policing effort will stem from the normal human tendency of individuals and organizations to resist change. Part of the resistance will also stem from the fact police departments are conservative, paramilitary organizations that view change with skepticsm. And some resistance will come from traditionalists who disagree with the effort on philosophical grounds, primarily those who feel that the police department's plate is already full enough dealing with serious crime, and that the police should not broaden their mandate to include problems where they may not have sufficient expertise. Added to them are people inside the department who are the *winners* under the existing system, those who may see themselves as relative *losers* under the Community Policing approach.

Regardless of their assignment, anyone who has loudly championed or defended the existing system risks becoming a loser, since the change implies a rejection of the system they probably continue to believe in, one they probably worked hard to make succeed. The change may not only be viewed as a betrayal, but as an insult as well. After all, if the existing system was working well, there would be no need to make any change, especially one as dramatic, fundamental, and far-reaching as Community Policing.

People who currently hold particular positions within the department can perceive themselves as becoming losers as a result of the change. While it seems axiomatic that the chief must support Community Policing or it will never be adopted, that has not always been the case. In at least one notable instance, a police chief offered sizable new funding to pay for positioning CPOs around the city initially rejected the money, until pressure from the community and city government forced him to relent.

Yet for the most part, though the police in general may have been reluctant to change, once educated to the benefits of Community Policing, many police chiefs were at least numbered among the primary proponents responsible for making the shift. But the chief often has the most to lose if the new approach appears to fail or produces embarrassing mistakes. One of the ways in which the traditional system makes the chief a winner is that it promotes predictability. By rewarding those who follow rules and procedures closely, the system emphasizes avoiding mistakes. As long as no one challenges whether those rules and procedures do as much to produce the results that people want as Community Policing, the traditional system often hums along relatively smoothly, causing little unexpected grief for the person at the top, though there have obviously been many examples where this has not been true.

The traditional system also provides at least some "protective cover" when problems erupt. Many times the chief can deflect criticism by pointing out that the mistake occurred because the officers involved violated or ignored the rules and procedures. When criminal violence erupts, an area suffers a dramatic rise in property crimes, or people complain about new drug problems, the chief in a traditional department can hope to deflect responsibility by pointing to the underlying social problems. Though the traditional approach emphasizes the role of the police as society's crime-fighters, the chief can usually elicit at least some sympathy by saying that police cannot do anything about the *slum* or *ghetto* conditions under which people live, the places that breed crime and drug problems. In a traditional police department, the chief can rail about how his officers are doing all they can to help, but the blame for decaying neighborhoods lies with city fathers who allow garbage to rot uncollected on the street and who fail to provide idle teens enough summer activities to keep them out of mischief.

Community Policing puts the chief on the hook for many problems that the traditional system does not. It says the department has a valid role to play in making sure that garbage is picked up and kids have something worthwhile to do. In granting the responsibility to line officers to tackle a broader range of community problems, it also provides them the authority and power to do more – which means more opportunities for mistakes. There was the embarrassing incident in Flint, in which a well-meaning officer inadvertently took a group of area youngsters to an X-rated movie.

The chief can also take heat if a creative problem-solving effort flops. The oft-discussed example of moving and re-designing the bus stop to help stop purse-snatchings could make embarrassing headlines if a reporter announces that the department *wasted* all that time and money and yet a purse-snatching occurred there the next day – and that could happen. The chief may be hard-pressed to explain that the effort was worth the investment if it reduces the purse-snatchings there over time.

Not only will some creative solutions fail totally, even if they help reduce overall severity or frequency, some people will still take potshots at involving the police in anything that does not focus on arresting the bad guys and putting them away. Doing anything else seems to them to ignore getting tough on the people who break the law. Others fear that re-designing the bus stop may even make it tougher for the police to catch the predators. Now they can strike anywhere; at least the bus stop acted as a predictor of where they will strike, which might offer the police a better chance of catching them in the act.

By granting officers greater autonomy, some officers will potentially put the chief on the spot by abusing their new freedom. In one actual case, a person called the department to report that a male CPO and his female counterpart appeared to be sneaking away to an apartment for an afternoon tryst every day. The bad news was that an investigation proved the allegations were true, but the good news was that this shows people become so involved in the police process as a result of Community Policing that they not only act as unofficial supervisors, but trust their department well enough to call and complain.

The same problems the chief faces extend to the people in top command, as well as middle managers and especially supervisors. Supervisors, who usually feel caught in the middle regardless of which system is in place, have reason to worry about becoming big losers with a shift to Community Policing, because the worst part of their job is carrying any bad news to the boss. Middle managers can also feel threatened by a loss of status and control, because Community Policing requires them to share decision-making with officers beneath them in the hierarchy. It is also demonstrably more difficult to supervise CPOs, since a true assessment of their performance requires making personal visits to the beat areas to see firsthand how well the CPO is doing.

It would seem that all line officers would benefit under a Community Policing approach, because of the greater responsibility, authority, and freedom to explore new ways to solve problems. Yet experience shows that much of the resistance to

Community Policing comes from motor patrol officers. This was often more true in the past, when Community Policing was adopted piecemeal. This often meant that the ranks of the department's motor patrol officers were thinned to field the new CPOs required. Instead of educating and energizing everyone in the department about how to become community problem-solvers, many departments focused first on using CPOs as their new, creative thinkers, while motor patrol officers were pretty much told to keep doing the same old thing, with fewer officers.

Eager, open-minded CPOs enthusiastic about their new opportunity to work with people directly on a host of challenging new initiatives are obvious winners, yet it is easy to see why their motor patrol peers resented their greater autonomy – especially since CPOs may not work nights or weekends, and they often have additional flexibility in setting their schedules. Motor patrol officers who take great pride in their role as crime-fighters and who see themselves as potentially risking their lives daily for people in the community they often perceive as ungrateful can see themselves as losers if the department begins to emphasize broader goals. Many openly resent the social work approach of Community Policing, dismissing CPOs as *lollicops* or the *grin-and-wave squad.*

Building Internal Support

It is easy to suggest that all problems in implementing and sustaining a successful Community Policing effort depend exclusively on strong support from the top, but the truth is that support from the chief and the top command is essential, yet that constitutes just the minimum of what it takes. On occasion, the biggest potential threat to a new Community Policing effort is that the chief himself does not fully understand the concept. The biggest problem is often that the chief mistakenly sees the elements that make up a true Community Policing effort as a shopping list from which he can pick ones he likes and reject ones he does not like or thinks are too expensive.

For starters, Community Policing is not a simple tactic that can be applied to a specific problem that can then be abandoned once the problem appears to be solved. A criminal justice policymaker once raved openly about how great Community Policing had worked in his community – so well that the department was able to withdraw the officers in the community even sooner than expected.

Community Policing is a permanent shift in the way the department views and handles the job. It implies both a broader mandate that focuses on community problem-solving, and a structural shift to deliver decentralized and personalized police service to the community by means of CPOs, who are permanently assigned a portion of the community as the department's outreach specliasts.

Community Policing is not simple. Educating officers to see their function differently is not easy. Helping everyone in the department to become efficient and effective community problem-solvers takes time. Some motor patrol officers are so frustrated with the existing job that often means doing the equivalent of visiting that same bus stop and just writing another report leap at the chance to do more. Others groan at the mere suggestion.

Community Policing does not mean that the chief just takes part of the force and deploys them to play the role of the *nice cops,* as an antidote to the *tough cops* of motor patrol. In some departments, CPOs are not supposed to make arrests or respond to calls for service, except in emergencies – which means they are not real CPOs. CPOs must be full-fledged law enforcement officers or the effort does not qualify as Community Policing. Not only does this tend to increase friction between motor patrol officers and CPOs, but it robs the community of the full benefits of the approach. (It should be noted, however, that at least one department intends to phase in having its CPOs carry guns and make arrests, because their particular internal dynamics appear to make it easier to introduce Community Policing more slowly.)

The hottest debate surrounds whether CPOs can use patrol cars, full time or part time, or whether that destroys their ability to function as true community outreach specialists. The easy answer, of course, is no – that freeing CPOs from the isolation of the patrol car and the incessant demands of the police radio are vital in allowing the department full expression of what Community Policing can offer. Yet many departments that allow CPOs to use patrol cars at least part of the time insist they have improved the officers' efficiency without seriously compromising their ability to make the concept work. It should be remembered, however, that when the foot patrol officers in Flint were later put back into cars, critics said that *park and walk* quickly degenerated into *park and watch.*

The bottom line on this issue may depend more on the commitment of the department to allow CPOs the time and opportunity to interact directly with the greatest number of people in the beat area – and the enthusiasm and commitment of the individual CPOs – than on the mode of transportation. Yet it is also true that the larger the city or the more calls for service a department receives, the more likely that once the CPO is placed in a car that he becomes a slave to the radio. And this also highlights how the approach must be tailored to fit both the department and the community.

It is also important to remember that simply freeing the CPO from the patrol car is also not enough. CPOs must be assigned to particular beat areas and left there *unmolested* so that they can develop the rapport and trust the philosophy depends on.

Edmonton (Canada) Superintendent Chris Braiden cited an incident that underscored the importance of allowing CPOs to "own" specific beat areas. Braiden said he watched for weeks as officers walked by a rickety bike parked in front of the station, yet no one took the initiative to find out if it was stolen – when it is everyone's job, it is no one's job. "The easiest way to understand the importance of this feeling of ownership is to remember that no one bothers to wash a rental car," says Braiden.[2] Departments that succumb to the temptation to rotate CPOs from one area to another or that use them to fill holes elsewhere in the system can damage a CPO's potential effectiveness.

For Community Policing to succeed, it is vitally important that it gets off on the right foot, since that can determine its reputation forever. Past experience shows the two keys are advance planning and department-wide education. In Morristown, New Jersey, for example, the department elected not to seek press coverage when the department launched Community Policing, since they did not want to run the risk of hyping the effort before it had a chance to prove itself. Other departments might opt to do the reverse, for reasons particular to their community or as a means to inform the community. It is not the choice that Morristown made that is important, but the fact that the top administrators took the time to develop a coherent plan tailored to their particular needs. It is vital to look at the potential issues in advance, to develop a strategy for implementation, one that is also flexible enough to adjust to changing realities.

A good administrator will involve the top command in the initial phases of the planning process, then extend the opportunity for input to everyone else in the department as well. The announcement that the decision has been made to embrace Community Policing provides a unique opportunity to make everyone feel they are part of the same team. A common problem in the past was that the potential for resistance did not seem as important as getting things started. In Clearwater, Florida, for example, Lieutenant Frank Palombo said it seemed logical that the first priority was to get the CPOs in place and operating in the community, but they could have avoided problems if they had realized the first priority should have been to educate everyone in the department about how and why the changes were being made.[3]

"The main difference is that Community Policing is risky – it's risky for the administration, the supervisors, and the officers," says Palombo. "In traditional policing, there is less chance of failure. The officer has clear-cut duties, he has a car, a zone, and he answers calls. If he does exactly what he's told to do, he's judged as being successful in his job. Community Policing is more creative. To be an effective Community Policing officer, you have to try new approaches and not all of them will work. But unless you educate the department that mistakes are the prices of success, they may not see why they should take the heat."

While support from the top is essential, experience shows that the group that has the greatest power to help or hurt Community Policing is middle management. Middle managers directly implement policy and supervise results, which provides them tremendous power within the department. According to Robert Lunney, who has been called the father of Community Policing in Canada, middle managers fall into three groups: those who will support the new concept's goals and orientation immediately, those who will become converts over time, and those who will never embrace the philosophy.[4] Lunney, who inaugurated new Community Policing efforts in both Edmonton and Winnipeg, says that the major problem obviously lies with that third group, but that the solution is both harder and easier than most people think.

According to Lunney, traditionalists who will never embrace Community Policing offer both good news and bad. The bad news is that you will never change their minds, no matter how long and hard you talk and how logical you may think your arguments are. The good news, however, is that traditionalists subscribe to the importance of following orders. The goal therefore is not to change attitudes, but to change behavior. That requires clear, constant, and consistent reinforcement from the top. "My advice to any chief who is introducing this kind of program is that he must nurture it carefully for at least the first three years," says Lunney.

Community Policing requires supervisors share power with underlings, at the same time they must be willing to work harder to find out if CPOs are doing a good job. The loss of status and control, as well as the new challenge imposed by finding new ways to assess performance, makes the job tougher. Supervisors who see the wisdom of the effort, at first or over time, find the change invigorating, while those who do not like what Community Policing entails find the new demands draining. Though they may never like the change, at least they can be made to accept the need to do the new job well.

"What the chief must remember is that you cannot simply issue an order once and expect it to be obeyed," says Lunney. "[The chief] must keep repeating the message to everyone who might be an obstacle. And sometimes when people are stubborn, you may have to use the *hammer.*"

Motor patrol officers also pose a thorny problem, since many automatically resent the fact that some CPOs may inappropriately keep bankers' hours, with weekends off, and they can also benefit from more flexible schedules. If the motor patrol officers share a commitment to community problem-solving as a valid goal and understand how their CPOs can help them, that will help. But many motor patrol officers will at least take time to grasp the benefits. Until or unless this happens, resentment risks becoming outright hostility.

Many motor patrol officers who believe bravery and toughness are "the right stuff" can rankle when they see people treat their CPOs as heroes. The macho myth says that people should not like police officers, but respect them, as if the two were mutually exclusive. Even though CPOs still use force, when appropriate, many motor patrol officers feel this new kind of officer is just not a real cop.

This reinforces why motor patrol officers must be educated to see that the new CPOs are not an elite new unit, but fellow patrol officers who are a resource that everyone in the deparment can use and whose contribution can directly help them. For example, in Clearwater, a motor patrol officer took off after a teenager in a stolen car, but when the teen screeched to a halt and fled on foot, the officer could not keep up. By the time the officer had returned to his patrol car, he was met by the CPO – with the boy's name, his address, and information about where the boy's father worked. "[The CPO] had such rapport with the kids in the area that they ran up to tell him all about the kid they had seen running away," says Palombo.

Early Community Policing efforts suffered because few departments could cite concrete examples like this to show how CPOs help their peers. Palombo said that it took a year and a half for the detectives in his department to see how the CPOs helped them in their jobs and that with proper education it should not have taken so long for that to happen. Administrators can also invite officers from other departments that have switched to Community Policing to offer sessions on how it works for them. The department can also send emissaries to Community Policing training sessions, so that they can bring back information and anecdotes to share.

Once the program is under way, it is important to make sure locker room talk does not get out of hand, because CPOs are already under unique pressures because of the intense emotional attachments they form with people in the community. "In a sense, you lose the protective armor you acquire as a motor patrol officer. In that role, it's easier to distance yourself from the problems of the people you deal with," says Palombo. "Unless you begin to take these concerns seriously and do all you can to improve the internal support within the department, you risk seeing officers suffer early burnout."

Lunney said that this is an especially important consideration with young or inexperienced CPOs, since they often suffer the additional worry of whether they are doing what is expected of them. This is a case where the chief may want to jump the chain of command and make periodic visits to talk with CPOs in the field, so that they know they have strong support from the top. "The chief must reassure them directly so that they can mature into the job," he says. These visits also send a message throughout the department that those who are tempted to sabotage the effort risk censure.

Encouraging sustained, informal communication between motor patrol officers and CPOs can help break down the barriers. The ill-fated *Take a Motor Patrol Officer to Lunch* effort in Flint was a disaster, but requiring the foot officers to attend roll calls more frequently did help. In Clearwater, CPOs made a special effort to invite motor patrol officers to use the substation. "We gave them a desk and phone to use. We made sure the place looked good, that the restrooms were clean. Our biggest successes came from lobbying officers one on one," says Palombo. "Eventually, three of the officers who stopped by on occasion ended up becoming part of the Community Policing program."

Michigan State University's Bruce Benson used this same approach when launching the new Community Policing effort on campus. He had seen the corrosive friction that can develop when he was a lieutenant in Flint during the foot patrol experiment. As a result, he has implemented what he calls community team policing, which involves assigning motor patrol officers and a CPO permanently to the same beat so that they can develop internal rapport and work together. The dissension he saw in Flint persuaded him that it is far easier to head off problems before they can become entrenched.

Another important issue concerns whether CPOs should all be volunteers. Many programs have been built on volunteers, because it makes good sense to use people who have an affinity for the job, but that must change in the future. Perhaps this will mean that civil service requirements should be changed to require all incoming candidates for police work must at least demonstrate some level of knowledge about what the Community Policing approach entails. Over time as well, when more former CPOs advance within the department, tensions will likely ease when fans of the approach hold more of the key jobs in the upper echelons in more departments nationwide.

George Kelling stresses the importance of reminding motor patrol officers that Community Policing also frees them to become community problem-solvers. Though their job may not provide them the time and opportunity to initiate the kind of long-term, proactive efforts that CPOs can create, they must understand the importance of moving beyond a narrow focus on individual crime incidents, to understand the process that produces problems and explore ways to alter the dynamics.

As more and more departments adopt Community Policing, the transition becomes easier simply because the issues involved in making the transition have clarified. Yet the concept continues to evolve and progress. At the cutting edge is the Aurora (Colorado) Police Department, which is currently phasing in Community Policing. Chief Gerry Williams has decided that every job within the department must be reviewed to see how it can be made part of the new Community Policing approach. The goal over time is to have everyone, both civilian and sworn personnel, express the commitment to helping people solve their problems in the most effective way. Each activity area within the department has been encouraged to submit a plan of action, showing the changes they can make to implement the philosophy. A review committee looks at the suggestions and prioritizes and coordinates a timetable for implementation. The changes are documented so that people clearly know what is expected of them.

Far from flinging CPOs into the community and hoping everything works out, Aurora has elected a slow and methodical approach to ensuring that everyone understands the importance of the new role they are expected to play. After changing their slogan from *Serve and Protect* to *Community Commitment,* the department adopted a new logo to match. Attention to detail even means they are developing a new directory, with the goal of ensuring that callers will be transferred to the right person on the first try, unlike the standard impersonal bureaucracy where people can bounce around so many times they give up.

People call the police department for help, often because they do not know where else to turn. Sometimes the call allows the police to save someone from being murdered. Sometimes the call is from someone who needs a copy of a report. Sometimes it is about noisy kids next door. The flaw in the traditional system is that only the first call is truly taken seriously. A department that has adopted the Community Policing approach recognizes that each caller thinks his or her problem deserves a response.

The police must always maintain the ability to respond immediately to life-and-death situations, but anyone who takes the time to ask for help deserves some level of concerned attention and assistance. The department need not dispatch a car immediately to the complaint about the noisy kids next door. But it might mean challenging the caller to talk to her neighbors about the problem – or talk to the kids themselves. Alienation between people in the community can be a problem just as it can between people and their police. It might even be worth asking the CPO to stop for a home visit when there is time. It could mean a serious problem of child neglect or abuse. It might mean the CPO challenges people in the community to work with him on developing worthwhile activities for young people in the area.

The worst thing the department can do is rudely dismiss any caller's concerns as trivial and bothersome. It is an honor, not an interruption, when people trust their police enough to see them as both a protector and as a friend to turn to. Both roles are essential, because the police must rely on the community's support as well.

Community Policing recognizes that the police must find new ways to help people cope with the myriad of problems they face. Depending on the nature of the problem, the police can offer help directly, show people how to help themselves, or direct them to where help is available. What the police cannot afford to do is ignore problems today and wait until they risk becoming a crisis tomorrow. By breaking down the isolation and alienation that the traditional system fosters, Community Policing allows the police to form a new partnership with the people they are sworn to serve.

While that makes it sound like Community Policing should be an easy sell, it is not. A chief in Texas called to say that he had implemented a Community Policing approach in his department and found that almost everyone he talked to initially seemed to hate it. People in the community warned him he was making a big mistake, and people in the department said worse. But he hung in there and, over time, former critics both inside and outside the department have become converts because they can see that Community Policing really works, particularly in the case of drugs. Perhaps the solution to overcoming resistance to Community Policing requires remembering that nothing succeeds like success.

NOTES

Concerning how to assess local police departments, see also *How To Rate Your Local Police,* David C. Couper, published by the Police Executive Research Forum, Washington, DC, 1983.

[1] *Report to the Nation on Crime and Justice,* Second Edition, U.S. Department of Justice (Washington, DC: Bureau of Justice Statistics, March 1988), p. 47.

[2] Braiden, Chris, at a presentation offered during the *Foot Patrol Training Seminar,* held by the National Neighborhood Foot Patrol Center at Michigan State University, April 1987.

[3] Palombo, Frank, as quoted in *Clearwater's Palombo Stresses Internal PR,* by Bonnie Bucqueroux, *Footprints,* Volume I, No. 1, Winter Issue 1987, p. 3. Winter Issue 1987, p. 3.

[4] Lunney, Robert, as quoted in *Success Depends on Support at the Top,* by Bonnie Bucqueroux, *Footprints,* Volume I, No. 3 & Volume II, No. 1, Fall/Winter Issue 1988, p. 11.

CHAPTER 13
The Future of Policing

As for the Future, your task is not to foresee but to enable it.

—Saint-Exupery

The Future of Public Policing

The history of modern policing is littered with the remains of promising ideas that faltered and died. Police/Community Relations and team policing are only two of the more obvious recent examples. Both undeniably addressed important problems. Both were launched with great fanfare and enthusiasm. Both attracted dedicated officers who cared deeply about making the programs work. And both are in danger of disappearing altogether.

Many supporters naively believe that Community Policing's demonstrated success ensures a bright future. Many also believe the movement is too firmly entrenched to be denied. Yet this ignores the fierce competition in the marketplace of ideas, especially in this era when voters balk at new taxes, so government agencies are routinely asked to do more with less. In the past 35 years, the murder rate has almost tripled, and motor vehicle thefts are roughly six times higher, yet virtually no police department has grown at a commensurate pace.[1]

As we approach the 21st century, this country finds itself confronting a new reality, in which we discuss limits more often than possibilities. We see many pressing needs left unmet – housing for the homeless, immediate drug treatment for all addicts who seek help, medical coverage for those who cannot afford to buy it. Even when we see an obvious problem and an equally obvious solution, this does not mean adequate funding will somehow magically appear.

Before tackling the specific challenges that Community Policing in particular faces, we must first address the threats to public policing in general. The unpleasant reality is that public policing has come under siege. Funding for local police efforts is often stagnant or declining. In addition, public policing has steadily lost ground to private policing, though few outside police circles realize that there are now far more people employed in private security than there are public police officers.

Even many within the police may not recognize the full ramifications of this trend. One consequence is that those who want more protection and can afford to pay more to feel safer often choose to buy service from private sources, which does nothing to support local police. Those who cannot afford to pay more therefore must make do with the level of service that the public police can provide. The added irony, of course, is that those who can afford to buy more private security are often those who are already less likely to be victimized.

The harsh reality today is that we have a two-tiered system of police protection, one in which the poorest and most crime-riddled areas depend on beleaguered public policing, while the middle and upper classes must spend more and more of what they make on a mix of public and private services.

On one end of the spectrum is a family in an exclusive apartment building (or suburban enclave) where a hired security guard monitors the entrance with a video camera, challenging anyone who tries to enter to prove they have a valid reason for being there. On the other end is the inner-city welfare mother who has no phone to dial 911 if she hears someone breaking in – a problem she is increasingly likely to face because the growing number of crack addicts in her neighborhood who steal to pay for their drugs.

Advantages tend to multiply the further up the economic pyramid a person climbs. Affluent areas benefit from a higher tax base, which means more tax dollars for public protection. Those who earn more also have more to spend for extra security, whether that means buying a burglar alarm or sharing the fee for a doorman or security guard. Even if someone penetrates those superior defenses, money can insulate people of means from many of the consequences of crime. Such people usually have insurance – medical, homeowner's or renter's, disability – in addition to being better able to bear any out-of-pocket losses in the first place. If necessary, most can also afford extra services, ranging from psychological counseling to household help, to ease the impact of any injury or emotional trauma.

This should not be misconstrued as an attack on the privileges enjoyed by those who have worked their way to the top. The capitalist system depends on providing incentives for embracing the hard-work ethic. Our values are based on the ideal of providing equal opportunity for all, with rewards for individual effort. Those who contribute most to society are entitled to enjoy a better standard of living.

Yet we also believe that government should temper the tendency of our system to allow money and power to concentrate over time into the hands of a few. We accept that those who benefit most from our system should pay a greater share of what it takes to maintain a decent standard of living and social safety nets for everyone. The progressive income tax is one tool that we use to transfer wealth from those at the top to those at the bottom who need a helping hand.

Public Police Funding

There is a significant difference, however, in how our system collects and uses resources depending on whether the perceived threat to our stability comes from the outside or the inside. We look to the federal government to fund national security, to protect us from external threats, such as repelling an attack or invasion from a foreign country or terrorists. We recognize the need to protect everyone equally, no matter whether the person lives in Maryland or Montana, Boise or Boston. We also understand that anything other than a unified federal response would be too risky. Allowing different areas to develop their own defenses would not only be foolish, but it would invite duplication, lack of coordination, and other abuses that would make the overall system dangerously unreliable.

Our response to internal threats is based on a different model, one that relies on a changing mix of federal, state, and local dollars to fund efforts to provide and promote domestic security. The United States was founded by people who worried about the potential tyranny of a strong centralized government, which explains why we so strongly embrace states' rights and local control. To meet internal threats, for example those posed by ignorance, crime, and disease, we blend federal dollars with state and local tax dollars, so that voters close at hand can exert greater control in tailoring the educational, law enforcement, and public health programs to fit local conditions.

In the case of the police in particular, fear of government repression resulted in a system where we greatly restrict the scope of our federally funded police forces, the FBI and now the DEA. We instead rely on state, county, and especially city and township police departments for the bulk of our public policing. The amount of federal government help in funding those efforts swings with the political pendulum, though not always in completely predictable ways.

The common wisdom is that the police fare better in a politically conservative administration, because liberals favor social work alternatives. Republican President Richard Nixon won election on a platform that proposed a War on Crime almost as an antidote to the liberals' War on Poverty. Yet a dozen years later, an even more conservative Republican, Ronald Reagan, won election to the presidency by placing an even higher priority on reducing the size and scope of the federal government. This resulted in more money for defense, with less to state and local government. Even

Reagan's War on Drugs did not boost federal funding for state and local police departments to the levels of the LEAA days discussed in Chapter 6. President George Bush, who inherited a massive federal deficit, announced a $1.2 federal anti-crime initiative in the early summer of 1989, and it followed in the Reagan tradition by not providing any funds for state and local efforts (and no funding for criminal justice research).[2]

The new political reality is that state and local public police cannot expect any massive new infusion of federal dollars, regardless of whether the administration is conservative or liberal. This is bad news for police departments who suffered cuts when federal LEAA funding disappeared and then saw their budgets slashed further when the recession of the 1970s caused local tax revenues to plummet. Increasing reliance on scarce local tax dollars, without the equalizing influence of federal funds to help depressed areas, has already contributed to an obvious gap between the level of police services available to decaying major cities and the wealthy suburbs that surround them.

Complicating the problem further, many cities face continued erosion of their tax base. To compete for new industries, many communities promise to grant tax abatements that stretch far into the future. Even the community that wins the nod often finds the new enterprise does not generate as many jobs as initially promised. Oftentimes as well, the highest-paid jobs are held by those who choose to live and spend their dollars in the surrounding suburbs. Society as a whole is also undergoing a wrenching economic dislocation, as high-paid jobs in industry disappear, and most of the new jobs created tend to be in the lower-paying service sector.

Not only policing but many other government services that must depend more and more on local funding as their primary means of support find it virtually impossible to maintain equitable levels of service in the inner city. In public education, for example, we see dilapidated and overcrowded city schools, with their outdated textbooks, standing in stark contrast to neighboring suburban districts where elementary students often have the chance to work with computers. The further irony is that middle- and upper-class students come from families who are better able to afford private help, such as tutoring and after-school classes and enrichment activities, to make up for any deficits in the public system. If we see entry into the work world as clearing the bar in the high jump, we have a system where the bar is often placed higher for those with the poorest coaching and training, yet we tend to blame those who fail for not trying hard enough.

The consequences of this growing disparity continue to add to the overall police burden, as despair contributes to the creation of a permanent Underclass. All public police have budget problems, but the danger is that the funding in many of this country's biggest cities may simply be inadequate to the task at hand. Many inner-city neighborhoods today have become the dumping ground for the elderly, the poor, the disabled, beleaguered minorities, ex-offenders, those on the public dole or unemployment, the mentally ill, individuals with alcohol and drug problems, and those without the education or skills to cope with today's work world, let alone tomorrow's. As the gap between rich and poor continues to grow wider, this often means the police departments that face the most staggering increases in violent, property, and drug-related crime are often those areas that are faced with the grim prospect of a dwindling tax base.

All too often as well, big-city police departments are not seen as the victims in the drama, but as part of the problem. Since the reform movement of the 1930s, the police have billed themselves first and foremost as crime-fighters. Against that narrow yardstick, many urban departments have failed – badly. Even people who would never risk venturing into the inner-city at night see the nightmare images on the nightly news. Teenage runaways who survive by selling their bodies or selling drugs on filthy, litter-strewn sidewalks. Merciless, angry, young, gun-toting gang members cruise by scanning their turf for signs of their enemies. Abandoned cars, drunks and junkies huddled in doorways, mainstreamed mental patients muttering to themselves, bag ladies scrounging in garbage cans for food. While that vision relates as much to decay as to actual crime, the taxpayers who pay for police protection and who are therefore the *consumers* of police service see this as proof the police have failed.

The general public understands that the police can do little to alleviate the underlying economic problems that spawn crime and decay. Many also realize the police are only one element in an embattled criminal justice system. Yet explaining to someone who has been mugged that the lack of jail and prison space means the attacker will soon be back on the street only adds to the perception that the system is careening dangerously out of control.

Faced with this reality, those who can afford to do so often cope with their fear of crime by paying the private and hidden tax for increased personal security. That tax is part of the cost of moving to the suburbs or renting an apartment with a doorman and video cameras in the lobby. It is part of the price paid for burglar alarms, bars for the windows, and guns. Many willingly accept the further trade-off in safety implicit in the fact that barred windows can cost lives in a fire and guns can discharge accidentally. There is also a hidden tax included in the price tag of goods sold at the upscale shopping malls, where the cost for all those security guards must be passed on to the consumer.

While it is easy to mount a convincing argument that it might prove cheaper – or at least fairer – to invest those hidden private tax dollars in public efforts, we have yet to generate the political will necessary to devise a palatable way to even out the glaring inequities in the levels of local government services place to place. City officials look longingly at the property tax base in the suburbs that encircle them, but without much hope that they can ever persuade people there to share. Most city officials have simply given up looking to Washington.

Policing for a Profit

In this troubled atmosphere, when many people appear to believe that government cannot handle any job well and that private enterprise would at least be a cheaper alternative, the future portrayed in the movie *Robocop* may prove prophetic. In that film, the city of Detroit contracted with a private corporation to provide city police service. Experiments with for-profit prisons demonstrate that private enterprise is willing to expand its range of services to fill new opportunities. In California, well-heeled litigants in civil cases who want speedier justice than the public system provides can now hire a private "rent-a-judge-and-jury" company to render a legally binding decision, by splitting the $15,000 a week fee.[3]

Those who say this cannot happen to public policing ignore how atractive such an option might seem to city officials eager to find a way to break their expensive police union contracts. We need only look to the recent case where unionized air traffic controllers found to their surprise that they could be so easily ousted from their jobs.

If the idea of privatizing the public police still sounds farfetched, remember that many departments have already abdicated part of their traditional role to the private sector. It remains an anomaly that public police officers routinely patrol downtown shopping districts, but fewer provide service at suburban shopping malls. On the one hand, it made good sense for local police agencies already strained to meet existing needs to argue that mall managers should pay for private security to handle their needs. In retrospect, however, that decision may be short-sighted because of the precedent it sets. It is worth noting that discussions about privatizing the U.S. Postal Service have increased now that private enterprises such as United Parcel Service and Federal Express have demonstrated that they can provide reliable and affordable service in the niches left open to them.

We see further signs of a two-track system, with private policing for those who can afford it and others totally reliant on the public system, in New York City's efforts to cope with crack. A 1989 article in *New York* magazine told how Community Policing helped residents in a Harlem housing project drive dealers out of the building, while residents of North Slope instead chipped in to pay $600 a week for a private patrol car to cruise the area eight hours each night.[4]

What may ultimately save public policing is the fact that many private security companies cost less simply because of the opportunity to piggyback on tax-supported public policing. Many private firms rely on moonlighting police officers, who are often educated and trained at taxpayer expense. Those officers are also more willing to work for lower wages in these part-time jobs, because they count on their full-time jobs as police officers to provide them their basic income and benefits. In some communities, off-duty officers can use their patrol cars for personal travel, because the department hopes this will increase overall police visibility. Some can wear police uniforms when they work for private firms. In essence, this allows private companies to merchandise the credibility of the public police as part of the package they offer their customers.

Many private firms can also cut costs because they are not held to the same standards as the public police. Many areas have no ordinances requiring specific levels of education or training for private police. Many communities do not regulate the levels of bonding and liability insurance such firms must carry. If someone is injured because of negligence on the part of a private security guard, the company can choose to go bankrupt, leaving the injured person with no recourse to collect damages. In comparison, many public police today face staggering increases in their liability insurance premiums, which has forced some cities to self-insure, putting local taxpayers at future risk.

Yet perhaps the biggest threat posed by encroachment of private security is the resulting loss of community control and accountability. Private enterprise, by definition, must put the needs of its stockholders first. The automatic loss of community control inherent in a private, for-profit police force poses a very real threat to our democratic civil rights. Who would set the police agenda? What guarantees would people have that their civil liberties would not be threatened?

Even today's common practice of hiring off-duty police officers as private security officers raises troubling ethical questions, including potential conflict of interest. Should an off-duty officer on private duty respond if he sees a crime in progress or some other emergency nearby, even if it means losing the job? Would failure to do so be immoral, unethical, illegal – or understandable?

What if an off-duty officer hired as a private security officer is asked to "hassle" particular groups – such as minorities, homosexuals, or the homeless – because the business owner views their presence as bad for business? If the officer accedes to the order, is he endangering the department's credibility? What if that off-duty officer works where alcohol is served and he is asked to look the other way when a rich patron staggers drunkenly to his car?

Does moonlighting contribute to burnout, so that taxpayers receive less of a return on their investment? Do police departments who allow off-duty officers to wear their uniforms on private jobs inadvertently risk being named co-defendants in future lawsuits?

Of concern as well is that people often make little distinction between public and private police, especially when many private officers are recognizably off-duty officers. Yet there is no formal mechanism for the public and private police to share valuable information (though it might prove logical to add this to the CPO's job). A private security guard patrolling the mall may well learn things the police department should know.

Because many of the economies currently enjoyed by private security companies would disappear if there were no public police system on which those savings depend, it may be that instead of replacing public policing, private efforts will simply continue to expand piecemeal into any niches that prove profitable. Public policing in many areas may be saved because few private firms would even consider tackling the entire job. Yet the threat is there, if not of total extinction, of a potential chipping away at the breadth and depth of service the public police currently provide.

Satisfied Customers

The healthiest response that the public police can make is to learn how to compete. Too many traditional police administrators fail to understand the importance of pleasing the consumer. Just because the public police depend on tax dollars and not discretionary dollars does not mean they ignore what their *customers* want and need. Increasing isolation from the community can mean that departments ignore valid community concerns. Police administrators start believing that they have the best answers to every problem, without realizing that if they persist in ignoring those they serve, they do so at their ultimate peril.

As the research shows, Community Policing is popular with taxpayers and voters. Some police officials continue to dismiss the importance of this popularity, with the argument that Community Policing wins friends by pandering to the public. Many traditionalists think Community Policing mollifies people by paying attention to their petty concerns. They often think average people are naive about how the system should work and that police resources would be better spent on efforts to deal directly with serious crime.

The story of how Community Policing went private in Flint after the foot patrol program ended tends to refute that argument. In one section of Flint, two large housing projects have long had serious crime problems. Many of the residents are poor, black, single mothers on public assistance. When the Flint foot patrol program was cancelled, the managers of both complexes initially hired private security companies to fill the gap, but they were not happy with perfunctory service provided. So the managers approached former foot patrol officers about hiring them for part time, after-hours' duty, to keep the spirit of Community Policing alive. Though the level of service provided did not equal what it had been when it was part of the overall public police initiative, it was still far better than what private security firms had offered.

It is important to understand that the out-of-state firms that owned the complexes received most rent checks directly from state or federal agencies, which meant that they had little reason to fund privatized foot patrol simply to keep their tenants happy - the owners received their rent whether the people were pleased with the service or not, and most tenants had few housing alternatives. Instead this proves that they invested in the service because it works.

The police should heed that message before frustrated taxpayers shift even more to *shopping* for police services in the private sector because it will try to listen to their needs. The police should also realize the potential loss of vital information that could be shared with the rest of the department when public efforts go private.

Yet this story also serves as a cautionary tale for taxpayers, who should be told what was lost when those foot patrol officers shifted from public to private duty. One casualty was the emphasis on developing creative, new, community-based strategies. The private job no longer stressed the role of community ombudsman, where the officer would link people to public and private agencies that could help. Another shift was that the managers had the ultimate power to set the agenda and veto new ideas.

Yet perhaps the most important difference was that the officers were not there as full-fledged law enforcement officers, though because they were off-duty officers, the information they gleaned could still be carried back to the department informally. This was especially beneficial because the area suffered major problems with drugs, so the officers involved could share valuable information with the department. But considering all that was lost, the fact that everyone involved – the officers, the residents, the managers, and the owners – still deemed private foot patrol a success testifies to Community Policing's contribution even when its potential impact has been watered down.

This incident also demonstrates that Community Policing could prove to be an important key to public policing's future health – and even its survival. Unlike other well-meaning social-action programs, Community Policing does not foster dependence, but instead it challenges people to assume greater responsibility for policing themselves. By allowing the police to share power and responsibility with people in the community, it helps break down isolation and alienation. It also provides people who do not currently pay taxes a way to make a valid contribution, through their cooperation, support, and participation. It moves beyond a narrow focus on crime, toward efforts to improve the overall quality of life in communities.

Threats to Community Policing

Because Community Policing is such a dramatic departure from the past, it faces a host of internal and external threats to its existence beyond what any other new police programs must contend with. Any change, even one obviously for the better, always inspires some resistance, at least initially. As touched on in the last chapter, the obstacles to the adoption of Community Policing go beyond the typical reluctance to embrace new ideas. What makes Community Policing so threatening is that it is not just a new strategy or technique, but a radical new approach to the business of policing, one that implies a reversal of winners and losers under the current system.

Community Policing challenges long-standing, fundamental assumptions about the business of policing. The Community Policing philosophy, grounded in a defined set of values that serve as its ethical and moral foundation, changes both the nature of the task, and it shifts responsibility for achieiving the desired means and ends. The assumptions upon which the Community Policing philosophy rests are a dramatic departure from the past, and they pose a threat to the values and beliefs that the traditional system embraces.

Concerning the community, Community Policing says:

- People – and not the police – have the ultimate power to control crime, enhance their own safety, and help improve the overall quality of life in the community.

- All people deserve a say in how they are policed, regardless of whether they vote or pay taxes.

- People are a vital police resource. To do their job, the police must have access to the information that people have about criminal activity in their communities. To encourage their cooperation, the police must educate them that they are no longer the passive recipients of police service, but important partners in the policing process. In exchange for allowing them input into the police agenda, community residents must provide active support and participation in community-based efforts to improve the overall quality of life in the community.

- People in the community become important arbiters in determining the relative success or failure of local initiatives, and they have a new role to play in helping supervise and assess the performance of the CPOs assigned to their neighborhoods.

Concerning the police role, Community Policing says:

- The police, as the only social agency open around-the-clock every day of the year, are the most logical, most powerful, and most respected candidates for the job of harnessing and directing people's efforts in addressing crime, fear of crime, social and physical disorder, and neighborhood decay.

- Police administrators must actively demonstrate their commitment to this new philosophy, by delegating some of their power and control to the community.

- Middle managers must shift to emphasizing trust as much as accountability, allowing all officers within the department the freedom and autonomy to move beyond responding to calls as isolated incidents. The system must treat police officers as true professionals, who bring unique judgment and expertise to the challenge of solving problems in the community. The system must also accept the inevitability of mistakes as the price of taking innovative and creative action.

- Motor patrol officers must be educated to think of themselves as community problem-solvers, not just as crime-fighters. Within the limits imposed by their role, they must move beyond responding to calls as isolated incidents, to identifying and altering the underlying dynamics that create the social and physical environment that allowed the problem to occur.

- Motor patrol officers must also understand the importance of cooperating and coordinating with CPOs, so that they can work together on proactive efforts designed to enhance both the safety and quality of life in the community.

- As the department's outreach specialists, CPOs establish the rapport that allows people to trust the police, so that they can work together on solving community problems together in new ways. CPOs continue to serve as full-fledged law enforcement officers, but their expanded role includes initiating short- and long-term proactive efforts aimed at crime, fear of crime, social and physical disorder, and neighborhood decay. They also enlist people's support and participation, both individually and collectively, in a broad range of proactive efforts. CPOs also monitor new community-based initiatives, to channel the impulse to vigilantism into lawful action, and they serve as the community's ombudsman and link to public and private agencies that can help.

- Police unions must change to accommodate the increasing professionalization of the police role. They must become active partners in the process of enhancing the flexibility that officers need to become community problem-solvers.

These issues are important in assessing Community Policing's future, because they help clarify where resistance is likely to come from and why. The first major obstacle Community Policing faces in making the transition to becoming the prevailing way that police provide service to the community is generating acceptance inside and outside policing. The second major obstacle is proving that the new approach is affordable within current budget constraints.

As we learned as well in the last chapter, the overall resistance to Community Policing both inside and outside police circles falls into six basic categories:

- Community Policing conflicts with the values and beliefs inherent in the existing system.

- Community Policing threatens those who currently exercise power and control.

- This also means Community Policing empowers other groups that previously had less power and control.

- Community Policing implies new risks, particularly embarrassing mistakes.

- Community Policing requires changes in the way that police resources are spent.

- Community Policing can inspire new jealousies.

Recapitulating what we learned in the last chapter, Community Policing implies a new relationship between the police and the community, with new winners and losers. We often talk about *the community,* as if it were a monolithic whole, yet as we learned in the chapter on the meaning of community in Community Policing, community means different things in different contexts. When we talk about the entire area that a police department serves, the unit of government to which the department must answer and upon which it depends for funding constitutes the political community whose support is essential for any new idea.

Community Policing implies a reduction in the power and control of local officials and the rich and powerful in the community – the beneficiaries of the existing system. Conversely, this also means increased empowerment of those groups that currently have less access and clout. Community Policing can also inspire jealousy among political leaders who find their constituents turn to CPOs for the kinds of help they previously sought from them, the kind of assistance that helps solidify political power. Adding to the bad news, the new shift allows for the increased possibility of embarrassing mistakes that could reflect badly on the power structure.

Overall as well, Community Policing implies changes in the kinds of services the department currently provides. A shift to Community Policing could mean that political leaders no longer have as much police protection as before. Powerful business interests may suffer a cut in the level of service that they had enjoyed. Non-emergency calls no longer demand the fastest possible response.

Within police departments, Community Policing redefines power, control, and accountability, allowing those at the base of the pyramid more autonomy and freedom to act independently in achieving the new goal of becoming community problem-solvers. Through its CPOs, the department also allows new community groups direct input into the police process, broadening the base of community involvement.

It has taken a decade for the glimmerings of what has come to be called Community Policing to overcome the internal and external resistance to its mission and structure in enough areas so that it is no longer just a promising experiment, but a widespread trend. As it continues to demonstrate its unique contribution, Community Policing no longer inspires as much resistance as in the past. In the early days, delivering a talk about what Community Policing offers to a group of police professionals meant girding for the inevitable hostile questions. Now it has become an established part of the dialogue about how the police can confront contemporary challenges.

The primary hurdle it must now cross is proving that it can be implemented without massive new infusions of funding. Many police executives who are receptive to the approach still balk at what they believe is its excessively high cost – or use that as an excuse to ignore the pressures to make the change. Though there are departments that may well need some additional funds to launch as many CPOs as they want and need, there are also many that can field enough new CPOs with no budget increase. To understand why the Community Policing approach has been tagged as costly again requires looking back at its roots.

Finding the Funding

The philosophical shift to Community Policing is free, but where departments balk is in making the structural changes that are required. Much of the perception of Community Policing as an expensive add-on, rather than as a department-wide reorganization, stems from those early experimental days, when research funds were used to put officers into the community to see what they could do. For example, the Mott Foundation provided the Flint Police Department an additional $2.6 million over three years to put 22 new officers into base stations in the community. Critics have long argued that putting hundreds of thousands of extra dollars into a department's coffers each year would undeniably make a positive impact.

The difficulty in Flint, as detailed in Chapter 7, is that the department faced a watershed decision concerning what to do when the funding ran out. The problem was complicated by the fact that the overall number of officers in the department never really rose. Though safeguards had been written in to prevent the additional funding from being offset by cuts in the regular funding, the economic crisis in Flint meant that this was, in essence, what happened. In that sense, Flint is misleading because, for the most part, the new venture was arguably funded without any real budget increase.

Yet faced with the loss of that money, the decision was made to ask the voters whether their support for foot patrol would translate into a willingness to pay for the effort. And despite the fact that the commitment to providing the authentic version that the community enjoyed during those early years has never been completely realized, voters there have still been willing on all three occasions when they have had the chance to do so to assess themselves the additional millage required to underwrite what has now come to be called Community Policing.

The lesson to be learned from that experience, according to Bruce Benson, who was a lieutenant involved in the foot patrol program, is that providing a separate pot of money to fund CPOs is a mistake. The inadvertent result is that those funds become a target whenever government officials look for a way to balance the books. In this era especially, it is dangerous for CPOs to have their future tied to a separate line item in the budget, when even previously sacrosanct resources such as pension funds are being eyed as a way to ease the current crunch.

George Kelling concurs that once you accept that Community Policing involves making a permanent, department-wide shift toward providing expanded police services in a new way, the question then is not one of funding but of managing resources. This recognizes that CPOs are a priority, as integral to the functioning of a modern police department as the job of motor patrol officer – or even chief. The question then becomes how to make the most of the existing resources to do the best job.

Obviously, this might still mean the department would look first at motor patrol, to assess whether current staffing levels will allow police managers to redeploy some motor patrol officers as CPOs. As noted before, the traditional system tends to overemphasize efficiency measures, such as speed of response, and undervalue effectiveness – what the officers accomplish once they arrive. Community Policing restores needed balance, by recognizing that resources should be deployed in a way that assures people the police can arrive as swiftly as possible, when the situation warrants, but that doing the same for non-emergency calls wastes precious resources.

As the research suggests, what often matters most to people to being told clearly how long it will be before an officer arrives – and why. A dispatcher who clearly explains the benefits they enjoy as a result of trade-off inherent in accepting a relatively minor delay in the response to non-emergency calls, most willingly accept the rationale.

To be able to thin the ranks of motor patrol even more, some departments look at the current services that the officers provide, to see if some can be trimmed. In some cases, the department first surveys citizens, asking them to help in prioritizing services.

Such a study often persuades departments to stop sending motor patrol officers to help people locked out of their homes or cars, instead referring them to locksmiths or towing companies that can help. Handled properly, this can provide what academics call a *teaching opportunity.* When someone pays $15 to $50 to a private company to handle a task previously done for *free* by the police, it helps people understand what economist Milton Friedman meant when he said there was no such thing as a free lunch. In this case, it helps people, particularly taxpayers, understand the hidden costs involved in policing, which can both make them appreciate the *free* services they receive and the payoff in taxing themselves to pay more if they want more.

Comparing the relative costs of CPOs and motor patrol officers is not as easy as it might seem at first. If the CPO walks the beat, there is no expense for a patrol car, with its attendant costs for maintenance, repair, and insurance, but in some cases, this is partially offset if the CPO uses a scooter, horse, bicycle, or other mode of transport. If the department must rent office space for the CPO in the community and furnish the space, this can also mean an additional expense. To cut those costs, many departments have secured low-cost or even free space for CPOs in schools, public recreation centers, or other facilities where space has been donated by the community. Many departments have also required new CPOs to furnish the office with donated items secured from businesses and people in the community, which also has the virtue of making the CPO move quickly to establish community ties.

CPOs also operate alone, while many departments put two motor patrol officers together in at least some patrol cars. In most cases as well, CPOs cover, at most, two shifts, while motor patrol must cover three. Because a CPO is not the beat cop of old, it rarely, if ever, makes sense to have them work the graveyard shift overnight, since what distinguishes the CPO's job is becoming deeply involved with the people in the community, not rattling doorknobs and looking for crimes in progress.

But what if a department analyzes its motor patrol deployment and finds that maintaining a speedy response for emergencies means that not enough officers can be retreaded as CPOs to fill the need? Obviously, prudent managers also have the option to reduce or eliminate efforts that duplicate what CPOs do. This is why many departments have reduced or completely eliminated positions in Crime Prevention and Police/Community Relations, since CPOs usually provide the same police services, but as part of being full-fledged law enforcement officers in the community.

Going even further, departments can reassess everything they do through the different priorities inherent in shifting from crime-fighting to community problem-solving. In essence, this means applying a problem-solving approach to the budget process, borrowing the concept of *zero-based budgeting* from business. Viewed in this way, resource management means more than tinkering with the existing budget. It says that each function of the department must be reassessed as if the department was being started from scratch, to see whether current efforts are justified at all or in part. This can mean taking a new look at the police service provided to protect politicians. In some communities, it means assessing fees for services that might have been free before, such as using the police to lead and follow runners in corporate-sponsored road races or using the police as escorts for visiting celebrities on tour. Some departments are even rethinking budgets for narcotics and undercover officers, to see whether Community Policing's contribution allows some shift.

Innovative Funding Solutions

The restructuring that has taken place over time in the North Miami Beach Police Department deserves special attention because it did not just look at services within the department. A major change there involved moving city code enforcement personnel into the police department and using CPOs to make the initial on-site calls. This recognizes that when someone is upset about an abandoned car, a dilapidated building, or an unmowed lawn, many of those people first call the police anyhow. Since making the shift to Community Policing, the department also has a greater role to play in solving these problems.

CPOs now sweep their beat areas at least once a month looking for violations, since the North Miami Beach Community Policing effort recognizes the best time to deal with neighborhood decay is before it starts. The CPOs work with the enforcement personnel on referring calls and monitoring progress. Technical calls involving plumbing and wiring are still referred to the building officers located in City Hall. As noted before, it also means the department is exploring the possibility that code violations can provide the police another tool that they can use to close dope houses. And in terms of budgeting, it also means that municipalities may be able to solve budget problems by taking a new look at how to structure services in ways that not only make better sense but that improve overall effectiveness in ways that could cost less.

North Miami Beach has also taken the bold step of making the entire property crime investigation function part of the CPOs role. A study of the department's existing structure showed that officers were bidding to become CPOs but not detectives, even though detectives were paid more. "We haven't done any actual research," said Lt. Robert Horowitz, "but I would say that our detectives spend 80% to 90% of their time behind a desk, making phone calls and handling paperwork."[5] Highly motivated officers, eager to make an impact, apparently found being a CPO was a more attractive option, despite the lower pay.

Making property crime investigation part of the CPO's duties meant shifting from a system where a few detectives handled such duties fulltime, to one where all CPOs spend roughly two hours a day on this assignment. Reportedly, the two detectives who became CPOs were delighted with this change, but the existing CPOs were less than thrilled to find they are now deskbound for one-quarter of their workday. "But that's the grim reality when resources are tight," said Horowitz.[6]

The success of this restructuring raises the possibility that all criminal investigations could be made part of the CPO's job, thereby eliminating the detective rank. This raises questions about whether CPOs should therefore be awarded higher pay, as the department's outreach specialists, and there are arguments both pro and con. Those who favor higher pay say the job of being a CPO is uniquely demanding, since these officers serve as the department's community outreach specialists, and they deserve higher pay reflecting their status, especially if crime investigation is part of their job description. The downside is that this might further increase the friction between CPOs and motor patrol officers.

Pay was the main issue that made it difficult to make property crime investigation part of the CPO's job in North Miami Beach, but the Police Benevolent Association gave its approval, demonstrating its continued willingness to accommodate the flexibility required by a Community Policing approach. When the department first launched its CPO program, the union contract required giving all officers two-weeks' notice before their hours were changed. But the union agreed to allow CPOs to waive this right voluntarily, since doing the job well often demands being able to shift work schedules quickly as situations change.

George Kelling also says that management should not be exempt from the re-evaluation process. Perhaps police departments should take yet another lesson from business, since many U.S. companies have learned that, to stay competitive, they must be run *lean and mean,* which means trimming back the number of executives. The oft-cited example against which other organizations are compared is the Catholic Church, which effectively manages a worldwide organization with only three layers of management, while many businesses – and police departments – insist they require four, five, or more. Kelling envisions a future where universities act as the departments *R&D Division* (Research and Development), so that they can continue to become more and more effective community problem-solvers.

Yet if a police department finds that it simply cannot do a good job with existing resources, Bruce Benson says that department should not hesitate to ask voters for more tax revenue. Contrary to the popular wisdom that taxpayers will refuse all pleas for help, Benson says that he has been encouraged to find many communities are willing to pay more for improved police service, especially as they become more aware of the burden imposed by drugs. Again, however, he cautions against tying any millage proposal to a specific service, because of the danger this will tempt government officials to offset the gain by cutting other elements in the overall police budget.

As these suggestions attest, the bottom line in police budgeting proves the adage that where there is a will, there is a way. The movement has outgrown the pilot project stage, where extra funds were needed to pay for experiments. As Community Policing gains acceptance as being a better way for departments to deliver police service to their areas, the question is no longer whether departments can afford to make the switch, but how best to make the change. Each day, more departments are understanding that they cannot afford not to make the change.

Today's Efforts Foretell the Future

The question now becomes what Community Policing will look like in the future, what forms it will take as it becomes the mainstream tradition. For clues, we can look to places such as Alexandria, Virginia, where Chief Gary Leonard says that he hopes it provides his department the help they need in combatting the escalating drug problems their community faces. We can also look to the Michigan State University campus, where Bruce Benson is exploring how the approach can be tailored to meet the needs of the college students who live on campus, as well as the faculty and staff who work there. Then there's the unique situation that Chief Alex Longoria faces in the Texas border town of McAllen, less than 10 miles from the Mexican border.

At the cutting edge as well is the Aurora (Colorado) Police Department, where Chief Gerry Williams is investigating new ways to break down the barriers between motor patrol officers and CPOs (which his department calls Police Area Representatives, or PARs). The department has proposed assigning six officers to each beat – five motor patrol officers and one PAR – so that the officers can trade off PAR duty as needed. This new configuration is designed to encourage the officers to coalesce into a permanent team that works together to solve community problems, sharing information and ideas among all officers, regardless of assignment or shift. The goal is to encourage *all* the officers involved to feel that they *own* their specific beat areas.

It is too early to tell how well this effort will fare, though a formal evaluation is in progress. Both Williams and Benson say they hope that using CPOs as part of a team approach will reduce internal tensions among line officers. Both also say they intend to provide strong leadership from the top in the hope they can prevent motor patrol officers from dumping unwanted or tedious duties on their community outreach specialists, because bogging them down will reduce their effectiveness.

Though research is in progress, Aurora can already point to successes that would not have been achieved in a traditional approach. In one instance, a local teen club was plagued by a rash of thefts from cars in the parking lot. Instead of just taking reports and focusing on finding the culprits, the Aurora team identified that the problem was that the young women who patronized the club did not want to fuss with their purses when they danced, so they would lock them inside their cars. Once word got around that this was common practice, predators began to poach on the easy pickings.

Instead of just responding to calls, taking reports, and attempting to find the culprits, the Aurora team assigned to the area looked for other ways to solve the problem. Warn the female patrons through signs or handbills? Find some way to guard the parking lot? The bold stroke that worked was to persuade the owner to install lockers in the club, so that everyone could store their purses and other valuables safely. And it was not hard persuading the club owner to make the investment, because the bad publicity from the thefts threatened his business.

As police departments like Aurora, Alexandria, and McAllen not only make the shift to Community Policing, but also embrace a vigorous research component to identify what works and what does not, Community Policing will continue to evolve and mature based on solid research. These departments at the cutting edge will be able to share what they learn, including how to make the Community Policing philosophy part of the selection and training of officers, their performance evaluations on the job, and their promotional exams. The police departments in Grand Rapids and Lansing that plan to implement their new Community Policing plan by the dawn of the new decade will also provide models for others, because the research evaluations that are built in as part of the process will help other departments that come after them.

An Ambitious Proposal

Progress relies on finding ways to see adversity as opportunity, to move from talking about problems to discussing new ways to meet challenges. Just as creativity is the hallmark of Community Policing in action, a discussion of the future of the public police role demands setting forth a bold new vision. Meeting the challenge of the 21st century requires envisioning where we want to go, so that we can begin to develop the will to get there.

Today, we see a society where rural and suburban areas have crime problems that must be addressed, but they pale compared to the crime and violence exploding in areas of many of our major cities. A recent book about the Detroit riot of 1968 notes that the level of violence there is actually higher today – that we now have a neverending "riot in slow motion." Detroit is far from unique, and we begin to see unfortunate signs that the crime, violence, and drug trafficking that we have too long ignored is contagious. Drug traffickers from Detroit have been linked to a spate of recent murders in other Michigan cities, because, like McDonald's, they are franchising in the hope of earning even more.

While there is undeniable truth in the contention that not all problems can be solved by money, these massive problems certainly cannot be solved without it. The federal government appears either unable or unwilling to help. The cities with the biggest problems are often those with a declining tax base. That leaves state government as the only possible source of support, but what is required is to find an innovative way to generate additional funds in ways that taxpayers will accept.

Since dreams are free, it costs nothing to propose an ambitious new model of how Community Policing could evolve in the future – and how the money could be raised to turn the vision into reality. About funding, the logical solution borrows from a novel approach various states have used to address specific needs – a check-off to create a special trust fund.

In Michigan, for instance, growing concern about the heartbreaking problem of child abuse and neglect led to enabling legislation in 1982 that created the Children's Trust Fund. It allows people entitled to a refund on their state income tax to donate $5 or more, simply by checking the appropriate box on their state income tax forms. (This is quite different from the check-off on federal income tax forms that allows people to contribute to presidential campaigns, because that check-off simply earmarks part of the revenues that are already being collected for a specific use.)

In 1987, the Children's Trust Fund check-off generated $927,000. The laws require that half stays in the fund, where the money earns interest. The other half, along with the interest from the previous year, additional donations, and money from special fundraisers, is then disbursed by a 15-member commission. The commission is made up of 10 members appointed by the governor and confirmed by the state senate and five representatives from the Michigan Departments of Social Services, Public Health, Mental Health, Education, and the State Police. Grants are made to local programs targeted at preventing child abuse and neglect.

Once the fund reaches $20 million, the check-off will end, since sufficient grants can then be made solely from the annual interest generated. Though the Children's Trust Fund has a long way to go before reaching this point, its success has now spawned a similar initiative, the Non-Game Wildlife Fund that raised $500,300 in 1987.[8]

If people in Michigan will contribute half a million dollars annually to protect songbirds in the wild, why not use this kind of approach to ask them for funds that might help with crime problems in Detroit? Wouldn't people prove even more willing to fund efforts that might help reduce statistics like the 54 young people 16 years old or younger who were shot to death there in 1988?[9] Have we truly become so inured to crime and violence that we worry more about protecting wildlife than people?

Establishing a new Police/Community Trust Fund or attempting a statewide bonding issue would allow people from all across any state a direct opportunity to provide the seed money for Community Policing initiatives in areas with the greatest need. It would allow a commission to make grants directly to community-based, CPO-supervised, proactive initiatives, bypassing the bureaucracy and thereby eliminating red tape. In one area, this might allow CPOs to invest in video equipment to allow kids to make their own anti-drug programming that could be aired at area schools. In another, it could provide funds to pay volunteers, perhaps particularly the elderly, to provide in-home assistance to teenage mothers raising babies alone. It could mean a small grant to pay for rototilling a vacant lot and buying seeds and plants to establish a community vegetable garden. Perhaps it would allow a department to fund a school bus to take seniors and juveniles on worthwhile excursions.

New Community Policing initiatives in various areas have demonstrated tremendous fund-raising ability. CPOs have become master marketers, persuading area busi-nesses and organizations to pitch in time, money, and supplies. The approach's abil-ity to make each dollar stretch as far as it can demonstrates how even relatively modest amounts of additional funding could be used to make a tremendous differ-ence in reversing downward trends.

But why would suburban and out-of-state residents agree to donate money or tax themselves to help urban areas? As a caring society, many people would at least feel a moral obligation to help. Others could be persuaded by appeals to their sense of fair play. After all, many suburbs that are now relatively self-sufficient would not exist at all, if it had not been for the cities that spawned them. And the ripple effect of the dollars generated by our once-proud cities no doubt benefited the entire state economy. Maybe people could be enticed into giving as a way to pay an old friend back for past favors.

If moral arguments are not enough, we need to explain that contributing would also be in each person's enlightened self-interest. We spend billions defending our-selves from foreign invaders, yet the biggest threat to our security may be collapse from within. Unless we meet the challenge posed by the violence and crime in our inner cities, we face spreading decay. Donating the price of a movie ticket – or taxing ourselves the cost of taking the family to dinner at a fast-food restaurant – might at least allow new Community Policing efforts the chance to slow or stem the flood of drugs and violence beginning to overflow our cities' borders.

Community Resource Centers

A vision of tomorrow could also include viewing CPOs as the vanguard that would stabilize our cities, so that a host of other professionals would feel safe enough to follow. Neighborhood Community Policing Centers could then grow into Com-munity Resource Centers, as new social services sent representatives to reach people where they live. Depending on local needs, it might make sense to move parole officers into the center, so that they could work together, share information, and share staffing the local office. The next step might be to employ drug counselors, who could work with the CPOs and the area parole officer to coordinate workable proactive outreach efforts.

Just by allowing those three new outreach professionals to work together as a community team would allow them to be far more effective together than they hope to be individually. Operating out of such a center, the drug counselor could work with the parole officer to field a roster of former drug offenders who will work the CPO on making presentations to kids at risk, warning them of the potential consequences they face and reminding them of the power they have in making positive choices. Unlike the *Scared Straight* approach of dubious value, where the goal is to frighten kids away from bad behavior, such an effort could encourage both ex-cons and kids at risk to work together on helping each other stay drug-free.

The center would also allow CPOs and parole officers to share information about ex-offenders in the neighborhood, so that they can help each other keep tabs on these individuals. Being in the same facility would give them a chance to work together on helping people on parole readjust and get their lives back together so that they do not fall back on bad habits. This might involve working with area businesses to find jobs, or enlisting the help of adult education teachers to help them sharpen their job skills. The center might provide a home for a volunteer-supported literacy effort.

Then imagine the explosion of possibilities if they were joined by a public health nurse. The nurse could work with everyone in the center on identifying and helping pregnant women get off drugs, because of the urgent need to prevent the damage that drugs can do to unborn babies. Doctors in places such as Cook County Hospital in Chicago warn that our urban health care centers risk being overwhelmed by the escalating number of babies born cocaine-addicted, many of whom may suffer life-long mental and physical problems.[10] Public health nurses could also work with the CPO to develop community-based initiatives to help single parents struggling to raise infants alone. The public health nurse also has a vital role to play in helping prevent the spread of AIDS among the IV drug users that the drug counselor sees.

The opportunities multiply exponentially each time a new outreach specialist joins the team – social workers, adult education teachers, parks and recreation specialists. Perhaps some spend a day each week, while others might move into the facility full-time. With the CPO leading the way to ensure their safety, these professionals may be able to enlist others in the cause. Perhaps a physician visits once a month, to provide immunizations and physicals to youngsters. Maybe a corporation frees a personnel specialist one afternoon a week to help counsel people in how to find and hold jobs. Businesses who recruit employees from the area might be persuaded that their long-term future depends on allowing their successful minority employees time off to spend working with minority youth in the area, to provide them positive role models to help counteract the negative role model of the drug pusher.

The Community Resource Center could become the hub of neighborhood activity, the outreach center where local churches and civic organizations hold meetings, coordinate projects, and disseminate information. It would become the place that people turn to for help first, because even if the help is not available there directly, there will always be someone there who can tell people where to go or whom to call. Perhaps the concern is finding safe shelter for the homeless. Maybe the challenge is to address minority health concerns, ranging from sickle-cell anemia to high blood pressure. The focus and scope of each effort would be bounded only by the collective imagination of the people involved and the particular needs of the community. And all would benefit from the involvement of the CPO as the community's first line of defense, providing both continuity and protection.

Ironically, of course, this future harkens back to the past, just as the CPO blends the old-fashioned cop on the beat with today's new reality. Not that long ago, social workers visited clients in their homes; the public health nurse made calls on the elderly, the sick, and young mothers; and truant officers tracked down kids who skipped school. Since then, however, we have pulled back from providing decentralized and personalized service, where professionals worked directly in the community.

Pressures to become more efficient and more "modern" have favored a centralized system, where the clients came to the professionals. But just as putting police officers into patrol cars inadvertently spawned isolation from the community, centralizing other public services has alienated these professionals from the people they serve. The results of that decision echo what happened when the police lost touch with the people who need them and on whom they depend.

The first thing that happened when the public system pulled back from direct involvement in the community was that the burden of receiving service fell onto those with the fewest resources. When the social workers of the past visited homes, their transportation expenses were covered as part of the job. Now instead, we demand that welfare clients must pay to take the bus, often with their children in tow, and they often have to wait for hours to be seen. This change sends a message that the system no longer cares about the client's wants and needs.

Pulling social agents out of the community also removed the visible symbols of social control. Though it may be somewhat unfashionable to say so, a visiting social worker was in some sense both a role model and a snoop. The social worker typically brought with him or her a middle-class set of values about what constituted proper behavior, backed with the power to approve or disapprove certain benefits.

When the system worked properly, those spot checks could uncover obvious cases of physical, mental, and sexual child abuse and neglect. The downside was the thought of an imperious bureaucrat, arriving unannounced, threatening fearful clients that they would lose their benefits simply because the social worker found the person's lifestyle or customs distasteful.

Another concern was that personalized service led to uneven distribution of aid. A kind-hearted social worker might bend the rules to find a way to give enough money to a struggling mother whose kids needed shoes to go to school. Another might slash benefits to the children of a mother deemed promiscuous. The line between offering help and interfering with individual freedom and dignity has never been easy to draw, which made it easier to retreat from a personalized approach that allowed professionals the opportunity both to use – and abuse – individual discretion.

Adding to our uneasiness about personalized service was the tinge of racism. In the past, many social workers were white, while many clients were minorities. The cynical view was that the white majority saw this system as a way to use economic coercion as a means of imposing its will and its customs on minorities, in the guise of providing charity and assistance. Yet reform has created a centralized system where people's benefits are determined purely "by the numbers," a system so impersonal that common sense plays no role. This also reduces the job of social work to paper shuffling that squelches opportunities for creativity and innovation. Though we have upgraded the job by demanding more education, we no longer allow our social work professionals as much opportunity to think.

Enabling a Healthy Future

Perhaps Community Policing has taught us that we have learned enough to be more sensitive to community concerns, so that we can again send professionals into the community, but this time as partners, not as experts with all the answers. It is not paternalistic, condescending, or racist to target the greatest level of service where the need is greatest. But just as today's CPO is not merely yesterday's beat cop by another name, we must reconsider the roles of the other social service agents who would follow the CPO into the Community Resource Center. The goal would be to provide full-spectrum public service – policing, drug treatment, education, mental health services, social services, health care. The center would also act as a catalyst to galvanize others to become involved – churches, public and private agencies, area businesses. Yet the primary resource chronically underutilized and ignored has been the people in the community, whose support and participation is paramount in turning communities around.

As proof of how quickly theory turns into action, in the six months between when this chapter proposing Community Resources Centers as a model for the future was written and when the final text was being readied for print, the authors discovered that Windsor, Ontario, Canada, had already implemented its Cooperation Stations in public housing, where social agencies and the police work together on community problem-solving. They serve as a testament that what a few months earlier seemed perilously close to pie-in-the-sky fantasy can quickly become reality in today's fast-changing world.

This vision of Community Resource Centers providing a concerted community-action approach, with CPOs as the vanguard, could be the proper model for high-crime, poverty-stricken areas of American cities. Extending the Community

Policing/CPO model to other public service agencies holds the promise that they can all work together on addressing the root causes of crime and disorder that risk escalating out of control with the emergence of new drug problems like crack. The synergy of filling a community-based center with this new breed of dedicated professionals working as partners with people in the community could spark new thinking that would help make blighted communities livable again.

Many economists have pointed to demographic profiles of the future with great optimism, since they show an ever-increasing need for new workers as Baby Boomers age and move toward retirement. But we can no longer tolerate allowing American jobs to be exported elsewhere in the world, when we have once-glorious cities pockmarked with pockets of poverty, despair, and anger. Yet we cannot expect business and industry to "buy American" when shopping for labor, unless we can compete by providing them safe, drug-free communities for those new enterprises that will provide all those new jobs we desperately need.

Many will argue that such a vision is an illusion, a dream that this country cannot afford. Yet perhaps the proper question is whether we can afford *not* to make these changes. Only history will show whether our embattled cities and their problems are simply in a transitional phase that will pass – or the first signs of a spreading cancer that will ultimately consume the body politic.

Demographic projections of the future offer some basis for overall optimism. The tail end of the big bulge of Baby Boomers has already passed out of their teens and, in a few years, will move beyond their mid-to-late twenties, the peak age for arrest and incarceration.[11] Yet those projections also offer cause for concern about urban hot spots, particularly poverty-stricken areas where single mothers cluster. According to a recent analysis by David E. Bloom of Columbia and Neil G. Bennett at Yale, "[M]ore than half of children who live with just their mothers are in poverty, over five times the rate for children who live with a married couple."[12] They note that these demographic trends are of particular concern for blacks, since half of all black babies were born out of wedlock in 1986, more than three times the rate for whites.[13] Of concern as well is that one in four black babies is born to a teenage mother, who is often unmarried, and studies show that teen mothers earn roughly half as much as women who wait until twenty to have their first child.[14]

We cannot risk missing this opportunity to protect our society's future health, by wasting time quibbling about price. The Community Policing approach is cheap insurance that offers society a promising new treatment for a variety of ills. Through better resource management or new funding initiatives, all police departments can find a way once they develop the will. Their example provides a new model for delivering decentralized and personalized service to people whose help is essential in making this society a place where everyone can enjoy feeling safe. Whether we are moralists or pragmatists, we must begin to see the wisdom inherent in the increasingly obvious truth that until we are all safe, no one is truly safe – and that Community Policing offers important answers to society as it is poised on the brink of the 21st century, answers about how ailing communities can begin to recover and become healthy, safe places in which to live and work.

NOTES

[1]Analysis of UCR data supplied by the FBI's Statistical Section in Washington, D.C., by telephone on March 22, compared to information in *Report to the Nation on Crime and Justice,* Second Edition, U.S. Department of Justice (Washington, DC: Bureau of Justice Statistics, March 1988).

[2]Malcolm, Andrew H., *Federal War on Crime Seems To See No End, New York Times,* May 28, 1989, p. 5.

[3]Lacayo, Richard, with Nancy Seufert/Los Angeles, *Tell It to the Rent-a-Judge, Time,* August 29, 1989, p. 50.

[4]Pooley, Eric, *Fighting Back Against Crack, New York Magazine,* January 23, 1989, p. 39.

[5]Bucqueroux, Bonnie, *North Miami Beach broadens the mandate, Footprints* newsletter, published by the National Neighborhood Foot Patrol Center (now the National Center for Community Policing) Michigan State University, East Lansing, MI, Vol. I, No. 3, and Vol. II, No. 1, Fall/Winter 1988.

[6]*Ibid.*

[7]Stanton, Barbara, as quoted in *A Once and Future Model City?,* by Jeanne May, *Detroit Free Press,* December 11, 1988.

[8]Information provided by the Children's Trust Fund, Lansing, Michigan, with additional information from the staff for Michigan State Representative Debbie Stabenow, during telephone interviews on March 23, 1989.

[9]Variously reported by the Detroit Free Press as 54 or 55 young people murdered; actual figures are difficult to determine, because the Detroit Police Department does not report data this way.

[10]*Babies at Risk,* a *Frontline* presentation, hosted by Judy Woodruff, aired on Public Broadcast Stations, May 30, 1989.

[11]Bloom, David E., and Bennett, Neil G., *Future Shock, The New Republic,* June 19, 1989, pp. 19-20.

[12]*Ibid.*

[13]*Ibid.*

[14]The Editors, *The Toni Award, The New Republic,* June 19, 1989, p. 9.

COMMUNITY CLOSE-UP
Philadelphia Police Department
Philadelphia, Pennsylvania

Willie L. Williams, Commissioner

Community Policing as a managerial and tactical police program has taken many forms across the United States. In Philadelphia, Community Policing means police accountability to the community for the quality of life in neighborhoods. This has involved the implementation of three interrelated programs to accomplish the mission of the department: to improve community quality of life; neighborhood advisory councils, decentralized experimentation; and the adoption of a problem-focus for management and tactical operations.

In each of Philadelphia's 23 police patrol districts, neighborhood advisory councils have been formed with the explicit purposes of (1) providing community access to police policymaking and (2) establishing an accountability linkage between the police and the consumers of police services, the public. These advisory councils meet regularly with district captains to identify and assess community problems, and jointly to determine strategies (police and community) to resolve those problems.

Linked to neighborhood advisory councils is broadening of operational discretion at the patrol district level, and the mandate that captains have the managerial latitude to experiment in programs aimed at reducing crime, fear of crime, and community disorder. In several instances, that has resulted in opening *mini-stations* to anchor deteriorating neighborhoods and to strengthen civic development. In others, this has resulted in the full-scale decentralization of a police division as an alternative to traditional, and, oftentimes, centralized, police functioning in the city. The central theme of this "spirit of experimentation" within the Philadelphia Police Department recognizes that problems and programs will, of necessity, vary according to community needs and available resources.

Finally, the Philadelphia Police Department has embraced a problem-oriented approach to policing, wherein managers, supervisors, and patrol officers are challenged to solve community crime and disorder problems, rather than reactively responding to problems once they are identified by the community. Here, the department is in the process of elaborating on communications and analytic systems to better capture demand, conduct repeat call analysis, and isolate persistent problems confronting the community.

The theme of Community Policing in Philadelphia is establishing a partnership with the community to reduce crime, disorder, and fear, and to improve community quality of life. Many individual efforts and programs contribute to this theme. Preliminary assessments of the effectiveness of these programs have been encouraging. The challenge of Community Policing in a large, urban police department is not to reduce the concept to a listing of programs that are implemented citywide. We have resisted this approach in favor of a strategy that provides incentive and initiative for local commanders to tailor programs to local needs. Each patrol district has a team of specalists that help to fulfill the many missions of Community Policing. In addition to the patrol force, Victim Assistance Officers, Police and Community Relations Officers, and Community Crime Prevention Officers are assigned to each patrol district. This core of community-oriented officers is not expected to become just another specialization within the department. Instead, the ultimate goal is to transfuse the patrol force with the Community Policing idea and practice, so that community-oriented and problem-focused policing become the *normal* operational practice of the department.

Community leaders have access to police decision-making that they did not have in the past. Command officers, most particularly those who are in the patrol and detective bureaus, have begun to make the transition from policing as reaction to policing as problem identification, analysis, and resolution. The police themselves have developed a better appreciation for Community Policing, although acceptance of this strategy in the face of drastically reduced manpower remains a problem. Business and residential communities, however, are squarely behind this initiative.

Submitted by: William T. Bergman, Inspector

COMMUNITY CLOSE-UP
Los Angeles Police Department
Los Angeles, California

Daryl Gates, Chief of Police

Since the establishment of the Crime Prevention Unit on June 25, 1927, the Los Angeles Police Department has recognized the need for a partnership between the public and the police. This relationship linked the department's mission to prevent crime with community involvement. Because the police are unable to patrol every potential crime location, crime can be reduced more effectively by citizen participation in Community Policing. To this end, the department added the Police Assisted Community Enhancement (PACE) program to its crime prevention efforts.

PACE was developed in response to Chief of Police Daryl Gates' concern about "resident fear" and "quality of life" issues. Chief Gates cited studies in other cities that indicated that these issues were not always linked solely to the existence of serious crime, but also to overall conditions in a neighborhood. PACE assumes that conditions such as graffiti, abandoned cars, and transients literally affect the *morale* of a neighborhood and, thus, the perception of the residents' control over their environment. Attacking these often-ignored conditions has the positive effect of lifting neighborhood pride, raising community standards, and thereby lowering the residents' tolerance for crime. This concept was articulated by James Q. Wilson and George L. Kelling of Harvard University in the March 1982 issues of the *Atlantic Monthly* in an article titled *Broken Windows*.

PACE expands the role of police officers in two important areas. First, the officers must enforce laws for minor violations. Second, they must serve as a catalyst to identify and use other resources to improve community conditions. This secondary role is a departure from traditional police work, but it is an essential part of the program, because the Police Department is the most visible component of city government.

To give the officers a framework within which to work, procedures were needed to facilitate the program. The Rampart Area of the Los Angeles Police Department was selected as one of the test areas to develop PACE. Their experience proved very successful and has had a positive impact on the community.

Resources had to be identified to effect such tasks as trash removal in alleys and abatement of abandoned houses used as gang hangouts. This required staff-level contact with other city departments, such as Sanitation and Building & Safety, to get them to commit their strained resources on a consistent basis. The courts were also persuaded to commit personnel sentenced to community service work to assist in graffiti removal. Although the department's staff was instrumental in obtaining formal commitments for inter-departmental cooperation, the really effective work was accomplished by the personal relationships established on a working level. The value of this individual commitment should not be underestimated. Logistical problems are usually solved by individual creativity and enthusiastic community support.

Other procedural methods are used to effect PACE. A short, easy-to-use manual was developed, one that allows enough flexibility to be useful in a wide variety of situations. A Community Enhancement Request citation-like form was developed to identify PACE-related problems. These forms document requests initiated by the officers or the citizens. The completed forms are forwarded to the appropriate agency for action. One of the key factors in making the whole program a success is that the process is simple.

The PACE program is now out of the experimental stage and is being implemented on a citywide basis. It is expected that it will have positive, long-term results. PACE has had the effect of uniting many of the city's department's toward the mutual goal of improving the quality of life in Los Angeles.

Submitted by: Chief of Police Daryl Gates

COMMUNITY CLOSE-UP
Baltimore County Police Department
Towson, Maryland

Cornelius J. Behan, Chief of Police

Launched in 1982 as an experimental approach to alleviating fear among the citizens of Baltimore County, Citizen Oriented Police Enforcement (COPE) identifies and corrects community conditions that contribute to citizen fear. COPE gains its initiative from the government's recognition that fear – real or imagined – is just as pervasive and threatening as crime itself; that to address problems that cause fear is a police responsibility.

COPE is unique as a citizen-oriented, rather than a police-oriented, approach that gives top priority to citizen perceptions, with an emphasis on community identification of problems and concerns. Using a refined problem-solving technique, COPE examines all facets of a community problem, looking beyond crime to identify the underlying causes of fear and doing whatever is necessary to restore the desired quality of life to a neighborhood. All strata of society are represented among COPE recipients: the elderly and the youth; minority and ethnic groups; the poor and affluent; the ordinary citizens of residential, business, and farming communities.

A key strategy of COPE, which involves 54 police officers (approximately 6% of the department's patrol force), is to establish a close and positive interaction with citizens. Attending community meetings, canvassing neighborhoods door-to-door, working with citizens to improve their efforts in crime prevention, tapping the resources of public and private groups, and using highly visible foot and motorcycle patrol are examples of tactics employed to instill or regain citizen confidence in the police, and to establish a rapport that encourages involvement of the community and its leaders in planned action to alleviate community problems.

COPE units tackle problems that are not normally considered to be within the realm of law enforcement responsibilities, but nevertheless contribute to fear among citizens, e.g., inadequate streetlighting, closed playgrounds, overgrown lots, neglected potholes, uncollected garbage, and dilapidated houses or buildings. As a result, COPE has acquired an ombudsman function; COPE officers hear community concerns, request action by appropriate government agencies, and stay with the problems until they are acted upon satisfactorily.

A three-year study by Dr. Gary Cordner and associates at the University of Baltimore concluded that COPE reduced fear by 19% in target communities, crime by 12%, and calls for service by 11%. Community awareness of police presence and satisfaction with police service rose 20% and 16%, respectively, a fact attributed to COPE's highly visible nature and its emphasis on creating positive interaction with citizens. Somewhat unexpected was a 26% improvement in the attitudes of COPE officers toward police work and the community.

Initially, officers in patrol perceived COPE as just another public relations *gimmick,* or that COPE was really a special crime-fighting tactical squad. These misconceptions were dealt with through in-service training to increase awareness of the COPE philosophy at all organizational levels. COPE is not directed at placating the citizen, but at actively working with the community to identify root causes of fear and then to pursue the optimal solution. And, while established police tactics may be used to handle selected problems, COPE's principal successes have been where it has transcended the traditional police response of merely deployiing additional patrol resources.

One underlying prerequisite became clear in this endeavor: support and leadership from the highest-elected officials are essential. COPE's success in combatting fear by getting roads paved, shrubbery cut, panhandlers convicted, and parks cleaned depended on the active help of other agencies. Only elected officials have the position and power to support and facilitate that sort of government-wide cooperation and coordination.

Submitted by: Chief Cornelius (Neil) J. Behan

COMMUNITY CLOSE-UP
New York City Police Department
New York, New York

Benjamin Ward, Commissioner

In 1984, the New York City Police Department was still feeling the aftershocks of the city's fiscal crisis and had not fully recovered from the manpower cuts of the late 1970s. The massive volume of calls for service in New York City, numbering some seven and one-half million calls annually by 1984, resulted in the vast bulk of the department's patrol force being assigned to emergency response cars on the 911 queue. While this strategy allowed the department to maintain a viable response during the lean years, it did not permit the department to devote resources to low-level crime and disorderly conditions. As a result, the police department struggled to devise ways to deal effectively with order-maintenance conditions and improve the quality of life at the neighborhood level.

Against this backdrop, the department implemented a pilot Community Policing program in Brooklyn's 72nd Precinct in July 1984. Named the Community Patrol Officer Program, or CPOP, the pilot sought to determine the feasibility of permanently assigning police officers to foot patrol in fairly large neighborhood beat areas and requiring them to perform a variety of non-traditional tasks in addition to their normal law enforcement duties. Police officers assigned as Commuity Patrol Officers, or CPOs, were asked to be full-service police officers and to serve as community resources, helping to organize community groups, attending community meetings, making service referrals, and helping to devise strategies to deal not only with local crime and order-maintenance problems, but also with social needs.

CPOP differs in significant ways from traditional patrol deployment strategies. All police officers in CPOP were volunteers, which permitted the department to authorize wide flexibility in patrol hours. CPOs were recruited on their agreement to work those hours that permitted them to focus on the problems peculiar to their beat areas and to change those hours on a daily basis, if need be. The officers were encouraged to solicit input from the residents and merchants on their beats in setting their patrol priorities, rather than being guided solely by crime incidence, and to involve the community in formulating solutions to neighborhood problems when possible.

Of all the ways in which CPOP differed from conventional patrol, the most notable was that the CPOs were given the responsibility to work on problems over time. Working in a police radio car is analogous to being a paramedic in an ambulance. Just as a paramedic's principal function is to stabilize the patient until he can be delivered to a hospital for appropriate medical treatment, the principal function of a police officer responding to an emergency call is to stabilize the situation, to prevent further harm or violation of the law, to make an arrest or issue a summons, to take a report of a past crime, or to make a referral for some follow-up action. That done, the police officer must make himself available for the next emergency call. The police department is not at all like a hospital, however, and is largely unable to provide follow-up services, except where serious, unsolved crimes require investigation by detectives.

CPOP sought to fill this gap by making the CPO available to follow up on community problems, and by allowing the officer sufficient time to deal with them effectively.

The pilot CPOP project was judged to be a success, both by department officials and community representatives. Based on these early results, the department began a careful expansion of the project. Finally, in September 1988, CPOP had been implemented in each of New York City's 75 patrol precincts. The program involves more than 800 police officers (including trained alternatives), 75 sergeants, and 75 administrative aides.

CPOP is based on the belief that regular and meaningful contact between the police and the community must be established to address the street conditions and other crimes that lower the quality of life in local neighborhoods. The program attempts to accomplish this by forming a functional partnership between the police, the community, and other public and private service organzations.

The CPO embodies the law enforcement activities of the traditional foot patrol officers, the outreach and organizational activities of the community relations officer, and the problem analysis, strategy development, and tactical implementation activities of the police planner.

Conceptually, the CPO role has four principal dimensions:

1. **Planner** – The first responsibility of the CPO is to identify the principal crime and order-maintenance problems confronting people within the beat area. The officer examines relevant statistical materials, records observations from patrolling the beat, and solicits input from residents and merchants in the community. The problems are then prioritized and analyzed, and corrective strategies are designed. These strategies are reviewed with the Unit Supervisor, incorporated into the CPO's Monthly Work Plan, and form the focus of the officer's patrol for the coming month.

2. **Problem-Solver** – CPOs are encouraged to see themselves as problem-solvers,

using four general types of resources: their own law enforcement capabilities; other police resources from higher levels of the department that can be brought to bear through the CPO Sergeant and the Precinct Commander; other public and private service agencies operating in the beat area; and individual citizens or citizen organizations living and working in that community.

3. **Community Organizer** – The CPO increases the community's consciousness of its problems, involves community people and organizations in developing strategies to address the problems, and motivates others to help in implementing the strategies. Officers are encouraged to identify potential resources and, where they are inadequate, to help in organizing and motivating members of the community to address these needs.

4. **Information Exchange Link** – The CPOs, through their links to the community, are in a position to provide the department not only with information about problem conditions and locations, but also insights into the community's perceptions of police tactics. In turn, the CPOs can provide advice to address the community's fears as well as explain the police view of conditions in the neighborhood.

Submitted by: The Vera Institute and Susan Herman, Assistant to the Police Commissioner

COMMUNITY CLOSE-UP
Madison Police Department
Madison, Wisconsin

David C. Couper, Chief of Police

The Madison Police Department implemented a community-oriented policing team in January 1986, after an employee planning group identified a need to "get closer to the people we serve." The team started with six officers and a sergeant. It was expanded to eight officers and a sergeant in March 1987. We are now looking into expanding into one or two other neighborhood areas.

The neighborhood officers are assigned to a specific geographical area (approximately one-half square mile or less). Each officer has an office provided free by a public or private agency within the neighborhood. Officers are equipped not only with a telephone and answering machine, but they each have their own computer terminal and printer that links them, via a modem, to the department's main computer. This gives officers access to all previous calls for service by name, address, date, case number, or sector. The system is also tied into the Department of Motor Vehicle files, Probation and Parole, and the City's E-Mail system. E-Mail gives the officer the capability to send messages to any other neighborhood officer or city department that is connected to the system.

The neighborhood officers handle all responses for calls for service except traffic accidents. (This is because they do not have access to a vehicle and conduct all their business on foot.)

The neighborhood officers attempt to follow up on as many cases as possible in which no detective is assigned. The officers receive copies of all reports of incidents occurring in their areas. If no detective is assigned the case, the neighborhood officer will re-contact the victim or complainant to see what the present status is and to see if any further information can be obtained. Most of these cases involve order-maintenance problems (i.e., loud stereos, noise complaints, domestic disputes, etc.). The neighborhood officer can check on their computers to determine the previous history of calls at a specific location, re-contact complainant and suspect, if any, and determine if any further action should be taken (i.e., verbal warning, citation, criminal complaint, or contacting the landlord, City Building Inspection, County Social Services, City Housing, or any other agency). Neighborhood officers investigate some criminal cases in which the officer is familiar with the participants. Many times, the detectives rely on the neighborhood officers to assist them with investigations because of the neighborhood officer's familiarity with the area and people. They also try to work closely with the district patrol officers, by sharing the workload and sharing information about the area.

Neighborhood officers are encouraged to try new, different, and non-traditional approaches to find long-term solutions to chronic problems. As an example, one officer designed and organized a Building Representatives Project. It deals not only with crime problems within a low-income housing project, but also with the quality of life within the project. It was built on the idea that people in public housing should take responsibility for helping themselves and working together to solve their problems. In this concept of Community Policing, the officer is not the person who must solve the problem, but the officer functions as a facilitator, organizer, planner, and information gatherer. The officer links the community with other agencies so that they can work together to solve the problem (power sharing). The project initially was set up in one eight-unit building. The officer organized a training program for building representatives. The people living in the building established their own norms, using a *bottom up* approach, not the typical *top down* authoritarian approach. They also elected a person from the building to be their representative to manage the housing. Calls for service decreased by 47% in a 10-month period after the program was under way.

A neighborhood officer also organized a grass-roots effort that provided part-time jobs for young people during the summer. Another officer solved a problem with people gambling and drinking in a local park by working with the community and city officials to pass an ordinance against gambling that could be used to stop the problem. In other instances, neighborhood officers have worked with city inspectors to close apartment buildings where problems congregated. The neighborhood officers have also been instrumental in working with the Department of Corrections to add restrictions to people under supervision who were causing problems and even to revoke their parole.

The neighborhood officers meet monthly as a team to discuss problems in their neighborhoods and to brainstorm about promising ideas. The sessions also provide an opportunity for neighborhood officers to learn about department matters and relevant information about city agencies. People from other agencies frequently appear to discuss how they can work better together on mutual problems.

The management style is also a *bottom up* approach. Officers share in decision-making, planning, and organizing. It is important that the unit work as a team in order to best use the various talents and knowledge of the group to arrive at better decisions. The officers must also rely on each other for mutual support.

Neighborhood officers report a high level of job satisfaction. An internal survey indicated a statistically significant difference in their job satisfaction levels compared to police officers working in other areas. Although patrol officers initially had a negative view of this type of policing, officers who have had the opportunity to work directly with neighborhood officers are now seeing the benefits.

Submitted by: Dennis L. Reno, Sergeant of Police

COMMUNITY CLOSE-UP
McAllen Police Department
McAllen, Texas

Alex Longoria, Chief of Police

First, a brief reminder of some unfortunate events in the history of the McAllen Police Department. In 1979 and 1980, the department was a party to several federal civil-rights complaints, lawsuits, and criminal trials. The department received national and even international publicity in the form of booking-desk videotapes that revealed verbal and physical abuse by the police of people who were arrested and in their custody. The department's morale plunged to an indescribable low. As the events were being played up by the media, officers were being stopped on the streets by citizens who would taunt them to brutalize them just like the prisoners on TV. That was a period when the department had virtually no pride, little effectiveness, and serious internal conflicts. In October 1981, the department reorganized from top to bottom, hiring a new chief and reassessing all management positions, and subsequently replacing the majority of managers and supervisors. Eventually, the federal courts placed the department under a temporary injunction that mandated certain changes. The main items were that the department was to provide in-service training for all police officers in certain categories – 96 hours per year per officer – and the City of McAllen was required to establish a civilian review board to oversee and hear citizen complaints of misconduct by the police.

The new Chief of Police, L.W. Spradlin, instituted efforts to accomplish a complete turnaround. Morale improved considerably and the department's image within the community began to improve. Lee Spradlin was an outgoing chief executive who exuded confidence and pride in policing as a profession. He opened up the department to the community, so that people could not only see but participate in helping to carry out the department's mission.

In 1985, several officers were sent to the National Neighborhood Foot Patrol Center (now the National Center of Community Policing) at Michigan State University in East Lansing, Michigan, where they received training in the principles of foot patrol and Community Policing. Shortly afterward, the officers made a site visit to Houston's Community Service Centers. When they returned from Houston, the officers established their first neighborhood office at a city-run housing project. They also opened a complete Community Service Center in a strip mall in a northern sector of the city. Cost to the city was minimal, since space and construction materials were donated. Since then, the department has established two more neighborhood beat offices and two community police stations. Unfortunately, we closed the station at the strip mall for lack of activity, but re-opened with the same crew at a large, enclosed shopping mall. Another portable Community Policing station was established during 1989, bringing to six the number of outreach points in the Community Policing Program, with another slated to be added by the end of the year.

To understand why the department undertook the change from the traditional forms of motorized patrol to a more community-based policing effort, we must first try to understand the make-up of the community and the different liaisons that were or were not established by the police. We do not need to discuss the reasons why the police in general have been changing to this form of policing, but it is important to understand why McAllen has had to change to be effective.

About 85 % of the population is Mexican-American. Traditionally, the relationship of the police to the majority of the population has been one of controller to those controlled. The perception was that the police represented the Anglo establishment and government, even though the majority of the police were Mexican-American themselves. This perception led to distrust, which was reinforced by complaints of police misconduct from the Chicano community. Whether the perception was merited or not is not the question, because the widespread perception strained the relationship between the police and the majority of the people in the community, particularly in the barrios and colonias. This meant the police received little help, in the form of information, to help them resolve crimes. Many suspects would also hide in these areas, with distrust and apathy providing the camouflage for such people. So the main goal of the organization was and is to win back the community's trust and loyalty, through direct police/neighborhood intervention, to establish a foothold in the barrios, colonias, and neighborhoods that was real and fruitful for both the community and the police, and to lift the camouflage (apathy) that cloaked the criminal element.

To establish this foothold, the department has had to and continues to have to share something the police generally are reluctant to talk about, let alone share, with the community – power – the power to determine police priorities, enforcement standards, levels of service, and other *exclusive* police rights. Not only had these never been shared with the community before, many police processes were treated as secret. The department feels that returning some power of government to those who feel they have none can most certainly have a positive effect on the overall police mission. With the sincere desire of this department to share directly with all the community the responsibilities of enforcement, policymaking, etc., the department embarked on decentralizing its patrol services. Targeted for direct intervention were those neighborhoods where the police were not commonly accepted – or desired, for that matter.

The department has now separated its patrol force into two units: one responds to calls for service and the other is responsible for the Community Policing mission. The uniformed services' missions are broken down in this manner:

- **Response Cars** – Mission:
  Answering ALL calls for service
  Selective traffic enforcement

- **Beat Cars** – Mission:
  Community Policing
  Crime prevention
  Crime suppression
  Neighborhood mobilization
  Quality of life and the environment
  Intelligence gathering

So far, the acceptance of the separation of duties has been met with some resistance and confusion. The resistance, I feel, is a result of the fear of the unknown, and the confusion is the result of little written direction, but that is being corrected. We have discovered that some officers are not cut out to be Community Police Officers because they tend to be introverted to some degree and just do not seem to function well within the framework of the mission.

Our Community Policing effort is multi-fold and is centered around the neighborhood officer or station. Officers are generally assigned hours that suit the neighborhoods served, and we use civilian police service officers to run the stations or offices during peak hours, when possible. We have also discovered that these PSOs are just as devoted and dedicated to this service as the police and, without them, the program would suffer serious setbacks. They are involved in crime prevention, neighborhood mobilization, and other station duties.

The success or failure of Community Policing will rest on the shoulders of the officers responsible for carrying out its mission and their first-line supervisors. No amount of training and written guidelines can replace desire and love of this type of work. It takes a very intense, yet flexible, officer, one who is willing to ask for help from the community and one who is willing to help in return. But rest assured that our experience has been that most officers were reluctant at first, but now they view their work as indispensable, constructive, and enjoyable.

If perceptions are a good measure of success, then the organization has done the right thing with its Community Policing mission. If cold statistics and beans are what measuring is all about, then the verdict is not in yet, and only time will tell if our efforts are meritorious. We are currently working on surveying the community to determine fear of crime and police services desired.

Our program is rough around the edges, to say the least, but it is working. Fiscal implications have not been a factor since most offices or stations used donated space or received HUD funding in the form of community block grants.

Without a doubt, the challenge for Community Policing will be to recruit and train officers who are willing to give of themselves and are willing to work as a team, with neighborhood members and other officers. Currently, the police are trained and re-trained to be independent and self-reliant. Much work needs to be done to develop a generation of officers who are more flexible and self-starting, more concerned with the total environment of a community, and more willing to share experiences and information with other officers to foster the "team approach" to problem solving.

Submitted by: Chief Alex Longoria

COMMUNITY CLOSE-UP
Newport News Police Department
Newport News, Virginia

Jay A. Carey, Jr., Chief of Police

The Problem-Oriented Policing (POP) approach to problem-solving was introduced in the Newport News Police Department in the latter part of 1984. This effort was conducted in collaboration with the Police Executive Research Forum (PERF) of Washington, D.C. A two-year, federally funded grant from the National Institute of Justice (NIJ) was awarded to the Police Executive Research Forum to develop, test, and evaluate a system for collecting and analyzing different kinds of information about criminal incidents in Newport News. The system was to be developed, and the experiences gained from it would serve as a model for other police departments nationwide. To accomplish the goals of the grant-funded project, a Crime Analysis Task Force was organized, involving a full range of police personnel of all ranks and positions from divisions and bureaus throughout the department.

Problem-Oriented Policing – the routine application of problem-solving procedures — is new in law enforcement, but problem-solving is not. Police officers are confronted with and resolve problems every day. POP emphasizes the analysis of a group of recurring similar incidents and the development of solutions that solicit a broad range of public and private endorsements. It is based on two premises. The first is that problem-solving can be applied by officers throughout the department as part of their daily work. Traditionally, problem-solving efforts are confined to special projects or specialized units. The second premise is that routine problem-solving efforts can be effective in reducing or resolving problems.

The use of the problem-solving system in the analyses of community issues, concerns, and problems was applied to 39 different problems from 1984 through September 1987. The 39 problems were representative of a variety of crime and disorder problems occurring in specific neighborhoods or citywide. Neighborhood problems consisted of crime problems such as burglaries and larcenies at various apartments, prostitution, drug trafficking, and traffic violations. Neighborhood disorder problems ranged from a problem with dirt bikes, to loitering, to disturbances at a convenience store. Citywide crime problems included commercial burglaries and robberies, assaults on police officers, driving under the influence, gasoline drive-offs (thefts), and domestic violence. Citywide disorder problems included runaway youths, accidents with city vehicles, teen alcoholism, false alarms, juvenile gangs, and suicide. These experiences demonstrated that problem-solving can be implemented on a routine basis and innovative approaches developed to provide officers with the freedom to examine underlying causes. Also, many officers derived the personal satisfaction of accomplishing quality results.

The Newport News Police Department's problem-oriented approach to policing is as much a philosophy as a set of procedures and methodology for accomplishing our goal and objective of effective and efficient service delivery. The active involvement and participation of citizens, officers, employees, city departments, community agencies, and various institutions in the resolution of crime, disorder, and service problems is a philosophy the department is committed to and is part of a value system that guides the organization.

Annually, all department managers and employees participate in the goals and objectives' process, incorporating innovative and creative approaches to difficult crime issues, disorder, and service problems, whether administrative or operational. Many goals and objectives are addressed by officers utilizing the POP approach.

POP is a department-wide effort and is widely accepted throughout the department as a way of life. The department has developed policy and procedures, newsletters, performance measures, an annual roundtable conference, and career development initiatives and rewards and recognition to support the institutionalization of POP. Also, the Problem Analysis Advisory Committee (PAAC), an annually appointed support group comprised of representatives from each rank and organizational level of the department, meets monthly to listen to and guide users through the identification, analysis, response, and assessment stages of their problem. PAAC offers recommended strategies, resources, and assistance to all users of POP.

POP is evaluated annually by the Police Planning Coordinator and a roundtable conference convened with users and first-line supervisors, to review and address identified issues and problems and to enhance the use of POP in the department, whether it is training, operational, administrative, or other concerns.

The results are as diverse as the problems themselves – many solutions were effective at reducing the size and seriousness of the problem, others at decreasing calls for service, fear reduction, and crime. Moreover, other solutions aided the department in dealing more effectively with the problem, and citizens proclaimed the enhanced cooperative police/community relations an extra plus. The local news media has been instrumental in publishing many of the POP efforts.

The following provides a closer look at four efforts:

- **Gasoline Drive-Offs** – Detective Laura Harwood's responsibility in the General Assignment Squad was investigating larceny – shoplifting. She noted that much of her time was spent investigating gas drive-offs. Using the analysis model checklist made it clear that the police officers were simply being used to chase down the culprits so that they would pay up, since none of the incidents resulted in a criminal prosecution – and as long as the police would continue to track down the offenders, no prosecutions would ever occur as long as restitution was made.

Detective Harwood realized the problem was not criminal, but it was instead that the police were being used as personal bill collectors by the gas companies. A plausible strategy was to implement a policy that required customers to pay in advance, but efforts to solicit support for this from the gas companies was unsuccessful, because the manager/owners believed their customers would not like the change.

Detective Harwood met with the manager/owners to share her findings, solicit recommendations, and to try to reduce the demand for police officers to respond to the scene. She recommended to PAAC the revision of Policy and Procedure #1301, Call Management, which was revised so that future calls concerning drive-offs were referred to the telephone operator assigned to the Tele-Serve desk. Tele-Serve is an alternative to handling calls for police service that utilizes telephone reporting rather than dispatching a field unit. The operator advised the complainant that if no prosecution was intended, a report would be filed for record only. Detective Harwood notified the gasoline association of the new policy in writing and requested their attendance at a meeting to review policy. Both Detective Harwood and the Chief of Police met with the local gasoline association to advise them of the new policy and respond to questions or concerns, and the policy became effective immediately.

- **Borrow Pit** – Officer Ron Hendrickson responded to a call about people shooting across the street from Mr. Woolridge's residence in an area known as the Borrow Pit. Woolridge complained that he had contacted the police several times about the shootings, but the problem had continued the past 15 years. After talking to Woolridge for more than 45 minutes, Officer Hendrickson then reviewed a computer printout from Crime Analysis and discovered 45 calls for service in that general area between April and September 1987. After showing Sergeant James L. Hogan the printout, they decided the problem should be analyzed using the problem-solving model.

  When Officer Hendrickson contacted several agencies and individuals to collect information about the Borrow Pit and the surrounding property, he learned that the boulevard and the interstate that formed the boundary for the area were 988 feet apart, which allowed the police to enforce the city code that prohibited discharging a firearm within 300 yards (900 feet) of a structure or highway. He also met with Traffic Operations to negotiate placing No Parking signs along the boulevard and warning signs on both sides of the railroad tracks that told people not to trespass or shoot in the area.

Analysis also showed that most of the people shooting in the area were military personnel stationed at several area bases, people target practicing, and sportsmen from the surrounding area. Letters were sent to military post commanders notifying them of the problem and the appropriate city code. The police also received cooperation from the property owners, their attorney, and the railroad that allowed the police to enforce the No Trespassing signs.

The department also met with the Criminal Court Judge, which led to developing an evidence and information packet that was left at the court to assist in obtaining convictions on the trespassing and firearms violations.

After these initiatives were implemented, 35 criminal summonses were issued and five field interviews taken. Officer Hendrickson's initial efforts have also led to additional long-range strategies, such as notifying gun shops of the enforcement efforts of the police, meeting to inform and solicit support from the Crime Council, confiscating all weapons from violators, and contacting the news media to assist in public education and awareness.

- **Neighborhood in Partnership With Police (NIPP)** – The department assigned Officers Vernon Lyons and Jeff Cross to the first modified foot patrol program, known as NIPP, in October 1985 and October 1986, respectively. NIPP resulted from the initial POP test problem, the residential burglaries at Briarfield Apartments. NIPP is designed to return the police officer to the neighborhood and make the officer responsive to the needs of the community. NIPP officers are issued a Honda 110 scooter, because it works well in densely populated areas.

  The reduction of criminal activity, daily presence of the "neighborhood cop," and the enhanced police/community relations resulted in the expansion of the police Community Policing efforts by the department. This led to the conceptualization of the Storefront Unit.

- **Storefront Unit** – The department established two police community service centers to respond proactively to an increasing crime problem in the southeastern part of the city. A statistical analysis showed that 43 % of the reported Part I crimes in the city occurred there.

  This new Storefront Unit was established to reduce those crimes, reduce fear levels, and increase interaction between the community and the police.

  Each Storefront Unit building was renovated with city funds, and they are staffed by a sergeant, eight patrol officers, and four community service officers. Two officers are assigned to patrol each target area using a modified walk/ride patrol technique that requires making daily contact with businesses to help identify problem areas and making arrests for criminal and traffic violations. The officers work hours according to the need of the target area, and, once a problem is identified, the patrol officers use traditional and nontraditional techniques to solve the problem. The patrol officers are also directed to field interview all suspicious persons; hundreds have thus far been interviewed. Many of the persons field interviewed were found to be fugitives from other states.

When the Storefront Unit opened in February 1988, Sergeant Carl Burt noted a large number of people loitering in front of businesses, and drug dealers were so dominating a local public housing project through their presence and intimidation that the children were afraid to play on the playgrounds.

As a result of meetings with the complex management, No Trespassing signs were posted at the borders of the complex, and the police and the management worked together on enforcement. A trespassing violation is a misdemeanor punishable by 12 months in jail and/or a $1,000 fine. Officers warned all first offenders that they would be arrested if they trespassed again, and their identities were documented on field interview cards. Within the first two months, several hundred people were arrested on trespassing and other charges. Not long after that, the playgrounds once again belonged to the children. (It should also be noted that the judicial system was part of the planning and enforcement of this initiative.)

Both residents and businesses have noted the impact made by the Storefront Unit. The unit also enjoys the complete support of the city administration. The mayor, city manager, city council members, department heads, residents, and business owners, approximately 200 people in total, attended opening day ceremonies and the open house. The local TV, radio, and print media also provided extensive coverage of the event.

The Storefront Unit has also established a Role Model Program for neighborhood young people that allows them to interact with professional people on a monthly basis. The unit is also actively seeking volunteers from the community for office duties, providing information to visitors, and assisting with the Storefront newsletter.

A survey of businesses showed that 95 % of those who responded felt the program was effective. The two target areas also showed significant reductions in Part I crimes over a three-year period, Jefferson Avenue down 59 %, and Chestnut Avenue down 79 %.

The many accomplishments from the use of POP by officers and personnel in the Newport News Police Department places it in the unique position of becoming the first law enforcement agency to implement this philosophy throughout all ranks, divisions, and bureaus of the organization. Furthermore, the increase in officer-initiated problem-solving efforts will enhance the opportunity of the department to realize the full potential of its policy statement: "The department shall institutionalize the use of this system so that problem-solving becomes a routine part of police activities. As this approach involves personnel and the community in the delivery of police serivces, it is consistent with organization values."

The use of the problem-oriented approach to policing in the department suggests it is a more practical, challenging, and a different way of thinking about doing the job. The quality of the results, the relationships developed with the community, city agencies, and people enhances the service we deliver. The participation, suggestions, and recommendations for improving POP will enable the department to have an impact on the future of policing and the quality of life in Newport News.

Submitted by: Edriene Johnson-Butcher, Police Planning Coordinator

COMMUNITY CLOSE-UP
Edmonton Police Department
Edmonton, Alberta, Canada

L. Chahley, Chief of Police

In 1987, the Executive Management Team, under the direction of L. Chahley, Chief of Police, set a new direction for policing in Edmonton, with the intention of incorporating the philosophy and implementing the practice of Community-Based Policing. The central idea was to combine the responsibility of taking calls for service with a problem-solving approach; to have the police officer and the community become a problem-solving group.

As a result of this new direction, the Edmonton Police Department embarked on a unique Neighborhood Foot Patrol Project in early 1988. Twenty-one areas were selected where the workload was intense, and foot patrol area boundaries were developed around these intense pockets of activity. Areas range from four to 48 square blocks. Twenty-one officers were chosen on the basis of their willingness to try something different and trained with an emphasis on innovation and risk taking.

To introduce the program, several publications were distributed internally, and information sessions were held with middle and senior managers. Members of City Council and the Police Commission were briefed, and the Chief of Police wrote to community groups and business associations to introduce the program and the Neighborhood Foot Patrol officers. Externally, the media cooperated fully and helped spread the word. Nearly everyone was enthusiastic.

In April 1988, the Neighborhood Foot Patrol Program got under way. Foot patrol officers work out of storefront offices and operate with the following mandate:

> To provide a police service that is community based and is directed at solving community problems in the interest of community well-being and co-existence.

Specifically, the duties of the Foot Patrol Officers are:

- to become community team leaders/facilitators within their desig-nated areas,
- to become intimate with the social structure and the problems that

are legitimate concerns,
- to work collectively with residents to identify problems and determine and apply solutions,
- to respond to and investigate calls for service,
- to decentralize service level calls to the storefront office,
- to take a problem-oriented approach in dealing with repeat problems,
- to eliminate the causes of repeat calls for service,
- to identify and organize volunteers to staff the storefront office,
- to recruit responsible people to form a Neighborhood Liaison Committee,
- to attend Neighborhood Liaison Committee meetings and act as a team leader/facilitator, and
- to recognize that information is the lifeblood of policing and to facilitate the flow of information within the neighborhood.

All foot patrol officers have a complete inventory of their "repeat" customers – names, addresses, occurrence type, and dates – as well a neighborhood historical profiles consisting of socioeconomic and demographic information.

Assuming responsibility for calls for service is an essential ingredient of this project. Within the first few months, the 21 Foot Patrol Officers, who comprise only 4% of the total number of constables, have taken 5% of the total dispatched calls for service. Clearly, they have handled more than their share of the work. Projected over a 12-month period, the foot patrol officers will take 6,840 dispatched calls for service.

The obvious question is, "Does it work?" To be honest, we do not know yet. What we do know is that there are many examples of ongoing problems that have been solved by the Foot Patrol Officers that would not have been solved by those in mobile patrol. A sense of ownership has surfaced; constables want to know what is going on in their areas and have the benefit of a modern computer system to search for incidents that have occurred within their areas during a previous 24 hours, before they commence their shifts.

The independent Canadian Research Institute for Law and the Family will provide both a "process" evaluation and an "impact" evaluation in July 1989. It is anticipated that the impact will be significant. Time will tell.

Submitted by: Dave Cassels, Superintendent, Neighbourhood Foot Patrol Project Manager

COMMUNITY CLOSE-UP
Evanston Police Department
Evanston, Illinois

Ernest A. Jacobi, Chief of Police

Evanston, located in northeastern Illinois, is a city with approximately 75,000 residents living within 8.3 square miles. The community is culturally and economically diverse, with neighborhoods consisting of single- and multiple-family residences, commercial areas, and large private institutions.

The Evanston Police Department, with an annual operating budget of almost $8.5 million, consists of 154 sworn officers, 34 of whom are command and supervisory staff, plus 47 civilians, including three supervisors. It is divided into six divisions, and, for operational and crime-reporting purposes, the city is divided into seven motor patrol beats.

The department accomplishes its law enforcement missions through a mixture of traditional and new policing methods. In response to the social changes of the 1960s and 1970s, the department broadened its style of policing beyond what has come to be known as *traditional policing*. Greater attention was paid to identifying and responding to the needs of individuals and special groups within the community.

At that time, the department began to emphasize programs for youth, such as Officer Friendly and School Liaison Officers, as well as a Youth Outreach Program staffed by in-house civilian caseworkers. For schools, the School-Focused Delinquency Prevention Program involved a crime prevention curriculum designed by the department and the local school district. Teachers and police Resource and Liaison Officers provided lessons for all students in kindergarten through eighth grade.

Efforts targeted at residential areas included a police/community advisory and planning group, called the Residential Crime Prevention Committee; a community crime prevention newsletter; Neighborhood Watch; free Home Security Surveys; and other efforts. Similar activities were initiated for the business sector: Commercial Advisory Committee, Security Surveys, Training Seminars, and Directed Retail Foot Patrols.

The Community Affairs Officer became the Community Relations Bureau, which later evolved into a very active Crime Prevention Bureau. A new beat structure was designed to better serve neighborhood needs, and beat officers were given crime prevention training. The department also established a crime-analysis bureau, tactical teams for specialized responses to serious crimes, and a gang crimes bureau.

During the middle to late 1970s, the department started one of the first police-based victim/witness units.

The department has had a long history and reputation for being in the vanguard of progressive and innovative policing, which continues today in Community-Oriented Policing. Over the years, some programs have been cut back or eliminated (the most notable absence is the school crime prevention curriculum, and the School Resource/Liaison Officers have been cut back in numbers and duties), but other new efforts have been added. These include the use of videos and public access to cable television; the Home Security Lock Program that provides free installation of security hardware in the homes of low- and middle-income residents; sponsorship of a law enforcement Explorer Scout Post; annual citizen surveys; a merchant survey; a crime prevention community outpost; and residential foot patrols.

The Partnership

In 1987, the department decided to adopt a formal name for its community-involved approach which is called, simply, The Partnership. The Partnership is not considered a program, but a department-wide value, philosophy, or policing style that is expressed through a broad spectrum of policies, procedures, programs, and activities. Some important elements include:

- **Department-Wide Commitment** – The Partnership is a total philosophy, a way of viewing policing that is not limited to specific bureaus or department members. To emphasize the importance of partnership policing to all members, it has been incorporated into the department's written policy statements that have been disseminated throughout the department. The message is reinforced through in-service training, and new officers are introduced to partnership policing through the foot patrol component of the Field Training Program.

  Even though it has been established as department-wide policy, some members or units are more directly involved in carrying out partnership policing than others. Among those most directly involved are:

  - **Foot Patrol Bureau** – With one sergeant, seven officers.
  - **Victim/Witness and Youth Outreach Bureau** – With one civilian supervisor and four civilian outreach workers.
  - **Crime Prevention Bureau** – With one sergeant, two officers, and one part-time civilian Crime Prevention Specialist.
  - **Planning Bureau** – With one civilian.

- **Foot Patrol** – The Partnership motto is "We Walk Together," and each of the seven foot patrol officers is assigned complete responsibility for one foot patrol beat. The officers handle planning – needs assessments and other research, goal setting, and problem-solving. Duties and activities range from traditional responsibilities to a wide variety of proactive and preventive community services. They perform regular and highly visible foot patrol, assist others with investigations, develop information, respond to calls, and make arrests. They also develop block clubs, perform security surveys, attend neighborhood and association meetings, and work with residents and merchants to identify problems and solutions. To meet the varying needs of the areas they serve, officers adjust their work schedules accordingly.

  Roughly three-fourths of the city's residential and commercial areas are covered by foot patrol. They are not assigned patrol cars and routinely ride public transportation or "hitch a ride" with motor patrol officers to get to their beats.

  To make the department's programs more accessible, two neighborhood Foot Patrol Offices were established in the community, using donated space.

- **Bottom-Up Planning** – Foot officers use a bottom-up planning process to manage their neighborhoods, which means the officers, rather than their supervisors or command staff, plan most of their objectives and activities. This assists in an upward flow of information from the community to department administrators.

- **Weekly Planning Meetings** – These sessions are chaired by the Commander of Patrol Operations and all foot officers, plus representatives from all major bureaus and divisions, attend. The meeting is structured to encourage information sharing, mutual goal setting, brainstorming, and internal networking, which not only assures thorough implementation of goals and objectives, but it reinforces the department-wide commitment to partnership policing.

- **Communication Network** – The department has taken an active role in promoting an extensive communication network throughout the city that allows neighborhood and community groups to communicate with each other and with the department. The Residential Crime Prevention Committee, made up of representatives from block clubs, Neighborhood Watch groups, and other community representatives, meets monthly with foot patrol and crime prevention officers. The committee and the department together publish *The ALERT*, a bi-monthly community crime prevention newsletter. Another innovation is to have successful neighborhood groups work as *consultants* to help other neighborhoods solve similar problems, just as consultants are used in private industry. Not only does this provide a means to share expertise, it helps improve communication between neighborhood groups, and it has even generated some friendly competition that helps keep the motivation and commitment fresh and vital. To stay in touch with all segments of the community, the department also regularly meets with other citizen advisory groups, city council, the clergy, and business and financial leaders.

- **Practical Research** – The department uses simple research methods to gauge the effectiveness of strategies and as a way of gathering information for planning and goal setting. Citizen surveys are used to generate feedback on performance. Foot patrol officers are developing written neighborhood needs assessments to facilitate developing long- and short-term plans for their specific beats.

- **Acceptance** – As initial research indicated, greater police/community involvement is what the community wanted. Outside of the department, The Partnership sells itself. Internal acceptance has come more slowly. Even the first foot patrol recruits were somewhat skeptical at first, but their attitudes soon changed drastically. Other members of the department wanted to be shown that this is part of *real* policing. Some foot patrol acitivities, crime prevention, and victim/witness and youth outreach programs are more accepted and appreciated now, but department-wide understanding, acceptance, support, and active participation are still in the future.

- **Evaluation** – The department has not conducted in-depth research on the effects of The Partnership approach, but an informal citizens' opinion survey conducted annually showed positive results. An unexpected but very important and welcome effect has been the greatly improved morale and attitudes of the foot patrol officers. While they express great appreciation of the increased freedom, variety, and involvement this form of policing allows, their greatest amazement is the strong support and appreciation from residents and businesses.

  Perhaps the best evidence of this mutual apprecation and enthusiasm is the creation of the Evanston Police Department Charity Fund by members of the foot patrol and gang crime units. The fund is financed through contributions from civilian and sworn members of the department and private donations. Funding currently allows two events each year:

- **Summer Playground Camp** – The fund provides financial assistance to the families of approximately 125 needy children, age 5 to 12 years old, so that they can attend an eight-week summer playground camp.

- **Holiday Food Basket** – The fund provides food baskets to approximately 70 needy families during the Christmas holiday season. The food baskets are assembled and delivered by volunteers from the department and the young people of the Explorer Scout Post.

Submitted by: Chief Ernest A. Jacobi, with assistance from Brian Scruggs, Police Planner

INDEX